S0-ARG-583

THE CAMBRIDGE COMPANION TO
THE ACTRESS

This *Companion* brings together sixteen new essays which examine, from various perspectives, the social and cultural role of the actress throughout history and across continents. Each essay focuses on a particular stage in her development, for example professionalism in the seventeenth century; the emergence of the actress / critic during the Romantic period and, later on, of the actress as best-selling autobiographer; and the coming of the drama schools which led to today's emphasis on the actress as a highly trained working woman. Chapters consider the image of the actress as a courtesan, as a 'muse', as a representative of the 'ordinary' housewife, and as a political activist. The collection also contains essays on forms, genres and traditions – on cross-dressing, solo performance, racial constraints and recent Shakespeare – as well as on the actress in early photography and on film. Its unique range will fascinate, surprise and instruct theatre-goers and students alike.

THE CAMBRIDGE
COMPANION TO
THE ACTRESS

EDITED BY
MAGGIE B. GALE AND JOHN STOKES

CAMBRIDGE
UNIVERSITY PRESS

CAMBRIDGE UNIVERSITY PRESS
Cambridge, New York, Melbourne, Madrid, Cape Town, Singapore, São Paulo

Cambridge University Press
The Edinburgh Building, Cambridge CB2 8RU, UK

Published in the United States of America by Cambridge University Press, New York

www.cambridge.org
Information on this title: www.cambridge.org/9780521608541

© Cambridge University Press 2007

First published 2007

Printed in the United Kingdom at the University Press, Cambridge

A catalogue record for this publication is available from the British Library

ISBN-13 978-0-521-84606-6 hardback
ISBN-10 0-521-84606-4 hardback
ISBN-13 978-0-521-60854-1 paperback
ISBN-10 0-521-60854-6 paperback

CONTENTS

ILLUSTRATIONS

CONTRIBUTORS

ELAINE ASTON is Professor of Contemporary Performance at Lancaster University, where she researches and teaches feminist theory, theatre and performance. Her authored studies include *Sarah Bernhardt: A French Actress on the English Stage* (1989), *Theatre as Sign-System*, with George Savona (1991), *An Introduction to Feminism and Theatre* (1995), *Caryl Churchill* (1997; 2001), *Feminist Theatre Practice* (1999) and *Feminist Views on the English Stage* (2003).

JACKY BRATTON is Professor of Theatre and Cultural History at Royal Holloway, University of London. She has written about music hall and other aspects of Romantic and Victorian theatre; her latest publications are *New Readings in Theatre History* (2003) and *The Victorian Clown* (with Ann Featherstone, 2006).

GILLI BUSH-BAILEY is Senior Lecturer in the Department of Drama and Theatre at Royal Holloway, University of London. She has published articles on practice-based research in early nineteenth-century theatre and her monograph *Treading the Bawds: Actresses and Playwrights on the Late-Stuart Stage* (2006) offers a revisionist history of writing and performing women on the seventeenth-century stage.

MARIA M. DELGADO is Professor of Drama and Theatre Arts at Queen Mary, University of London and co-editor of *Contemporary Theatre Review*. Her publications include co-edited volumes for Manchester University Press: *In Contact with the Gods? Directors Talk Theatre* (1996), *The Paris Jigsaw: Internationalism and the Paris Stages* (2002) and *Theatre in Crisis? Performance Manifestos for a New Century* (2002). Her studies of the Spanish actresses Maria Casarès, Margarita Xirgu and Nuria Espert are included in *'Other' Spanish Theatres: Erasure and Inscription on the Twentieth-Century Spanish Stage* (2003).

ELIZABETH EGER is Lecturer in the Department of English at King's College London and is currently completing a book entitled *Living Muses: Women of Reason from Enlightenment to Romanticism*. Previous publications include, as co-editor and contributor, *Luxury in the Eighteenth Century: Debates, Desires and Delectable Goods* (2003) and *Women, Writing and the Public Sphere: 1700–1830* (2001).

MAGGIE B. GALE is Chair in Drama at the University of Manchester. Author of *West End Women: Women on the London Stage 1918–1962* (1996), she is co-editor with Viv Gardner of *Women, Theatre and Performance: New Histories, New Historiographies* (2000) and *Auto/biography and Identity: Women, Theatre and Performance* (2004), and, with Clive Barker, of *British Theatre Between the Wars 1918–1939* (2000). She is currently working on a monograph on J. B. Priestley for the *Routledge Modern and Contemporary Dramatists* series (2007).

VIV GARDNER is Professor of Theatre Studies at the University of Manchester. She is co-editor with Maggie B. Gale of *Women, Theatre and Performance: New Histories, New Historiographies* (2000) and *Auto/biography and Identity: Women, Theatre and Performance* (2004). Her recent research is on Gertie Millar, Florence Farr and the 5th Marquis of Anglesey, and on British provincial theatre 1900–1939.

PENNY GAY is Professor in English Literature and Drama at the University of Sydney. She is the author of *As She Likes It: Shakespeare's Unruly Women* (1994), *William Shakespeare: As You Like It* (1999), *Jane Austen and the Theatre* (2002) and numerous essays on Shakespeare's female roles.

CHRISTINE GLEDHILL is currently part-time Professor of Cinema Studies at the University of Sunderland. She has published extensively on feminist film criticism, melodrama and film and British cinema. Her most recent publications include *Reinventing Film Studies* (co-edited with Linda Williams, 2003) and *Reframing British Cinema 1918–1928: Between Restraint and Passion* (2003).

LYNETTE GODDARD is Lecturer in Drama and Theatre at Royal Holloway, University of London. She has published articles on British black women's theatre in *Alternatives Within the Mainstream II: British Postwar Queer Theatres* (2007), *The Companion to Contemporary Black British Culture* (2002) and *Contemporary Theatre Review*. Her monograph *Staging Black Feminisms: Identity, Politics, Performance* will be published in 2007.

TONY HOWARD is Senior Lecturer in the Department of English at the University of Warwick. Publications include *Women as Hamlet* (2007), *Reading the Apocalypse in Bed: Selected Plays of Tadeusz Rozewicz* (1998) and *Acts of War* (co-edited with John Stokes, 1996). He translates Polish poetry and drama with Barbara Bogoczek.

GAIL MARSHALL is Reader in Nineteenth-Century Literature at Oxford Brookes University. She is the author and editor of books on Victorian theatre, literature and culture and is currently editing the *Cambridge Companion to the Fin de Siècle* and writing a monograph on Victorian women and Shakespeare.

DAVID MAYER is Emeritus Professor and Research Professor at the University of Manchester. His recent writing explores the interstices between late-Victorian stages and early motion pictures and he is currently completing a study of D. W. Griffith and the American theatre. Founder of the Victorian and Edwardian Stage on Film Project, he is also a contributing member of the Griffith Project.

JO ROBINSON teaches nineteenth- and early twentieth-century theatre and theatre history in the School of English Studies at the University of Nottingham. She has published in *Nineteenth Century Theatre and Film*, *Performance Research* and *Women's Studies: An Interdisciplinary Journal*.

JOHN STOKES is Professor of Modern British Literature in the Department of English, King's College London. His most recent book is *The French Actress and her English Audience* (2005) and he is a regular theatre reviewer for the *Times Literary Supplement*.

LUCIE SUTHERLAND is a Research Fellow in Theatre and Performance History at the University of Nottingham. She has written on aspects of late nineteenth- and twentieth-century British theatre, including the career of the actor-manager George Alexander. She is currently researching the performance culture of Nottingham in the mid-nineteenth century.

ACKNOWLEDGEMENTS

The editors and publishers have made every attempt to trace copyright holders: subsequent reprints of this volume will include any alterations to copyright acknowledgements of which the publishers are made aware. The editors would particularly like to thank Victoria Cooper and Rebecca Jones at Cambridge University Press for their enthusiasm and encouragement. Thanks are also due to Richard Mangan at the Mander and Mitchenson Theatre Collection, to Sarah Williams at the Museum of London, to Liz and Tony Gale and to Dame Eileen Atkins, Eve Best, Cordelia Monsey, Gillian Raine and Harriet Walter. Maggie B. Gale and John Stokes are grateful for the support of their respective institutions, Manchester University and King's College London, and of their partners Ben Partridge and Faith Evans.

MAGGIE B. GALE AND JOHN STOKES

Introduction

Historically, the figure of the actress has often been marked by absence and by exclusion. The theatre of the English Renaissance, like that of the Greeks, was famously without women, although it is true that in both cases scholars continue to debate why this might have been and how absolute the prohibition actually was. In Catholic Europe performers, both male and female, while sometimes much admired, were denied full religious burial rites. There was clearly an entrenched unease about their power. By the eighteenth century many European actresses were celebrated not only for their physical presence but for their special capacity for feeling, their unique insights into human behaviour. At the same time their public 'femininity' – culturally created and projected – may even have exceeded that of the female roles they played. Even so, their success depended upon the art of dramatists who were frequently, if not exclusively, male. Despite the more recent rise of feminist historiography, the ways in which modern actresses have confronted these situations, and their dealings with playwrights, image-makers, managers and entrepreneurs, are only now beginning to be being fully explored.

The first 'actresses', in anything like the modern sense of the word, were Italian and, according to the most recent scholarship, they were, at least until the fifteenth century, mainly courtesans. The most celebrated, however, was a learned and respectable woman, wife of an actor, who lived in both Italy and France: Isabella Andreini.[1] The early French actresses aspired to her example: Molière's partner and the driving force behind much of his work, Madeleine Béjart, is perhaps the most famous example of this independent spirit. In England, with its transvestite theatre, the situation was very different. The current edition of the *Oxford English Dictionary* says that the word 'actress' was 'at first used only in the general sense, not in the dramatic; now only in the dramatic, not in the general'. The 'general' sense here means 'a female actor or doer'; the 'dramatic' sense means 'a female player on the stage', and the first example of the latter in the dictionary is from Dryden in 1700. ('Actor', says the *OED*, was 'at first used for both sexes'.) However, earlier

1

instances have since been discovered of what looks like the 'dramatic' sense of 'actress', referring to female participation in masques.[2] These semantic shifts are important in two respects: they remind us that the very word 'actor' may imply not simply to play on stage but to take action, to 'do'; they suggest that we still need to make a distinction between the kind of performance required in musical and dance entertainments and 'acting' since, as Clare McManus has put it, the 'concept of masquing differed radically from that of acting, demanding neither the effacement of self nor the adoption of an alternative identity'.[3] Our concern throughout this *Companion* is as much to do with the construction, the loss and the disguise of the self in dramatic performance as it is with the ideological and practical relations between 'acting' and 'action'.

The special skills of the 'actress' are mimetic, to do with characterization, as well as interpretative: she gives voice to texts. While these abilities can sometimes mesh with prevailing sexual ideologies to make her seem dangerous, a seductive dissembler, they can also signify a truth-teller whose art powerfully and accurately expresses the reality of the surrounding world. As a contemporary theorist such as Judith Butler would argue, performance in daily life plays an essential part in the creation of our sense of self.[4] To 'act' theatrically, to become another, even 'the Other', is to engage in a reflexive activity through which socially constructed individuals, either on stage or in an audience, encounter the conditions of their own survival. In an essay cited more than once in this collection, Ellen Donkin asserts that 'the history of women's performance is the history of a struggle for a subject, rather than an object, position in representation'.[5] Here, at least, is one dominant element in the actress's insistent but precarious status, her occasional invisibility coupled with her all-pervasive significance.

It is precisely because of these ambiguities that we have restricted the field to the areas where they are historically most apparent, deliberately concentrating upon performers from Europe or North America, and confining ourselves to those women whose talents are unquestionably mimetic, where imitation controls expressive potential, and whose skills are predominantly, though not exclusively, verbal.

We have also, perhaps more contentiously, confined ourselves to professionals, to women who get paid for acting. The very word 'professional' hovers between public and private: the 'professional actress' is defined by what she does, and yet what she does is imitate other people, which means that her work may have a problematic relation with the rest of her life. Nevertheless, we begin with the paid female performers of the English Restoration – allowing for, but not exploring, the precedents among amateur ladies at the English court and parallel careers in continental Europe. The English

Restoration marks a moment when, as professionalism takes over in the theatre, the division in women's lives between public and private is simultaneously reconceived.

The Cambridge Companion to the Actress pursues the professional actress across the centuries and across two continents. But, rather than present its findings in a simply chronological fashion, which might suggest an untrammelled progression from apparent absence to full presence, the essays are grouped into three parts. While the story of the actress obviously cannot be separated from shifting concepts of gender, contributors also account for the particular manifestations of her art by referring to cultural determinants – political, economic, and technological – as well as to modifications in dramatic form and modes of theatrical representation.

In Part I: 'Turning points', the essays concentrate upon key historical moments, all of them driven by widespread uncertainties about what the actress might now represent. Gilli Bush-Bailey establishes many important themes: the equation between actress and 'whore', between theatrical performance and sexual availability. This, as she shows, is very much of an historical phenomenon, yet something similar will be found to recur at later periods. In addition, she stresses social configurations that have 'gossip' as their product, and these too will continue to operate long after, although in new ways. Bush-Bailey's technique is to concentrate on a small group of representative figures: Mary Saunderson, Elizabeth Barry, Anne Bracegirdle. Elizabeth Eger continues with this approach when, in her survey of eighteenth-century actresses, she focuses upon Elizabeth Griffiths, Mary Robinson and Sarah Siddons. But Eger's special interest is in the ways in which experience in the theatre conditioned personal expression away from it. The actress as writer and critic was a powerful and lasting phenomenon who not only brought out the distinctive significance of literary texts for a female readership but who understood the risks and rewards involved in any act of self-presentation.

In France actresses such as Hippolyte Clairon (1723–1803) and Marie-Françoise Dumesnil (1713–1803) had become acknowledged objects of intellectual fascination for *philosophes* of the order of Voltaire and Diderot, a theoretical interest that also captured the attention of the English actor David Garrick. But in the nineteenth-century the actress becomes fully international. For the legendary artists who feature in Gail Marshall's essay on global touring, opportunities for universal exposure (brought about by the combination of immensely improved facilities for long-distance travel and patterns of emigration that had created huge potential audiences in the New World) turned them from local or national heroines into modern phenomena. Harriet Smithson, Rachel Félix, Adelaide Ristori, Charlotte Cushman,

Helena Modjeska and Eleonora Duse are the key names here, all of them, in a term that will become increasingly relevant, 'celebrities'.

David Mayer remarks in his detailed study of the actress and the photograph that 'Fame, publicity, adulation, collecting, fan-dom, and the full apparatus of fan-worship – even celebrity stalking – would be impossible without the attendant development in photo-engraving and print technologies and national rail and transport systems which could move the actress and her various images in various formats to all parts of the country and, beyond, to the Empire.' This is undoubtedly true. Some familiar names reappear in Mayer's census but other, rather less well-known women also claim his attention: Isabella Glyn, Kate Saville, Annabelle Moore.

By the end of the nineteenth century the successful actress has become, in another word that is overused but hard to avoid, an 'icon'. She may be internationally known, her image may be widely disseminated, she may be famous even to those who haven't witnessed her in a theatre and, of course, she may be an inspiration to ambitious young women who see in her a role model of seeming independence. Yet that freedom may, in some respects, be illusory or precarious. Chance may play as large a part as talent, and the actual business of theatre is, as Tracy C. Davis has shown in early research that has done more than any other to determine this whole field, a guarded male preserve.[6] Although opportunities for administrative and financial power could sometimes be found, the dominant mode of production revolved around the figure of the male actor-manager who relied upon a steady supply of attractive young female performers for his popular commercial repertoire. It was one of the ironies of the new drama schools that developed in the early years of the twentieth century, whose impact is described by Lucie Sutherland, that although women dominated the student intake, the schools should have been largely founded and directed by men. Sutherland connects the schools with unionisation, linked as symptoms of a 'professionalisation' that would, eventually, lead the way forward.

So far the 'turning points' have been largely to do with the profession as it grew and developed in relation to technology and social organisation. But the arts of performance also reflect and contribute to great political events. In his essay on the English actress in the post-war years John Stokes shows how a world-wide catastrophe, which had imposed new responsibilities upon women in the domestic and the industrial spheres, resulted in what looks at first like a contradiction: a renewed stress upon the 'ordinary'. Matters were not, of course, quite what they seemed. In the tense, unstable performances of actresses such as Celia Johnson, Peggy Ashcroft, Yvonne Mitchell and even Vivien Leigh, internal struggles – with class, with sexuality, with intellectual expectations, and with professional status – are made apparent in subtly

4

visible discontent. In Mitchell's partly autobiographical book published in 1957, simply entitled *Actress*, the stress is mainly upon the technicalities and, indeed, the ethics of performance. Popular success is incidental to self-discovery.

All this at a period when the cult of the fabulous movie star is reaching its peak with the careers of Marilyn Monroe, of Jane Russell, of Doris Day and of Jayne Mansfield in the USA and, in the UK, of Diana Dors and Shirley Eaton. Yet, in publicity ploys even the 'sex symbol' is the girl – or wife – or mother – next door. This provides a kind of reverse glamour in which the very 'normality' of the actress's personality is said to enable her exceptional performances. It's the time, too, when sophisticated theories of acting, often Stanislavski-based, begin to take a hold, especially in America. And it's a time when a new medium, television, will bring high drama into the home on a daily basis.

It was probably no accident, then, that even those women who were mainly renowned for their portrayal of the quotidian should have displayed on many occasions a highly developed social conscience. Even this was nothing new. By rehearsing her potential in plays an activist prepared for her political life. The 'political' actress has her origins in the role of national figurehead adopted on occasion by Rachel Félix (who chanted the 'Marseillaise' in 1848), in Bernhardt's response to the crises of 1871 and of 1914–18, in Modjeska's fierce Polish patriotism. Feminist historians such as Julie Holledge, Sheila Stowell, Viv Gardner, Carole Hayman, Sally Ledger and Barbara Green have stressed the wider cultural importance of the New Woman and unearthed the continuities between the literary, political and theatrical activities that lay behind the broad banners of the suffrage movement. The Actresses' Franchise League (AFL), founded in 1908, and the Pioneer Players, founded in 1911, were in many ways the culmination of the actress-led Ibsen campaign of the 1880s and 1890s. The AFL provided an organisation which questioned the interface between professional theatre women and the politics of gender in their industry, campaigning on behalf of actresses, playwrights and managers (fig. 1). It gave a focus for politicized actresses who understood the relationship between the gender inequalities in the theatre and those which existed in society at large. The AFL also created opportunities for training in political oratory and campaigned for suffrage outside the context of the theatre itself, recognizing the usefulness of actresses' skills as public speakers and public women who could galvanize attention and direct it towards a particular political topic.

Tony Howard takes the historical existence of political actresses one step further and in his chapter focuses on those who used their celebrity and enhanced access to public forums to campaign about all varieties of political

Fig. 1. The Actresses' Franchise League, assembled for the Women's Coronation Procession, 17 June 1911 (Museum of London).

issues. Here the actresses, many of them taking a radical as opposed to a liberal stance, assume extraordinary levels of responsibility as citizens who can use their professional status, and their theatre or film and TV personalities, as a means to inspire and create political change, often at the 'cost' of their own careers. Howard picks up the story with Maud Gonne, the Irish revolutionary, orator and sometime actress, and continues with a broad survey, again based on selective examples, in which he draws attention to the roles of actresses in the American witch-hunts of the 1940s, in the Civil Rights struggles in the USA and South Africa, in the campaigns against the Vietnam war and in the subsequent activities of such powerful spokeswomen as Vanessa Redgrave (fig. 2), Jane Fonda and Glenda Jackson. It seems fitting that this section on 'turning points' should conclude with women who have contributed so powerfully to the history of today.

In Part II: 'Professional opportunities', the essays are more concerned with matters of status, with the strategies through which women have created or seized a chance to advance their influence over the theatre of their time. These range from developing managerial power to creating or recreating their own histories in the burgeoning market for autobiographies, to establishing their position within the new industry of cinema, to the overcoming of race prejudice and, following on from that, challenging the 'victim status' that, paradoxically but no less oppressively, can accompany public acceptance.

6

Fig. 2. Vanessa Redgrave as Mrs Pankhurst in the film of *Oh! What a Lovely War* (1969). (Corbis)

As Jo Robinson explains, actresses were motivated to become managers by a number of ambitions: 'financial ambition or security; control over artistic repertoire and staging; and control over reputation and representation'. Some of the names of the actress-managers she discusses are familiar: Bernhardt, again, and, a little later, Elizabeth Robins and Lena Ashwell – but

7

not all. Marianne Saville worked in the provinces, yet her achievements were none the less solid for that, since she commanded an influential position in the cultural history of a whole city. She was, to a large extent, mistress of her own fate. Similarly, Viv Gardner's introduction to the phenomenon of the theatrical autobiography stresses the fact that, whatever the 'truth' of autobiographical writing, it allows the actress a heightened level of agency in terms of the way she 'presents' herself to the world. Taking a broad range of examples, Gardner looks at the ways in which actresses' autobiographies often acknowledge the participation of others in the construction of a persona – from family to editors to secretaries. Autobiographies enable the manipulation of such creations; a parallel reconfiguration of the individual career is very much the focus of Christine Gledhill's chapter on the actress in early film.

Gledhill examines the early film industry in Britain and the United States in terms of the possibilities that allowed actresses to cross from theatre to silent film and then to the 'talkies'. Notions of beauty and femininity, rooted in emerging national cultural identities as well as in tradition, were key to the success (or otherwise) of actresses when they undertook the professional journey between continents. Equally important in determining the position of actresses in early film were the different acting techniques favoured by competing sections of the industry. The careers of Florence Turner, Mary Pickford and Betty Balfour are as varied as those of later screen actresses such as Madeleine Carroll who was more able, in some respects, to command the directions taken by her career. Ideas of agency and self-determination link actresses in early film with actresses and autobiography and the work of the political actress. At the close of the previous section, Tony Howard ended by proclaiming that in today's culture of 'manipulated images, perhaps the actress might protect the word'. Yet, images, not always 'manipulated', have played their part in her history too. The actress is always a physical presence in autobiography and a visual sign whether on the stage, on film or in the street as a public protester.

Gardner points to the fact that we should be particularly cautious with autobiographical accounts which set out to please their readership or to confirm current views, rather than to record the actuality: we have to read such narratives with great care. Lynette Goddard makes the same point when she challenges the myth of obstacles finally and triumphantly overcome that tends to characterise the 'life-writing' of black performers. The objection is not to the representation of the obstacles, which are always real enough, but to the simplification of the success. As Goddard explains, despite the international prominence of Oscar winner Halle Berry and a handful of other black stars, the position of the black actress in still disadvantaged, still complicated and unresolved. Taking the British actress Josette Simon as one of her main examples, Goddard explores the doubleness of a situation in which the usually welcome principle of 'colour-blind' casting (in, for example, Shakespeare) coexits uneasily with the urgent need for major roles for black women in new plays.

In Part III: 'Genre, form and tradition', the essays are more specifically concerned with practices and conventions within the theatre itself. 'Cross-dressing', 'solo performance', 'the function of the erotic', 'collaboration', 'the Shakespearean heroine': these are all topics with which recent feminist theatre history has been much concerned. By putting the actress, rather than the writer or the text, at the very centre of enquiry, it becomes possible to see how matters of gender can be primary rather than secondary, how they can determine a generic tradition, how an actress can initiate as well as respond.

Allowing for the rule that operates throughout all these essays, that 'the material culture goes its own way', Jacky Bratton nevertheless announces that 'the enactment of the male by women seems to me to be always specific to the immediate, historical negotiations of interpersonal power through gender'. She goes on to concentrate upon the phenomenon of the cross-dressed woman as 'boy'. If it is true that the crossed-dressed figure of woman as 'man' deconstructs a basic patriarchal assumption about 'nature' and the normative, the image of the 'boy' stands for something deeper, more primordial. The popular drag artist who plays at being a boy constructs a 'male/female reality' that challenges 'the gender divisions itself, and so the pre-existence of man'. Bratton's survey ranges from Margaret Woffington to Vesta Tilley, proving her underlying assumption that as sexual ideologies change so do genres and conventions. Even in the case of 'drag' with its legendary stars (Bratton brings fascinating new research to bear on the figure of Tilley), we should still look for discontinuity within a celebrated 'tradition'.

As with 'drag' so with 'stand-up' and 'monologist': popular generic names change according to content and structure. Maggie B. Gale's emphasis is on the women who had careers as 'solo performers', many of whom wrote their own work, their own one-woman dramas. This is as different from the one-woman 'show' in which a single performer does a series of turns – recitations, songs, anecdotes – as it is from the *comédienne* (Lily Tomlin, Jo Brand or Helen Lederer, say) who recounts anecdotes supposedly from her own life in so condensed and exaggerated a form that they serve as 'gags'. Gale points to the fact that performers like Beatrice Herford and Ruth Draper capitalised on a growing interest in 'identity' and 'character' to make careers out of creating and performing social types. Following on from Charlotte Cushman and Fanny Kelly, for whom the solo form had enabled a reinvention of their careers, Draper developed the art of the monologue into a form in which a whole personal career history could be contained.

Modes of erotic attraction are as vulnerable to change as anything else. Elaine Aston concentrates upon a crucial phase in the history of sexuality in an essay on the 'hysteric' who is aptly described as inspiring both 'fascination and terror'. Aston's key figures are Bernhardt and Mrs Patrick Campbell; her main texts *La Dame aux camélias* and *The Second Mrs Tanqueray*, plays that feature 'fallen women'. The advantages and disadvantages of personal identification with the scandalous are, of course, relevant to 'celebrity', as is the strangely mixed morality that allowed an actress to flaunt her sexual power and then, symbolically, to pay the ultimate price for having done so.

Were the actresses who specialised in fallen women roles complicit or conflicted? There is a good deal of evidence that both Bernhardt and Campbell had very firm ideas about what they wanted to bring to these men's stories about women's lives. This made them, in a sense, 'collaborators' in the final theatrical outcome. But 'collaboration' is always a vexed, unequal business and, as Maria Delgado insists, we should not accept the habitual assumption that the only role for the actress who 'collaborates' with a male writer is that of muse to artist. Delgado opens with a list of those partnerships in which the woman has played a far more active and exploratory role than the stereotype allows. And, to further prove her point, she turns to two women who worked in a theatre – the Hispanic – which is often overlooked or misunderstood by anglocentric histories. Detailed accounts of the extraordinary careers of Maria Guerrero and Margarita Xirgu reveal them to have been leaders not followers, figures whose significance, political in the widest sense, is only now being fully realised and commemorated.

We conclude, as we did not begin, with Shakespeare. The very fact that the most celebrated repertoire in the western tradition, that of Shakespeare and his contemporaries, was generated by a transvestite theatre has, ironically enough, meant that decisions about the role of gender in casting have, in more recent years, become excitingly volatile. Penny Gay's tough-minded estimation of the opportunities currently available for women who wish to work with Shakespeare, whether as actresses or directors, is optimistic only in the longer term. The present she sees as merely a transitional or stalled phase in the continuing history of Shakespearean production – and that despite the magnificent achievements of Judi Dench, of Vanessa Redgrave, of Harriet Walter, of Janet McTeer, of Fiona Shaw, of Kathryn Hunter and of Frances de la Tour, all of whose performances Gay warmly and appreciatively evokes.

It would, of course, be possible to trace other patterns in these essays by noting elements that feature in more than one part. Lucie Sutherland's perception that the training offered by drama schools parallels the notion of the performing self made current by Judith Butler connects, in turn, with Howard's politically aware rebels, with Gale's monologists and with Aston's sexual outlaws. Gledhill's recognition and questioning of English 'restraint' provides an historical backdrop to Stokes. One can find in Bernhardt's assertive eroticism a continuation of the provocative sexuality deployed in the English theatre as far back Nell Gwynn, as well as the transgressive aura that had once, for instance, inspired the French playwright Jean Racine to try to accommodate his mistress, the actress Champmeslé (1642–98), within the neoclassical tragedy of *Phèdre*. The freedom to act at certain moments on stage leads to an increased freedom to express oneself away from it – both Bush-Bailey and Eger elaborate this idea. In convoluted ways the 'hysteria' of the late nineteenth century and the deceptive 'ordinariness' of the mid-twentieth both lead to the 'liberation' of today. Yet cautionary notes are everywhere struck, most notably in Gay's reading of Shakespearean production and in Goddard's essay on black actresses. One might even trace an alternative line back from the actresses of the Harlem Renaissance to the Ibsenite pioneers at the turn of the century who, although their cultural circumstances were very different, had to take control of the production process before they could play the parts that they believed told the truth about themselves.

It would also be possible to use the *Companion* as a starting point for a study of the uses that women have made of comic personae from the Restoration to today, touching upon Nell Gwynn, Ellen Terry, Judy Holliday, Ruth Draper, Joyce Grenfell and beyond. Equally, one could think about the *tragédienne* and ask why that designation seems to have lost the prestige it once possessed. Finally, there are the names that seem recur over and again: Siddons, Robins, Bernhardt, Duse, Ashcroft, Redgrave. What made these actresses, in particular, seem so pivotal, not just as individual performers but as women whose careers affected the profession as a whole? What enabled them to capture the times?

At which point we think again of the countless women we have been obliged to leave out, each of whom made her own entirely distinctive contribution: Shirley Temple, Helene Weigel, Mary Frith, Franca Rame . . . Our only defence is that we make no claim for the *Companion* to be exhaustive, an encyclopedia, but rather to be a preliminary survey of a rich and extraordinarily diverse history in which certain typical narratives might be usefully highlighted.

We noticed, near the outset, some scholarly uncertainty as to when the term 'actress' achieved general currency, and an accompanying worry as to whether, in fact, that moment accurately reflected what was happening on stage. As the female performer came to represent the dangerous, destabilising intoxication of theatre itself, might not the feminine noun be, in some respects, more appropriate and more powerful than the masculine? Not because the women were subservient to men (as nearly all these essays suggest, this was usually far from the case) but because the material conditions of employment, of perception and of success were fundamentally different. We can conclude, though, by noting the announcement, perhaps premature, of its demise. 'Actor' is now the preferred term for obituaries and many other forms of curricula vitae. It indicates a professional status, it buys back the useful ambiguity of 'one who takes action', and it may indeed point to a future of professional equality. It does not, however, accommodate a unique and turbulent history.

NOTES

1. Isabella Andreini (1562–1604), born Isabella Canali at Padua, she married Francesco Andreini, who later had his own company, in 1578. In addition to her fame as a performer she was a considerable writer, producing a pastoral and volumes of poems and letters. See Virginia Scott, *Molière: A Theatrical Life* (Cambridge: Cambridge University Press, 2000), pp. 41–2. Also see chapter 1.
2. Sophie Tomlinson, 'She that Plays the King: Henrietta Maria and the threat of the Actress in Caroline Culture', in Gordon McMullan and Jonathan Hope, eds., *The Politics of Tragicomedy* (London: Routledge, 1992), pp. 189–207, p. 189.
3. Clare McManus, *Women on the Renaissance stage: Anna of Denmark and Female Masquing in the Stuart Court 1590–1619* (Manchester: Manchester University Press, 2002), p. 9. Also see Stephen Orgel, *Impersonations: The Performance of Gender in Shakespeare's England* (Cambridge: Cambridge University Press, 1996).
4. See Judith Butler, *Bodies that Matter* (New York: Routledge, 1993) and *Undoing Gender* (New York: Routledge, 2004).
5. 'Mrs Siddons Looks Back in Anger', in Janelle G. Reinelt and Joseph R. Roach, eds., *Critical Theory and Performance* (Ann Arbor: University of Michigan Press, 1992), pp. 276–99.
6. See Tracy C. Davis, *Actresses as Working Women* (London: Routledge, 1991).

I
TURNING POINTS

I

GILLI BUSH-BAILEY

Revolution, legislation and autonomy

Hard by Pell-Mell, lives a wench cal'd *Nell*,
  King *Charles* the second he kept her,
She hath got a trick to handle his . . . [prick]
  But never lays hands on his Scepter.
All matters of State, from her Soul she does hate,
  And leave[s] to the Pollitick Bitches,
The Whore's in the right, for 'tis her delight,
  To be scratching just where it Itches.
                              Anonymous lampoon

From the moment the first British professional actress appeared on the London stage in 1661 she became an object of fascination. She was both admired and derided, desired and vilified. The very public sphere in which her craft was practised quickly led to parallels with prostitution in a patriarchal society employing the binaries of private/public, virgin/whore as constructs of femininity. Seventeenth-century society was enthralled by the actress's craft on stage and simultaneously engrossed by the stories surrounding her sexual liaisons off stage. The elision between her public and private identity, the visual spectacle of her acting body *on* stage and the availability of her sexually active body *off* stage, reveals a bifocal perspective that has captured the popular imagination, underpinned biographies and histories of the actress and, as the quotation above demonstrates, fuelled a lucrative trade in gossip for over three hundred years. Here, the cultural embodiment of the early actress, Nell Gwynn, is represented in her most famous role: the fun-loving whore of the 'Merry Monarch', Charles II. As one of His Majesty's Servants, Gwynn's public/private performance is focused on the pleasures of the flesh: her interest in and enjoyment of the private body royal, favourably set against interests in the public body politic enjoyed by the king's much-hated aristocratic mistresses, especially his French mistress, Louise de la Kéroualle. Nell Gwynn's mythical status as one of the first actresses casts her in the role of the ultimate English sexual Cinderella: she was allegedly born into the whorehouses of London's Covent Garden, and rose through the ranks as orange-seller at the playhouse to become a popular comic actress and ultimately the king's mistress. In spite of Gwynn's quite considerable achievements as an actress over a comparatively short career of only five years, her sexualised representation has become emblematic of all the early actresses and is indelibly inked into the many pages that have recorded the history of the arrival of the British actress, irrevocably linking her newly established professional status with the oldest profession for women.

In order to begin to unpick this tightly woven knot we need to consider the broader social and cultural context in which women were licensed to perform on the London public stage and cast the net beyond British shores to the playhouses of Europe, where women had been part of theatre companies since the sixteenth century. The English Civil War and the subsequent eighteen-year closure of London's public theatres under Oliver Cromwell's Puritan Interregnum also play a significant role in the opposition to performing women and the whorish designation of their profession. The Restoration of King Charles in May 1660 marks another turn in the social revolutions of the seventeenth century, one that now had to embrace the autonomy achieved by the rise of an expanding merchant class intent upon determining their own economic, political and religious role in society. The economic expansion saw, among other things, a rise in the importation of foreign goods and the concomitant establishment of new social spaces, including the reopening of the playhouses and the establishment of coffee houses and parks in which to parade a public self, all playing a crucial role in establishing a social discourse which was increasingly interested in the processes of power. As Michel Foucault has so convincingly argued, the late seventeenth century can be seen as a key point in the development of the bourgeois society and the establishing of a repressive sexual discourse that is concerned with the surveillance and control of sexual identity and activity.[1] This emergent discourse of gender definition and, specifically, the construction of femininity within the private sphere, coincides with the licensed appearance of the actress on the British public stage. Although there were a series of public debates about the immorality of the stage, notably coming to a head in the publication of Jeremy Collier's treatise *A Short View of the Profaneness and Immorality of the Stage* (1698), such debates were underpinned by less serious commentaries on the arrival of the actress. These are contained in private/public accounts such as satires, lampoons and, most famously, in the diary entries of a rising civil servant that record visits to the playhouse by that inveterate theatre-goer Samuel Pepys, who provides gossipy accounts of the goings-on in the royal box and visits to the actresses behind the scenes in the "tiring rooms' with an equal measure of delight and disapproval.[2]

Gossip is at the heart of largely male-authored histories of the actress and plays an essential role in understanding the social and cultural construction of the work of the professional female theatre practitioner. Gossip is largely (and pejoratively) identified as a female activity in which attention to the micro-detail of the story is essential and yet, by this definition, renders the story unimportant to the macro-politics of the public and thus traditionally male sphere. Joseph Roach argues that gossip guards against cultural forgetting: '[o]ften the best hedge against amnesia is gossip',[3] but by its concomitant interest in things notorious, gossip also works to reinforce hegemonic sexual values, particularly in relation to constructs of women in the much-contested space of power – the public sphere. Gossip then plays an essential role in the ongoing social negotiations surrounding sex: relations between the sexes and sexual relationships accepted or rejected by society at any given moment. But what is really at stake here is the matter of women's influence, power and autonomy and the way that gossip has worked to elide her public and private identity in a bid to contain her within the dominant constructs of female social behaviour. The arrival of the first professional actress on the London stage certainly marks a new departure in a social discourse concerned with hegemonic constructions of class, gender and morality, demonstrated through the case-studies of the actresses with which this chapter concludes. But the debates around women's participation in the commercial sphere of theatre can be seen to have begun before Charles II's triumphant return to the throne and the start of the period in theatre history we know as the Restoration. The potential financial independence achieved by the actress from that point and, crucially, her autonomous action and public influence had disturbed her critics long before the royal warrant permitted British women to perform on the public stage.

A question of morality

The *OED* records the first reference to the 'actress' in the context of theatrical performance in 1700, some forty years after women were professionally employed to perform on the public stage. Prior to this point, it has been assumed that the term referred only to female action: the 'actress' as 'female doer'. But Sophie Tomlinson presents a convincing argument for the theatrical use of the term some three-quarters of a century earlier. In her discussion of Caroline court production and, specifically, a contemporary reference to Queen Henrietta Maria's private/public performances at court, Tomlinson demonstrates that Henrietta Maria is identified as 'a principal actress' by a contemporary witness, not only marking a shift in language but also opening the discourse surrounding women's actions and agency.[4] As Tomlinson points out, William Prynne's (in)famous attack on actresses as 'notorious whores' in *Histrio-Mastix* (1633) was seen as a clear attack against the queen and 'quickly turned female acting into a livewire issue'.[5] Prynne's objections also gave voice to a mounting hatred among Protestants of all things foreign and especially of the perceived immorality of Roman Catholicism – personified it seems by actresses.[6]

Prynne had already publicly expressed outrage at an earlier appearance of 'some French-women, or monsters rather' who appeared on the stage as part of a French company visiting the playhouse at Blackfriars in 1629. This event in English theatre history frequently repeats a contemporary account detailed in a letter by one Thomas Brande which relates that the actresses were 'hissed, hooted and pippin-pelted from the stage'.[7] Stephen Orgel revisits this account and notes that as the company went on to visit two other playhouses in the following weeks, not all of London's audience were averse to paying to see women on the stage.[8] Orgel's point is that traditional English male-only theatre companies did not include *English* actresses: 'the distinction they maintained was not between men and women but between "us" and "them" – what was appropriate for foreigners was not appropriate for the English, and women on display became increasingly associated with Roman Catholicism'.[9] But Prynne's sexualised equation of performing women as 'notorious whores' surely reveals an even deeper set of anxieties about women and the private/public sphere. Tomlinson suggests that the 'threat of the actress in performance lay in the potential for presenting femininity as a vivid and mobile force' which 'disrupted the symbolic ordering of gender . . . provid[ing] a model for female insubordination in the public sphere'[10] and acknowledges that '[f]or the culture at large . . . Prynne's equation between female performance and sexual immodesty held firm'.[11] The move from equation to construct had certainly taken shape by the time the professional actress stepped onto the public stage in 1661.

Revisionist histories have worked to separate the performing woman from the actress/whore trope, rightly arguing that this historical narrative limits an understanding of women's agency and power in the public sphere. Kirsten Pullen considers this a semiotic problem, suggesting that '[d]uring the Restoration, the word "whore" was an insult, certainly, but one along the lines of the contemporary "bitch", designating an unruly woman rather than one who engaged in commercial sex', and her series of case-studies demonstrate the ways in which actresses through the ages have used their sexualised identity to 'wrest personal agency'.[12] Perhaps it is the moment to move beyond the either/or arguments and consider the both/and perspective suggested by Tomlinson's summary: 'The perception of the actress as whore

18

is essentially a perception of woman as wrong-doer, as (sexual) malefactor. It is a short step from this notion to the combined threat of female agency and feminine counterfeit or duplicity.'[13] In other words, the actress/whore trope works to focus on the immoral sexual activity of the private female body in a hegemonic move to limit women's agency in the public body politic. She may well use her sexual and sexualised body to achieve levels of independence and autonomy but her success will always be circumscribed by that same sexuality. The actress clearly poses a threat to the stability of male/public, female/private construction but, interestingly, her introduction to the British Restoration stage was framed as part of a moral imperative to *reinforce* sexual/gender difference; a move that had already been well rehearsed on the theatrical stages of Europe.

Actresses were officially permitted to appear on the Spanish stage from the 1580s, although there is evidence that they appeared as early as 1530. Over the next twenty years they were variously banned and then reinstated by a final regulation in 1600 which was concomitant with a prohibition against cross-dressing for both boy players and actresses – an issue we will return to later in relation to actresses cross-dressing in 'breeches roles'. In her study of transvestism on the Spanish public stage, Ursula Heise notes that the 1600 licence insisted that 'actresses not be allowed to dress up as men on stage, but that they be forced to wear long skirts instead, [and] they should be married'.[14] Such edicts were repeated in 1641 and 1644 and extended to men in the companies who also had to provide evidence that they were married and had their wives living with them. As Heise notes, '[t]hese continued attempts at regulating and enforcing a norm in performances as well as in the everyday life of the troupes reveal an intense anxiety over the sexual dynamics of the public theatre and its possible impact on social order'.[15] France and Italy also admitted actresses to the stage from the mid-sixteenth century, and it is generally accepted that Charles II's determination to introduce actresses to the London stage arose, at least partially, from his familiarity with European theatre during his years of exile.[16] But in the light of earlier fears about performing women as one of the worst examples of foreign imports, why was it that, as Katharine Eisaman Maus observes, 'attitudes toward women on the stage seem to have changed radically. The new actresses were accepted almost immediately into the life of the British theatre, and there was surprisingly little controversy over their suitability for the stage.'[17] Tomlinson suggests that the answer lies in the fact that the 'cultural event provoked by women's acting had already taken place' in Caroline discourse.[18] There is a gap of some twenty years between Henrietta Maria and her 'actresses' at court and the inclusion of the professional actress in the newly formed commercial theatre companies of 1660.

The unanswered and, I suspect, unanswerable questions surrounding where the first English actresses came from must be considered in the context of the apparent silencing of all public theatrical performance between 1642 and Charles II's Restoration. In this apparent 'gap' in public theatrical performance, the cultural conditions for the commercially driven playhouse were forged, with the on- and off-stage body of the actress serving as a site for some well-rehearsed constructs of women, morality and the private/public sphere.

A question of licence

In August 1660, Charles II issued a warrant granting exclusive rights for theatrical performance in London to 'the art and skill of our trusty and well-beloved Thomas Killigrew, Esq., . . . and William Davenant, Knight'.[19] The royal patent also included the injunction that 'all the womens [sic] parts to be acted in either of the said two companies for the time to come, may be performed by women'.[20] It is worth noting that at this point men were not forbidden to play female roles (the most famous actor, Edward Kynaston, continued to do so for some years), but both patentees set about recruiting women into their companies. Elizabeth Howe notes that '[w]ith the eighteen-year gap in theatre production . . . there was of course a shortage of boy-actresses',[21] but goes on to discuss the more significant matter of Killigrew and Davenant's involvement with French theatre during the period of Charles's exile where women were firmly established in theatre companies. Killigrew and Davenant had both contributed to theatrical entertainment in the Caroline court, but perhaps the most significant move heralded by Charles's decree to reopen the theatres in England was the erosion of the gap between public and private theatrical performance. Paula Backsheider demonstrates that Charles II took every opportunity to reinforce his monarchical authority and that the way he chose to do this was essentially theatrical.[22] His seven-hour procession into London in May 1660 was one of many public appearances that worked to impress the people with the splendour and authority of the king and, above all, his presence among his people. The two playhouses, hastily converted from tennis courts by Killigrew and Davenant, each contained a royal box in the heart of an auditorium packed with people loyal to and eager to forward the royal cause. Support for the actresses may have begun in the private court theatre but the court theatre was now in the public and, crucially, the commercial sphere – and the actresses were a central part of that move.

The 'first' actress is thought to have appeared in Killigrew's King's Company production of *Othello* performed on 8 December 1660, but William

Davenant is known to have used a female 'singer' in his private production of *The Siege of Rhodes* in the late 1650s. Davenant had returned to London and tested out the theatrical water by presenting it as an 'opera', thus circumventing the ban on plays, and mounting the production in the relative privacy of Rutland House. With the royal warrant in his hands in 1660, Davenant set about forming the Duke's Company (so called in honour of James, Charles's brother), the only theatrical competition to Killigrew's King's Company permitted by the terms of the royal patent. Killigrew appears to have initially recruited at least four actresses and, according to Howe, 'may have had them perform in public before they were ready'[23] – if we are to believe Pepys's account that they did not know their lines.[24] Davenant evidently took a rather different approach, building a new wing to the playhouse in Lincoln's Inn Fields which his family shared, initially at least, with four of the six actresses recruited into the Duke's Company and for whom Davenant claimed extra shares from the company profits to recompense him for their upkeep.

John Downes, prompter at Lincoln's Inn Fields, provides one of the few first-hand accounts of the recruitment of women into the patent companies in *Roscius Anglicanus* (1708). He lists the first eight actresses recruited by Davenant, including Mrs Davenport, Mrs Davies, Mrs Saunderson and Mrs Long, adding that '[t]hese four being his Principal Actresses, he [Davenant] boarded them at his own house'.[25] Downes's modern editors note that Jane Long 'left the stage in 1673 to become the mistress of George Porter'[26] and a few pages later Downes himself makes the observation that Davenport and Davies were also among those who 'by force of love were Erept the Stage'.[27] This much-quoted extract from Downes has been used to reinforce the trope of the actress/whore, with the attendant implication that Davenant housed them in a vain attempt to control these unruly women and curtail their socially aspirant sexual adventures. But there is another interpretation (besides the obvious one that might suggest Davenant was no more than a pimp) which reveals a social shift between the old guild system, under which theatre companies of the past had gained a degree of respectability and protection, and the new patent system in which His Majesty's comedians participated in the royally sanctioned commercial sphere of theatre business.

In his consideration of the apprentice system for boy actors in Renaissance theatre companies, Stephen Orgel shows that histories have ignored the presence of women as apprentices and as full guild members in the fifteenth, sixteenth and seventeenth centuries.[28] In a convincing argument that draws on a range of social and cultural histories, Orgel points out that female apprentices were not confined to 'ladylike pursuits' but pursued a full range of trades 'as fully independent, legally responsible craftspersons'.[29] Orgel's point is that 'the fact that there were no English actresses on the Elizabethan and early Stuart stage [was] a matter of social convention, not statute . . . When they started to represent competition to men . . . women were gradually either eased out, or eased into clearly gender-linked crafts as the needle trades.'[30] The creation of a new craft for women, the role of the actress, marks a moment when a new, specifically female craft was opened up. Davenant, identified more closely with an interest in the craft of theatre than his fellow patentee Killigrew, appears to have taken up something of the model of the guilds' training systems by including the actresses in his household and, as we shall see later, by 'adopting' at least one young actress. The problem with the notion of women operating independently within a highly visible trade in the public sphere is that it disrupts constructs of women and their perceived role in the domestic, private sphere – the very anxiety Prynne identified thirty years earlier. The representation of the actress as socially aspirant, sexually active and, therefore, immoral fits the construct of the woman working out-side the boundaries of domestic propriety and control by operating in the highly visible public sphere of the playhouse. There are clearly a number of women who did improve their social positions via this route but, interest-ingly, there is one actress in Davenant's theatrical household who became the emblem of the virtuous female theatre craftswoman: Mary (Saunderson) Betterton.[31]

A question of identity

The actress/whore trope has been reinforced by its setting up in a binary with its opposite: the virtuous wife and dedicated professional artist. The construction of the actress as wholly dedicated to her craft is personified in numerous accounts of the life and work of Mary (Saunderson) Betterton. She is identified as one of the first 'striking exception[s] to the general run of light-hearted and light-headed ladies who adorned' the Restoration stage, and seen as a 'steady worker' who, as Rosamond Gilder goes on to explain, 'was fortunate enough to find in the man whom she loved and married not only a devoted and faithful husband, but a leader in her own profession'.[32] The romanticism attached to the happily married woman Gilder presents may be somewhat cloying to modern feminist sensibilities, but it is interesting to note that, as in European theatre troupes, actresses married to actors in the patent companies are generally spared the slander and gossip aimed at their unattached fellows. Even though actors were, in a term coined by Kristina Straub, 'sexual suspects', and far from a social position in which they might resist the pressures placed on them to make their wives available to a wealthy and influential protector, there is little evidence to suggest that this ever occurred.[33] The most vehement gossip, however, is launched against those actresses who used their on-stage performance to raise their off-stage position in society by marriage.

Mary Lee joined the Duke's Company around 1670. She was married to a minor actor in the company, John Lee, who died in 1680. Soon after his death she married again, but this time becoming Lady Slingsby, releasing a stream of invective circulated in a contemporary lampoon, 'A Satyr on the Players'.

> Imprimis *Slingsby* hath the fatal curse
> To have Ladies Honour with a Player's Purse
> Tho' now she is so plaguy [sic] haughty grown
> Yet 'Gad my Lady; I the time have known
> When a dull Whiggish Poet would go down.
> That Scene's now chang'd yet prithee dandy beast
> Think nor thyself an Actress in the least
> For sure thy Figure ne'er was seen before
> Such Arse like breasts; stiff neck; with all thy store
> Are certain Antidotes against a Whore.[34]

This attack works on the premise that the actress is *pretending* to be other than she really is and that the lampoonist is merely exposing her *real* identity, but then goes further, undercutting her fit with the whorish label by focusing on that ever-vulnerable target: women's looks. As Susan Bassnett puts it: 'The notion of acting as disguise, the connections between disguise and deceit, and between deceit and immorality' are crucial in a society that marks difference of rank by appearance; 'a female performer was . . . an example of a woman who crossed legal boundaries in terms of dress and who had greater licence than other women'.[35] Behind the superficial entertainment value of the satire (the whole reaching depths to which today's Sunday tabloids only aspire) there is a profound sense of social anxiety around the transgressive position of the actress in the social order. The fact that the actress can be *seen* to be a 'Lady' on the stage, carrying the signs of dress, language and movement associated with that status, is one thing. If she then *becomes* a Lady, as Slingsby did, the stability of social hierarchies is threatened.

Mary Betterton is not included in this vituperative attack against the players (although her actor husband, Thomas Betterton, is certainly not spared), but her escape from gossip and slander works to reinforce the alternative female construct of faithful wife and, in the absence of her own children to raise into the family business, devoted teacher. The *Biographical Dictionary* records that Mary 'had a flair for teaching . . . and an interest in playing foster mother to young actresses . . . [A]fter the turn of the century her chief function in the theatre was training the young performers.'[36] In this construction of the actress, Mary Betterton represents a safe alternative to the model of the social climbing Mary (Lee) Slingsby and the rags-to-riches stories attached to Nell Gwynn. There is little information concerning Mary Betterton's social background, and although it is assumed that 'her origins may have been humble',[37] there is also an implicit understanding that she was of a 'respectable' family, and only the mildest hint of gossip surrounding the fact that she took Betterton's name a year before the young actor 'brought Mary Saunderson honestly to the altar in December 1662'.[38]

The creation of notions around a domestic sphere operating *within* the public space of the patent companies allows for the reinstatement of a relatively stable patriarchal construct which can contain and control professional women working as actresses. Actresses earned considerably less than actors (Howe notes that an experienced actor could expect 50 shillings per. week, whereas an actress would be unlikely to command more than 30 shillings).[39] and married women's pay and playing conditions were negotiated by their husbands.[40] Actresses did, however, enjoy some individual protection as His Majesty's Servants, marked by their right to wear liveries at state occasions. As Howe notes, 'These liveries made them recognized servants of the king and meant most usefully that they could not be sued or arrested for debt without the express permission of the Lord Chamberlain.'[41] The best protection against gossip and accusations of immorality, however, was to belong to a theatrical family, as wife or daughter. By the turn of the eighteenth century theatrical dynasties, notably the Cibber family, were clearly established and the long tradition of young actresses beginning their careers as child performers in the family business was soon underway. Thomas Percival, a minor actor with the Duke's Company, had a daughter, Susannah, who began her career with the King's Company but returned to the Duke's and married their rising young actor/playwright William Mountfort. Notions of the family and the implications of adoption in the seventeenth century are far from our modern understanding, as John Gillis makes clear.[42] The connections between household, family and business are crucial to an understanding of the emerging theatrical community and the moves to construct the actress as belonging within its domestic sphere (virtuous) or beyond those boundaries (whorish). This binary, working under the broader constructs of women in the public/private sphere, can be seen most clearly in the representation of the life and work of the two most prominent and successful actresses of the

Restoration stage, both of whom were adopted into theatrical families as children.

A question of connections

Biographical accounts of Elizabeth Barry suggest a number of explanations concerning her adoption into the Davenant family and her theatrical training. It is generally accepted that she was the daughter of a barrister, Robert Barry, a royalist who lost his fortune during the Civil War, and that she was taken into the Davenant family when she was around ten years old. John Harold Wilson seems unable to spare the whorish brush or avoid the rags-to-riches story in his account of Barry's early life:

> Lady Davenant, a friend of the family, took her in, gave her a genteel education, and, about 1674, put her on the stage. This, we may presume, was Mrs Barry's own version of her parentage and background. Anthony Aston wrote, 'She was woman to Lady Shelton of Norfolk (my Godmother) – when Lord Rochester took her on the Stage; where for some time they could make nothing of her. – She could neither sing nor dance, no, not in a Country-Dance.' According to Cibber she was so unsuccessful that she was discharged at the end of the first year. Curll insists that she was rejected three times and did not succeed until her lover, the Earl of Rochester, gave her private lessons for about six months.[43]

Wilson here continues to build on a series of historical accounts that work to undermine not only Barry's middle-class rank/origins but also, crucially, her creative ability and agency. The picture here is of a malleable young woman being groomed: first, by the 'genteel' education she received in the Davanant household in order to be made fit to be 'put' on the stage by Lady Davenant, and second, following her initial failure to impress, by the intervention of Rochester, an aristocratic libertine playwright, to whom she owed her eventual success on stage.

Barry's private connections with Rochester are well, if not always accurately, documented and it is certain that she bore his child in 1677; but the Svengali-like story can also be read as yet another example of the appropriation of women's work to male control. As the 'adopted' daughter of Sir William and Lady Davenant, the young Barry was brought into a household that revolved around the family business: the activities of the playhouse. Barry's first role is recorded in 1675, seven years after William Davenant's death, during which time Lady Davenant acted as manager of the Duke's Company. With Mary Betterton (the dedicated teacher) a leading actress in the company, if not actually still living with the family, there are grounds for questioning the stories that credit Rochester, rather than Mary Betterton, for 'training her' in the business of theatre. It is interesting to note that Barry did not marry, either in or out of the playhouse community. Throughout her long career (1675–1708) she remained firmly outside the boundaries of domestic constructs and her independent wealth and prominence made her a clear target for gossip and slander. Reports of her ability to move her audience to tears in tragedy are contrasted with stories of her hard-hearted treatment of her admirers, especially the playwright Thomas Otway who wrote many of her early and most successful roles. She excelled in comedy and is named as the speaker for numerous prologues and epilogues, a sure sign of her public popularity, but she was also dubbed a 'mercenary whore', who 'will prostitute with any / Rather than waive the getting of a penny'.[44] Elizabeth Barry created numerous roles for rising and established playwrights of the day, including those for the 'first' professional female playwright, Aphra Behn. By the time the Duke's and King's Companies united in 1682, Barry was the leading actress in the only patent theatre company in London. She was the first actress to negotiate a benefit payment, whereby she received the entire profits for a performance as additional income to her weekly salary. Rumours of profitable affairs with the Earl of Dorset and Sir George Etherege are mixed in with accounts of on-stage fights with a fellow actress over a piece of costume – all part of the well-worn trope of female jealousy. As Elizabeth Howe concludes, 'All documentary evidence suggests that her income was largely made through acting – hence her interest in carving her share from the company profits. The vicious satires against "that mercenary Prostituted Dame" represent, above all, a dislike of a remarkable female professional success.'[45] Barry's strongest and lengthiest alliance was with another, younger actress, who had also been adopted into the theatrical community.

Anne Bracegirdle joined the Bettertons' household when she was six years old. In stark contrast to Barry, Bracegirdle was almost immediately represented in the same light as her adoptive mother, Mary, and the same virtuous label attached to her. The *Biographical Dictionary* goes to some lengths to establish a respectable background and suggest a possible connection to 'the Staffordshire Bracegirdles, in which case she would have been distantly related to the Astons and the Congreves'.[46] This last connection is most interesting as, if true, it might cast a quite different light on the supposed relationship between Bracegirdle and playwright William Congreve. Like Barry, Bracegirdle never married and there were numerous stories concerning romantic entanglements – notably with actor/playwright William Mountfort, who lost his life defending Bracegirdle from the attentions of a jealous admirer. Under the respectable, domestic realm of the

Bettertons, Bracegirdle escaped the vituperative attacks endured by Barry, as a contemporary account by that other theatrical patriarch Colley Cibber demonstrates:

> never any Woman was in such general Favour of her spectators, which, to the last Scene of her Dramatick Life, she maintain'd by not being unguarded in her private Character. This Discretion contributed not a little to make her the *Cara*, the Darling of the Theatre: For it will be no extravagant thing to say, Scarce an Audience saw her that were less than half of them Lovers, without a suspected Favourite among them: And tho' she might be said to have been the Universal Passion, and under the highest Temptations, her constancy in resisting them served but to Increase the number of her Admirers . . . It was even a fashion among the Gay and Young to have a taste or *Tendre* for Mrs. *Bracegirdle*.[47]

The crucial shift in this representation of Bracegirdle is that the 'virtuous' actress might be seen as a figure worthy of being *admired* from afar, rather than her appearance in the public sphere being a demonstration of her availability to the highest bidder. The public display of virtue on stage is a reflection of her virtuous 'private character' off stage, not a veil to hide her true character.

The contrasting on-stage identity and off-stage representations of both actresses led to a formidable acting partnership forged by Barry and Bracegirdle over eighteen years. In the seven-year partnership played out in the United Company (1688–95), they performed together in sixteen plays, with Barry playing the dark *femme fatale* and Bracegirdle the innocent and virtuous foil. This collaboration played a vital role in the success of Congreve's first two plays, and when the actresses broke away from the patent house in 1695 to form a players' co-operative with Thomas Betterton at Lincoln's Inn Fields Theatre, William Congreve moved with them. The creation of contrasting female characters on stage by actresses with contrasting public identities off stage is a tried and tested model in modern film drama. The partnership between Elizabeth Barry and Anne Bracegirdle offers an early example of that model. Its most interesting aspect is the way in which they exploited their public identity, perhaps even using gossip to fuel their success at the box office. The female perspective their characters presented *on* stage and the new opportunities their working partnership suggested for theatre women *off* stage demonstrated the potential for actresses as agents. The development of their own professional status began to reshape the discourse around the actress and women's role in the public and private sphere.

A question of autonomy

On 25 March 1695 the Lord Chamberlain granted the licence for a new theatre company in London.[48] This licence not only marks an end to the thirteen-year monopoly enjoyed by the United Company at Drury Lane but also provides documentary evidence of a new status for actresses. Until this point actresses had been hired on weekly salaries, but now they were named as 'sharers' in company management and, crucially, company profits. The licence is issued to eleven named players. Four of these were actresses, with Barry and Bracegirdle at the head of the list (after Thomas Betterton). As leading actress/managers, Barry and Bracegirdle brought the works of five new female playwrights to the public stage, performing in at least seventeen new plays in a period of ten years (1695–1705) and played a crucial part in launching the most successful female playwright of the eighteenth century, Susannah Centlivre.[49]

With such a high profile in the public sphere, it is little wonder that gossip about Barry and Bracegirdle stepped up as the satirists set about undermining the collaboration between actress and female playwright. At Drury Lane an anonymous satirical play, *The Female Wits* (1697), openly mocked the female playwright and attacked Barry and Bracegirdle's company as over-the-hill players with outmoded acting styles. The rise of the anti-theatrical lobby provoked a further wave of invective against the immorality of women in the public sphere of the playhouse. Barry's financial dealings in company matters evidently continued to vex her critics, notably a playwright adopting the pseudonym 'Frank Teltroth' for the dedicatory epistle to his published but unperformed play *The Lunatick* (1705) which unleashes a swingeing attack on the managerial operations of Barry, Bracegirdle and Betterton, 'the three B–s':

> There will be no more clandestine sharing betwixt you without the rest; no more private accounts, and double Books; no more paying Debts half a score times over out of the Publick Stock, yet never paying them in reality at all ... no more sinking the Court-money into your own Pockets, and letting the Sallary people and Under sharers Starve without pay; no more taking Benefit-Days in the Best Season of the Year, and dunning the quality for Guinea-Tickets to help out the Defects of all the other above named Prerequisites ... no saving Coals at Home, by Working, Eating and Drinking, &c. by the Stock-Fire; nor, in short, any Advantage to be made but by stated Sallaries or the best Improvement of Naturall Gifts, as far as Age, Ugliness and gout will permit.

The accusations of financial impropriety are matched by attacks aimed at Anne Bracegirdle's virtuous identity in several lampoons, with one satirist setting the female playwright and actress against one another in a fictional cat-fight entitled: 'From Worthy Mrs Behn the Poetess, to the Famous Virgin Actress':

> I am sensible 'tis as hard a matter for a pretty Woman to keep her self Honest in a Theatre, as 'tis for an Apothecary to keep his Treacle from the Flies in hot Weather; for every Libertine in the Audience will be buzzing about her Honey-pot, and her Vertue must defend it self by Abundance of Fly-flaps, or those Flesh-loving Insects will soon blow upon her Honour, and when once she has a Maggot in her Tail, all the Pepper and Salt in the Kingdom will scarce keep her Reputation from stinking; therefore that which makes me admire your good Housewifery above all your Sex is, that notwithstanding, your powdering-Tub has been so often polluted, yet you have kept your Flesh in such Credit and good Order, that the nicest Appetite in the Town would be glad to make a meal of it.[50]

Published in the year that Bracegirdle retired from the stage, one year before Barry also gave in her parts and retired to her farm in the countryside of west London, it seems that the actress/whore trope prevailed over alternative stories of independence and creative and financial autonomy.

In the centuries that follow, actress/managers/writers become increasingly involved in theatrical production, even if their work has been occluded from many of our theatre histories. The evidence of their success can be found in theatrical documents, contracts, playbills and calendars of performance, but the most vivid representations are to be found in the gossip columns of their day. Michael L. Quinn sees gossip as an essential part of celebrity, arguing that '[g]ossip presumably allows every spectator to see the truth behind the mask, to project the knowledge that similar events in the life of actor and character converge'.[51] For the actress, that 'truth' is generally focused on her sexualised identity and her sexual activity. The more successful she is, the more interest/suspicion she attracts for, as Quinn puts it, 'The first requisite for celebrity is public notoriety, which is only sometimes achieved through acting.'[52] The performing woman who achieves public recognition, agency and autonomy is deeply connected with notions of female immorality forged in historically distant cultural discourses. The social and cultural revolution of the seventeenth century brought changes in legislation that undoubtedly created a new professional status for women operating within the commercial business of theatre. The evidence for her success and influence, in this and later centuries, may lie in the very documents that seek to undermine her: we should perhaps pay rather more careful attention to gossip.

NOTES

1. Michel Foucault, *The History of Sexuality*, vol. 1: *The Will to Knowledge* (1976), trans. Robert Hurley (London: Penguin Books, 1998).
2. Samuel Pepys, *The Diary of Samuel Pepys*, ed. Robert Latham and William Matthews, 11 vols. (London: G. Bell and Sons, 1970–83).
3. Joseph Roach, *Cities of the Dead: Circum-Atlantic Performance* (New York: Columbia University Press, 1996), p. 30.
4. Sophie Tomlinson, 'She that Plays the King: Henrietta Maria and the Threat of the Actress in Caroline Culture', in Gordon McMullan and Jonathan Hope, eds., *The Politics of Tragicomedy: Shakespeare and After* (London: Routledge, 1992), pp. 189–207, p. 189.
5. Ibid., p. 190.
6. Prynne, quoted ibid., p. 195.
7. G. E. Bentley, *The Jacobean and Caroline Stage*, 7 vols. (Oxford: Clarendon Press, 1948–61), vol. 1, p. 25.
8. Stephen Orgel, *Impersonations* (Cambridge: Cambridge University Press 1996), p. 7.
9. Ibid., p. 11.
10. Tomlinson, 'She that Plays the King', p. 192.
11. Ibid., p. 198.
12. Kirsten Pullen, *Actresses and Whores: On Stage and in Society* (Cambridge: Cambridge University Press, 2005), pp. 22–3.
13. Tomlinson, 'She that Plays The King', p. 198.
14. Ursula K. Heise, 'Transvestism and the Stage Controversy in Spain and England, 1580–1680', *Theatre Journal* 44 (1992), pp. 357–74, p. 359.
15. Ibid., p. 360.
16. The work of sixteenth-century Italian actress Isabella Andreini is followed by a discussion of seventeenth-century French actresses Madeleine and Armande Béjart in Rosamond Gilder, *Enter the Actress* (London: George Harrap, 1931), which still remains a key resource in histories of the actress.
17. Katherine Eisaman Maus, '"Playhouse Flesh and Blood": Sexual Ideology and the Restoration Actress', *ELH* 46 (1979), pp. 595–617, p. 595.
18. Tomlinson, 'She that Plays the King', p. 190
19. BL Add. MS 19, 256, fn. 47, quoted in David Thomas, ed., *Restoration and Georgian England 1660–1788* (Cambridge: Cambridge University Press, 1989), pp. 11–13.
20. Allardyce Nicoll, *A History of English Drama 1660–1900*, vol. 1: *Restoration Drama 1660–1700* (Cambridge: Cambridge University Press, 1952), p. 324.
21. Elizabeth Howe, *The First English Actresses* (Cambridge: Cambridge University Press, 1992), p. 20.
22. Paula Backsheider, *Spectacular Politics* (Baltimore, MD: Johns Hopkins University Press, 1993), pp. 3–31.
23. Howe, *First English Actresses*, p. 24.
24. Pepys, *Diary*, 8 January 1661.
25. John Downes, *Roscius Anglicanus* (1708), ed. Judith Milhous and Robert D. Hume (London: Society for Theatre Research, 1987), p. 49.
26. Ibid., fn. 127.

27. Ibid., p. 74.
28. Orgel, *Impersonations*, pp. 71–4.
29. Ibid., p. 73.
30. Ibid.
31. See Antonia Fraser, *The Weaker Vessel* (1984, repr. London: Arrow Books, 1997), pp. 476–9.
32. Gilder, *Enter the Actress*, pp. 150–1.
33. Kristina Straub, *Sexual Suspects: Eighteenth-century Players and Sexual Ideology* (Princeton, NJ: Princeton University Press, 1992).
34. 'A Satyr on the Players', in *Satyrs and Lampoons* (ca. 1678–90), BL MS Harley 7317, pp. 96–100. Parts of the lampoon are published in many standard histories. The full version, which includes scandalous attacks on all the main actors and actresses in the patent company, can be found in Gilli Bush-Bailey, *Treading the Bawds: Actresses and Playwrights on the Late Stuart Stage* (Manchester: Manchester University Press, 2006).
35. Susan Bassnett, 'Struggling with the Past: Women's Theatre in Search of a History', *New Theatre Quarterly* 5.18 (1989), pp. 107–12, p. 111.
36. Philip H. Highfill, ed., *A Biographical Dictionary of Actors, Actresses, Musicians, Dancers, Managers and Other Stage Personnel in London 1660–1800*, 16 vols. (Carbondale: Southern Illinois University Press, 1973), vol. 1, pp. 96–9, p. 97.
37. Ibid., p. 96.
38. Ibid., p. 97.
39. Howe, *First English Actresses*, p. 27.
40. Ibid., p. 27.
41. Ibid.
42. See John R. Gillis, *A World of their Own Making: A History of Myth and Ritual in Family Life* (Oxford: Oxford University Press, 1996), pp. 3–19, for his explanation of the organisation of family/household in relation to the industry/work they depended upon.
43. John Harold Wilson, *All the King's Ladies: Actresses of the Restoration* (Chicago: University of Chicago Press, 1958), p. 110.
44. Robert Gould, *The Playhouse* (1700), quoted in Highfill, *Biographical Dictionary*, vol. 1, p. 320.
45. Howe, *First English Actresses*, p. 31.
46. Highfill, *Biographical Dictionary*, vol. 1, p. 269.
47. Colley Cibber, *An Apology for the Life of Mr Colley Cibber* (ca. 1740), with notes and supplement by Robert W. Lowe, 2 vols. (London: John C. Nimmo, 1889), vol. 1, pp. 170–2.
48. Judith Milhous, *Thomas Betterton and the Management of Lincoln's Inn Fields 1695–1708* (Carbondale: Southern Illinois University Press, 1979); see Appendix D for a reproduction of the licence and Bush-Bailey, *Treading the Bawds* for more on Barry and Bracegirdle's involvement in creating the new company.
49. Nancy Cotton, *Women Playwrights in England c.1363–1750* (London: Associated University Presses, 1980); Fidelis Morgan, *The Female Wits* (London: Virago, 1981); *The Plays of Mary Pix and Catherine Trotter*, ed. Edna Steeves, 2 vols. (New York: Garland Publishing Inc., 1982); and Diana Kendall, *Love and Thunder: Plays by Women in the Age of Queen Anne* (London: Methuen, 1988), for more on the playwrights.

50. Thomas Brown, *The Works of Mr. Thomas Brown*, 3 vols. (London: Sam Briscoe, 1707), pp. 165–70.
51. Michael L. Quinn, 'Celebrity and the Semiotics of Acting', *New Theatre Quarterly* (May 1990), pp. 154–61, p. 155.
52. Ibid., p. 156.

FURTHER READING

Backsheider, Paula. *Spectacular Politics*. Baltimore, MD: Johns Hopkins University Press, 1993.

Bush-Bailey, Gilli. *Treading the Bawds: Actresses and Playwrights on the Late Stuart Stage*. Manchester: Manchester University Press, 2006.

Gilder, Rosamond. *Enter the Actress*. London: George Harrap, 1931.

Howe, Elizabeth. *The First English Actresses*. Cambridge: Cambridge University Press, 1992.

Kendall, Diana, ed. *Love and Thunder: Plays by Women in the Age of Queen Anne*. London: Methuen, 1988.

Morgan, Fidelis. *The Female Wits*. London: Virago, 1981.

Orgel, Stephen. *Impersonations*. Cambridge: Cambridge University Press, 1996.

Pullen, Kirsten. *Actresses and Whores: On Stage and in Society*. Cambridge: Cambridge University Press, 2005.

Straub, Kristina. *Sexual Suspects: Eighteenth-century Players and Sexual Ideology*. Princeton, NJ: Princeton University Press, 1992.

Tomlinson, Sophie. 'She that Plays the King: Henrietta Maria and the Threat of the Actress in Caroline Culture', in George McMullan and Jonathan Hope, eds., *The Politics of Tragicomedy: Shakespeare and After*: London: Routledge, 1992.

Wilson, John Harold. *All the King's Ladies: Actresses of the Restoration*. Chicago: Chicago University Press, 1958.

2

ELIZABETH EGER

Spectacle, intellect and authority: the actress in the eighteenth century

Nicholas Rowe's play *The Fair Penitent*, which was first performed in 1703, provided the eighteenth century with one of its most popular heroines, Calista. In the following speech, she vents a rare moment of anger in a play that paints a bleak picture of women's fate:

> How hard is the condition of our sex,
> Through ev'ry state of life the slaves of man!
> In all the dear, delightful days of youth
> A rigid father dictates to our will,
> And deals out pleasure with a scanty hand;
> To his, the tyrant husband's reign succeeds;
> Proud with opinion of superior reason,
> He holds domestic business and devotion
> All we are capable to know, and shuts us,
> Like cloistered idiots, from the world's acquaintance
> And all the joys of freedom; wherefore are we
> Born with high souls but to assert ourselves,
> Shake off this vile obedience they exact,
> And claim an equal empire o'er the world?[1]

The Fair Penitent was designed to inspire an overwhelming sensation of pity rather than to make an intellectual argument for equality between men and women. Nonetheless, Calista became famous in the popular imagination as an advocate for the female sex and was often cited as a model of endurance by proto-feminist writers. Rowe asks the audience to see through Calista's eyes, if only for a moment, offering a woman's assessment of the world she lives in rather than a more stereotypical vision of passive femininity. Such moments of dramatic intensity were known as 'hits' or 'points' and often remained fixed in the public memory long after the play's plot had been forgotten. These 'hits' created a space in which women's voices could be heard, forming important moments of resistance in a scheme of representation that tended to allow women little agency (even of this male-authored variety).[2]

'She-tragedy', a genre coined by Rowe himself, had become increasingly popular with female audiences from the beginning of the century and contributed to the rise of the professional actress by foregrounding strong heroines under the pressure of sentimental situations, sustaining a remarkably durable presence on the London stage. Rowe's plays provided Sarah Siddons with two of her most famous roles, as Calista and as Jane Shore, figures of feminine strength and pathos that undoubtedly influenced contemporary attitudes to the female sex. With hindsight, Calista's speech can be read metaphorically as a premonition of the rise of the actress over the course of the eighteenth century – a period during which she asserted herself with unprecedented force in the theatre and beyond.

Actresses had a more regular and highly charged relationship with the public than any other group of women of their day. They were frequently open to accusations of immorality and tended to be associated with the prostitutes, or 'public women', that frequented the pit, rather than the aristocratic ladies who occupied the boxes above. However, as the century progressed and more and more women of the middling classes attended the theatre, a gradual moralisation of the stage occurred so that women of virtue could perform and become respected as professional actresses. In addition to tracing the positive moral shift in the reputation of the actress, this essay suggests that acting formed a realm of possibility and independent action for women concerned to push against the social and political boundaries marked out for their sex. Figures such as Charlotte Charke, Hannah Pritchard, Lavinia Fenton and Sarah Siddons developed new styles of performing, acquiring a prominent role in the public imagination and provoking anxieties about women's place in society.

The theatre was a space for cultural innovation, in which the relationship between actress, audience, managers and playwrights was dynamic and mutually influential. From being a court institution, shaped by the taste of the monarch, it became a commercial business formed by the taste of a general public. As such, it was in touch with the contemporary cultural spaces of the coffee house, the exhibition hall, the booksellers and circulating libraries. Women were closely involved in shaping the public sphere, and it is in this context that the agency of actresses must be understood.[3] Actresses came to see their work in active terms, as something over which they had considerable control and in which they could invest as a means to both material and intellectual improvement and independence. Acting came to be valued as a vocation that required education but which could also educate. The complex relationship between spectacle, intellect and authority in the lives and texts of actresses such as Elizabeth Griffith, Sarah Siddons and above all Mary

Robinson confirms their contribution to the broader cultural definition of the time.

Women's increasing involvement in the theatre can be associated with licensing agreements enacted in England after the Restoration of the monarchy in 1660, when Charles II allowed women to play female roles on the legitimate stage. The Licensing Act of 1713 reduced various laws relating to rogues and vagabonds into a single Act of Parliament, raising the status of the profession as a whole to a respectable legal standing. For the first time the Lord Chamberlain's relation to the theatre was given statutory recognition. These stipulations gave women new access to the stage as a space for public identity and professional reward. Having been too often overshadowed by the prominence of male 'stars' such as Colley Cibber and David Garrick, women developed an increasingly confident theatrical presence. As Sandra Richards maintains, 'women's pioneering performances of roles old and new, acted in experimental or emerging styles, prepared the way for actresses to supersede their male colleagues as performers during the latter half of the eighteenth century'.[4] Robert Walpole's Licensing Act of 1737 effectively restricted the appearance of spoken drama to the licensed playhouses, Covent Garden and Drury Lane, and all new plays had to be approved by the Lord Chamberlain in his role as censor. One result of this was an increase in the number of productions of Shakespeare. Actresses particularly enjoyed the range and breadth of characters offered by Shakespearean drama, often becoming associated with particular characters. Sarah Siddons's Lady Macbeth, for example, was among the most discussed and analysed roles of the era.

Theatre managers favoured the use of actresses, including Hannah Pritchard and Dora Jordan, in 'breeches roles', partly because it offered audiences the titillating and usually forbidden sensation of viewing female legs. The 'breeches role' was also adopted by actresses who wanted to extend the possibilities of transvestite acting in order to compete directly with men for the most coveted roles. Charlotte Charke's performance of Hamlet had a freshness and daring that gave her the edge over her male contemporaries. Apart from countless productions of Shakespeare, the heavy tragedies of Otway and Rowe dominated the first half of the century while sentimental comedy became more popular during the second half – a genre that bordered on the mawkish until made crisper by Sheridan and Goldsmith. Actresses and an increasingly female audience helped to shape the popularity of these genres, both of which highlighted virtuous heroines in distress.

Joseph Roach has used acting manuals published between 1730 and 1780 to analyse the ways in which actors were taught to represent the passions of love, hate, sorrow, jealousy and scorn in a detailed series of facial configurations and formal bodily gestures.[5] However, the most successful actresses of the period managed to break out of formulaic moral language, creating their own modes of dramatic expression. Reviews of Siddons's performances suggest that she built upon this highly developed practice but took it further by managing to evoke a swift succession of emotions or even several emotions at once. This presented a difficult challenge to visual artists of the time, who had been used to the relative ease of being able to record the exaggerated 'points' or 'stills'. Shearer West's work on the image of the actor has alerted us to the sense in which it is almost impossible to understand fully the effect of particular actresses' performances or even to be able to imagine their methods on stage.[6] But it is possible to gain a sense of how the performances of actresses could connect with and influence different aesthetic, social, political and literary concerns during this period by looking at their writing.

A significant number of eighteenth-century actresses, including Susannah Centlivre, Charlotte Charke, Catherine Clive, Elizabeth Griffith, Eliza Haywood, Elizabeth Inchbald, Susanna Rowson, Sarah Siddons and Mary Robinson, made the transition from acting to writing, several producing the sort of plays they wished to see on stage, rather than merely acting in and inspiring the works of men.[7] All demonstrate a remarkable capacity for self-invention across a range of different literary genres.[8] Eliza Haywood, actress, journalist and novelist, spoke the Prologue to one of her own plays, *A Wife to be Lett*, when it was first performed at Drury Lane in 1723:

> *Criticks! be dumb to-night – no skill display;*
> *A dangerous* Woman-Poet *wrote the Play:*
> *More than your Match, in every thing, but Railing.*
> *Give her fair Quarter, and when'er she tries ye,*
> *Safe in superior Spirit, she defies thee:*
> *Measure her Force, by her known Novels, writ*
> *With manly vigour, and with Woman's Wit.*
> *Then tremble, and depend, if ye beset her,*
> *She, who can talk so well, may yet act better.*[9]

Haywood had first acted at the Smock Alley Theatre in Dublin in 1714, coming to London to join the Lincoln's Inn Fields Theatre three years later. She kept up her acting career until 1737 when the Licensing Act threatened the non-patent theatres. Here she connects her acting and literary careers in her general advertisement of her 'manly vigour' in taking on the theatrical establishment. This productive confusion of gender recurs among actresses of the period. Sarah Siddons attracted the traditionally masculine label 'sublime', suggesting the extent to which she had broadened the range of virtues and attributes previously associated with women.[10] A *Wife to be Lett* is a shrewd portrayal of woman's vulnerability in a world of human interaction as economic exchange. Haywood was proud of her own commercial success in the literary marketplace and the theatre, aware that she offered a model of resistance to the iniquities of institutions still dominated by men. Later in the century, women playwrights continued to attack establishment attitudes but often softened – or even distorted – their criticism by displacing the action of their plays to distant times and places. The British-born actress and playwright Susanna Rowson, for example, who emigrated to America in the 1790s, managed to express her sympathies for the abolition and feminist movements by writing a play called *Slaves in Algiers* (1794), a diverse blend of historical tragedy and musical comedy.[11]

In 1799 the actress, poet and novelist Mary Robinson published *A Letter to the Women of England, on the Injustice of Mental Subordination*, under the pseudonym Anne Frances Randall.[12] This pamphlet carried an epigraph from Calista's speech, quoted at the outset of this essay: 'Wherefore are we / Born with high Souls, but to *assert ourselves*?' By identifying with Calista, Robinson placed herself in a distinguished tradition of feminist writing, as well as self-consciously joining the ranks of radical writers of the 1790s: 'For it requires a legion of Wollstonecrafts to undermine the poisons of prejudice and malevolence.'[13] Her *Letter* forms a spirited interrogation of contemporary legal and social prejudice, demanding that women should be allowed to 'speak and write their opinions more freely'.[14] It has the freshness and emotional intensity of theatrical dialogue and can be interpreted as a mode of dramatic performance. The address is direct, intimate and impassioned, often explicitly echoing the speech of familiar dramatic characters. In one passage, for example, she reworks Shylock's appeal in *The Merchant of Venice*:

> Let me ask this plain and rational question – is not woman a human being, gifted with all the feeling that inhabits the bosom of man? Has not woman affections, susceptibility, fortitude, and an acute sense of injuries received? Does she not shrink at the touch of persecution? Does not her bosom melt with sympathy, throb with pity, glow with resentment, ache with sensibility, and burn with indignation?[15]

Here Robinson asks the reader to imagine the female body in a series of poignant tableaux or 'attitudes', in a visible state of emotional conflict.[16] She highlights the vexed relationship between passion and reason that was

37

experienced by many of her contemporary female writers, aiming to elicit a pitying response that is nonetheless a recognition of woman's moral fibre. This rhetorical strategy is akin to that employed in eighteenth-century tragedy, in which the female protagonist emerged as dramatic focus, often in the role of victim and always associated with the display of correct moral sentiments. Robinson relies on the reader's sympathy with private feeling in order to make a more universal, public point. This tactic was not, of course, the exclusive property of women writers. More famously, Burke had adopted a similar method in his *Reflections on the Revolution in France* (1789), in which he compared the feelings excited in him by the revolution to those aroused by the spectacle of tragic drama, recalling 'the tears that Garrick formerly, or that Siddons not long since, have extorted from me'.[17] Where Burke aimed to make his readers feel for the fall of the great, however, Robinson wanted to elevate the concerns of the oppressed. Her experience as an actress heightened her literary sense of audience and gave her a particular sense of authority in representing her sex.

While borrowing much from the spirit of Wollstonecraft's *Vindication of the Rights of Woman* (1792), Robinson's work is less theoretical and more personal in structure. In a short essay, 'Society and Manners in the Metropolis of England', in 1800, she combines her pride in British women writers with a celebration of the wider range of contemporary female cultural activity: 'We have also sculptors, modellers, paintresses, and female artists of every description. Mrs Damer, Mrs Siddons, Mrs Cosway, and Miss Linwood have produced specimens of art that will long be admired and cherished as ornaments to the country.'[18] Unlike several encomiums by male critics, in which the actress Sarah Siddons appears as an abstracted and objectified work of art, here she is praised as an artist, in the company of writers, sculptors and painters: all professions concerned with creating works of art for public display and all requiring female agency.

Robinson's tract was published the end of a century that had witnessed a transformation in women's involvement in their culture and the emergence of a new attitude to women's work. Any consideration of the role of the actress in this period must take into account the broader cultural canvas upon which women were making their mark, finding expression. By the same token, any close engagement with literary culture of this time must acknowledge the actress as a significant, even central force in the contemporary imagination. If, as Ellen Donkin has claimed, 'the history of women's performance is the history of a struggle for a subject, rather than an object, position in representation', it is not surprising that the actress should come close to achieving such a subject position in an era when the nature of citizenship was debated with particular urgency.[19] Strongly influenced by the French Revolution in articulating their desire for full citizenship, women aimed in their polemical writings 'to fashion all women as actors within a more generous conception of the public sphere'.[20] In her *Letter to the Women of England*, Robinson is aware of the historical significance of the moment she documents, presenting her sisters' literary productions as evidence of women's right to wider freedoms, answers to Calista's call.

Women writers and actresses never became free of the public's fascination with their private lives. Mary Robinson's *Memoirs*, published posthumously and completed by her daughter, provide an unusual response to this pressure, and constitute a document of self-justification and explanation – both an attempt to answer the 'gossip' that had supported (and undermined) her career, and a shrewd means of providing for her daughter by satisfying a public still hungry for 'authentic' information about the famous 'Perdita', actress, royal courtesan and poet.[21] As Stella Tillyard has written, 'celebrity was born at the moment private life became a tradeable public commodity. It had, and still has, a more feminine face than fame, because private life, and the kind of virtue around which reputations could pivot, were both seen to reside in femininity and in women.'[22]

Mary Robinson, aware of the power of her beauty from an early age, had a profound knowledge of the world of celebrity.[23] Her *Memoirs* catalogue her effect on the public in minute detail. She was constantly on display: 'Whenever I appeared in public, I was overwhelmed by the gazing of the multitude. I was frequently obliged to quit Ranelagh, owing to the crowd which staring curiosity had assembled round my box . . . Many hours have I waited till the crowd dispersed, which surrounded my carriage, in expectation of my quitting the shop.'[24] The following extract from her *Memoirs*, in which she sees her marriage at the age of fourteen as an impediment to life on the stage, reveals the extent to which she was unable, or perhaps reluctant, to distinguish between life and performance in fashioning her own identity:

> My heart, even when I knelt at the altar, was as free from any tender impression as it had been at the moment of my birth. I knew not the sensation of any sentiment beyond that of esteem; love was still a stranger to my bosom. I had never, then, seen the being who was destined to inspire a thought which might influence my fancy, or excite an interest in my mind; and I well remember that even while I was pronouncing the marriage vow my fancy involuntarily wandered to that scene where I had hoped to support myself with *éclat* and reputation.

Mary Darby's marriage to Thomas Robinson was arranged by her mother in order to prevent her imminent debut as an actress. The *Memoirs* recall

Mary's youthful ambition to become 'an ornament to the theatre', and her attempts to enlist her mother's support by citing examples of 'females who, even in that perilous and arduous situation, preserved an unspotted fame'.[25] She was introduced to the elderly Garrick, who resolved to appear as Lear to her Cordelia. Mary's mother, however, feared for her daughter's reputation, particularly in the light of her father's absence (Matthew Darby, a merchant sailor, had abandoned his family for a mistress in the fishing territories of Labrador). Mary was forced by her mother to relinquish her plans for 'a thousand triumphs' on stage. However, it soon became clear Thomas Robinson had lied about his inheritance and had gambled away any money he once had. After a spell in debtors' prison, Mary rekindled her acting career in an effort to support the couple financially.

Robinson's vivid description of her debut as Juliet at Drury Lane describes the courage it took her to master her relationship with her audience. She is acutely aware of herself as an object of the audience's gaze:

> The theatre was crowded with fashionable spectators; the Green-room and Orchestra (where Mr Garrick sat during the night) were thronged with critics. My dress was a pale pink satin, trimmed with crape, richly spangled with silver. My head was ornamented with white feathers, and my monumental suit, for the last scene, was white satin and completely plain; excepting that I wore a veil of the most transparent gauze, which fell quite to my feet from the back of my head, and a string of beads round my waist, to which was suspended a cross appropriately fashioned.
>
> When I approached the side wing my heart throbbed convulsively; I then began to fear that my resolution would fail, and I leaned upon the nurse's arm, almost fainting. Mr Sheridan and several other friends encouraged me to proceed; and at length, with trembling limbs and fearful apprehension, I approached the audience.
>
> The thundering applause that greeted me nearly overpowered my faculties. I stood mute and bending with alarm, which did not subside till I had feebly articulated the few sentences of the first short scene, during the whole of which I had never once ventured to look at the audience.[26]

She writes of her sense of failure as she returned to the greenroom after the first scene and realised that while her looks had been admired, her powers as an actress were still unknown, 'my fears having as it were palsied both my voice and action'. While she revels in the visual beauty of her costume, she is aware that without 'voice and action' she is nothing more than an object of desire. Robinson goes on to describe the moment of transformation that occurs when she returns to the stage and decides to look out towards her audience, watching them in the act of looking at her:

I never shall forget the sensation which rushed through my bosom when I first looked towards the Pit. I beheld a gradual ascent of heads: all eyes were fixed upon me; and the sensation they conveyed was awfully impressive: but the keen, the penetrating eyes of Mr Garrick, darting their lustre from the centre of the Orchestra, were beyond all others, the objects most conspicuous.[27]

Robinson recounts this moment with a sense of revelation, as the time when she became initiated into the dynamics of her profession and developed, under the tutelage of Garrick, a sense of personal ambition:

I then experienced, for the first time in my life, a gratification which language could not utter. I heard one of the most fascinating men and the most distinguished geniuses of the age honour me with partial approbation: a new sensation seemed to awake in my bosom: I felt that emulation which the soul delights to encourage, where the attainment of fame will be pleasing to an esteemed object.[28]

Despite the brevity of her stage career, Robinson retained a fierce attachment to the profession until the end of her life. Her ambition to succeed and her experience as an acclaimed performer helped to shape her literary career and enabled her to enact a series of literary, political and cultural transformations that combined intellect, spectacle and authority in a dazzling array of styles and voices.[29]

If the lives of actresses were public property, publicity could be manipulated both for and against women's interests. More often than not, women exploited publicity for professional reward, and their visibility could also become a useful resource for other professions experiencing a process of transformation. As British art made claims for a new authority and confidence, galvanised by Reynolds's project to found a national school of painting, its painters turned to actresses in order to attract the attention of the public. From 1780, aesthetically ambitious and innovative portraits of actresses by Reynolds, Gainsborough, Romney and Hamilton appeared to great acclaim in the annual exhibitions of the Royal Academy, jostling amongst nobility and royalty on the crowded walls of Somerset House. The mode of display in these exhibitions favoured an unsystematic mode of juxtaposition, so that the hierarchies of class and gender were often visually confused or openly placed in confrontation. Portraits of actresses played upon the cultural visibility and fame of their subjects, but also sought to elevate actresses through mythical allusion in order to raise portraiture to the level of history painting. As Gill Perry argues, portraits of actresses thus created a profound tension between the aesthetic and the commercial, combining associations of 'high' and 'low' forms of display.[30]

Reynolds's *Mrs Siddons as the Tragic Muse* was exhibited at the Royal Academy show of 1784. Her posture in this impressive portrait is based on a pose by Michelangelo, lending an air of classical authority to the composition.[31] Siddons appeared in a revival of Garrick's 'Shakespeare Jubilee' in the pose of Reynold's picture the following year, art imitating art in the most self-conscious sense possible. The eulogistic reviews of Reynolds's portrait in the *Public Advertiser* of 1784 refer to his artistic 'performance', while Siddons's performance in the theatre was labelled as that of an 'artist'. In his portraits of Mary Robinson and Sarah Siddons, Gainsborough chose to elevate them to the level of fine ladies, isolating them from the tools of their profession and presenting them as captivating and assertive individuals in their own right. He seems to play upon the ambiguity inherent in luxurious images that are faintly redolent of earlier portraits of royal courtesans yet also advertise a new breed of professional beauty. Kimberly Crouch has written of the sense in which actresses occupied a place between the whore and the artistocrat, both literally in the physical dynamics of their interaction with the audience – actresses played to the prostitutes who displayed themselves in the pit below and the fine ladies in the boxes above – and more metaphorically in the contemporary imagination: 'In the grey area between aristocrat and whore, the actress was sometimes allowed and even forgiven for the freedoms of both.'[32] Yet as Crouch's phrasing implies, such freedoms were constrained and actresses could not necessarily control their image in the public sphere across the whole spectrum of representation. While Mary Robinson was aware of exerting a certain degree of control in her relationship with Joshua Reynolds, for example, conscious of her ability to bring him fame, she could not control her image in the realm of satirical print culture, which often distorted the meaning of her portraits in 'high' art through means of graphic sexual innuendo and cruel wit.

While acting never completely lost its morally ambiguous character for women, there was a new sense in which the very visibility of the actress became an argument for her improved social status. Even the morally cautious Quaker philanthropist Priscilla Wakefield cannot dismiss actresses completely from her guide to suitable professions for the genteel but distressed females of her day. She also makes the link between the literary and theatrical professions:

> The stage is a profession, to which many women of refined manners, and a literary turn of mind have had recourse. Since it has been customary for females to assume dramatic characters, there appears to have been full as great a proportion of women, who have attained celebrity, among those who have devoted themselves to a theatrical life, as of the other sex; a fact which argues

that there is no inequality of genius, in the sexes, for the imitative arts; the observation may operate as a stimulant to women to those pursuits which are less objectionable than the stage; which is not mentioned for the purpose of recommending it, but of proving that the abilities of the female sex are equal to nobler labours than are usually undertaken by women.[33]

Wakefield is reluctantly impressed by the success and sheer number of actresses upon the British stage, using their example in her argument for the expansion of suitable, 'less objectionable' professions for women in need of financial independence.

The actress most successful in achieving a virtuous reputation during this era was Siddons, who was frequently praised for combining her acting talent with a blameless private life.[34] Siddons drew vast audiences, who admired, above all, her ability to convey several types of passion all at once through her tremendously versatile range of facial expressions. She also self-consciously connected her private and public roles by appealing as a mother to her audience's emotions. Before her second London debut, for example, she brought her three children on to the stage during a speech about her 'three reasons' for leaving her loyal provincial audiences in the Bath and Bristol theatres. She also allowed herself, and her audience, to add a personal gloss to some of her most popular roles, creating a risky amalgam of fact and fiction that was to work in her favour.[35] By 1789 Siddons's status was such that her roles included serving as the symbol of the entire nation, dressed as Britannia at the service in St Paul's to celebrate the recovery of George III from his madness. As John Brewer writes, 'During the 1780s and 1790s, when she enjoyed the support of George III and Queen Charlotte, her admirers touted her as an exemplary Englishwoman of noble feelings and high moral character. After her triumphant return to the London stage in 1782 she became *the* muse of tragedy.'[36] Embodying a convergence of symbolic and actual female power, Siddons became a compelling figure in the public imagination: an example of women's cultural and intellectual potential that could not be ignored.

Siddons's example served as a positive encouragement to actresses who sought a career on the stage but did not want to blemish their personal reputation. However, one can sense the precarious fragility of such an elevated position in Siddons's constant monitoring of her own social contact with other actresses of more ambiguous fame. She refused to return Mary Robinson's poetic compliments for fear of moral corruption by association. While Robinson idolised Siddons, Siddons could only pity her:

If she is half as amiable as her writings, I shall long for the possibility of being acquainted with her. I say the *possibility*, because one's whole life is one continual sacrifice of inclinations, which to indulge, however laudable or innocent, would draw down the malice and reproach of those prudent people who never do ill . . . The charming and beautiful Mrs Robinson: I pity her from the bottom of my soul.[37]

Siddons's reaction suggests the effort of maintaining a reputation in the contemporary world of celebrity. It also suggests that perhaps there was room for only one paragon of virtue on the British stage.

Contemporary notions of spectacle, celebrity and virtue all played a part in shaping moral and intellectual reputations, and the literary work of actresses is frequently concerned with disturbing the customary boundaries between subject and object, fact and fiction, spectacle and spectator. Elizabeth Griffith, who spent her early career on the Dublin stage, made her literary debut with her husband by publishing their courtship letters under fictional names: *A Series of Genuine Letters between Henry and Frances* (1757). They followed this in 1769 with *Two Novels in Letters by the authors of Henry and Frances* ('Frances's' *The Delicate Distress* and 'Henry's' *Gordian Knot*) in which they included prefaces under their pen-names, extending their unusual literary conceit whereby the distinctions between fact and fiction were blurred. While other novelists had aimed to deceive their readers as to the authenticity of their epistolary fictions, few had used real letters to weave a sentimental narrative. Elizabeth Griffith's epistolary style has the immediacy of dialogue and draws upon her experience on the stage in developing the psychology of her female narrator through a series of letters that frequently have the intimate progression of a dramatic soliloquy – essays in self-revelation that are intended to be overheard.

As an actress, Griffith had specialised in tragic roles. She made her debut as Juliet to Thomas Sheridan's ageing Romeo in Dublin's Smock Alley Theatre on 13 October 1749. Subsequent performances included Andromache in Ambrose Philips's *Distrest Mother* (an adaptation of Racine's *Andromache*), Cordelia in *King Lear* and Calista in Rowe's *Fair Penitent*. These plays all depict the spectacle of feminine virtue in distress and are resolved by the death of their heroines. In one of her earliest attempts at writing a play, Elizabeth Griffith resolved to create a more realistic view of womanhood for her audience (fig. 3). *The Platonic Wife*, her first comedy, was taken immediately for production on the stage at Drury Lane, where it premièred on 24 January 1765.[38] The heroine of the play was modelled on Frances in the *Letters*, a learned and witty woman who insists that her husband treat her with tenderness and politeness after their marriage. When he refuses, she leaves him, and while separated entertains (but rejects) the propositions of two lovers. She repents and returns to a husband who is similarly remorseful and treats her with all the civility she desires. While Griffith's writing is

Fig. 3. Portrait of Elizabeth Griffith in the pose of confident author and actress, surrounded by visual icons of her stage and literary careers. The image forms the frontispiece to a collection of short fiction she edited: *Novelettes Selected for the Use of Young Ladies and Gentlemen, Written by Dr. Goldsmith, Mrs. Griffith &c.* (London, 1780). Fourteen of the seventeen tales are by Griffith and the preface, written by herself, contains a glowing account of her success as an instructor of the young and, moreover, an example to her sex: 'Mrs. GRIFFITH, the ornament and pride of her country, has strove to open the flood-gate of Literature to her own Sex, and purifying the stream from the filth with which it was impregnated to make it guide with meandering invitation through the vallies of Britain. She is one of the many examples in the present day, that have served to explode the illiberal assertion that Female genius is inferior to Male.' (Bodleian Library, University of Oxford.)

spritely and she has a sure sense of dramatic pace, critical reactions were extremely harsh. The London theatrical establishment resented the audacity of a woman playwright's claims for respect and admiration. To support her children as a writer, Griffith needed to conform to contemporary sexual stereotypes rather than challenge the orthodoxy. Readers can detect a significant change of tone in Griffith's subsequent four plays, in which she abandoned her concern for improving the status of intelligent women and created a host of female characters who are the passive and long-suffering companions of errant and often violent men. While Griffith managed to become a professional playwright by manipulating contemporary opinion rather than allowing herself to be its victim, she was never entirely free from others' sexist prejudice against her work.

Griffith's most significant intervention in literary history was her ambitious work of dramatic criticism, *The Morality of Shakespeare's Drama Illustrated* (1775), dedicated to David Garrick. While interested in Shakespeare's distinctive poetic language, Griffith focuses above all on his female characters. She describes his evocation of the female mind as part of his depiction of a common humanity that transcends the boundaries of gender, praising his capacity to reform and educate both sexes in their knowledge of each other: 'What age, what sex, what character, escapes the touches of Shakespeare's plastic hand!' (p. 169). Here she praises his evocation of Imogen's shock when accused of infidelity:

> False to his bed! What is it to be false?
> To lie in watch there, and to think on him?
> To weep 'twixt clock and clock? If sleep charge nature,
> To break it with a fearful dream of him,
> And cry myself awake? that is false to's bed! is't?

Nothing, in situation or circumstance, in thought, or expression, can exceed the beauty or tender effect of the above passage. It catches such quick hold of our sympathy, that we feel as if the scene were real, and are at once transported, amidst the gloom and silence of the forest, in spite of all the glare of the Theatre, and the loud applause of the audience. It is in such instances that Shakespeare has never yet been equalled, and never can be excelled. What a power of natural sentiment must a man have been possessed of, who could so adequately express the kind of ingenious surprise upon such a challenge, which none but a woman can possibly feel! Shakespeare could not only assume all characters, but even their sexes too.[39]

The reader senses Griffith's experience as an actor – of transporting herself and her audience under the bright lights of the theatre. She interprets *Cymbeline*'s underlying moral message as advocating the equality of humankind: 'Human nature is the same throughout; it is education alone that distinguishes man from man. There are, indeed, great differences often observable between the talents and intellects of the species; but this distinction is remarked in *individuals*, only, not in the *classes* of mankind.'[40] Like Mary Robinson, Griffith was conscious of belonging to an age in which her sex was in the ascendant. Having felt the pain of exclusion from the highest theatrical and literary establishments, both felt impelled to contribute to their redefinition.

For such women acting could serve as an important intellectual resource. Of all her contemporaries, Mary Robinson was perhaps the actress who expressed most directly the extent to which sympathy, impersonation and dialogue could be developed and refined into highly articulate literary modes. As one of the female characters in her novel *Angelina* explains, being an actress formed an education in itself:

> We have many females on the stage, who are ornaments to society and in every respect worthy of imitation! For my part, I adore the Theatre, and think there is more morality to be found in one good tragedy, than in all the sermons that ever were printed.
>
> With regard to acting; it is an act which demands no small portion of intellectual acquirements! It polishes the manners; enlightens the understanding, gives a finish to external grace, and calls forth all the powers of mental superiority![41]

For Robinson, the theatre had a central role in society and the actress could inspire virtue in her audience, the theatre forming a moral realm that is analogous to the church. Her definition of actresses as 'ornaments to society' foreshadows Hazlitt's famous verdict on the life of Sarah Siddons: 'She was Tragedy personified. She was the stateliest ornament of the public mind' (*Examiner*, 15 June 1816). The word 'ornament' carries a certain moral weight in this context, suggesting the sense in which the actress could embody virtue, design and display. While never entirely free from the threat of scandal or public disapprobation, by performing virtue on the stage (and page) women could divert some of the contemporary social and sexual prejudice against their work. In her many and diverse manifestations, the actress could combine spectacle, intellect and authority in a performance that started on stage but asserted itself powerfully in the broader sphere of eighteenth-century and Romantic culture.

NOTES

1. Nicholas Rowe, *The Fair Penitent*, ed. Macolm Goldstein (Lincoln: University of Nebraska Press, 1969), Act 3, lines 39–52, p. 34.

2. See Ellen Donkin, 'Mrs Siddons Looks Back in Anger: Feminist Historiography for Eighteenth-Century British Theater', in Janelle G. Reinelt and Joseph R. Roach, eds., *Critical Theory and Performance* (Ann Arbor: University of Michigan Press, 1992), pp. 276–90, p. 278.

3. See Hannah Barker and Elaine Chalus, eds., *Gender in Eighteenth-Century England: Roles, Representations and Responsibilities* (London: Longman, 1997) and Elizabeth Eger, Charlotte Grant, Cliona O Gallchoir and Penny Warburton, eds., *Women, Writing and the Public Sphere, 1700–1830* (Cambridge: Cambridge University Press, 2001).

4. Sandra Richards, *The Rise of the English Actress* (Basingstoke: Macmillan, 1993), p. 30.

5. Joseph R. Roach, *The Player's Passion: Studies in the Science of Acting* (London: Associated University Presses, 1985).

6. Shearer West, *The Image of the Actor: Verbal and Visual Representation in the Age of Garrick and Kemble* (London: Pinter Publishers, 1991).

7. For an overview of women's contribution to stagecraft, see Derek Hughes, ed., *British Women Playwrights*, 6 vols. (London: Pickering and Chatto, 2001). See also Ellen Donkin, *Getting into the Act: Women Playwrights in London, 1776–1829* (London: Routledge, 1995).

8. Elizabeth Inchbald (1753–1821), for example, ran away from home at the age of eighteen to pursue a career as an actress. After a successful period touring the provincial theatres she decided to become an author, writing her first novel, *A Simple Story* (1791). She then turned her mind from the novel to drama, writing over twenty plays, including her translation of Kotzebue's *Lovers Vows* (1798) which appears in Jane Austen's *Mansfield Park* (1814). In 1793 Inchbald's *Every One Has his Fault* was attacked for encouraging women to think they should have more choice in marriage and that society's wealth could be more justly shared. In addition to writing her own plays, Inchbald published a vast critical edition, *The British Theatre*, in twenty-five volumes (1806), in which she developed a sophisticated language of dramatic criticism that assesses the moral lessons of her chosen dramas. She is particularly original in drawing on her own experience in order to discuss plays as read and performed experiences. See Paula Byrne, *Jane Austen and the Theatre* (London: Hambledon and London, 2002) for a discussion of the relationship between the stage and the novel in the Regency period, and Marvin Carlson, 'Elizabeth Inchbald: A Woman Critic in her Theatrical Culture', in Catherine Burroughs, ed., *Women in British Romantic Theatre: Drama, Performance, Society, 1790–1840* (Cambridge: Cambridge University Press, 2000), pp. 207–22.

9. Eliza Haywood, *A Wife to be Lett*, in Magarete Rubik and Eva Mueller-Zettelmann, eds., *Eighteenth-Century Women Playwrights*, 6 vols. (London: Pickering and Chatto), vol. 1, p. 167.

10. See Pat Rogers, '"Towering Beyond her Sex": Stature and Sublimity in the Achievement of Sarah Siddons', in Mary Anne Schofield and Cecilia Macheski, eds., *Curtain Calls: British and American Women and the Theatre, 1660–1820* (Athens: Ohio University Press, 1991), pp. 48–67.

11. See Katherine Newey, 'Women and History on the Romantic Stage: More, Yearsley and Mitford', in Catherine Burroughs, ed., *Women in British Romantic*

Theatre: Drama, Performance, Society, 1790–1840 (Cambridge: Cambridge University Press, 2000), pp. 79–100.

12. I refer to Sharon Setzer's edition, drawing upon her introduction: Mary Robinson, *A Letter to the Women of England* and *The Natural Daughter*, ed. Sharon M. Setzer (Peterborough, Ont.: Broadview Press, 2003).

13. Ibid., p. 41.

14. Ibid., p. 83.

15. Ibid., pp. 43–4.

16. For a discussion of the formal language used to describe the actress's body on stage and in art, see Shearer West, 'Body Connoisseurship', in Robyn Asleson, ed., *Notorious Muse: The Actress in British Art and Culture, 1776–1812* (New Haven, CT: Yale University Press, 2003), pp. 151–70.

17. See Christopher Reid, 'Burke's Tragic Muse: Sarah Siddons and the "Feminization" of the Reflections', in Steven Blakemore, ed., *Burke and the French Revolution: Bicentennial Essays* (Athens: University of Georgia Press, 1992), pp. 1–27.

18. *Monthly Magazine* 10 (1800), pp. 138–9.

19. Donkin, 'Mrs Siddons Looks Back in Anger', p. 276.

20. Felicia Gordon, '*Filles publiques* or Public Women: The Actress as Citizen: Marie Madeleine Jodin (1741–90) and Mary Darby Robinson (1758–1800)', in Sarah Knott and Barbara Taylor, eds., *Women, Gender and Enlightenment* (Basingstoke: Palgrave Macmillan, 2005), pp. 610–29, p. 629.

21. *Memoirs of the late Mrs Robinson, Written by Herself, with some Posthumous Pieces in Verse*, ed. Mary Elizabeth Robinson, 4 vols. (London: R. Phillips, 1801). For a modern edition, see Mary Robinson, *Perdita: The Memoirs of Mary Robinson*, ed. M. J. Levy (London: Peter Owen, 1994). Also see Linda H. Peterson, 'Becoming and Author: Mary Robinson's *Memoirs* and the Origins of the Woman Artist's Autobiography', in Carol Shiner Wilson and Joel Haefner, eds., *Re-visioning Romanticism* (Philadelphia: University of Pennsylvania Press, 1994), pp. 36–56.

22. Stella Tillyard, ' "Paths of Glory": Fame and the Public in Eighteenth-Century London', in Martin Postle, ed., *Joshua Reynolds and the Creation of Celebrity*, Exhibition Catalogue (London: Tate Publishing, 2005), pp. 61–9, p. 64.

23. See Paula Byrne, *Perdita: The Life of Mary Robinson* (London: HarperCollins, 2004), for an account of the relationship between Mary Robinson's life and work.

24. Robinson, *Memoirs*, ed. Levy, pp. 178–9.

25. Ibid., p. 34.

26. Ibid., pp. 87–8.

27. Ibid., p. 88.

28. Ibid., pp. 88–9.

29. Judith Pascoe and Anne Janowitz have written of Robinson's chameleon-like ability to absorb the cultural currents of her time but also to reinvent herself in response to historical change. See Judith Pascoe, *Romantic Theatricality: Gender, Poetry and Spectatorship* (Ithaca, NY: Cornell University Press, 1997), and Anne Janowitz, *Women Romantic Poets: Anna Barbauld and Mary Robinson* (Horndon: Northcote House Publishers, 2004).

30. Gill Perry, 'The Spectacle of the Muse: Exhibiting the Actress at the Royal Academy', in David Solkin, ed., *Art on the Line*, Exhibition Catalogue (New Haven, CT: Yale University Press, 2001), pp. 111–25.

31. See Michael Booth, 'Sarah Siddons', in Michael R. Booth, John Stokes and Susan Bassnett, *Three Tragic Actresses: Siddons, Rachel, Ristori* (Cambridge: Cambridge University Press, 1996), pp. 10–65.

32. Kimberly Crouch, 'The Public Life of Actresses: Prostitutes or Ladies?', in Hannah Barker and Elaine Chalus, eds., *Gender in Eighteenth-Century England: Roles, Representations and Responsibilities* (London: Longman, 1997), pp. 58–78, p. 77.

33. Priscilla Wakefield, *Reflections on the Present Condition of the Female Sex; With Suggestions for Its Improvement* (1798), from ch. 6: 'Lucrative Employments for the First and Second Classes Suggested . . . With Strictures on a Theatrical Life'.

34. Mary Pilkington, *Memoirs of Celebrated Female Characters, who have Distinguished Themselves by their Talents and Virtues in Every Age and Nation; Containing the most Extensive Collection of Illustrious Examples of Feminine Excellence ever Published; in which the Virtuous and the Vicious are Painted in their True Colours* (London, 1804).

35. See Shearer West, 'The Public and Private Roles of Sarah Siddons', in Robyn Asleson, ed., *A Passion for Performance: Sarah Siddons and her Portraitists* (Los Angeles: J. Paul Getty Museum, 1999), pp. 1–40, pp. 6–7.

36. John Brewer, *The Pleasures of the Imagination: English Culture in the Eighteenth Century* (London: HarperCollins, 1997), p. 346. For the nationalist context of Siddons's role as feminine ideal, see Linda Colley, *Britons: Forging the Nation, 1707–1837* (New Haven, CT: Yale University Press, 1992).

37. Sarah Siddons to John Taylor, quoted in J. Fitzgerald Molloy's introduction to *Memoirs of Mary Robinson* (London, 1895), p. xiv. See also Judith Pascoe, *Romantic Theatricality: Gender, Poetry and Spectatorship* (Ithaca, NY: Cornell University Press, 1997).

38. See Betty Rizzo, 'Introduction', in Derek Hughes, ed., *British Women Playwrights*, vol. 4: *Elizabeth Griffith* (London: Pickering and Chatto, 2001).

39. Elizabeth Griffith, *The Morality of Shakespeare's Drama Illustrated* (London, 1775), p. 481. See Elizabeth Eger, '"Out Rushed a Female to Protect the Bard": The Bluestocking Defense of Shakespeare', *Huntington Library Quarterly* 65. 1 and 2 (2003), pp. 127–51.

40. Griffith, *Morality of Shakespeare's Drama*, p. 483.

41. Mary Robinson, *Angelina: A Novel*, 3 vols. (London, 1796), vol. 2, p. 80.

FURTHER READING

Asleson, Robyn, ed. *Notorious Muse: The Actress in British Art and Culture, 1776–1812*. New Haven, CT: Yale University Press, 2003.

    ed. *A Passion for Performance: Sarah Siddons and her Portraitists*. Los Angeles: J. Paul Getty Museum, 1999.

Burroughs, Catherine B. *Closet Stages: Joanna Baillie and the Theatre Theory of British Romantic Women Writers*. Philadephia: University of Pennsylvania Press, 1997.

Byrne, Paula. *Jane Austen and the Theatre*. London: Hambledon and London, 2002.

Perdita: The Life of Mary Robinson. London: HarperCollins, 2004.

Donkin, Ellen. *Getting into the Act: Women Playwrights in London, 1776–1829*. London: Routledge, 1995.

Galperin, William. *The Return of the Visible in British Romanticism*. Baltimore, MD: Johns Hopkins University Press, 1993.

Pascoe, Judith. *Romantic Theatricality: Gender, Poetry and Spectatorship*. Ithaca, NY: Cornell University Press, 1997.

Robinson, Mary. *Memoirs of the Late Mrs Robinson, Written by Herself, with some Posthumous Pieces in Verse*, ed. Mary Elizabeth Robinson 4 vols. London: R. Phillips, 1801.

Perdita: The Memoirs of Mary Robinson, ed. M. J. Levy. London: Peter Owen, 1994.

Schofield, Mary Anne, and Cecilia Macheski. *Curtain Calls: British and American Women and the Theatre, 1660–1820*. Athens: Ohio University Press, 1991.

West, Shearer. *The Image of the Actor: Verbal and Visual Representation in the Age of Garrick and Kemble*. London: Pinter, 1991.

3

GAIL MARSHALL

Cultural formations: the nineteenth-century touring actress and her international audiences

The theatre has always been an itinerant art which recognises the need to take its product to its audiences, as well as a responsive art which identifies its financial survival in its ability to meet audience demands. For some English companies in the mid- and late nineteenth century, survival was ineluctably bound up with the need to support the opulent central London locations which were both a huge financial burden, and a necessary part of the theatre's effort to attract and to sustain a middle-class audience. Henry Irving's Lyceum was one of the most luxurious and socially successful of these theatres. Secure in its social reputation, with visits from royalty and the leading figures of British, European and American cultural life, nonetheless the Lyceum's London productions made a loss between 1875 and 1899 of almost £22,000.[1] The company's financial stability was only secured by its exhaustive domestic and international tours. North America proved its most valuable source of income, with each performance grossing over £80, as opposed to the loss of £5 10s for each London performance. Thus, as Tracy C. Davis points out, touring should not be understood as a bonus or residual profit, building on London profits; rather, touring made being in London possible.[2] The splendours which signified the Lyceum's London stage were only made possible by the company's tours in the United States, Australia and the provinces.

But other reasons existed too for the national and international tours that were increasingly becoming a regular part of the theatre company's routine. Provincial audiences might provide a testing ground for new material, and new international audiences might provide an important boost for the performer who, like Sarah Bernhardt, might be finding her home company too constraining. It was during the visit of the Comédie Française to London in 1879 that Bernhardt, perhaps buoyed by her enthusiastic reception in England, made her definitive break with a company that she felt had been hampering her financial and artistic independence for too long. Increasingly, the phenomenon of the international tour might also be fuelled by political reasons. The Comédie's 1871 tour to London occurred at the time of the Prussian invasion of Paris, when the Comédie was in need of a home overseas. Furthermore, the touring company might reflect its home country's trading status and characteristics. Whilst Britain was the recipient of a number of visits from distinguished European companies, it rarely exported its own drama to those countries in the mid- and late nineteenth century, preferring instead to trade its theatrical goods on the English-speaking stages of North America and Australia, and other outposts of former or current British dominion.

Earlier in the century, however, Harriet Smithson's appearances in Paris in 1827–8 as a member of Charles Kemble's company did much to fuel European Romanticism, were in part the inspiration for Berlioz's *Symphonie fantastique*, and introduced a sceptical French audience to the visceral possibilities of Shakespeare on the stage. In the part of Ophelia, which was happily dependent for much of its impact on non-linguistic effects, 'the emotional surge imprinted itself upon the audience's imagination in a rare and heightened way'.[3] Alexandre Dumas *père* was later to recall that 'It was the first time that I saw in the theatre real passions, giving life to men and women of flesh and blood.'[4] As Peter Raby notes, the performances fuelled the debates between the champions of Classicism and Romanticism, but were perhaps most effective as a means of promoting the export of Shakespeare as a national product. French writers were inspired to translate Shakespeare for their own stage, Delacroix produced a series of lithographs and paintings based on Shakespeare, and there was, of course, the continuing musical impact on Berlioz, who went on to compose works based on *The Tempest*, *King Lear*, *Romeo and Juliet*, *The Merchant of Venice* and *Much Ado about Nothing*.

Smithson's visit to Paris was a highly successful export trip. The plays had been adapted for French taste so successfully that such language difficulties as existed were no barrier to the company's effecting a lasting impact. The visit took Shakespeare to a new audience, was lucrative for Charles Kemble's company, and established its leading lady's fame for an international audience. It also established the parameters for subsequent international tours. Smithson herself was followed in the winter of 1844–5 by Helen Faucit's successful appearances with William Macready's company, which proved similarly crucial for her fame, both in France and at home. Received as a specifically English actress – Théophile Gautier wrote of her 'slightly mannered English grace of the keepsakes and books of beauty'[5] – she was pitted in the minds of critics against the potential skills of Rachel Félix, the leading proponent of French neoclassicism, who was in 1844 briefly away from the stage following the birth of one of her illegitimate children. Throughout their careers, the two women would be compared on moral and artistic grounds which could not help but have their grounding in definitions of national culture.

Smithson and Faucit demonstrate the terms and conditions upon which the touring actress occupied the international stage in the early nineteenth century. She would be compared with indigenous performers, defined by expectations based in often the crudest forms of national prejudice, and judged as an ambassador for her country's arts of writing and acting. She would also, however, as was the case for both Smithson and Faucit, be able to garner substantial praise which would have a lasting impact on her domestic career, and achieve a form of determining significance which outstripped the possibilities of her often apparently dependent position as part of a theatre company at home. Arguably, popular perceptions suggest that the fate of their tours was determined by the reception meted out to the two leading ladies, and not to their partners, Charles Kemble and William Macready. These actresses, taking advantage of the infancy of the star system which would come to dominate theatre over the coming century, and exploiting their audiences' readiness to be attracted to the difference and exoticism of their appeal, however quotidian it might appear at home, used the practice of touring to augment substantially their own reputations, that of their own theatre, and the writing of Shakespeare.

In this chapter I will be concerned to map the progress of a pattern of international reception for some of the best known of the vast number of European and American actresses who appeared in England during the nineteenth century. Examining the work of Rachel Félix, Adelaide Ristori, Charlotte Cushman, Helena Modjeska, Sarah Bernhardt and Eleonora Duse in particular, we will see the extent to which they appeared and were received as figures specifically determined by a code of national expectations, and will see how those expectations arose and were transformed throughout the century. We will assess the extent to which the concept of the tour itself was dependent on the reception of its leading lady, and how those women fared when they made their apparently inevitable attempts to perform in Shakespearean roles for their English audiences. Though there are undoubtedly continuities between these women's experiences and those of Smithson and Faucit, there are also significant differences between the latter's experience of a cross-Channel visit which was not in itself innovatory,[6] and the experience of the actresses whose lives were increasingly determined, and their renown defined, by their international tours, and by audiences who shared neither their language nor their cultural history.

The first of the international actresses of the nineteenth century was Rachel Félix, the French *tragédienne* credited with restoring the reputations of her country's neoclassical playwrights, Racine and Corneille. Born in 1821,

54

Rachel first appeared in England twenty years later, when she achieved her first major overseas success. Rachel was an inveterate touring actress who relished the challenges and triumphs of touring, finding them fundamentally restorative, both of her fortune and her artistry.[7] In 1851, Rachel traveled 800 leagues by rail, one of the crucial factors facilitating the touring actress's success, and gave twenty-five performances in one month across Belgium, Prussia, Saxony, Bohemia and in Vienna.[8] As would be the case later for Sarah Bernhardt, an equally indefatigable international actress, the French press and public chided her for what they perceived as the greed that was driving her efforts, but enjoyed the evidence of cultural conquest that she wrought, especially in England, where she made a devotee of the Duke of Wellington, thus reversing the sting of the latter's defeat of Napoleon,[9] and of Queen Victoria.

Rachel also shared with Sarah Bernhardt the power to influence the English artists of her day, and became the inspiration behind a number of fictional actresses, most notably Josephine in Benjamin Disraeli's *Tancred* (1847), Vashti in Charlotte Brontë's *Villette* (1853), and Alcharisi in George Eliot's *Daniel Deronda* (1876). Vashti and Alcharisi were in part inspired by the ways in which Rachel had been refracted through the theatre criticism of G. H. Lewes. In his essay on Rachel in his collected reviews, *On Actors and the Art of Acting*, Lewes writes of her that 'Rachel was the panther of the stage; with a panther's terrible beauty and undulating grace she moved and stood, glared and sprang. There always seemed something not human about her. She seemed made of different clay from her fellows – beautiful but not loveable.'[10] He also effects an interesting continuity between the French actress and the Romantic actor Edmund Kean: 'Those who never saw Edmund Kean may form a very good conception of him if they have seen Rachel. She was very much as a woman what he was as a man. If he was a lion, she was a panther.'[11] He goes on to add that as Phèdre, 'she left us quivering with an excitement comparable only to that produced by Kean in the third act of *Othello*'.[12] Phèdre would become an iconic part for the continental European actress in the nineteenth century, and it was Rachel who provided in this, as in other, cases, the achievement to which others aspired. Her example was, however, not wholly well received. As late as 1882, Theodore Martin was denigrating her classical aesthetic, which masked the 'natural deportment which was ever eloquent of character', and the actress's 'unsympathetic nature'.[13] Concealed by the practice of anonymous periodical authorship, Martin was perhaps taking the opportunity strategically to revive his wife Helen Faucit's ancient rivalry with Rachel on the eve of the publication of Faucit's essays on Shakespeare, but was more transparently intent on promoting English womanliness over European, self-conscious artistry. This would be a dyad that would endure throughout the century, but was an ideological issue which did not register with Lewes, who compared Rachel rather on affective than moral grounds with Edmund Kean.

The same impulse to draw comparisons with a male actor coloured early responses to the American actress Charlotte Cushman, who premièred in London in February 1845. She shared her audience's language, but it was far more enthralled by her difference than by any such similarity. The *Illustrated London News* from that month helpfully reminds us that the London stage on which Cushman appeared was fundamentally cosmopolitan. The week before Cushman first appeared, 'The Theatres welcomed the advent of the Italian opera, and the opening of the season of French plays, starring Plessy and Lemâitre, as a sign that spring was coming, and that London life could begin again.'[14]

Cushman, however, despite her extraordinarily favourable reception, was less easily assimilated into the round of London entertainments. From the first, critics explored a whole new vocabulary of language and images in which they sought to convey her considerable impact, and to recognise the import of her international otherness and the specificities of her American identity. Notoriously masculine and physically powerful in her appearance and bearing, the *Illustrated London News* reviewer wrote, when she first appeared in Britain in the part of Bianca in Henry Hart Milman's *Fazio*, that Cushman most strongly resembled Macready, 'in face, and occasionally in her manner and the tones of her voice. She has a tall and well proportioned figure, a commanding deportment, and features which, although not regular, bear an impress of unusual intelligence.'[15] The comparison was one which would dog Cushman's early years in London, and signals the extent to which she was appreciated as not inhabiting a realm of expectations determined by earlier actresses. Indeed, it is possible that the virility implied by the comparison was the key to an apprehension of the Americanness of Cushman's appearances. Lisa Merrill suggests that, for British audiences, Cushman 'reinforced their beliefs about powerful, dynamic Americans'.[16]

What is most notable, however, about early British responses to Cushman is the way in which the actress's vigour is reflected in the excited delight of her reviewers, whose language glows with the effort both to reflect and account for her vitality and invigorating energy. They note her uniqueness, her efforts to reform and redeem the stage, and crucially draw together apprehensions of the naturalness and intelligence of her performances. Whilst that 'naturalness' might, for an English actress, secure her exoneration for being on the stage, in responses to the American, 'nature' is appropriately recognised as being something profoundly created. Appropriate forms of femininity are not 'at stake' in reviews of Cushman, and her reviewers, and presumably her audiences too, are liberated to apprehend and to be able to articulate the ways in which Cushman's roles might challenge both stage conventions and conventions of femininity; indeed, femininity might be tacitly recognised as a convention through her acting. This possibility is very visually demonstrated in the *Illustrated London News* review of Cushman's first appearance in London as Lady Macbeth in March 1845 (fig. 4). The busy and oddly configured page upon which the review and its illustration appear juxtaposes Cushman's Lady Macbeth with elegantly dressed young women displaying the Paris and London fashions for March. Their meek gentility contrasts forcibly with Cushman's energetic physical support of her husband, and their eye contact both similarly enforces the lack of such sympathetic recognition between Cushman and Edwin Forrest (as Macbeth), and suggests a complicit and knowing recognition of the extent to which they too have assumed roles and appropriate costumes in their occupation of their own social stages.

Such an assumption of gendered character was most forcibly demonstrated later that year with Cushman's debut performance as Romeo (fig. 5), which she played opposite her sister Susan's Juliet. Acting Shakespeare's text rather than David Garrick's adaptation, Cushman appeared to the critic of *The Times* to be 'far superior to any Romeo that has been seen for years. The distinction is not one of degree, it is one of kind. For a long time Romeo has been a convention. Miss Cushman's Romeo is a creative, a living, breathing, animated, ardent human being.'[17] That it was an actress who had thus animated one of the most notable romantic heroes of the English stage is a fact that goes unnoticed in a review which even finds Cushman's fighting exemplary, and is not discernible in the illustration which accompanies the *Illustrated London News* review. With this part, Cushman leaves the environs of the theatre review column to take up the top third of a page which is dominated by her unambiguously male and dominating Romeo towering over a beseeching Juliet. It answers the prurient curiosity of how a female Romeo would look, and is backed up by the review's assertion of her continuing 'singular resemblance' to Macready, 'even to his attitudes and inflections of voice'.[18] Like *The Times*, the *Illustrated London News* declares that the character has never been better played, and that in Cushman's 'energy and passion, coupled with an extraordinary assumption of manly character and bearing … we altogether lost sight of the woman'. The woman still inhabits the journals, in Romeo's tiny waist, and in the feminised language with which *The Times* seeks to recount the passion of the Italian youth, but she is a curiously muted presence, whose proximity to the masculinity which is being depicted is designedly incidental.

"ICE-TREE," MIDDLE TEMPLE.

The subject of our Engraving represents one of the most curious effects of the late frost, in the metropolis. A great portion of our readers must remember the solitary little fountain in one of the courts of the Middle Temple—a spot enshrined in the annals of Miss Lamb—we mean by the humour of Mr. Pickles' "Martin Chuzzlewit." Upon the north side of the fountain pool stood a low tree and, during the severe weather, the spray from the jet of water, as it fell upon the branches, became incrusted into icicles, and a kind of fairy frost-work, which had a very beautiful appearance. The phenomenon (for such it really was) attracted the notice of several persons; but, in the midst of their admiration, the tree broke down with the weight of its incrustations.

Our Engraving is from a Daguerréotype, taken for this journal: it shows the beautifully frozen tree, with the winter background, and a portion of the Middle Temple buildings. Whilst the artist was preparing for a second Daguerréotype, the tree fell, as we have described.

In the "Illustrated Magazine" for the present month, we find the following graceful lyrical address to this tree:—

Colitis incurvus comis.

Exigue stranger, whence and what art thou?
A spectre rais'd from Flora's winter tomb,
In ghostly bloom:—
Fair Beauty sits upon thy snowy brow
As gracefully as e'er was seen
In summery woodland green,
Where weeping willow o'er some gentle brook
Hath seem'd to look
Into its mirror for the memory
Of happy hours that long have ceas'd to be—
(Alas!)
No glass
Can show us what we once could see,
And well descry,
Through Nature's own intending eye!]
Thou dost appear
A love-lorn Dryad come
From northern forest drear,
To weep a tear
Over the wat'ry tomb

* Miss Landon penned some very beautiful Lines to this Fountain.

"ICE TREE," MIDDLE TEMPLE.

costumes,—those of the most enduring favour. A still more singular and picturesque costume consists of a dress whose skirt is embroidered with five rows of border à la Grecque, defined by golden threads; the corsage also in Grecian form, and very short sleeves looped up above with golden tassels. Placed over the braided hair at the back of the head, and as if to confine the knot of hair behind, is a golden resille, encircled by a branch of small wild grape-leaves.

Great preparations are already being made, and brilliant are the properties of the well informed. We hear of nothing but drawing-rooms, fancy balls, children's balls, *tableaux vivants*, reviews, and concerts, at the palace of the Sovereign and the mansions of the peerage, and other millionaires. Amongst those bright visions, one that is on the eve of being accomplished is the opening of the Grand Italian Opera, which will prove too small to contain the crowd eager to behold the extraordinary assemblage of artists from all countries, covered with the laurels they have each separately reaped in capitals distinguished for their fastidious taste, and who have come to lay them at the feet of John Bull, and receive from him the applause that is alone wanting to complete their European fame. But whilst such is the aspect of things on the stage, that of the house before the proscenium will offer scarce less interest, and we speak of costumes adapted for effect. Who that has ever witnessed it can forget the effect produced by the singing of the National Anthem at the Italian Opera in London? How much is the solemn and magnificent effect of the music given forth by so many voices, heightened by the sight of the concourse of beauty set off by the costliest attire, and the *prestige* of rank and birth standing around in sympathy. The costumes, therefore, for such an occasion must be of the greatest importance, and are with ladies the pressing concern of the moment.

Dresses of blue, white, or rose-coloured satin, open and displaying beneath, under skirts of silver-coloured moire, edged with silver embroidery, over which hang embroidered scarfs; others opened over under skirts of brocaded gold, the extremity of the opening being caught up by a rose or a diamond, and round the waist a cordelière of plain gold, gracefully twisted, and terminating in two tassels; or, dresses of gold and cherry-coloured satin, made à la Agnes Sorel, trimmed with gold chefs, and opening over a magnificent guipure skirt dress, caught up by gold ornaments of a spiral form, will be of the highest vogue. A turban of gold net-work, forming a small calotte, fastened on each side by two golden tulips, and the point of each leaf formed by a diamond, or ruby, present an admirable accompaniment to this style of dress.

DESCRIPTION OF THE FIGURES.

FIGURE 1.—For full toilette. A satin petit-bord (Dress Hat) ornamented with feathers. A satin dress with train, ornamented with furbelows of the same, and with bouquets of flowers. Petticoat of guipire or antique lace, with two deep volants.

FIGURE 2.—A Ball Dress of coloured tulle, trimmed with narrow bouillons of the same, and with broad satin ribbon, with silver border and fringe. A coiffure ornamented with roses, without leaves, and a chaplet of smaller roses.

FIGURE 3.—A walking toilette. A velvet nut-brown hat, trimmed with lace. A silk dress trimmed with narrow velvet ribbons of the same colour.

FIGURE 4.—A morning toilette. A hat of pink satin, trimmed with lace. A striped silk dress.

SCENE FROM "MACBETH," AT THE PRINCESS'S THEATRE.

PARIS AND LONDON FASHIONS FOR MARCH.

To form an idea of present fashions, the Paris and the London Vogues must be combined in one rapid glance. Paris is at this moment in a state of widowhood, lamenting the departed spirit of pleasure. The uninterrupted succession of brilliant *fêtes*, routs, and concerts, to the incessant whirlwind of amusement has succeeded general silence and quietude. The court ceasing its *receptions* has given an example which all have of necessity followed; brilliant reunions are now all that is left. The King and his suite, who forget nothing that can increase their popularity, and who are fully conscious of the high influence exerted by the pleasures of a nation over its graver interests, have this season received more than usual, and the *fêtes* of the Tuileries have recalled, by their magnificence, the palmy days of Louis XIV. The necessity of luxury and expenditure amongst the aristocracy is well understood in France, and if the costumes of the mass yet recall the days of the Directory, the ladies, with better taste and finer tact, now adopt toilettes which, by their splendid elegance, at the same time mark the distinctions of the different classes of society, and promote the welfare of the manufacturer and tradesman.

The novelties of the past season are beyond enumeration; but amongst the coiffures, those à la Marie Stuart, the poufs à la Maintenon, the charming petits bords, surrounded with garlands of diamonds, on little hats à la Raphael, with a slender waving white feather, are those chiefly destined to survive; whilst amongst the dresses, those in the lightest Tulle, trimmed with puffings of the same material, and interspersed with roses, giving an aerial and fairy-like appearance to their youthful wearers; and for the married ladies, those embroidered in gold and silver-coloured silk in the most exquisite designs, harmonising admirably with the dazzling brilliance of the jewelled

Of some false breast, sad
From thy cold arms to wed
A Nymph of warmer sky;
And thither next to die;
To find his shallow grave
Beneath the tiny wave
That freezes o'er thy sigh!
Or not that seems to say, poor man
Shall here be trysting as before—
Fond hearts expectant shall not thrill
To meet beneath my icy chill!

If so, vain Tree
I tell to thee
Fond hearts will leave the thunder shower;
And when thou'rt gone—
Vanished before the warming sun,
Tree Love will keep th' appointed hour!   W.

FASHIONS FOR MARCH.

THE THEATRES.

PRINCESS'.—
Miss Cushman appeared as *Lady Macbeth*, on Friday evening last, and fully answered the expectations we had formed of her acting in this character. Her success was most complete; indeed, it is some time since we have heard such genuine and repeated bursts of applause as those which greeted her, throughout her performance. There was the same perfect absence of anything like a straining after an effect which we have before remarked in this lady's acting; and yet wherever it was required her energy had something in it that was really terrible. The part which appeared to make the greatest impression on the audience, was in the banquet scene of the third act. The effect of her earnest anxiety to talk away the suspicions excited in the breasts of the visitors by *Macbeth's* horror at the apparition of *Banquo*, was electrical. Mr. Forrest was less successful as *Macbeth*. From his previous performances we had expected better things; and we were grievously disappointed. His long pauses were wearisome and tedious to an insupportable degree; and there was a total absence of expressive passion to compensate for the winddrawn periods of silence. It is true that he ranted at times, but it was with the half-energy of a man, who thinks such physical exertion beneath him, although he must do it to please his audience. They applauded vigorously, it is true; but they also hissed, and sometimes tittered, which was worse. The other characters were respectably played, which is all we can say for them. The choruses were given with much effect, and comprised the

principal members of the operatic company, including Messrs. Allen, Leffler, and Hime; Misses Condell, Emma Stanley, and Grant; and Madame Feron. Some *entr'actes*, by Mr. C. Horn, were introduced; but there was such a noise in the house, which was densely crammed, that we cannot offer an opinion upon their merits.

Miss Cushman was announced to appear, on Thursday, as *Rosalind*, in "As You Like it." Her engagement appears altogether to have been a most fortunate stroke of policy on the part of Mr. Maddox.

DRURY LANE.—
Notwithstanding the entire failure of the last ballet, "Les Danaïdes," the business at this establishment has been above the average, even to such old performances as "The Bohemian Girl" and "Der Freyschütz," which have drawn one or two good houses. In the latter opera Miss Romer and Mr. King have obtained and merited very considerable applause; and their exertions in "La Somnambula" have been similarly successful. Mr. Bunn announced his benefit for Monday evening next. The programme is attractive, commencing with the "Elixir d'Amore," followed by a divertissement conducted by Jullien and Keening; then a concert, sustained by the principal artistes of this theatre; and, lastly, the ballet of "Giselle." A mistake is made in the bill, in allusion to this ballet, which should be rectified. It is stated that it will be performed "for the first time on the English stage." This is wrong; the ballet of "Giselle" was produced, and with very good effect, at the Princess' Theatre, where is attracted for some time, the principal character being

THE ILLUSTRATED LONDON NEWS.

MISS CUSHMAN AS "ROMEO," AND MISS SUSAN CUSHMAN AS "JULIET," AT THE HAYMARKET THEATRE.

Fig. 5. Miss Cushman as Romeo, and Miss Susan Cushman as Juliet, at the Haymarket Theatre, *Illustrated London News*, 3 January 1846. (Cambridge University Library.)

In some ways, Cushman acts as the precursor of those strong American women such as Henrietta Stackpole and Wallachia Petrie who would stride through the later Victorian fiction of James and Trollope, unperturbed by the disturbance they spread around them, but Cushman is far more significant in her disruption of English viewing practices which would traditionally centre around the spectacle of the actress's 'natural' appearance on stage. In the case of Cushman, nature was recognised as the effect of intelligence, and her part, rather than her own person, was allowed textual space. In her reception in Britain, recognition of her intelligence and her popularity were jointly enabled by physicality impossible to accommodate within the traditional practices of spectating, and by the freedom from a particularly prescriptive form of femininity which was accorded by her nationality.

The conjunction of femininity and forms of national identity is evident in reviews throughout the century, from the rivalries engineered between Rachel and Helen Faucit which made of each the exemplar of their respective country's national drama, to accounts of later Victorian theatre which became part of an editorial function to promote patriotism. In 1881, the *Saturday Review* takes an anonymous Henry James to task for his slighting review of Ellen Terry's Portia, which she performed at the Lyceum in 1880. James's extremely wide-ranging review is a digest of the London theatre in 1880, and the *Saturday Review* finds in it 'an undertone of contemptuous indulgence towards our efforts in the art of acting which is highly characteristic of a certain school of modern critics'.[19] In all the lengthy article, the *Review* takes most exception to what it describes as James's 'French-inspired' distaste for Ellen Terry's Portia's bearing towards Bassanio. James notes that

> When Bassanio has chosen the casket which contains the key of her heart, she approaches him and begins to pat and stroke him. This seems to us an appallingly false note. "Good heavens she's touching him!" a person sitting next to us exclaimed – a person whose judgment in such matters is always unerring.[20]

The *Saturday Review* could not, of course, know that James's companion was none other than Fanny Kemble, herself a noted – English – Shakespearean actress. James goes on to suggest that

> The English would be greatly – and naturally – surprised if one should undertake to suggest to them that they have a shallower sense of decency than the French, and yet they view with complacency, in the high glare of the footlights, a redundancy of physical endearment which the taste of their neighbours across the channel would never accept.[21]

In a curiously self-negating put-down, the *Saturday Review* dismisses James as typical of the 'American who has worshipped at the Comédie-Française',[22] and ridicules his distaste for Terry as one among 'many other curious specimens' in his review. The singling out of James's comments on Terry is telling, as James challenges not only the acknowledged leading English actress of the Victorian stage, but also, of course, the taste which put her in that position, a taste which he suggests is willingly beguiled by that 'natural quality' about Terry that is 'extremely pleasing – something wholesome and English and womanly which often touches easily where art, to touch, has to be finer than we often see it'.[23]

Both James and the *Saturday Review*'s writer invest in a sense of the fundamental sympathy and symbiosis between the actress and the expectations of an appropriate form of national identity held by her audience. James has then to be dismissed as tainted by foreign, and specifically French, tastes in order that his critique of Terry and of English audiences be dismissed as a mere curiosity. This is all the more important because James ends his review with a postscript in which he writes:

> By far the most agreeable theatrical event that has lately taken place in London is the highly successful appearance of Madame Modjeska, who is so well known and generally appreciated in America. This charming and touching actress has hitherto appeared but in two parts; but in these parts she has given evidence of a remarkably delicate and cultivated talent . . . Madame Modjeska is the attraction of the hour; but it only points the moral of these desultory remarks that the principal ornament of the English stage just now should be a Polish actress performing in a German play.[24]

The review's implicit comparison of the Polish actress with Ellen Terry gives a clue to the extent of the *Saturday Review*'s hostility to James.

At that stage, Modjeska had, as James notes, only appeared in a bowdlerised version of *La Dame aux camélias* (under the title *Heartsease*), adapted to bypass the vigilance of the British censor, and in Schiller's *Mary Stuart*. She was received sufficiently warmly that she was able to report in letters quoted in her autobiography that she had 'conquered': 'My success surpassed all expectations; everyone here seems to think it quite extraordinary.'[25] Modjeska's appearances in late Victorian Britain were heralded by the paraphernalia of the new celebrity and advertising culture of the day. She recalls her advertisements, which consisted of

> Nothing but 'MODJESKA' in letters three feet long. We often stand nearby to listen to the remarks of the passers-by. Some of them, having read the name, ask each other: What is it? Is it alive? Others remark to their friends that it surely must be some new tooth-powder, or some sanitary cereal, or a medicine for rheumatism.[26]

Modjeska goes on to remark that her name was 'less known here than that of the ruler of the smallest of the Fiji islands; still I have the audacity to brave the audience by giving them samples of my native art – and my individuality'.[27] Modjeska's start in Britain had indeed been inauspicious. Invited to recite at an evening party by Hamilton Aïdé, she had found herself, for the first time in her life, 'being observed by some women as an interesting object of curiosity. Against all rules of good breeding and politeness, they looked me over from head to foot with their lorgnettes, and their supercilious smile was quite aggravating.'[28]

Modjeska had arrived in London, under the auspices of Wilson Barrett's management, as an international star who was particularly well known in America, but of whom, as she ruefully notes, Britain was entirely ignorant. Her autobiography suggests that equal measures of ambition and resentment of her English hosts, whose ways often seem to her disrespectful and uncouth, determine her efforts to succeed on the English stage. Unusually for the touring actress, Modjeska took on the difficult task of appearing in English on the London stage, and, as she records, practised her English for up to seven hours a day in order to succeed, 'to be worthy of myself and of the appreciation of great Albion'.[29] Modjeska's writings on the subject of her English tours display a mixture of self-abasing unworthiness that she should be acting in the land of Shakespeare and other great dramatists, and a pronounced sense of the degraded nature of contemporary England, in which Good Friday is celebrated with jollity, and the birthplace of Shakespeare is treated with a great lack of respect. There is a sense in both her writings and in the responses of reviewers to Modjeska that some form of cultural authority is at stake in the acting of the foreign visitor, some question of ownership of appropriate forms of interpretation. Modjeska might be able to find success as a sanitised Marguerite Gautier, and in plays such as *Adrienne Lecouvreur*, *Odette* or *Froufrou*, plays which had an accepted European provenance, but in the legitimate, and more specifically Shakespearean repertoire, Modjeska struggled to achieve success.

After a largely successful year in London and the provinces, where she toured with Wilson Barrett's company, Modjeska attempted Juliet at the Royal Court Theatre in April 1881. This part had in England both an extraordinary cultural and theatrical status. One of the best-recognised markers of the *tragédienne*'s skills, it also functioned throughout the Victorian period, especially during the 1880s when there were an unprecedented number of high-profile performances, as a form of display of female sexual attraction which was doubly authorised by Shakespeare and by the erring heroine's death at the play's conclusion, and which thus enabled that display to coexist with a persistent sense of the character's exemplary young femininity. This licensed and paradoxical sexual attraction was part of a theatrical tradition which the more high-minded Modjeska was either not aware of, or chose to ignore. She writes in her autobiography of Act 3, scene 5 of the play that if Romeo and Juliet

> succumb to the natural law and the calling of their southern blood, it is not done with premeditation. There is no necessity, either, to remind the audience of what had just happened in Juliet's room by such naturalistic details as a disarranged four-posted bed, or the turning of the key of a locked door at the

nurse's entrance or Romeo's lacing his jerkin, and a dishevelled Juliet in a *crêpe de chine* nightgown. Such details are cheap illustrations and unworthy of a true artist. Shakespeare's plays do not require such commonplace interpretations in order to produce a genuine, vivid, and refining impression upon the audience.[30]

Thirty years on, Modjeska's rejection by the critics clearly still rankles and gives extra vigour to her self-justification and implicit slighting of the taste of English audiences.

Her reviewers found in her acting a self-conscious artistry which militated disastrously against the dimensions of her role. She was, according to the *Saturday Review*, 'everything that study, and care, and intelligence can provide, but lacking freshness and spontaneity'.[31] Liking her best when she was 'least herself', the *Review* goes on to invoke another Juliet so as to remind its readers of the iconic potency of the role. Fanny Kemble's timidity is found to be more fitting, at least in some degree, because it is more natural to the actress. On leaving the stage, indeed, the *Review* records how Miss Kemble rushed for reassurance to her mother in a way which was very 'fitting to the part'. Modjeska is tasked with being both visibly 'artistic' and insufficiently 'natural', which in this case can only mean young and English. Unable to rise above nationalist prejudices as Cushman had done, Modjeska never achieved the status in Britain that she had won elsewhere. Curiously, she seems to have fallen victim to ignorance about precisely what her nationality might signify. Reviews make few references to her status as a foreigner beyond noting her accent, which for most was not a problem. Unlike Cushman's American identity, Modjeska's Polish nationality offered few recognisable signifiers to her audience. She herself notes that in England, 'I never yet felt so far from my country and my own people as I feel here.'[32] Without nationally derived expectations which Modjeska might be expected to fulfil, or at least to be read against, critics simply rejected her as falling short in the qualities of 'naturalness' and 'charm' so beloved of English actresses, and particularly of Ellen Terry, at that time. Even the celebrity machine was unable to make the name 'Modjeska' sufficiently familiar to potential audiences, lacking, as they seemed to have done, any sense of what a Polish identity might even begin to mean.

Modjeska also stood apart from her international peers in deviating from the tragic repertoire that they practised. It is notable that all of the major touring actresses of the nineteenth century who made a name for themselves in Britain – Rachel, Cushman, Modjeska, Adelaide Ristori, Sarah Bernhardt and Eleanora Duse – were *tragédiennes*. With the exception of Rachel, who was primarily defined by the neoclassical French drama, all of them essayed Shakespeare at some time during their time in London and the provinces.

Bernhardt would perhaps become the most notorious Shakespearean with her 1899 Hamlet, but before then, she like most of her peers had played Lady Macbeth. The part seems to have had something of a talismanic quality for the international actress, but it was one which Modjeska resisted. Her chosen Shakespearean tragic heroine was Juliet, and in that choice she seems to have trespassed too fundamentally upon cherished conceptions of English theatrical womanhood. English audiences wanted to believe in the transparency of Juliet, hence her choice as the debut role of Helen Faucit and her iconic place in the early career of Fanny Kemble, women who could activate the part's ideological dimensions as a means of excusing their appropriation of the theatrical space. Modjeska's efforts in the part disrupted that aesthetic of the natural, though its persistence was reinvigorated the next year by Ellen Terry's Juliet, a performance about which few but Henry James found anything to quibble. James concluded that Terry 'is almost always interesting, and she is often a delightful presence: but she is not Juliet; on the contrary! She is too voluminous, too deliberate, too prosaic, too English',[33] precisely those qualities which signalled her popular success, and Modjeska's relative failure. It was less Modjeska's temerity in approaching Shakespeare that her audiences objected to, for they had been welcoming for decades overseas actresses who did just that, but Modjeska's choice of part, for that revealed, as did James's comments on Terry the next year, the precisely English femininity with which that part had come to be invested. No matter that the role was that of a young Italian heroine, Juliet had been definitively appropriated as English.

This was not the case with Lady Macbeth, a role which Ristori, Cushman and Bernhardt had all attempted, and which had a recognised part in an English theatrical tradition going back most notably to Sarah Siddons, but which did not have a similar role within expectations of English femininity. There was less to feel protective about in this role, and more to assess by way of theatrical tradition. Sensing both possibilities perhaps, the part became a seminal one for the international actress, whose own performances subsequently added to that tradition, and may indeed have helped to inspire the Lyceum production of *Macbeth* in 1888, when Ellen Terry gave a performance which is usually read in comparison to Sarah Siddons's innovations in the part, but which may just as well have been responding to recent European and American performances.

Adelaide Ristori first appeared in Britain in 1856, following a season in Paris in which she had been set up, unwillingly, as a rival to Rachel, and during the run of the Italian Opera at Her Majesty's Theatre where Alboni was singing. She appeared first as Medea in Legouvé's adaptation, and, according to the *Saturday Review*, made the 'ill-written play endurable'.[34] From that very first production, she was encouraged by critics to think of playing Lady Macbeth: 'If Madame Ristori can make as much as she does of this, what would she not do if she played Lady Macbeth – a part exactly suited to her?'[35] It was not until the following year that Ristori began her gradual assault on the part of Lady Macbeth, in a season in which it was preceded by her appearances in a revival of *Medea*, in *Rosamunda*, and in *Camma*, a classical motif which Tennyson would adapt as *The Cup* for the Lyceum in 1881. Each part was greeted with more superlatives than the last by most critics, though George Henry Lewes finds in her primarily a conventional actress. He notes that

> Ristori has comparative mastery of the mechanism of the stage, but is without the inspiration necessary for great acting. A more beautiful and graceful woman, with a more musical voice, has seldom appeared; but it is with her acting as with her voice – the line which separates charm from profound emotion is never passed.[36]

Of her conventionality, he adds that

> The conventional artist is one who either, because he does not feel the vivid sympathy, or cannot express what he feels, or has not sufficient energy of self-reliance to trust frankly to his own expressions, cannot be the part, but tries to act it, and is thus necessarily driven to adopt those conventional means of expression with which the traditions of the stage abound.[37]

Reviews of Ristori's 1857 Lady Macbeth certainly engage with that stage tradition: 'To be able to act Lady Macbeth is to come up to the English traditionary standard of excellence in an actress', and her interpretation varied from the English tradition and was 'slightly coloured by the habits of Southern life'.[38] It should perhaps be noted that Ristori's performances were the only theatrical productions being noticed by the *Saturday Review* at this period. The references to tradition, and the comparisons to Siddons which Ristori had feared would be made,[39] are, however, despite Lewes's dissenting voice, a measure of her success. Despite, or perhaps even because of, the visibility of a 'fundamentally Italian'[40] aspect to her acting, Ristori is eligible to become part of a tradition of playing Lady Macbeth which may supplement, but will not supplant, her English predecessors, most notably Siddons.

This 1857 production was, however, just the first stage of a career-long assault on this part, and perhaps on the sensibilities of an English audience whom she and Modjeska both found lacking in respect to Shakespeare.[41] In 1873, Ristori gave the sleep-walking scene in English, and in 1882, once assured of the 'perfection' of her acquisition of an English accent, she performed the whole role in English at Drury Lane, and claims that she was acknowledged a 'splendid success'.[42] Other critics were, however, less enthusiastic, most notably on account of the poor cast with whom she acted, who undermined her performance, and who gave some cause to bewail the star system and the lack of systematised theatre training in Britain.

Eight years earlier, Matthew Arnold had used the visit of another foreign company to lend his voice to the agitation for an English national theatre along the lines of the Comédie Française. He ends his account of that company's visit to London thus:

> And still, even now that they are gone, when I pass along the Strand and come opposite to the Gaiety Theatre, I see a fugitive vision of delicate features under a shower of hair and a cloud of lace, and hear the voice of Mdlle Sarah Bernhardt saying in its most caressing tones to the Londoners: The theatre is irresistible; organise the theatre![43]

Bernhardt's is an ironic authority to cite in this debate, as by the time of the company's visit to London her relationship with the Comédie was coming under profound strain, due to disagreements over her roles and her opportunities to earn money in addition to her salary from the company. However, such as she was, she was a product of the national theatre system in France, which was an object of envy for theatre reformers in Britain. During that first London season, Bernhardt played roles largely made up of the tragic characters popularised, indeed epitomised, by Rachel, who, as John Stokes points out, many British theatre-goers (including Matthew Arnold) still remembered.[44] Arnold found something lacking in Bernhardt in comparison with Rachel, whom he had adored, a something he described as 'high intellectual power',[45] but, as he notes, Bernhardt's was the more popular success.

In part this is a measure of the changing times. Bernhardt arrived in London, as Henry James notes, as an acknowledged celebrity whom the British were eager to admire. Her success, he writes,

> has been the success of a celebrity, pure and simple, and Mlle Sarah Bernhardt is not, to my sense, a celebrity because she is an artist. She is a celebrity because, apparently, she desires with an intensity that has rarely been equaled to be one, and because for this end all means are alike to her.[46]

He goes on to suggest that she may justifiably be called 'the muse of the newspaper',[47] and that so potent is her celebrity that it has made her into 'a sort of fantastically impertinent victrix poised upon a perfect pyramid of ruins – the ruins of a hundred British prejudices and proprieties'.[48] One of those prejudices was that there was no need for a state-subsidised national theatre or training institution in Britain. The *Saturday Review* anticipated the French company's visit with an article entitled 'Mlle Sarah Bernhardt and Miss Ellen Terry'. In it, the journalist defended the lack of state intervention in Britain with the evidence of greatness provided by Ellen Terry herself, 'who may be said to be to the English something of what Mlle Sarah Bernhardt is to the French'.[49] In that comparison, all sorts of (im)moral equivalencies are made too, but subdued, as were hints of Terry's impropriety, by a desire for the overwhelmingly moral aesthetic of the English stage. The article is interesting in setting up the familiar motif of the 'rival queens' in its actual celebration of Terry rather than Bernhardt, and also in using as one of its grounds of comparability the actresses' as yet unperformed versions of Lady Macbeth. Both actresses are geniuses, both have the 'semblance of spontaneousness', both are identified with 'every thought and habit of every character that [they represent]'. '[T]he difference is one of personality': if both were to play Lady Macbeth, both performances would be 'equally true', but each would be 'marked by the personality of the actress who gave it'.[50] The judgement proved, to Bernhardt's cost, to be prophetic.

Bernhardt appeared in Jean Richepin's version of *Macbeth* in 1884, first in Edinburgh in June, and in the following month in London. *The Times'* reviews of both productions are revealingly contradictory, and invoke their own nationalist sympathies in response to Bernhardt. In Scotland, in the country with which the play was associated, and which, it is suggested, has its own distinct stage traditions, Bernhardt is allowed to have the courage 'to challenge comparison' with her illustrious predecessors, and to create a Lady Macbeth which is 'doubtless . . . one of her most original and most carefully elaborated characters', and which is recognised as being for her, as it was for Ristori, 'the one character in the list of Shakespeare's heroines that exactly and completely suits her idiosyncracies'.[51] This review praises the ways in which the softer touches of the character, her tenderness for her husband, and the spark of love which animates her even when Macbeth has most need of her 'diabolical determination' are in evidence throughout, and play alongside 'the extraordinary energy of her concentrated devilry'.

The later review of Bernhardt's London production recasts this energy as a specifically sexual one which, allied with a translation which is deemed unworthy of the original, makes for a performance which is 'more inadequate and unsatisfactory' than any Shakespeare play seen in London by the reviewer.[52] In modern terminology, *The Times* accuses Bernhardt of sexing up her performance of the role. Where the Scottish reviewer saw feminine wiles, the London writer sees 'an unromantic Cleopatra, who wheedles and cajoles where she should command, and whose influence over Macbeth's rugged nature is exercised not by means of masculine force but of feminine blandishment'. Added to this are the accusations that her conception of the role is 'wholly at variance with stage tradition', and thus 'wholly un-Shakespearean'. Ristori was felt at least to have engaged with a discernible tradition. Bernhardt threatened to overturn it completely for the sake of originality and the fulfilment of that 'character' of serpentine sexuality which was her trademark, and which would determine reception of her performances in England, no matter what her motivations.

In the 1890s, that character took on a new complexion in the context of the decadence which was the hallmark of the time, and of which Bernhardt, with her French nationality, overt sexuality and raffish personality, seemed to personify one aspect. In that decade, theatre in Britain was a highly conflicted form, where the 'new' theatre of Ibsen and Strindberg and the domestic 'problem' play of Pinero squared up against the more legitimate fare of the Lyceum, and where the influence of the international female performer figured more largely than ever before. Bernhardt was joined on the English stage during that decade by Eleonora Duse, against whom Bernhardt was pitted in a duel which began to articulate the terms of the new theatre's influence on British theatre and culture, and within which the parameters of decadence were explored.

Duse arrived in Britain in 1893 with a reputation for playing the heroines of what Bernhardt had famously dismissed as 'Nordic trash'.[53] Duse had been Italy's first Nora, in Milan in February 1891, and had followed up that performance with work in *Rosmersholm*, *John Gabriel Borkman*, *Ghosts* and *The Lady from the Sea*. Her first London season was in the spring and summer of 1893, an important year for English theatre, in which *A Woman of No Importance* and *An Enemy of the People* were both seen at the Haymarket, J. T. Grein's Independent Theatre had produced the grimly realistic melodrama *Alan's Wife*, Elizabeth Robins had premièred *The Master Builder*, and there was a well-received series of Ibsen performances at the Opera Comique. The most sensational event of the year, however, was arguably the appearance of Stella Campbell as *The Second Mrs Tanqueray*. In its 'Dramatic Notes' for 30 May, the *Pall Mall Gazette* recorded that the two dominant topics of the theatre were *The Second Mrs Tanqueray* and Duse.[54] Duse's own participation in that season was highly eclectic. She appeared first as Fédora and as Margaret Gautier in *Camille*, an Italian version of Dumas's play, following these Bernhardt roles with Nora in *A Doll's House*, and Cleopatra, a role in which William Archer found that there was 'nothing in the least voluptuous, sensuous, languorous about her performance. Her very embraces are chilly, and she kisses like a canary-bird.'[55]

Bernhardt's sensuousness in some measure provided the means by which to judge Duse's effectiveness in some of her roles, but the latter's primary appeal,

Fig. 6. Eleonora Duse on her last visit to London, 1923, pencil sketch by Marguerite Steen. (Private collection.)

and her methods, were completely opposed to Bernhardt's. Duse was taken up enthusiastically by theatre critics, and Decadent writers, in particular Arthur Symons, as a sign of the new possibilities of the theatre. She became also a figure who could represent, as Helen Zimmern suggests in 1900,

> the modern actress, the fin de siècle woman par excellence, with her hysterical maladies, her neurotism, her anaemia, and all its consequences . . . Eleonora Duse's repertoire largely consists of a collection of these abnormal types whom she renders with all their weaknesses, their paradoxes, their fantasies, their languors, their fascinations.[56]

As John Stokes notes, 'If Bernhardt was the type of star, Eleonora Duse was the type of anti-star',[57] and an actress who fundamentally disputed the terms of contemporary theatre: 'To save the theatre the theatre must be destroyed, the actors and actresses must all die of the plague: they poison the air, they make art impossible.'[58]

William Archer and Bernard Shaw, the leading theatre reviewers of the 1890s, both responded enthusiastically to Duse's innovative acting, its reserve, judgement and, above all, its intelligence. Archer wrote that 'her art is so delicate as to suffer her temperament always to shine through it', and goes on to compare her to Bernhardt, whom he describes as seeming

> no longer a real woman, but an exquisitely-contrived automaton, the most wonderful *article de Paris* ever invented, perfect in all its mechanical airs and graces, but devoid alike of genuine feeling and artistic conscience. Of course, this is a gross, an ungrateful, exaggeration. Sarah Bernhardt has been, and still is, a great actress, to whom we owe countless artistic pleasures. But there is a noble simplicity, a searching directness, in the art of Eleanora Duse, which certainly comes as a relief after the excessive artifice of Sarah's later manner. One has a sensation of passing out into the fresh air from an alcove redolent of patchouli.[59]

The artifice and cosmetics of Bernhardt were replaced by the simplicity of a Duse who spurned cosmetics, and whose greatest effect, as commemorated by Shaw, was the perfectly natural blush with which she was overcome as Magda in Sudermann's *Heimat*, when she meets her old lover. Shaw uses this blush as the main grounds of his comparison of Duse and Bernhardt, when the women appeared simultaneously in the same play in London in 1895. Whereas Bernhardt was always the same: she does not enter into the leading character, she substitutes herself for it, 'Duse produces the illusion of being infinite.'[60] Her blush epitomises her effect: 'it seemed to me a perfectly genuine effect of the dramatic imagination',[61] with no hint of that painted effect which Bernhardt had perfected.

In this duel between these two actresses, Ellen Terry was displaced as the leading female performer in London. The 'rival' dynamic still persisted, but the rivalry was between a French and an Italian *tragédienne*, with little space left for the charm which had for so long been a central element of English theatre. The emergence of the 'literary drama' onto the stage of the 1890s had definitively shifted the grounds of the actress's work, leaving Terry immersed in an aesthetic which was coming to seem outdated. Terry was the final Victorian practitioner of a national tradition which Bernhardt and Duse had sidestepped, bringing their own repertoire to the English stage, a repertoire which echoed, but also exceeded, the European parts played by their predecessors.

The touring actress was a fundamental part of the international theatre scene in the nineteenth century because her career worked variously either to complement theatrical traditions which evolved as needed, or to overthrow them altogether. She challenged concepts of femininity as given and natural, often by inviting comparison with male rather than with female actors, and her performances threw light upon the construction of theatrical and social concepts of gender. Made visible by the technological developments of the nineteenth century, the global presence of the touring actress ensured that the theatre of the twentieth would learn from her cosmopolitan example.

NOTES

1. Tracy C. Davis, *The Economics of the British Stage, 1800–1914* (Cambridge: Cambridge University Press, 2000), p. 221.
2. Ibid., p. 222.
3. Peter Raby, *Fair Ophelia: A Life of Harriet Smithson Berlioz* (Cambridge: Cambridge University Press, 1982), p. 63.
4. Alexandre Dumas as quoted in Raby, *Fair Ophelia*, p. 68.
5. Théophile Gautier, *Histoire de l'art dramatique en France depuis vingt-cinq ans*; quoted in Carol Jones Carlisle, *Helen Faucit: Fire and Ice on the Victorian Stage* (London: Society for Theatre Research, 2000), p. 132.
6. In *The French Actress and her English Audience* (Cambridge: Cambridge University Press, 2005), John Stokes examines aspects of the long-established experience of theatrical and cultural exchanges between England and France.
7. Rachel M. Brownstein, *Tragic Muse: Rachel of the Comédie-Française* (Durham, NC: Duke University Press, 1995), p. 197.
8. Ibid., p. 197.
9. Ibid., p. 141.
10. 'Rachel', in *On Actors and the Art of Acting* (London: Smith, Elder, 1875), pp. 23–31, p. 23.
11. Ibid.
12. Ibid., p. 27.
13. [Theodore Martin], 'Rachel', *Blackwood's Magazine* 132 (1882), pp. 271–95, p. 294.
14. 'The Theatres', *Illustrated London News*, 1 February 1845, pp. 72–4, p. 73.
15. 'The Theatres', *Illustrated London News*, 8 February 1845, pp. 108–10, p. 109.
16. Lisa Merrill, *When Romeo Was a Woman: Charlotte Cushman and her Circle of Female Spectators* (Ann Arbor: University of Michigan Press, 1999), p. 128.
17. 'Haymarket Theatre', *The Times*, 30 December 1845, p. 5.
18. 'Haymarket Theatre', *Illustrated London News*, 3 January 1846, p. 9.
19. 'The Theatres', *Saturday Review*, 15 January 1881, pp. 80–1, p. 81.
20. Henry James, 'The London Theatres', in *The Scenic Art: Notes on Acting and the Drama, 1872–1901*, ed. Allan Wade (London: Hart-Davis, 1949), pp. 133–61, p. 144.
21. Ibid.

22. 'The Theatres', *Saturday Review*, 15 January 1881, p. 81.
23. James, 'The London Theatres', p. 142.
24. Ibid., p. 161.
25. Helena Modjeska, *Memories and Impressions of Helena Modjeska: An Autobiography* (New York: Blom, 1969 [1910]), p. 402.
26. Ibid., p. 399.
27. Ibid.
28. Ibid., p. 396.
29. Ibid., p. 399.
30. Ibid., p. 398.
31. 'The Theatres', *Saturday Review*, 2 April 1881, p. 434.
32. Modjeska, *Memories and Impressions*, p. 398.
33. Henry James, 'London Plays', in *The Scenic Art*, pp. 162–7, pp. 163–4.
34. 'Madame Ristori in the Medea', *Saturday Review*, 14 June 1856, pp. 149–50, p. 149.
35. Ibid.
36. G. H. Lewes, 'Foreign Actors in our Stage', in *On Actors and the Art of Acting*, pp. 126–77, p. 166.
37. Ibid., p. 150.
38. 'Lady Macbeth', *Saturday Review*, 11 July 1857, p. 37.
39. Adelaide Ristori, *Memoirs and Artistic Studies of Adelaide Ristori* (London: Doubleday, Page, 1907), p. 44.
40. 'Lady Macbeth', *Saturday Review*, 11 July 1857, p. 37.
41. Ristori, *Memoirs and Artistic Studies*, p. 44.
42. Ibid., p. 107.
43. Matthew Arnold, 'The French Play in London', *Nineteenth Century* 6 (1879), pp. 228–43, p. 243.
44. Stokes, *The French Actress and her English Audience*, p. 141
45. Ibid., p. 230.
46. Henry James, 'The Comédie-Française in London', in *The Scenic Art*, pp. 125–32, p. 128.
47. Ibid., p. 129.
48. Ibid., pp. 128–9.
49. 'Mlle Sarah Bernhardt and Miss Ellen Terry', *Saturday Review*, 24 May 1879, pp. 643–4, p. 644.
50. Ibid.
51. 'Madame Bernhardt's Lady Macbeth', *The Times*, 25 June 1884, p. 10.
52. 'Gaiety Theatre: Madame Sarah Bernhardt in *Macbeth*', *The Times*, 5 July 1884, p. 7.
53. Quoted in Giovanni Pontiero, *Eleonora Duse: In Life and Art* (Frankfurt: Lang, 1986), p. 218.
54. 'Dramatic Notes', *Pall Mall Gazette*, 30 May 1893, p. 4.
55. William Archer, '*Antony and Cleopatra* – The Comédie-Française', in *The Theatrical World for 1893* (London: Scott, 1894), pp. 172–9, p. 175.
56. Helen Zimmern, 'Eleonora Duse', *Fortnightly Review* 67 (1900), pp. 980–93, p. 993.
57. John Stokes, 'The Legend of Duse', in Ian Fletcher, ed., *Decadence and the 1890s* (London: Edward Arnold, 1979), pp. 151–71, p. 154.

58. Ibid.
59. William Archer, 'Eleanora Duse – Ibsen Performances – The Independent Theatre – Five English Plays', *The Theatrical World for 1893*, p. 147.
60. George Bernard Shaw, 'Duse and Bernhardt', in *Our Theatres in the Nineties* vol. 1 (London: Constable, 1932), pp. 148–54, pp. 150–1.
61. Ibid., p. 154.

FURTHER READING

Brownstein, Rachel M. *Tragic Muse: Rachel of the Comédie-Française.* Durham, NC: Duke University Press, 1995.

Jones, Carol. *Helen Faucit: Fire and Ice on the Victorian Stage.* London: Society for Theatre Research, 2000.

Davis, Tracy C. *The Economics of the British Stage, 1800–1914.* Cambridge: Cambridge University Press, 2000.

Merrill, Lisa. *When Romeo was a Woman: Charlotte Cushman and her Circle of Female Spectators.* Ann Arbor: University of Michigan Press, 1999.

Modjeska, Helena. *Memories and Impressions of Helena Modjeska: An Autobiography.* New York: Blom, 1969 [1910].

Pontiero, Giovanni. *Eleonora Duse: In Life and Art.* Frankfurt: Lang, 1986.

Raby, Peter. *Fair Ophelia: A Life of Harriet Smithson Berlioz.* Cambridge: Cambridge University Press, 1982.

Ristori, Adelaide. *Memoirs and Artistic Studies of Adelaide Ristori.* London: Doubleday, Page, 1907.

Weaver, William. *Duse: A Biography.* London: Thames and Hudson, 1984.

4

DAVID MAYER

The actress as photographic icon: from early photography to early film

Of the many surviving relics of the Victorian and Edwardian actress, the photograph is among the most enduring and more ubiquitous. These images, most often sepia prints mounted on stiff beige cardboard on whose front is imprinted the name and address of a photographic studio and on whose reverse appear testimonials to the photographer's prowess and patronage, fill the cabinets of collectors or inhabit museum file boxes and display cases. Some images are fixed upon glass or china, some upon thin iron plates. Some images are reproduced and reach their consumers through early or advanced print technology; some are even printed in colour. By and large the images are stable enough to resist deterioration. Although made from light directed at surfaces sensitised with silver and treated with chemicals, the images remain unless dampness, mould or unusually strong sunlight causes them to fade. They survive. Thus these once inexpensive, supposedly ephemeral objects come readily to hand – valuable (and now comparatively expensive) when we query the actress's identity, her career trajectory, her professional, social and private status. They address the question: if the actress isn't seen upon the stage, how else – and where else – is she seen, identified, celebrated, memorialised, turned into an icon? What connects the spectator or former spectator or would-be spectator to the actress? How have photography and the photograph impacted on the professional and private lives of greater and lesser actresses?

The focus of this essay is the photograph as a testimonial to the actress's existence, talent, appearance and career in two discrete performance media: the Victorian and Edwardian stage and, some decades on, in early motion pictures. However, the very existence of the photograph raises discussions of the actress's relationship to the photographer and to the consumers of, or clients for, these images. How did actresses and photographers meet? At whose instigation were their encounters? Who benefited from these relationships, and what was the nature of the benefit? As important, this essay insists upon discussion of the various Victorian photographic and print technologies which aided the dispersal and marketing of the photographs. Indeed, there will be an absolute subtext to my essay: my insistence that recognition, fame and subsequent notoriety or celebrity are functions and achievements of existing and arriving print technologies and that, without the several commercially viable technical advances, photography would barely have served the actress's or theatre's purpose. Fame, publicity, adulation, collecting, fan-dom and the full apparatus of fan-worship – even celebrity stalking – would be impossible without the attendant development in photo-engraving and print technologies and national rail and transport systems which could move the actress and her various images in various formats to all parts of the country and, beyond, to the Empire.

Moreover, although superficially at least, photographs appear to explain themselves and their subject matter, there are questions which must be posed of each image: why and for whom was this image made? Is this a reliable likeness? What is the appeal of a likeness and for whom? Where – in what locale, under what conditions – was this image made? Had the actress exercised any control in determining how she was photographed and in selecting who the recipients of her images would be? Was there a tacit agreement between actress, photographer, vendors, and consumers which shaped or dictated the overall process of making and distributing photographs? What is the appeal of the photograph as a private possession? As modern historians, what are we likely to miss from this larger narrative? For example, we usually encounter early theatrical photographs as illustrations to essays and books, the image removed from the contexts of collectors' albums and – even more significantly – separated from the cardboard mountings to which they originally adhered when they left the photographer's studio. These mountings and their texts, front and back, are essential to understanding the photographs. Again, if the image has been taken from a postcard or from another printed or published source, we are not made aware of such sources. Yet these sources, too, help to explicate the photograph. In short, until all elements of contact between the sitter and the photographer, technical process, and commercial exchange are explored, and, insofar as is possible, made known, the photograph ceases to be self-explanatory and becomes an object which insists upon further scrutiny.

Whilst this chapter deals chiefly with images of the actress as a female appearing in the 'legitimate' or spoken drama and in music-based entertainments where their attire identifies them as principals and coryphees in burlesques, extravaganzas and pantomimes, it is necessary to distinguish the actress's photographs and the corresponding conventions of photographing the actress and circulating her photographs from those images of other female performers whose careers happen in variety theatres: aerialists, acrobats, gymnasts, contortionists, cyclists, Indian-club virtuosi, boxers and other females exhibiting physical skills. Between the legitimate actress and the variety performer differences in professional and social class intrude, compelling different choices in photographers, studio practice and marketing strategies. It is rare, but not entirely unknown, that there are crossovers between the two.

The first commercial depiction of actors and actresses, derived from daguerreotypes – but, because there is no extant print technology to reproduce photographs, substantially separated from their photographic origins – is to be found in the so-called Tallis Shakespeare.[1] Dating from 1850–1, it is our earliest representation of performers in their roles, their portraits and costumes unidealised but their few gestures energised, many of them inhabiting a role or depicting a character for the camera. The Tallis Shakespeare, a three-volume compendium of Shakespeare's known plays and pieces of the Shakespearean apocrypha edited by J. O. Halliwell, is illustrated with 150 plates, most of them of known actors and actresses in Shakespearean roles. Those plates of identified performers (as opposed to engravings which simply illustrate scenes from plays), are composite engravings.[2]

The several photographs of Phelps's leading actress Isabella Glyn are typical of this process and afford some of our earlier (near)-photographic likenesses of the actress. Glyn appears in character, her eyes closed or fixed somewhere in the middle distance. Her gaze never seeks the camera's lens, as she might do when sitting for a portrait. Although we know that she has been obliged to hold thirty-second poses to avoid an unwelcome blurring to the daguerreotype's sensitised plates, the strong downward thrust of her gesture, as she enacts an embittered Queen Constance, appears arrested by the camera before it can travel its full length. Some years later, the French-born, London-based photographer Adolphe Beau was to describe the method he used to induce actors into recreating a stage pose before the camera. Entering his studio, actors, sometimes bemused by the photographic apparatus and removed from the paraphernalia of the theatre, the company of other actors and supporting music – an environment that is conducive to acting, unlike a photographer's studio – lost concentration on the role they were to depict. Beau remarked,

> It is a very remarkable fact that most actors, when finding themselves in broad daylight, seemed, as it were, quite *dépaysés* and to have lost the actual remembrance of their exact poses and expressions before the footlights, and I had often to quote the words to promote the attitudes.[3]

Beau's reference to the actors' 'actual remembrance of their exact poses and expressions before the footlights' suggests that he believed pose, gesture and expression were rehearsed and committed to bodily memory to the degree that exact replication of stage performances could be coaxed from the actress as she stood before the camera. Although some modern investigations of early film acting, which compare 'verisimilar' screen acting to hackneyed 'histrionic' theatrical performance, assert that the Victorian performer drew upon a personal repertoire of gestural clichés,[4] there is much evidence to contradict this assumption,[5] and many of the gestures recorded by photography over six decades are individual and, although the subject-actress may have posed for dozens of photographers in the course of her touring, reasonably fresh. Poses staged (or assisted in their staging) by photographers vary considerably in intensity and effect. Some photographs of the actress in role can be matched to moments in the text or to a specific stage production. However, there are many photographs of actresses which, whilst depicting them costumed, find them striking poses which declare either their beauty or their apparent genial accessibility as private persons or their inaccessible spirituality. And there must also be poses more or less suited to the camera and to the photographer's particular expertise or house style and, of course, to the mise en scène and properties the studio can offer.

Isabella Glyn's 'remembered' poses and gestures are supplemented by fragments of text, printed in the floral cartouche below her image, which further specify the dramatic moment represented (fig. 7). Elsewhere in the three Tallis volumes are studio portraits of actresses, but these are in repose and in ordinary dress. The choice of actress's image, thereafter, will be between that of her engaged in a role and visibly interpreting that role or, regrettably and more frequently, in portrait mode. In realising the portrait option, she is costumed, but costumed without reference to the essential contexts of the drama or seen in fashionable modern attire (an extensive fashionable wardrobe which could be worn upon the stage in 'modern' plays was an essential part of the actresses's professional equipment). Thus, she may appear exotic and appealing and, at her best, half-heartedly in role. The camera, a noted instrument of scientific investigation in depicting phenomena and human physiognomies, is never used to probe the actress's psyche to find deeper truths which the actress, employing her acting skills, is thought to conceal. Actresses' portraits show little awareness that the actress is under investigation or that she has anything to hide from her public. Often images are conspicuous for their blandness.

Shearer West, writing on eighteenth-century theatrical portraiture, includes any painted, engraved or printed likeness of the actress – costumed for a role or enacting that role or in civilian's mufti – as a portrait.[6] Because of the manner in which theatrical photography will emerge, by the end of the nineteenth century, in the direction of showing enactment and, eventually,

MISS GLYN AS CONSTANCE

To me, and to the state of my great grief,
Let kings assemble; for my grief's so great
That no supporter but the huge firm earth
Can hold it up. Here I and sorrow sit;
Here is my throne; bid kings come bow to it.

KING JOHN.
Act 3 Sc 1

Fig. 7. Miss Glyn as Constance in *King John*. Engraved by George Greatbach from a Daguerreotype by Paine of Islington. (Author's collection.)

on-stage enactment, I am intentionally forcing a distinction between the image which depicts the actress undertaking and physically engaged in that role, and the portrait: a pictorial likeness of the passive, almost expressionless actress with no visible agenda apart from presenting an image of an attractive, well-gowned woman.

The unanswered question is what remuneration or advantage Glyn and her fellow performers received from being photographed for these volumes. Their actual photographic images were unmarketable and probably undisplayable. They may have achieved some kudos for being described as 'the greatest and most intellectual Actors of the age, taken in the embodiment of the varied and life-like Characters of our great National Poet', and there may have been some novelty in sitting for the Tallis cameras, but photographers are too new at their profession and actresses too inexperienced in negotiating their celebrity to have arrived at a *modus vivendi*. Such rules of exchange will be formulated in the near future.

The first theatrical use of the Victorian wet-plate-dry-print process is seen in the remarkable 'salt-print'[7] images by Martin Laroche, the studio pseudonym of the photographer William Henry Sylvester who advertised himself as a 'photographic miniature painter'. From his Oxford Street studio near the Princess's Theatre, Laroche photographed the Charles Kean company in both individual portraits and staged groupings from plays in Kean's repertoire. Backgrounds visible in these photographs are studio backcloths, not stage scenery. Groupings of actors were arranged by the photographer and cannot be confirmed as replicating Kean's stage directions. The adult Ellen Kean as Lady Macbeth, Caroline Heath as Olivia, Ellen Chapman as Viola and the nine-year-old Ellen Terry as Mamillius in Kean's 1856 *The Winter's Tale* are thus the first actresses whose images appear in photographic prints. However, the Laroche images were not to be viewed as photographs displayed on an easel or mounted within a collector's or family's album. Each photograph was taken in a camera fitted with two parallel lenses, the lenses separated by the average distance between human eyes. The images through the lenses were cast upon two adjacent plates, and these images, printed and mounted side by side, were made to be viewed in an expensive stereopticon viewer, manufactured in polished rosewood or carved walnut with burnished brass-ringed viewing lenses. We might think of Laroche's Kean company photographs as promotional or supporting software for the newly patented viewing equipment,[8] an immodest showy addition – a brief one, as it happened – to the Victorian parlour.

If, for our purposes, there is a significance to the stereopticon viewer and the daguerreotype beyond the theatrical subjects caught by various photographers in Paris, London, New York and Washington, it is that photography attracted the notice of the British royal family. Amongst the royals and nobility it soon became a consuming passion. The monarch, her consort and her offspring were frequent subjects for appointed photographers and – equally – themselves avid collectors of photographic portraits of relatives, royal in-laws and the more ethnographically distinct and distant of her subjects.[9]

A further technical development in 1854 was to nullify the exclusivity of the photograph as an upper-class possession. This development was the manufacture of an inexpensive camera and an inexpensive, easy to conduct developing process which put the cost of photographs so low that anyone might be photographed and anyone might acquire images of celebrity actresses and actors and other notables. The camera, patented, but not invented, by the French photographer André-Eugène Disdéri, simultaneously produced four, then six, then eventually twelve images, each approximately 9 cm × 7.3 cm

($3\frac{1}{2}$ in $\times$ $3\frac{7}{8}$ in). The small photographs were hand-pasted onto cardboard mounts 10 cm $\times$ 8 cm ($3\frac{7}{8}$ in $\times$ $3\frac{1}{4}$ in), the approximate size of a calling or visiting card, and became known as *cartes de visites* or, popularly, 'cdv's'. The cost of *cartes de visites* to the sitter at the more exclusive studios in the early 1860s was 10s 6d per dozen, but by the decade's end the price had been halved and some studios charged as little as 6d a dozen. Studios appeared in most cities and towns, their locales often chosen for their proximity to cafés, shops, theatres and their more fashionable patrons. Itinerant photographers with portable studios and darkrooms – 'smudgers' – stood at street corners and invaded fairs and coastal resorts, undercutting the prices of established studios. The acquisition, collecting and hoarding of *cartes de visites*, usually stored in ever more elaborate albums fitted with metal clasps and systems of internal framing, became an international obsession, and it is from this initial craze, 'cardomania', that the numerous photographic images of the actress first sprang.

Until the 1890s – and only in certain circumstances after that – theatrical photographs were made in a photographer's studio, never on a stage. Theatres did not offer the lighting and other facilities with which to make an acceptable photograph. The actress who wished to be photographed in costume and in character depended upon the photographer to provide a simulacrum of the theatrical settings in which she appeared at the theatre nearby, but these settings are notional rather than explicit. Hand properties might be brought along from the theatre, but it is not at all remarkable to find the same furnishings and identical properties appearing in photographs of civilians and actresses who have no connection with one another other than their choice of photographic studio.

Just as it must be emphasised that theatrical photographs were made in photographers' studios, not in theatres, so it must be stressed that all *cartes de visites* made before the early 1860s were intended as portraits – likenesses of the theatrical personalities caught by the camera and revelling in the tensions between the public face of the actress and her private personality. Actresses were photographed to display their faces, necks, and shoulders. There is no intent to depict action – and, given the duration of exposure times, scant technical possibility of achieving such representation of movement. However, by 1864, Adolphe Beau and Camille Silvy, another French photographer with a London studio in Porchester Terrace, began to photograph clients in full-length views. At first, such views met with derision. *Cartes de visites* already offered small images; facial expressions were harder to read when the total length of a body was seen. But full-length views revealed an actress's complete ensemble and invited gesture and a semblance of action rather than static poses. Gradually, the actress, her entire physical self visible, begins to emote, but her emoting is aestheticised and controlled by the photographer and is unlikely to be as overtly theatrical as it would have been on a stage before an audience. Gestures are rarely expansive. Arms stay close to her body. The body rarely contorts. Kate Saville, as May Edwards in the Olympic Theatre's 1863 production of *The Ticket-of-Leave Man*, is several times photographed by Beau, costumed as if she were appearing in the first-act and fourth-act concert hall scenes. In some images her guitar is visible, but she stays huddled in her shawl, her arms covered in its folds. In one single image she clasps the neck of the guitar and, her left hand pointing downstage accusingly, appears to defend herself against the slurs of dissatisfied auditors. Other actresses simply stand, still and elegant and amiable in full crinolines. Almost alone, Ada Isaacs Menken is repeatedly photographed in active poses taken from *Mazeppa*, *The Child of the Sun*, *Les Pirates de la Savane* and other physically expressive roles. At about the same date, a young Edwin Booth is photographed for *cartes de visites* in Napoleon Sarony's New York studio at 37 Union Square. Booth's head and shoulder images depict him as a handsome man with a wardrobe suitable for a stage-walking gentleman. His full-length views, in contrast, emphasise the physicality of his roles. His Iago crouches sword in hand, his rapier point leading his advanced knee, as if he were stalking an out-of-shot Cassio. In showing unambiguous action, Booth is typical of male actors. Actresses, too, will use the option of the full-length *carte de visite* for views which relate to specific stage moments, but they are likely to be more restrained in their enactments, limiting gestures and not as likely to compromise their good looks.

This description applies to the stage actress. It is not applicable to other species of female performers. Females whose careers were spent in variety theatres, music halls, circuses and fairground portables and who, as a part of these careers, performed feats of dexterity, strength and daring were depicted, in so far as photography technology allowed, as if they were in mid-performance. Female aerialists hang from ropes or trapezes, acrobats and wire-walkers balance precariously on one leg, some cyclists execute Edwardian 'wheelies' or balance on handlebars. Close examination of the photographs reveals, however, that these moments of perilous equilibrium are posed and that the subject is supported in her pose with metal bracing. Even though the focal-plane shutter and faster film somewhat reduced exposure times, the subject was likely to wobble and blur her image if actually attempting these feats in the studio. Iron clamps and other devices held the subject still, and these obtrusive supports which might otherwise give the game away were removed from the negative with the retoucher's brush.

Fig. 8. Theatrical photograph of Mrs John Wood, b. 1845, née Vining. (Author's collection.)

When *cartes de visites* are introduced and until the early 1880s, there is no means within existing print technologies to publish photographs of performers. Half-tone printing and photolithography do not yet exist, and, especially in the early years of these technologies, will be expensive processes, too expensive to reproduce photographs in small-circulation theatrical journals. Instead, the photograph became valued for its own sake and – as the core of an intricate commercial transaction – generated a long-enduring symbiotic relationship between the subject of the photograph (the actress), the maker of the photograph (the photographer), the theatrical sponsor of the photograph (the theatrical management or the theatre itself) and the photograph's consumer (the theatre-goer, the collector, the fan). We must recognise and acknowledge a largely unwritten and unspoken but widely understood agreement, subject to many local variations, trade-offs and variations in reciprocity and compensation, between these four parties involved.

It was a species of contract which largely met their several needs. The actress, seeking recognition for her work, a fan base, future acting contracts and local publicity at each touring stop, needed to have her photograph made at each touring stop – in portrait and in role – so that each local photographer would display her photographs in his studio window and in the large outdoor display kiosks before his shop. Moreover, the actress needed some photographs to send to agents or to managements booking further tours or to give to fans and admirers who came to meet her at the stage door. The management company or the theatre employing the actress needed the publicity that the interest in her photographs generated, and benefited from being able to exhibit photographs of the performers in role in the theatre foyer and in framed glass cases outside the theatre's doors. The photographer needed the attention given to his studio and to his work as each new batch of photographs was displayed in his shop window. Customers entered his shop to buy these photographs as soon as they were available for purchase, and the photographer further advertised his wares in the programmes of local theatres. In some instances, actresses paid to be photographed, the fee depending upon how well known she was and whether her image would attract paying customers. In other instances actresses were courted with the gift of free photographs if they would deign to sit for the photographer who stood to profit from sales to fans. Notices were placed on backstage notice boards inviting actors to call at local studios immediately upon their arrival in town, and photographers' advertisements in theatre programmes confirmed to the actress that there was an immediate local market for her image.

The fan, more simply, desired the actress's photographs, and it was the obligation of the other three to meet her or his demands for current images.

We know that some fans carried their photographs to the actress to have them autographed or to have personal messages written upon them, thus to a degree fetishising the photograph and signifying to the fan (an imagined) closer relationship to the actress than merely that of a spectator who had observed her from the theatre's auditorium. Laurence Senelick points to a further, clandestine, market for the actress's photographs. He identifies a subculture of men, unlikely to be able to afford mistresses, gathering in cigar cases photographs of actresses, female variety performers and prostitutes for viewing in fantasy 'seraglios'.[10] Some actresses appear to have voluntarily abetted this hidden trade. Studios which kept archives of their work offer evidence that some actresses paid for their professionally necessary sittings by posing for semi-nude photographs which, rather than being sold as albumen (sepia-coloured) prints, were peddled through the studio's back door as cheaper gelatine-silver (black-and-white) prints. There is, however, no evidence to indicate how widespread this practice may have been.

Parallel to this four-cornered exchange was another commercial process. Photographs made at local, little-known studios were bought and copied – or simply plagiarised – by retailers of photographs. H. N. King, a stationer in Bath who also sold sheet music, journals and writing supplies and who styled himself 'Photographer to the Queen',[11] became one of Britain's chief outlets for celebrity photographs. Many of these images are unlikely to have been made in his studio. King's customary advertisement, printed on the back of published sheet music, announces that for a shilling apiece he can supply, postage free, *cartes de visites* of some 350 noted actors and actresses, politicians, members of the bar and judiciary, editors, singers and composers, theatrical managers, military and naval officers, society beauties, academics, the nobility and minor royalty. Elsewhere, photographs found their way into music shops and booksellers, thus offering collectors and fans access to current photographs without obliging them to travel to the photographer's studio-shop. Through the agency of such photographer-distributor-retailers as King and lesser suppliers, and inviting comparison with the commemorative statuary of which the Victorians were so fond, portrait photography was transmuted into public art.

It is in the context of denoting source that the photograph's pasteboard mount achieves significance. The mount is our most reliable indication of provenance for the photograph, a means of assessing individual photographers' work and an index to the professional and social standing of the actress. The card's front will ordinarily proclaim the photographer's name, often a stylised signature, and studio address. The mount may also provide the name of the actress photographed and the role in which she is portrayed. Photographers' names denote the actress's current professional standing.

In major cities, such as London, Paris, Havana, New York, Philadelphia, Washington, Boston and Chicago, the actress's choice of a photographer was deliberate and rarely random. There were observed hierarchies and degrees of exclusivity which affected the client's choice of the photographer and, presumably, the photographer's willingness to accept his clients: actresses, operatic divas, mistresses, lesser performers and civilian sitters. We can follow the trajectory of an actress's career by reading the names of the photographers' studios in which she has sat for portraits and costume shots. To have one's photograph made by Alexander Basano at 25 Old Bond Street or by Barraud at 263 Oxford Street was to have arrived at a career pinnacle. Barraud in particular boasted a royal and noble clientele and the upper echelons of acting. He was especially skilful at photographing the actress's wardrobe, and it was not at all unusual for a sitter to arrive with numerous changes of clothing and to wear an entire season's wardrobe – hats, gowns and furs – in the course of a sitting.[12] Lesser but still successful actors had their photos made by Alfred Ellis or Elliott and Fry or W. and D. Downey (who also photographed royal and titled sitters) and thought themselves privileged. Barraud regularly exported photographs of his clients to the New York dealer Dr Joshua Roth at 5 Union Square. Foreign actresses arriving in New York might expect their photographs to be already in circulation. Female variety performers were largely excluded from these studios, although on provincial tour, when the choice of photographers was limited and sources for clients equally restricted, actresses and variety artistes patronised the same studios. In London, however, variety artistes, although occasionally seen on the premises of the London Stereoscopic Company, were photographed by more down-market portraitists such as Rodolfo & Co. in his Bolinbroke (sic) Studios at 108 Northcote Rd., Clapham Junction. Photographs were sold in variety theatres, in tobacconists and in newsagents, and nationally distributed by William Spooner from his shop in the Strand, London. On the mounting card's back were testimonials to the photographer's skills: medals won at international expositions, prizes, crests indicating royal patronage, boasts that the top-floor studio was served by a lift, drawings of the studio building and its exhibition kiosks. The card's back was not a stable text but was often changing, testifying to the photographer's mounting skill, reputation and prosperity. Thus, to separate a photograph from its mount is to deprive the image of important contextualising information.

The passion for collecting celebrity photographs and for having one's own likeness taken never slowed. From the late-1870s, the small *carte de visite* was replaced by a larger standard size, the cabinet photograph, 14 cm × 10.2 cm ($3^{1}/_{2}$ in × 4 in), an albumen print similarly mounted, 16.5 cm × 10.8 cm ($6^{1}/_{2}$ in × $4^{1}/_{2}$ in), and soon thereafter by a sequence of still larger images, the 'boudoir' print and the 'Paris Panel' which, backed with heavy gilt-edged cardboard, were intended to stand, unframed, upon domestic easels (see fig. 9). Studios quoted prices of £1 1s for mixed batches of *cartes de visites*, cabinets and boudoir prints. Celebrity images retailed for approximately 10d apiece. Photographers who had struggled to hand-tint the diminutive *cartes de visites* now found that colouring prints in the larger formats further increased photography's customers. It is to the cabinet photograph, popular and available until approximately 1910, that we look for the great proliferation of actresses' photographs. Most of the great modern collections of surviving theatrical photographs are cabinet photographs sent to actors' agents. Many of these images of actresses, taken both in role and in fashionable modern attire, bear notes pasted to their backs reminding the agent of current touring dates or citing laudatory reviews of successful engagements. Because the photographed image might now be applied to a durable metal surface, actresses also sent cabinet-size ferrotypes – 'tintypes' – to their actual or would-be agents.

The end of the 1870s also saw the first photographic images of theatrical personages – actresses, actors and dramatists – within a printed journal. These images, perhaps the most familiar of all Victorian individual and group theatrical portraits, are found in the *Theatre*[13] between 1877 and 1897. Sepia images, none of these printed on the pages of this monthly journal but hand-pasted in, are prints which, to the untrained eye,[14] are indistinguishable from conventional cabinet photographs. However, the image – which to us looks like a genuine Victorian cabinet-size photograph – is not, technically, a photograph (i.e. made directly from a negative) but a 'Woodburytype'. Woodburytypes were among the early attempts at reproducing photographs and were made in a process which pressed an engraved image into a waxy surface on a flat-bed press. Each Woodburytype image then had to be cropped from a larger sheet of similar images, trimmed and hand-pasted into the journal, an expensive and labour-intensive process which raised the price of the *Theatre* and limited its circulation. Because the Woodburytype process required expensive hand labour, its commercial use was limited.

As early as 1869, William Legge had devised a 'half-tone' process for printing photographs onto a page, the image now appearing in black, white and shades of grey, the greys made of miniscule dots or 'benday' screen. Legge's invention, however, appeared nearly twenty years before other print technologies had advanced to the point that commercial exploitation of the new process was possible, and even then, half-tone printing was restricted to the more expensive journals. We find an early example of the actress and the new technology meeting in correspondence between Henry Spielman, the editor of the upmarket *Magazine of Art*, and Charles Abud, the manager of the

86

DAYLIGHT SUPERSEDED BY ELECTRICITY. BY THE VAN DER WEYDE LIGHT. 182, REGENT STREET, W. LONDON, AND PARIS.

Fig. 9. Mary Anderson – a 'Paris panel' ca. 1895. (Author's collection.)

American actress Mary Anderson. Anderson, at London's Lyceum theatre in 1887 to play Hermione in *The Winter's Tale*, was invited to be photographed for this prestigious journal – by Barraud's, naturally. All parties to the photo session conceded that '[her] dress should be that worn in the statue scene'.[15] By 1891, the *Theatre* had attempted the half-tone process in two views of stage settings, but the results were disappointing, and these images appeared adjacent to yet another Woodburytype portrait.

Thus the travelling actress was endowed with the possibilities of being, sequentially or concurrently, a local, London (or capital city), national and international figure, her photograph taken by local photographers at every play-date on her tour, again by photographers in London, and her various images sold by these studios and by national and international dealers to collectors and fans at all of these national and foreign venues – where, of course, she was photographed again. The trajectory and vectors of the actress's career are consequently traceable through these sequenced images. The images convey her roles and the modes in which she sought to be portrayed; the mounts tell us who photographed her and theatre-stops through which she passed; distributors' and retailers' labels superimposed on the photograph's mount inform of her foreign tours and celebrity abroad. With print technologies improving to the point that the actress' photographed image could be transformed into a half-tone photo-engraved plate and enlarged and placed on a poster or sheet music covers, published in a newspaper or weekly magazine or a trade journal and – eventually – in a fan magazine, the actress might be recognised by people who had never seen her perform on a stage. Her image sold tickets. Her image also sold cosmetics and couture and issues of the journals which published her picture. The technical and commercial apparatus of celebrity were coalescing.

Additional copies and increased circulation brought down the cost of the half-tone process to the point that, in turn, the inclusion of photographs became a necessity for competing journals. Actors and actresses were advised to have their best photographs processed into zinc or copper printing blocks and to carry these blocks with them on their travels so that their pictures, a column or two columns wide, might be inserted into local newspapers at every touring venue.[16] The challenge for the would-be and lesser-known celebrity was to have his or her image in print where it would be viewed by theatrical agents and managers assembling variety bills and casting stage plays. By 1896, the weekly professional press of the acting profession, the *Era* and the *New York Clipper*, began to publish photographs, first in accompaniment to news items and features, but subsequently and more prolifically in columns of advertisements inserted by actors looking for situations. The former photographs were made by photographers at the behest of publishers;

the latter photographs featured actresses seeking publicity or bookings who had shown the foresight to have their photographs engraved onto printers' blocks and had paid for their photograph's insertion. Images of actresses, most often seeking roles for themselves in pantomime – where physical attributes were especially important in obtaining roles – regularly appeared in the advertising columns of the *Era*.

The most ambitious and successful exploiter of these new technologies were the photographers W. & D. Downey, operating from studios in Ebury Street, near Victoria Station. Already well established as theatrical photographers by the mid-1890s, the Downeys undertook a programme of publication which included photographic souvenir books of plays, photographic 'birthday books', coloured photo-lithographs of leading actors and royalty, decals which were stuck to chocolate and biscuit-tins and – inevitably – photographic postcards. The most remarkable Downey example of collotype colour printing is a large photo-lithograph of the American actress Maud Jeffries who, from 1894 to 1896 appeared in the leading role of Mercia in *The Sign of the Cross*. Jeffries, photographed in three-quarter view from the waist upward and clutching to her breast a crude wooden cross, gazes praying toward Heaven. The picture, simply titled *The Sign of the Cross*, appears to have been marketed as a devotional picture and, framed, survives in the homes of people who have no idea of its theatrical origin.

Until the early 1890s, it had been hugely difficult (although not entirely impossible) and financially unrewarding to attempt to photograph actors on stage in scenes from a theatrical production. This situation changed in 1893 when, coinciding with the widespread introduction of electric lighting in West End and Broadway theatres, the British-born New York photographer Joseph Byron devised a method for successful on-stage flash photography and persuaded theatre managements to display his large (8 in × 10 in and 11 in × 14 in) photographs in glass cases at theatre entrances and on easels in theatre foyers. Byron and his son Percy attended final rehearsals to make their photographs, obliging entire casts to hold poses whilst a combination of magnesium flash powder, electric lights and reduced shutter speeds enabled effective simulations of action which, even today, fool viewers into assuming that they are interrogating action photos. In Britain, the London Stereoscopic Company copied the Byrons' method and surpassed the Byrons in persuading actors to return to their studio in groups and to restage moments of their performances against neutral backcloths to meet a new market for theatrical photographs, the monthly illustrated theatre magazine.

With the success of on-stage photography and with cheaper photo-lithography and printing, it was possible to rethink popular theatre journals. The first of these journals, the *Play-goer* in New York (1902) and the *Play*

Pictorial (1902) and the *Playgoer and Society* (1909) in London, offered their largely female readerships numerous photographs of stage productions and leading actors, brief synopses of the plays and fashion tips. Individual or grouped photographs of actresses and matinee idol actors, as well as full-stage views of key scenes, dominated. Addressing this female readership and publishing on a high-quality coated (i.e. glossy) paper which added a lustrous surface to the photographs, the *Play Pictorial* remained in print until 1939. Similar developments in theatre souvenirs also exploited these technologies. Souvenir programmes offered photographs of key scenes, actors in role, and minimal texts. Concurrently, inexpensive colour photo-lithography was also an option in the making and exploitation of celebrity. Various large-format publications, often linked to the publishers' monthly journals, displayed colour photographs of stage celebrities in role. Large-format folios were sold through newsagents and stationers' shops. Actors presumably collaborated in the production of these publications, receiving fees and benefiting from the circulation of their images. Photographs which appeared in these souvenirs did double duty as picture postcards.

Photographic postcards were sold in their millions. The popularity of cards featuring theatrical subjects and stage personalities and their preservation by a newer generation of collectors has yielded a seemingly bountiful pictorial source which modern scholars have been hesitant to query and have been too ready to accept as reliable production photographs. But these images, too, were more often produced in a photographer's studio, far less often a theatre. Not surprisingly, the images of such well-known actresses as Mrs Patrick Campbell, Dorothea Baird, Maud Jeffries and Constance Collier, which had been available as cabinet photographs only a few months earlier, reappeared as postcards, cheaper and without any pretence of being the work of exclusive West End studios. The market for cards was so lively and competitive that performers were now induced to have their likenesses taken for the new card photographers who, forsaking the photographers' studio kiosks and other traditional markets for photographs, sold their products through newsagents and tobacconists. Variety artistes and those with physical abnormalities managed to exert some control over the sale of their images, giving or selling these at the stage door or from their fairground booths or caravans. To these marginal performers, the sale of photographic cards was a major source of income. Actors, and actresses especially, had far less control over the distribution of their images, and most were obliged to contract the number of cards and poses with the card publishers or with the studio photographers who acted on the card publishers' behalf. So immediate and compelling was the demand for photographs of attractive actresses that an entire genre of cards, 'professional beauties', soon appeared, their subjects portraits of musical comedy actresses and chorines from popular musicals and some women whose connections with the stage were, at best, tenuous. Leading the lengthy list of theatrical 'beauties' were the Dare sisters, Zena and Phyllis, and Gabrielle Ray, 'the most beautiful woman in the United Kingdom', who regularly appeared in Gaiety Theatre musical plays mounted by George Edwardes or other West End pieces devised by Seymour Hicks. Almost invariably, their portrait images underline their appeal as women of exquisite grooming and fashion. Rarely are they depicted in stage costume and even more rarely – if ever – do they gesture as if singing or enacting a role.

In terms of technical innovation and perspicacious marketing, there was only a short step between the studio photographer and the motion picture maker. Indeed, 'movies' began with machines which manipulated still photographs. The earlier and better known of these devices was the mutoscope – more commonly known today as a 'what-the-butler-saw' machine – essentially a viewing lens focusing upon a still image, behind which, fastened to a circular core, were 849 additional photographic prints. When a penny was dropped into a slot, the core was rotated by either a hand crank or an electric motor, and the 850 photographic images were flicked in quick order. In approximately a minute and a half, the entire core completed a full rotation, and the viewer – who had inserted the penny and turned the crank – witnessed a brief narrative drama or variety turn. Some of the mutoscope episodes depicted flirtatious males, obliging chorus girls, and less-than-obliging matronly wives, the actors in these brief dramas forever anonymous, the narratives appealing to a predominately male audience. However, some mutoscope rolls held images of known female variety theatre dancers. These women are the first identifiable movie celebrities.

Probably the best known of these mutoscope performers and one of the very few females whose name was known to cinema audience before 1911 was Annabelle Moore, who performed as Annabelle Whitford. Employed by the Thomas Edison studios in 1894, she reproduced two of Loïe Fuller's dances, dressed in diaphanous gowns and rhythmically waving large panels of transparent gauze. Whitfords's 'Annabelle Serpentine Dance' and 'Annabelle Butterfly Dance' were immediately popular, attracting so many patrons and wearing out mutoscope rolls with such frequency that her dances required frequent refilming at Edison's Black Maria studio.

Shortly after supplying rolls to other mutoscope entrepreneurs, Edison launched his own invention, the Kinetoscope, another persistence-of-vision device for viewing images through an eyepiece. Kinetoscope viewers now watched transparent film rather than the opaque images of the mutoscope. Whitford's gowns and gauze panels were hand-coloured, the irregularity of the colouring adding a remarkable luminescence and iridescence to the films. When, in April 1896, the first true cinema film – termed by Edison the Vitascope – was projected onto a screen at Koster & Bial's music hall in New York city, 'Annabelle Butterfly Dance' was the first film to be seen. The same year, only two years after filming the first mutoscope roll, Annabelle Whitford had become known internationally. In October 1896, her Kineto-scope 'Annabelle Serpentine Dance' introduced the first film programmes seen in New Zealand. In the same year her 'Annabelle Butterfly Dance' and 'Annabelle Flag Dance', in which she was draped in stars and stripes, were restaged for Biograph, drawing crowds to 'Kinetoscope parlours' in London. World-wide distribution of Whitford's image and a more pruri-ent interest in Whitford's identity as a performer were assured when it was reported, although never confirmed, that she had been approached to appear naked at a private party in New York. Annabelle Whitford's photographs, some showing her costumed for dances on the American variety stage, and others – still frames from her mutoscope dances – survive in small quanti-ties, but both Edison and Biograph mutoscope and Kinetoscope films sur-vive, initially in archives, but now more commonly and availably on video and DVD.

Film, invariably silent in its several early forms, based its appeal on visible – preferably strong – physical action. Equally, stage actors cost money; famous actors cost more. A singular exception to this reluctance to film known per-formers again dates from 1896. May Irwin, a popular Canadian actress, performing in New York city from the mid-1880s, had appeared in numer-ous photographs. Her name and image were well known to the public. When she and her co-star John C. Rice shared a lingering affectionate kiss in John J. McNally's 1895 musical farce *The Widow Jones*, Edison engaged the couple to repeat their kiss on screen. The result was 'the first screen kiss' and immediate accusations that film was a decadent medium. 'The May Irwin Kiss' frequently appears on video and DVD.

All of the above actresses – the early ones to be recorded by daguerreo-type or salt-print, the ones whose images sold thousands of *cartes de visites* or cabinet or boudoir prints, the ones whose images sold many more thou-sand of picture postcards, the actresses who appeared in plays photographed for monthly fan magazines, and the actresses and dancers whose moving, flickering, occasionally iridescent image appeared in viewing machines and on early cinema screens – shared a common problem: their fame was both restricted by and enhanced by the technologies of their eras. All depended on the skill of the photographer to record their images, and all were dependent upon the available means to distribute and reproduce that image. Fame, applause, celebrity, notoriety – or simple neglect – walked hand in hand with affordable and viable commercial technologies. Shrewd and intelligent actresses exploited these links. Naive actresses ignored them at their peril.

NOTES

1. *The Complete Works of Shakespere* [sic], *Revised from the Original Editions, with Historical and Analytical Introductions to each Play, also Notes Explanatory and Critical, and a Life of the Poet: by J. O. Halliwell, Esq., F.R.S., F.S.A., etc.; and Other Eminent Commentators. Elegantly and Appropriately Illustrated by Portraits Engraved on Steel, from Daguerreotypes of the Greatest and Most Intellectual Actors of the Age, Taken in the Embodiment of the Varied and Life-like Characters of our Great National Poet* (London: Tallis and Co., 1850–1). Images of performers were taken from daguerreotypes, most made in the Islington studio of William Paine, others made in the New Bond Street studio of John Jabez Mayall, and a few of American performers made in the St Louis studio of J. H. Fitzgibbon.

2. Each daguerreotype, necessitating the actor holding a pose for thirty or more seconds, was taken against a plain studio backcloth. The daguerreotype was then passed to an engraver who reproduced the photographed image as a stipple-and-line engraving, the engraver further superimposing this image upon or within an imagined or previously drawn setting. There is no evidence that these are actual stage sets.

3. Adolphe Beau, letter in appendix to Frederic Whyte, *Actors of the Century* (London: George Bell and Sons, 1898), p. 191.

4. Roberta E. Pearson, *Eloquent Gestures: The Transformation of Performance Style in the Griffith Biograph Films* (Berkeley and Los Angeles: University of California Press, 1992), and Ben Brewster and Lea Jacobs, *Theatre to Cinema: Stage Pictorialism and the Early Feature Film* (Oxford: Oxford University Press, 1997).

5. David Mayer, 'Acting in Silent Films: Which Legacy of the Theatre?', in Alan Lovell and Peter Krämer, eds., *Screen Acting* (London: Routledge, 1999), pp. 10–30.

6. Shearer West, 'The Theatrical Portrait', *The Image of the Actor: Verbal and Visual Representation in the Age of Garrick and Kemble* (London: Pinter Publishers, 1991), pp. 26–57.

7. So termed because of the chemical salts used to 'fix' the image and prevent its fading.

8. Just as early motion pictures were made and marketed in various formats and dimensions by competing manufacturers as inducements to purchase complete systems of motion picture cameras and projectors. Not until 1908 was agreement reached on industry-standard formats and dimensions.

9. Think of Hjalmar and Gina Ekdal in Ibsen's *The Wild Duck* (1882).

10. Laurence Senelick, 'Eroticism in Early Theatrical Photography', *Theatre History Studies* 11 (1991), pp. 1–49.

11. Images of the royal family are not listed in his advertisement. This sobriquet indicates that he may have sold photographs to the Queen, a noted collector.

12. One of the larger archives of cabinet and *cartes de visites* theatrical photographs is held by the Harry Ransom Center for the Humanities in Austin, Texas. Many

of the holdings offer evidence of actors using their photographs to obtain situations in nineteenth-century touring companies. Other images provide evidence of the sitter, most frequently an actress, arriving with a substantial wardrobe of fashionable attire and having herself photographed in each change of clothes. Her wardrobe, as much as the actress, is on display.

13. Clement Scott, ed., *The Theatre: A Monthly Review and Magazine*, 16 vols. (London: Wyman and Sons, 1877–97). Each monthly issue has a Woodburytype print hand-tipped in.

14. A Woodburytype, an image formed by pressing several layers of wax upon a paper surface, is distinguishable from a conventional photograph by peering at the image's surface with the surface held horizontally, against the light, close to eye-level. An albumen photograph will appear smooth. A Woodburytype will show surface contour, as the various layers of wax create visible variations in texture.

15. Letter in the author's possession.

16. Frank Vaughan, 'Process Engraver to the Profession', Melville Chambers, 50a Lord Street, Liverpool, ca. 1900 published a broadsheet-size poster intended for backstage theatre notice boards: *To the Members of the Musical and Dramatic Profession only.* Vaughan's poster depicts 'a few [fourteen] Specimens of our Process Engraving . . . Specially offered to Members of the Musical and Dramatic Profession alone'. Vaughan quotes prices and emphatically notes: 'The better the original Portrait, the better the Block, so send us as good a Photograph as you possess, and satisfaction can be assured.'

FURTHER READING

Brewster, Ben, and Lea Jacobs. *Theatre to Cinema: Stage Pictorialism and the Early Feature Film.* Oxford: Oxford University Press, 1997.

Mayer, David. '"Quote the words to prompt the attitudes": the Victorian performer, the Photographer, and the Photograph', *Theatre Survey* 43.2 (November 2002), pp. 223–52.

Pearson, Roberta E. *Eloquent Gestures: The Transformation of Performance Style in the Griffith Biograph Films.* Berkeley and Los Angeles: University of California Press, 1992.

Scott, Clement, ed. *The Theatre: A Monthly Review and Magazine.* 16 vols. London: Wyman and Sons, 1877–97.

West, Shearer. 'The Theatrical Portrait', *The Image of the Actor: Verbal and Visual Representation in the Age of Garrick and Kemble.* London: Pinter Publishers, 1991.

5

LUCIE SUTHERLAND

The actress and the profession: training in England in the twentieth century

When assessing the changing status of actresses in the twentieth century, attendance at drama school provides an obvious starting point since formal training is part of what Susan Bassnett calls the 'wider cultural context' that contributes to the status of women in the professional theatre.[1] In this chapter, the focus throughout remains with the Royal Academy of Dramatic Art (RADA) in London, although reference is made to other schools. Founded on 25 April 1904 by actor-manager Herbert Beerbohm Tree, the academy is generally recognised as the first institution to offer a prescribed course of training. This is owing to the temporary nature of all previous acting schools: to use Adrian Cairns's term, their poor 'standards and staying power'.[2] However, the chapter also draws upon the published experiences of professional actresses, as well as material from interviews conducted with three highly successful British actresses from different generations who have first-hand knowledge of drama schools and subsequent entry in to the profession: Eve Best, Gillian Raine and Harriet Walter.[3] By concentrating upon a number of performers, the chapter seeks to examine the particular significance of vocational training for the female performer.

Although other sources for potential employers are tapped by agents and casting directors, drama schools are now the preferred route into the profession, as attested by a 1994 report for the Arts Council, which estimated that 86 per cent of working actors had received vocational training.[4] The schools initially emerged in the first decade of the twentieth century to serve the needs of commercial and most often male actor-managers, who desired junior members of their companies, male and female, to have received some formal training. For Elizabeth Robins (1862–1952) the 'stage career of the actress was inextricably involved in the fact that she was a woman and that those who were the masters of the theatre were men'.[5] Thus the first two London drama schools, RADA and the Central School of Speech and Drama (CSSD), attracted a significant majority of female students in the early part of the twentieth century: drama schools supplied an enhanced status that was particularly valuable for the actress, when moves towards increased professional regulation had so far been of little advantage to female performers.

Although prominent actresses mobilised to provide support for women in the entertainment industry and their children through the Theatrical Ladies Guild in 1891, and subsequently to alter franchise legislation through the very important pioneering work of the Actresses' Franchise League in 1908, the progress towards regulation of their particular field of employment was dominated by male contemporaries. Indeed, when female theatrical labourers were granted membership of the Stage Operatives' Union, also in 1908, there was no such option available to actresses,[6] and an actors' union was not established until the second decade of the twentieth century.

The precursor to a union for the acting profession was founded in Manchester on 1 February 1891. By the close of the nineteenth century, the Actors' Association was the clearest evidence that there was a demand for a governing body that would attend to workers' rights: it aimed to improve the economic status of the actor and initial objectives included payment for rehearsals and daytime performances. In 1912, member Clarence Derwent described it as 'a protective society which exists primarily for the purpose of regularising and, wherever possible, ameliorating the conditions under which actors and actresses carry out their work . . . it supplies a real need to the profession'.[7] Derwent's insistence, albeit understated, that the association aimed to reform working conditions is evidence of demand from within for a universal bureaucratic structure that would challenge the control of professional theatre by metropolitan actor-managers. Paradoxically, however, the influence of the association was at first limited, because in order to provide it with sufficient status to implement comprehensive changes to employment conditions, prominent managers were invited on to the administrative council. Henry Irving became the first president on 5 March 1891.

As a consequence, metropolitan managers were able to resist legislation that had the potential to curtail their authority, and there was a growing need for a dedicated actors' union, which became more urgent as managers were superseded by production syndicates. Tracy C. Davis has described the 'combinatorial power amongst entrepreneurs' that had occurred after the Companies Acts of the 1860s.[8] Gradually, individual managements dependent upon private, often anonymous, investors were replaced by large production companies which came to dominate the market. In 1918, the Actors' Association was reconstituted as a union, and then replaced by Actors' Equity in 1929. A union was the inevitable result of such market control – the individual manager (male in the majority of cases) and the small number of actors that he employed were replaced by large firms, held to account by a trade union organisation.[9]

Joseph Macleod notes that some actresses, including Dames Sybil Thorndike and May Whitty, were prominent early members of Equity. Thorndike, for example, sat on the Equity council from 1934 to 1951.[10] She saw 'the fetish of "the dignity of the profession"' as a hangover from the actor-manager system.[11] An appeal to uphold this 'dignity' by the managerial, and later producer, class discouraged actors from campaigning for better working conditions, and consequently allowed managers and producers to maintain autonomous control. In an introduction to H. R. Barbor's *The Theatre: An Art and an Industry* (1924), an analysis of the work undertaken by the fledgling union in the early 1920s, Thorndike argued for the importance of accepting that professional actors were part of both an art and an industry, and that industrial conditions should be attended to:

> A short spell of personal success or a run of personal ill-luck is quite sufficient to blind us to the fact that the whole basis of our work and employment has been changing, and that while we have been pondering on the problems of the interpretation of our parts (if we were working) or the more concrete problems of where next week's money was to come from (if we were not) the theatre has passed out of the hands of the artist into those of the tradesman.[12]

The presence of these leading professional actresses provides evidence of the union's immediate engagement with the particular experience of women in the acting profession. However, the concerns of actresses were not directly addressed until as late as the mid-1970s, when a women's subcommittee was founded within Equity.[13] The need to regulate minimum terms and conditions of employment remained paramount in these early decades.

However, one notable appeal for actresses, particularly, to join Equity, may be found in a book published by Britain's first, formal drama school. *The RADA Graduates' Keepsake and Counsellor*, first published in 1941 and given to graduates of the academy, points out the particular challenges facing actresses embarking upon their professional careers. Although the publication was attributed to no single author, George Bernard Shaw, who had by this time been a member of RADA's council for twenty-nine years, was largely responsible for writing the book.[14] In the first pages of the volume he notes the erratic wage levels graduates were soon to experience:

> The competition among players for engagements would reduce their salaries to bare subsistence point, and even below it in the case of women, if there were not among them an understanding that they must not obtain employment by underselling one another or playing without payment for the fun of it.[15]

Shaw then appeals for all graduates to join Equity, advising them that a

> standard salary is fixed by a professional association formed by the players for their own protection, all the members agreeing to accept the limits which the association sets to their individual liberty in business matters. This association is called The British Actors' Equity Association, called shortly Equity. Join it at once if you have not already done so.[16]

The author elaborates upon the particular importance of the union to actresses, suggesting that 'it is not yet possible to allow a woman to enter on a stage career without warning her that if she plays for less than a standard subsistence wage she will not only commit a grave professional misdemeanour, but class herself with disorderly persons'.[17] Shaw reiterates the particular importance of the actors' union for female graduates, a focus upon the 'case of women' that becomes even less surprising when the presence of two female Equity council members, Athene Seyler and Thorndike, on the administrative council of the Academy is taken into account. Yet the advice is characterised by Shaw's own brand of feminism, particularly the fervent belief that there should be no professional distinctions along gender lines although, as he notes in the *Counsellor*, in fact there were.[18] His argument implies that the familiar association of two groups of public women – the actress and 'disorderly persons' (prostitutes) – might be disrupted through membership of Equity. Actresses were vulnerable to prejudices that affected all women working in the public sphere, but the professional status afforded by membership of the actors' union might help counteract such discrimination.

The *Counsellor* notes inequalities of professional standing and income, defined by gender, and suggests both Equity and the guidance provided by RADA as potential antidotes to this situation. However, although the *Counsellor* seems to indicate that RADA was concerned with the particular needs of female graduates, its early history provides evidence that this was not the case. Reviewing the origins of formal drama schools in 1975, a Gulbenkian Foundation report made the important point that they emerged 'in response to changing needs in the profession, almost entirely in the independent sector'.[19] This is true; the 'needs' of actor-managers dominated professional institutions in the first decade of the twentieth century.

The free trade in legitimate drama made possible by the 1843 Theatres Regulation Act had resulted in more commercial entertainment venues. Theatre had become a career option for a greater number of individuals and employment opportunities for middle-class entrants to the profession increased. Indeed, during the final decades of the nineteenth century performers would often progress from amateur companies to professional theatre,[20] and the style of these actors and actresses epitomised Richard Schechner's view of

98

performance as 'behaviour heightened, if ever so slightly, and publicly displayed; twice behaved behaviour'.[21] Middle-class recruits were a calculated investment by managers who reaped the benefits of this 'behaviour' in their productions of problem plays and society comedies. Women recruited from this class had received a particular, restricted form of education, focusing upon 'feminine' accomplishments including singing and recitation, that provided some preparation for the stage. Entry into the acting profession was in no way systematic, and the only available schooling for aspirants with some experience in amateur theatre was provided by either regional and touring managements, or individual actors giving classes, in a period which saw the decline of the stock company. Individual tuition was, however, available, and during the 1890s, courses of instruction were offered by London-based actors and actresses, including Mr and Mrs Hermann Vezin, Mrs Charles Young, Ben Greet, Henry Neville, Geneviève Ward and Rosina Filippi.[22] A significant number of these tutors were women, who were able to supplement their income by preparing younger performers. Such training was perceived to be suitable work for women long before the more prominent commercial and artistic roles of producer and director were available.

Significantly, one notable figure training actors at the end of the nineteenth century was the actress and manager Sarah Thorne at the Theatre Royal, Margate. Although Thorne was lessee and manager of this venue first from 1867 to 1873, and then from 1879 until her death in 1899, it is for her training programme that she has been remembered. From 1885, performers with some previous experience in amateur theatre enrolled at Margate, and her training provided necessary experience of performing in a wide repertoire. Her company was a recognised route into the profession for students who could afford the twenty pounds for three months under her tutelage. However Irene Vanbrugh, in a talk to students at RADA in the 1940s, described her dislike of the old-fashioned imitative technique employed by Thorne:

> Her method of teaching was to show you how to do a thing but *not* to explain *why* you did it, which is not really the best method because of all things in acting the least wise is to imitate . . . The art of acting is not imitation, and however much we may admire the movements, or voice, or even method of a certain actor or actress, it would be definitely a mistake to copy it.[23]

This imitative approach was by no means unique to the Margate programme. Learning through imitation had evolved in the stock companies, and was employed by individual tutors who, like Thorne, had begun their stage careers in that earlier period. For example, an actress who became one of RADA's first permanent staff members, Elsie Chester, was renowned for this

99

way of teaching. The novelist and playwright Dodie Smith, who attended the academy in 1914, recalls that she 'liked them to say every line after her and if they dashed ahead and read three or four lines on their own she would irritably take them back. This made most of us feel so demented we found ourselves imitating her without any idea of what the lines meant'.[24]

There were evident similarities between the instruction initially offered by RADA and the work of precursors. Although Tree aspired to emulate the thoroughness and rigorous selection policy of the Paris Conservatoire, he received no state funding, and initially his school, rather like Thorne's, was an attempt to provide some training for middle-class aspirants who could afford the fees, and it was staffed by professional colleagues.[25] The performer was the manager's most essential material asset, and both the academy and two years later CSSD originated because of the needs of two commercial managers: Tree and Frank Benson.

Although it was a woman, Elsie Fogerty, who founded Central at rooms in the Royal Albert Hall, the transition to a training school for actors resulted from her professional relationship with a man, Benson. Fogerty had already been teaching elocution for almost a decade, and in her own words:

> His school was housed up at Hampstead; but the place was not a good one: there was no proper theatre, and the students' minds were too much fixed on the happy day when they could join the Tour . . . So I asked Sir Frank if I might take his remaining students to the Albert Hall, and suggested that – if he would become president – we could found a dramatic school with a full training-course and examinations. To my great joy, he agreed, and promised to examine us. So came into being the Central School of Speech-Training and Dramatic Art – in 1906.[26]

In 1901, Benson had founded a drama school that travelled with his company. It consisted of both fee-paying students and actors already appearing for him whom he considered were in need of more training. Of significance here is the fact that Fogerty incorporated Benson's project and used his professional status to provide recognition for her school. Her teaching may have been founded upon the training she had received at the Conservatoire in Paris, but the school, like the academy, came into being because of the requirements and the influence of a prominent male manager.[27]

However, Fogerty managed Benson's school at her own premises, and she was succeeded at Central by another female principal, Gwynneth Thurburn. Fogerty, particularly, was prominent in the fields of vocational training for the stage and what would now be considered speech therapy (she established the first speech clinic at St Thomas's Hospital in 1914). This is an obvious example of how opportunities for employment in the developing sector of training for the stage were recognised by women. Importantly, the foundation of the London drama schools coincided with the growth of companies contracted to do work that had previously been undertaken in-house. For example, during the 1890s, women opened two-thirds of new costume businesses supplying wardrobe to commercial theatres.[28] As with these new businesses, the drama schools offered opportunities for women who might otherwise have sought work in the theatre itself to become teachers. They also provided a way for professional actresses to supplement their income. Fogerty had trained for the stage before progressing directly to teaching, and at RADA prominent West End artistes, male and female, instructed the students. Irene Vanbrugh was the first woman to sit on the Academy's administrative council in 1912, and she taught there until the 1950s, and Athlene Seyler, who received the Bancroft Gold Medal in 1908, taught there in the 1940s. Judith Gick, a member of Benson's company in the 1920s, and a professional actress before she embarked on a teaching career, was employed at RADA in 1955, and later, in the 1970s, by Raphael Jago at the progressive Webber Douglas Academy of Dramatic Art. Gick worked there 'for 23 years, encouraging and inspiring the very young and weening [sic] them away from the practice of learning chunks of Shakespeare by helping each of them to create and present a short one-man show based on a character from Shakespeare'.[29] The growing professional recognition afforded to dedicated drama school teaching is also evident in the success of publications by CSSD teacher and Voice Director for the Royal Shakespeare Company, Cicely Berry.[30]

The early prominence of women in this field of education is notable, but of equal significance is the considerable number of women who attended the new schools as students. In 1907, one early member of RADA's administrative council, the actor-manager George Alexander, publicly acknowledged this by making a direct appeal for men to attend the academy. In an interview Alexander remarked that 'if the young men who intend to go on the stage will enter the school, they will learn more there in six months than they can hope to learn in any theatre, in these days of long runs, in a year',[31] an appeal that in the early decades of the twentieth century went largely unheeded.

Because we have few accurate records from the first decades in which drama schools were in operation, student numbers must be assessed from such comments, and also from biographical material.[32] This cannot, of course, provide unequivocal accuracy, but rather what Jim Davis and Victor Emeljanow have described as 'recurring descriptive patterns and rhetorical formulas' that remain suggestive of particular environments, in this case RADA.[33] Kenneth Barnes recollects that when he became the Academy's first principal, in 1909, the ratio was four women to every one man. He also writes that most applications in this first decade came from 'stage-struck young ladies with "temperament"'.[34] At this time, there was also a class for children, with a majority of girls. The actress Fabia Drake, now best remembered for her film and television performances during the mid-1980s in *A Room with a View* and *The Jewel in the Crown*, entered the academy at the age of nine, in 1913. In her autobiography, she explains that there was an afternoon class for children between the ages of ten and sixteen who had an 'identical adult curriculum with that of the senior students'.[35] By implication, during the first decades of the twentieth century the majority of students attending RADA were female, and this majority was even greater than the ratio of actresses to actors during the same period.[36] The 1911 Census provides a nationwide ratio of 101.05 women for every 100 men in the profession. This figure differs if London is taken alone, where there were 121.54 women in the profession for every 100 men.

The painfully slow improvement in the status and respect afforded to the actress in the latter part of the nineteenth century, while in line with the increasing number of women working in a variety of professions, had resulted in the perception of the stage as a suitable interim career for middle- and upper-class women and, because they could pay fees, they were taking most of the places at the new training institutions. There is also some evidence that the schools were attended by a number of female students admitted merely to increase prestige. Certainly, the 'finishing school' identity stuck to RADA for a long time. John Elsom, describing the instruction students received there as late as the 1940s, suggests that 'the Royal Academy of Dramatic Art was used as a finishing school when the other finishing schools were closed'.[37] In her autobiography, Joan Littlewood also focuses on this perception of RADA. She entered in 1930, having received one of two annual London County Council scholarships, and although she acknowledges the introduction to Laban's work as an enduring influence, her attitude remained overwhelmingly negative. It is not surprising, when Littlewood's subsequent career is considered, that she would have become rapidly disillusioned. The two pages she gives to her time at RADA in a lengthy autobiography emphasise the number of 'debs' enrolled:

I made for the cloakroom. It was crowded with girls wriggling their rubber girdles, comparing lipsticks and making bee-sting lips in the mirrors. They were all debs or rich Americans acquiring an English accent . . . At the end of the first term, the head of the Academy told me he was disappointed in me. I said I wasn't too happy either. In fact, I thought the place was a waste of time. I only fancied Madame Gachet's French classes and Annie Fligg's Central

European Movement, but the one cost a guinea a term and for the other you needed a pair of tights and I couldn't run to either on my scholarship grant, eleven shillings a week.[38]

Another prominent and even earlier student provides an account which also observes that 'debs' were a distinctive presence. In 1993, John Gielgud contributed an article to RADA's magazine in which he recorded impressions of his time at the drama school, during 1922 and 1923. Gielgud lists memorable individuals he encountered there, including the female tutors Helen Haye, Alice Gachet, Elsie Chester and a Mrs McKern. He goes on to acknowledge the prominent students Beatrix Lehmann and Veronica Turleigh, whose Cleopatra impressed him greatly. Next, he mentions two of his contemporaries in less adulatory terms:

> Two of the girl students were titled and known to us commoners as 'The Duchesses'. We felt that they did not take theatre quite as seriously as we did, and suspected they had been sent to the Academy by their parents to keep then out of mischief. I think they both pursued stage careers for a little while, after which they both got married, one to Kenneth Barnes himself, the other to the impresario Henry Sherek.[39]

Gielgud is here recollecting Pamela Boscowan, stage name Pamela Carme, and Daphne Graham, who acted under the name Mary Sheridan. In fact the chronology of Gielgud's account, which implies acting was little more that a pastime before marriage for these women, is not completely accurate. Carme, the daughter of Viscount Falmouth, did cease acting when she married Sherek in 1937, but she continued to work in professional theatre as his business partner in management. Graham, a granddaughter of the Earl of Feversham, married Kenneth Barnes only months after completing her diploma, but continued to work on stage after her marriage, until the Second World War.

Barnes recollects his wife's attendance and career in more sympathetic terms, but does little to dispel the impression that the Academy was admitting a number of female students according to their economic means and social status, in the hope that they might also afford some kudos to the school. He recalls that both students initially enrolled for a term in Alice Gachet's French class (the guinea providing no barrier for them).[40] This preliminary attendance for instruction in French does suggest that their families accepted RADA as a form of 'finishing', and it is likely that the royal charter awarded to the academy in 1920 encouraged such acceptance. After the initial term with Gachet, Barnes recalls that he had to assure Graham's parents of her abilities:

Asked by Daphne's parents for my opinion of her capabilities, I was able to assure them without hesitation that she showed promise of talent in both emotional and comedy parts, and to praise unreservedly the resonant quality of her voice.[41]

Although both Graham and Carme progressed to the full diploma course, the casual entrance procedure via Gachet's course, and dependence upon the approval of Graham's parents rather than an admissions panel, speaks for itself.

An awards system had been introduced to help identify the most promising actors, both male and female, among those who completed the diploma course each year. The Bancroft Gold Medal was initiated in 1905, when the academy moved to its Gower Street premises and Squire Bancroft was made first president of its newly instituted administrative council. In the first twenty years that it was awarded, between 1905 and 1925, fourteen of the twenty recipients were female. The RADA Silver Medal was then introduced in 1917, and over the first two decades twelve recipients were female. The modest majority of female recipients for both awards is surprising when the much greater majority of female students attending the academy overall is taken into account. In addition, both these figures are calculated for a period including the First World War, when the number of men attending the academy was further reduced. It is evident that the members of the council – prominent actors, managers and playwrights – had a direct interest in providing an equal number of male and female performers to work in the commercial theatre, and might therefore seek to develop latent talent in the minority of male students. It is also apparent from these awards that the school did attempt to promote equal numbers entering the profession, and that there was, therefore, an acknowledged disparity between numbers of students attending the academy and the number who were expected to become professional actors; female students intent upon an acting career needed to supplement their training at RADA with additional experience to fully establish their professional status (fig. 10).

One example of such supplementary work is provided by the early career of the accomplished British theatre and television actress Gillian Raine, a former student of RADA. In April 1945, Raine left the two-year diploma course to work for Alec Clunes at the Arts Theatre Club in a production of *The Italian Straw Hat*.[42] She progressed from that part, for which she was paid at the Equity minimum rate of £4 per week,[43] to employment with H. M. Tennent Ltd, where she played minor and understudy roles for five years. Tennent's monopolised West End theatre management, and being employed by them was like signing on with an agent today. Tennent's

Fig. 10. Training not finishing: a mid-twentieth-century photograph showing RADA's first Principal, Kenneth Barnes, addressing some of the Academy's students. (Kenneth Barnes, *Welcome Good Friends*, 1958.)

provided a select group of performers with more consistent employment than could be hoped for by most of the profession. Clunes only employed Raine on the condition that she found a fellow female student of the same height and a similar appearance to appear alongside her.[44] However, Raine decided her own route into the profession; she seized the opportunities offered by Clunes and by Tennent, before choosing to move into repertory theatre.

At this point Raine moved to weekly rep at Salisbury, followed by periods in fortnightly and three-weekly companies. This provided her with experience that she did not receive either on a drama school course or working for commercial producers in London. Today, she describes the repertory system of brief rehearsal periods and varied parts as 'thorough' training, enabling a performer to 'know how to deal with your audience'.[45] She distinguishes the experience from her time with Tennent:

> I think however much you understudy and play small parts ... you really don't know what you can do and, very important, what you can't do.[46]

Repertory provided both actors and actresses with a breadth of experience in a community of new entrants to the profession. These companies were, to use George Rowell and Anthony Jackson's word, 'nursing' actors.[47] In a 2005 edition of RADA's magazine, former student Christine Ozanne, who attended the Academy in the early 1950s, provides a familiar, nostalgic recollection of such 'nursing', contrasting it with the challenges facing Academy graduates now:

> Back then, repertory companies were abundant and most of us could look forward to several years in theatre jobs playing dozens of different roles. Now, the 'few' will get snapped up by the big theatre companies and most students are likely to find their first few professional jobs will be in front of a camera.[48]

The experiences of Raine and Ozanne occurred immediately prior to a distinctive shift in the kind of training provided by drama schools, which was initiated in the mid-1950s. The needs of the profession were changing and new drama, broadcast to a new audience, was the most apparent symptom. Sheila Hancock, who was at the Academy in the very early 1950s, remembers that 'RADA was doggedly preparing students for classical theatre for which received pronunciation was deemed essential. No one questioned yet why the majority of people who received it didn't talk like that,' adding very pertinently, 'particularly not the audiences whose knowledge of drama was through their new TV sets'.[49] Noting developments at the school after fifty years, Ozanne acknowledges the technical facilities that are now available to students:

> The greatest differences between then and now seem to be: the extension of academic facilities (we had no screen training, for example) ... and the extension from a two- to a three-year course.[50]

After the theatre director John Ferald replaced Barnes as principal of RADA in 1955, significant changes were initiated in the range of training available.[51] In this volume (see chapter 6), John Stokes notes the conventions of 'received pronunciation' that perpetuated at the school under Barnes, but such standardisation began to alter under Ferald, who made a further important change. As many as two hundred students took the diploma in the 1950s, but RADA's second principal in four decades began the process of reducing numbers to the level found now, of up to thirty-two students in every year on the acting course.[52] Ozanne notes the change in numbers, but adds significantly that 'altogether there are more students training in this country today than there are actors working at any one time'.[53]

The community theatre pioneer Ann Jellicoe, a former student of CSSD who returned there to teach in 1954, notes the impact that Oliver Reynolds's improvisation work at the school had upon her subsequent career as a dramatist:

> One day I was watching one of Oliver's students improvising: he was playing a trumpet and it turned into a bird and flew away. Such freedom would be common today but, in 1954, watching that image develop, I suddenly felt, amidst all the welter of ideas and impressions crowding and shouting at one, that this was something tangible and strong. The germ of an idea of theatre not poetic, symbolist or literary: a theatre of direct action and concrete images.[54]

Another example of the growing influence of drama school training is provided by Harriet Walter, who attended the London Academy of Music and Dramatic Art (LAMDA) in the 1970s. In *Other People's Shoes*, her memoir and meditation on acting as an art and a career, Walter describes the progressive ethos she encountered there, which combated the dominance of the commercial sector:

> There were those who believed that drama school should give students a taste of the ideal work model, which would remain as something to strive for in the outside world; and there were others who took the view that ideals were all very fine, but there was no room for them in the Real Commercial World and students had better get used to that now. For me, the latter had nothing to offer but the legacy of their own disappointment.[55]

In fact, during Walter's final year at the school, the proponents of 'the ideal work model' left LAMDA to establish the company she was to join after graduation, the community group Common Stock.[56] Post-war drama schools had developed rapidly to provide more than just alternative approaches to performance, and the split within LAMDA in the 1970s provides an extreme example of this process.

Further opportunities were provided by an increasing number of schools and by developments in training. As early as 1923, Fogerty had gained the recognition of London University for a two-year diploma course in speech therapy and teaching, the first university-recognised qualification afforded to a drama school. This provided Central, and its students, with a new level of professional standing. Peggy Ashcroft, who entered the school in that year, was only allowed by her mother to apply on the condition that she took the teachers' course, although Fogerty intervened and she eventually studied straight acting.[57] There was funding available for these alternative courses, and this resulted in a particular opportunity for women who, as has been noted, were already prominent in the professional field of teaching. Certainly, there is some evidence that students who could not afford to attend to train in acting gained some valuable experience in this way. For example, in 1950 Eileen Atkins attended the Guildhall School of Music and Drama on a funded course, explaining: 'I did a teaching course as it was the only way to get a grant and did the drama course as well as no-one checked who was in what classes.'[58]

Acting students were still required to find their fees, at least until local education authorities provided a limited amount of funding for drama schools in the late 1950s. Judi Dench attended CSSD from 1954 to 1957, the final years of the drama school's location at the Royal Albert Hall. Dench, the daughter of a doctor, followed her brother to the school, and had the economic means to complete a full course of study. Her biographer John Miller notes that her parents 'knew that they would have to pay for her three years there . . . but they were confident that she had the talent to succeed, having watched it blossom as she grew up'.[59] Dench's parents, keen amateur actors, were willing to support two of their children at CSSD. This suggests that in the absence of funding there was a continuing reliance upon personal affluence and family support.

Despite such financial restrictions, however, drama school training had come to the fore as a recognised route into the profession. In the late 1950s, Barnes defined a drama school as 'an institution with a past, present and future, whose members meet on common ground, aware that association with the school has had a vital effect on them and on their careers . . . A three-dimensional contact is thus created between the former student, the school and the present student',[60] and certainly by mid-century, prestigious alumni were a valuable advertisement for the efficacy of drama schools. Significantly, Miller notes that although Dench's ability was apparent, it was her attendance at CSSD that brought her to the attention of prominent London producers:

> Julia Wootton had been sent by the Old Vic, which decided to act quickly on her report and called Judi for an audition at Waterloo Road a couple of days later. Tennent Productions was also interested in her, but they were slower off the mark.[61]

By mid-century, therefore, as well as providing technical instruction, drama schools were providing *access*. It was during this decade that Equity implemented a 'closed shop' entry system, as the actress Miriam Karlin, who attended RADA in the 1940s, recalls:

> Regulated entry began in the 50s, when things became very protectionist. That familiar Catch 22 no job no card, no card no job, frustrated many a would-be actor and of course by then, after the war, the profession was expanding enormously.[62]

The system that controlled the granting of an Equity card was a response to overcrowding in the profession, and at this time training at a recognised drama school, with the access it provided to professional employment, became far more important. Additionally, schools began to facilitate introductions to agents. In the 1940s, performers still established their careers at the behest of individual producers (except for the control exercised by the Equity minimum wage). Raine recalls:

> I didn't have an agent all the time I worked for Tennent's, because you didn't need one. They said 'you go here, you go there, and do that'. And of course you didn't need an agent in rep.[63]

This experience contrasts with that of Eve Best, who graduated from RADA in 1999. Since that time, Best has played leading roles at the Young Vic, the National and the Almeida, and she recognises the importance of finding representation at the beginning of a professional career.[64] She appeared in a number of productions at Oxford University, and acknowledges that several of her contemporaries began professional theatre work immediately after university.[65] However, after two and a half years acting in London fringe productions, it was attendance at drama school that provided Best with an agent and greater access to professional work. She recalls that RADA provided 'so much support in terms of getting into the business . . . you literally have to turn yourself into a product . . . what really does help is being given that support to understand that it is, ultimately, a profession'.[66] Best also describes a professional network that was initiated by the end-of-year show in her final term at RADA, which resulted in a leading role in *'Tis Pity She's a Whore* at the Young Vic:

> I got an agent from having done the showing and then got my first job through the fact that the casting director for the particular play had seen me in a role that was similar to the character in this play at a RADA production . . . so that when my agent suggested me for an audition she was able to say oh yes . . . suddenly this world that had seemed to me impossible to enter seemed to open up.[67]

Best's experience shows that what was an advantage to Dench four decades ago has subsequently become much more of a necessity. Drama school training is perceived as a particular type of professional endorsement, as the levels of employment found by RADA graduates each year demonstrate. In 2000, 50 per cent of graduates had found professional employment within three months of leaving the academy; in 1996, the figure was as high as 90 per cent.[68]

This is proof that the most established training schools in existence today – certainly the twenty-two in Britain that are members of the Conference of Drama Schools – are a primary, recognised route into the profession. However, what has also proved to be beneficial is the development of individual technique through a formal training system. Interviewed in June 2005, Walter explained this particular advantage:

> In my case and I'm sure in lots of people's cases, there's a talent there but it's inhibited, and the whole practice of drama school is to disinhibit . . . There are other people who are the other way and who are over-confident and think that acting is just about showing off and need to learn all the other things it is.[69]

Fiona Shaw, who attended the Academy in the early 1980s and was awarded the Gold Medal, provides a strikingly similar account of the training she received. In the centenary brochure produced by the Academy in 2004, she recalls that it 'was the first place I had studied where the student and her development was what really mattered. It was a place where judgement was only about improvement, it allowed faults to be exposed and replaced with control.'[70] Eve Best describes her training at RADA almost two decades later in similar terms, as 'a process of opening yourself up'.[71] What these schools provide now in the 'opening up' of performers is, to put it mildly, a more comprehensive form of training than the imitative techniques that predominated at the end of the nineteenth century. Now, to echo Judith Butler, the actress is encouraged to investigate the performative acts that make up the self, and to employ that exploratory process throughout her ensuing career.[72]

The creative benefits of a significant period spent developing particular skills and subjective potential has always, arguably, been the most immediate appeal of vocational training for individual performers. Indeed Thorndike, writing in the RADA magazine in 1946, claimed that 'techniques' learned at drama school were secondary to the 'flexibility' developed in the course of training:

Technique is only the making flexible and use-able the medium with which we have to do. To make our bodies and our limbs flexible – the voice and mind flexible – able to take on whatever incarnation – whatever human life we are called on to portray.[73]

This resembles Best's concept of 'opening yourself up', and is a valuable part of drama school training. A further interesting comparison can be made with Billie Whitelaw, who did not attend a drama school and who writes in her autobiography:

Had I done this, I might not still be carrying a permanent school satchel on my back. I might not have felt for the rest of my life as permanent amateur.[74]

However misplaced, given her actual achievements, Whitelaw's anxiety about the continued immaturity of her work, caused she feels by her lack of vocational training, contrasts strongly with the openness and flexibility described by these other actresses.

Of course, it must be acknowledged that such benefits are by no means gender-specific, and that training is invaluable to all who require a level of artistic skill and access to professional networks, in order to operate in a commercial marketplace.[75] What is particularly significant for actresses, however, is whether developments in training, which have resulted in relative equality of opportunity for men and women, can inform the vast entertainment industry. Research commissioned by Equity's Women's Committee in 1996 found that women in theatre, film and television were paid, on average, 34 per cent less than their male colleagues.[76] In trying to address such a gross disparity, this industry could do worse than to study the levels of professional and artistic support that have evolved to serve all students in vocational training.

NOTES

1. Susan Bassnett, 'Introduction', in Lizbeth Goodman, ed., *The Routledge Reader in Gender and Performance* (London: Routledge, 1998), pp. 87–91, p. 87.
2. Adrian Cairns, *The Making of the Professional Actor* (London: Peter Owen, 1996), p. 71.
3. These interviews were conducted in May and July 2005. I would also like to thank Dame Eileen Atkins for completing a questionnaire on training in July 2005, which is quoted later in this chapter.
4. Statistics are taken from the article 'Staging Post' by Liz Ford, *Guardian*, 23 August 2004.
5. Elizabeth Robins, *Theatre and Friendship* (London: Jonathan Cape, 1932), pp. 28–9.

6. See Tracy C. Davis, 'Victorian Charity and Self-help for Women Performers', *Theatre Notebook* 41.3 (1987), pp. 114–27, and 'Laborers of the Nineteenth-Century Theater: The Economies of Gender and Industrial Organization', *Journal of British Studies* 33 (January 1994), pp. 32–53.

7. Clarence Derwent, 'The Actors' Association', in Cecil Ferard Armstrong, ed., *The Actor's Companion* (n.p.: Mills & Boon, 1912), pp. 155–69, p. 155.

8. Tracy C. Davis, *The Economics of the British Stage 1800–1914* (Cambridge: Cambridge University Press, 2000), p. 271.

9. Ibid.

10. Joseph Macleod, *The Actor's Right to Act* (London: Lawrence and Wishart, 1981).

11. Sybil Thorndike, 'Introductory Note', in H. R. Barbor, *The Theatre: An Art and An Industry* (London: Labour Publishing Company Limited, 1924), pp. vii–viii, p. viii.

12. Ibid.

13. See Julie Holledge, 'Innocent Flowers No More: The Changing Status of Women in Theatre', in Goodman, ed., *The Routledge Reader in Gender and Performance*, pp. 92–6.

14. Barnes explains that Shaw wrote most of the *Counsellor* (4,000 words), although the book also contains brief passages written by the eleven other council members, as well as advice from the principal himself. Kenneth R. Barnes, *Welcome, Good Friends*, ed. Phyllis Hartnoll (London: Peter Davies, 1958), pp. 167–70.

15. *The RADA Graduates' Keepsake and Counsellor*, 3rd edn. (London: privately printed for circulation to graduates, 1953), pp. 3–4. Shaw funded publication of the first 500 copies of the *Counsellor*.

16. Ibid., p. 4.

17. Ibid.

18. See Sally Peters, 'Shaw's Life: A Feminist in Spite of Himself', in Christopher Innes, ed., *The Cambridge Companion to George Bernard Shaw* (Cambridge: Cambridge University Press, 1998), pp. 3–24.

19. *'Going on the Stage': A Report to the Calouste Gulbenkian Foundation on Professional Training for Drama* (London: Calouste Gulbenkian Foundation, UK and Commonwealth Branch, 1975), p. 17.

20. Note the numerous periodicals for amateur actors that appeared between 1867 and 1918. See Carl J. Stratman, *Britain's Theatrical Periodicals 1720–1967* (New York: New York Public Library, 1972).

21. Quoted in Nicholas Abercrombie and Brian Longhurst, *Audiences: A Sociological Theory of Performance and Interpretation* (London: Sage, 1998), p. 40.

22. Vezin was a noted teacher of elocution from the 1880s until his death in 1910; his wife prepared Eleanor Marx and other aspiring amateurs. Ward notes in her autobiography that she began 'coaching for the stage' in 1890: Geneviève Ward, *Both Sides of the Curtain* (London: Cassell, 1918), p. 140. The actress Rosina Filippi, half-sister to Eleonora Duse, had begun to teach in the 1890s in Chandos Hall, Maiden Lane, and she subsequently moved to premises in King Street, Covent Garden. In the first decade of the twentieth century, her students included Owen Nares and Hermione Gingold, but by July 1910 she was forced to appeal for endowments to run the school, and during the second decade

of the twentieth century her own school ceased and she became a teacher at RADA.

23. Vanbrugh trained with Thorne at Margate in 1888. This training is described in her autobiography *To Tell my Story* (London: Hutchinson, 1951), pp. 16–18, and *Hints on the Art of Acting*, (London: Hutchinson, 1951), pp. 43–4.
24. Dodie Smith, *Look Back With Mixed Feelings: Volume Two of an Autobiography* (London: W. H. Allen, 1978), p. 38.
25. The only discounts available were for the children of actors, who paid half price. Full fees were six guineas per term in 1905, and twelve guineas per term from 1906 until 1914. A limited number of scholarships were available from autumn 1910.
26. Elsie Fogerty, quoted by Marion Cole in *Fogie: The Life of Elsie Fogerty* (London: Peter Davies, 1967), p. 38.
27. Ibid. In 1883, Fogerty studied for the stage at the Conservatoire in Paris.
28. Statistic taken from Davis, 'Laborers of the Nineteenth-Century Theater', p. 52.
29. Ruth Gorb, 'Still Working, at a Late Stage', in *RADA: The Magazine* 11 (1998), 18–19, p. 19.
30. See Berry's *Voice and the Actor* (London: Harrap, 1973); *The Actor and the Text* (London: Harrap, 1973); *Text in Action* (London: Virgin, 2001).
31. *Pelican*, Christmas 1906. Cutting in the New York Public Library, Billy Rose Theatre Collection: anonymous scrapbooks containing clippings about George Alexander, T: MSS MWEZ. Tree's Academy of Dramatic Art is 'the school' referred to here.
32. Although in the wake of centenary celebrations at RADA attempts are being made to compile accurate databases, this process is made difficult by the absence of early records, largely due to bombing of the Malet Street premises in 1941.
33. Jim Davis and Victor Emeljanow, *Reflecting the Audience* (Hatfield: University of Hertfordshire Press, 2001), p. 99.
34. Barnes, *Welcome, Good Friends*, p. 67.
35. Fabia Drake, *Blind Fortune* (London: William Kimber, 1978), p. 19.
36. Statistics are taken from Tracy C. Davis's calculations in *Actresses as Working Women* (London: Routledge, 1991), pp. 10–11.
37. John Elsom, *Post-war British Theatre* (London: Routledge and Kegan Paul, 1976), p. 24.
38. Joan Littlewood, *Joan's Book: Joan Littlewood's Peculiar History as she Tells It* (London: Methuen, 1994), p. 68.
39. John Gielgud, 'A Year to Remember', *RADA: The Magazine* 1 (1993), pp. 4–5, p. 4.
40. Barnes, *Welcome, Good Friends*, p. 177.
41. Ibid.
42. The production ran from 19 April to 20 May 1945 at the Arts.
43. At this point, Equity minimum wage was as follows: West End 'Chorus' £5, West End 'Straight' £4; Provincial 'Chorus' £4, Provincial 'Straight', £4. In September 1948 a recognised minimum wage for repertory of £4 10s per week for eight performances was also introduced.
44. Gillian Raine described this condition when interviewed, July 2005: 'They were doing a play called *The Italian Straw Hat* and he [Clunes] said you can be a

bridesmaid if you can find someone else the same height as you. So I rushed back to RADA found a girl and said "we've got a job". So we left RADA.'

45. Raine, interviewed July 2005.
46. Ibid.
47. George Rowell and Anthony Jackson, *The Repertory Movement: A History of Regional Theatre in Britain* (Cambridge: Cambridge University Press, 1984), p. 56.
48. Christine Ozanne, '50 Years On', *RADA: The Magazine* 28 (2005), pp. 9–10, p. 10.
49. Sheila Hancock, *The Two of Us: My Life with John Thaw* (London: Bloomsbury, 2005), pp. 67–8.
50. Ozanne, '50 Years On', p. 10.
51. See *Proceedings of the International Conference on Speech Training* (London: F. J. Milner, 1928), p. 75.
52. This reduction is noted by Ozanne, '50 Years On', p. 10.
53. Ibid.
54. Ann Jellicoe in Margaret McCall, ed., *My Drama School* (London: Robson Books, 1978), p. 119.
55. Harriet Walter, *Other People's Shoes* (London: Viking, 1999), p. 34.
56. Walter's early career was characterised by work in notable fringe companies. After graduating from LAMDA in 1973, she appeared in *Tales from Whitechapel* and *Watch the Woman* for Common Stock Theatre Company. After two years working at the Duke's Playhouse, Lancaster, she was employed in the touring companies 7:84 (1975–7), Paines Plough (1977) and Joint Stock (1978).
57. Richard Findlater, *These our Actors* (London: Elm Tree Books, 1983), p. 13.
58. Dame Eileen Atkins, in a questionnaire completed July 2005.
59. John Miller, *Judi Dench: With a Crack in her Voice* (London: Weidenfeld and Nicolson, 1998), p. 20.
60. Barnes, *Welcome, Good Friends*, p. 137.
61. Miller, *Judi Dench*, p. 26.
62. Miriam Karlin, interviewed by Hilary Tagg in 'State of the Union', *RADA: The Magazine* 11 (1998), pp. 14–15, p. 14.
63. Gillian Raine, interviewed July 2005.
64. Best appeared as Annabella in Ford's *'Tis Pity she's a Whore* at the Young Vic in 1999, and received the *Evening Standard* and Critics' Circle Best Newcomer awards. Subsequently, she has appeared in repertory at the National, including performances as Masha in *Three Sisters* and Lavinia in *Mourning Becomes Electra*. In 2005, Best appeared in the title role of *Hedda Gabler*, an Almeida production that transferred to the West End.
65. When interviewed in July 2005, Best stated: 'a lot of my friends from Oxford got agents straight away . . . and had gone off and done movies and worked at the National'.
66. Ibid.
67. Ibid.
68. These statistics appear in *RADA: The Magazine* 7 (1996), p. 10, and 16 (2000), p. 9.
69. Harriet Walter, interviewed June 2005.

70. Shaw is quoted in the brochure printed on the occasion of RADA's centenary, *RADA 100: 1904–2004* (London: Dewynters, 2004), p. 31.
71. Eve Best, interviewed July 2005.
72. Butler's work on 'the performative structure of gender' (*Undoing Gender* (New York: Routledge, 2004), p. 10) is part of her broader analysis of gender and sexuality. See also *Bodies that Matter* (New York: Routledge, 1993), pp. 1–5.
73. Sybil Thorndike, 'Personality', in *The Royal Academy of Dramatic Art Magazine* n.s. 1.1 (May 1946), p. 19.
74. Billie Whitelaw, *Billie Whitelaw . . . Who He?* (London: Hodder and Stoughton, 1995), p. 41.
75. During the late 1950s and the 1960s developments in the LEA grants system enabled a broader range of students to attend drama school. Now that the majority of acting courses have degree status they receive some state funding, and up to 60 per cent of students per year can receive grants from the Dance and Drama Awards and some degrees are supported by the Higher Education Funding Council for England.
76. See Jean Rogers, 'Boys Town: Or How the Feature Film Industry Conspires to Exclude Older Women', *Equity* (Winter 2005), p. 24.

FURTHER READING

Cairns, Adrian. *The Making of the Professional Actor*. London: Peter Owen, 1996.

Cole, Marion. *Fogie: The Life of Elsie Fogerty*. London: Peter Davies, 1967.

Davis, Tracy C. 'Victorian Charity and Self-Help for Women Performers', *Theatre Notebook* 41.3 (1987), pp. 114–27.

'Laborers of the Nineteenth-Century Theater: The Economies of Gender and Industrial Organization', *Journal of British Studies* 33 (January 1994), pp. 32–53.

Drake, Fabia. *Blind Fortune*. London: William Kimber, 1978.

Ferard Armstrong, Cecil. *The Actor's Companion*. London: Mills and Boon, 1912.

Jellicoe, Ann. 'Ann Jellicoe', in Margaret McCall, ed., *My Drama School*. London: Robson Books, 1978.

Littlewood, Joan. *Joan's Book: Joan Littlewood's Peculiar History as she Tells It*. London: Methuen, 1994.

Miller, John. *Judi Dench: With a Crack in her Voice*. London: Weidenfeld and Nicolson, 1998.

Peters, Sally. 'Shaw's Life: A Feminist in Spite of Himself', in Christopher Innes, ed., *The Cambridge Companion to George Bernard Shaw* pp. 3–24. Cambridge: Cambridge University Press, 1998.

Robins, Elizabeth. *Theatre and Friendship*. London: Jonathan Cape, 1932.

Smith, Dodie. *Look Back With Mixed Feelings: Volume Two of an Autobiography*. London: W. H. Allen, 1978.

Vanburgh, Irene. *Hints on the Art of Acting*. London: Hutchinson, 1951.

Walter, Harriet. *Other People's Shoes*. London: Viking, 1999.

Ward, Geneviève. *Both Sides of the Curtain*. London: Cassell, 1918.

Whitelaw, Billie. *Billie Whitelaw . . . Who He?* London: Hodder and Stoughton, 1995.

6

JOHN STOKES

Out of the ordinary: exercising restraint in the post-war years

In 1954 a magazine tribute to the actress Celia Johnson conceded that although she had, unquestionably, 'a touch of the quality of greatness', nevertheless it was 'the greatness of our own particular time . . . a little ordinary, suburban, rather dull greatness'.[1] This, no doubt, was tacit acknowledgement of a voice-over heard early on in Johnson's most celebrated film, *Brief Encounter*: 'I'm an ordinary woman. I didn't think such violent things could happen to ordinary people.'

There's a self-deprecatory air about British drama, on stage and on screen, of the post-war period – self-confessedly 'ordinary, suburban, rather dull' – that encourages us even now to take its 'ordinariness', its 'unobtrusiveness',[2] on its own terms, to accept its modesty at face value, and consequently to patronise its achievements. Public protestations of essential decency muffle the deeper resonances that films and plays had for performers and audiences alike, as well as what it meant to be an actress in a cultural atmosphere that was secure but stifling. After all, the star actresses of the 1940s and 1950s included, among others, Margaret Leighton, Pamela Brown, Barbara Jefford, Diana Wynyard, Claire Bloom, Dorothy Tutin, Vivien Leigh, Peggy Ashcroft, Brenda Bruce, Sylvia Syms, Joyce Redman, Margaret Rawlings, Yvonne Mitchell, Constance Cummings and Mai Zetterling. None of them, in retrospect, seems in the least bit 'ordinary'.

Brief Encounter, directed by David Lean in 1945 but set in 1939, straddles the pre- and post-war periods. Based on *Still Life*, a short play by Noel Coward, it is about a truncated sexual relationship. Laura (Celia Johnson), a middle-class wife and mother who lives outside a pleasant country town, is in the habit of making a weekly trip to change her library books and visit the cinema. As a result of a chance incident in a railway buffet, she meets a doctor of her own age and class (Trevor Howard). They spend time together, fall in love, but the affair comes to an end when, with shared stoicism, they accept that he must go abroad and she must stay home with her children, with her dull but worthy husband and with her conventional, though far from uncomfortable, lifestyle. This whole episode is told as a backwards looking day-dream on the part of Laura, whose voice introduces and punctuates the visual narration of events.

Although sometimes characterised as a 'woman's film', the appeal of *Brief Encounter* is much wider than that possibly limiting term may suggest. For film aficionados and critics, of whom Richard Dyer is the most perceptive, it remains a classic of its time. As Dyer says,

> if *Brief Encounter* recognises the difficulty of going with one's feelings for a certain strain of Englishness, it also recognises the strain, fully registers the surging of emotion. It is because of both the social pressures toward and the genuine appeal of comfy conformity, both so meticulously realised, that the desire to love against the grain comes across so powerfully.[3]

'To love against the grain' is to risk social ostracism, a brutal punishment in a class-bound world, particularly if the transgressor is a woman. Yet, if in *Brief Encounter* the heroine decides to stay safely put, in Terence Rattigan's play *The Deep Blue Sea*, first staged in 1952,[4] she decides to leave. Hester Collyer, the wife of an eminent judge, has fallen hopelessly in love with a younger man named Freddie, an ex-flying ace and Battle of Britain hero who is finding it hard to settle back into post-war life. Deserting her husband (sufficiently affluent to run a Rolls Royce and to play golf at Sunningdale), she and Freddie move into dismal digs in Notting Hill. Here she stays home while he looks for work, not very wholeheartedly and not very successfully. Hester's husband tracks her down and begs her to return; she refuses even when, later, Freddie decides to leave. Although the play begins with her failed attempts at suicide, it ends with Hester – again stoically – accepting her isolation, strengthened in her resolve by the austere wisdom of a fellow lodger, like herself a social casualty and outsider, a doctor who has been struck off the register for reasons that are unclear, possibly for carrying out an abortion, possibly for some homosexual offence.[5]

Despite the contrasting situations, these two post-war classics have a good deal in common. Sex is at the heart of both crises but there is, in both cases, very little mention of the subject and absolutely nothing explicit. They both involve middle-class women, admittedly from different parts of the class range and with correspondingly different lifestyles. Both conclude, at least temporarily, with a kind of stasis, though not necessarily with the status quo. And both appeared after a period when, according to most testimonies, there had been considerable sexual freedom – coupled with a relaxing of class barriers. As Elizabeth Bowen put it in her novel *The Heat of the Day*, which was set during the conflict but first published in 1949, 'wartime, with its makeshifts, shelvings, deferrings, could not have been kinder to romantic love'.[6]

The trembling tension about the sex that we sense but don't actually see in *Brief Encounter* and *Deep Blue Sea* is the product not so much of pre-war repression, nor yet of a wartime freedom, so much as of a *post-war* attempt to reconstruct a now distant, and probably half-fictionalised, past. It was, though, a view of the past that had been sanctioned by some of the most popular films made during the actual conflict. In *Waterloo Bridge* (1940, directed by Mervyn LeRoy, starring Vivien Leigh), brief glimpses of recent history frame an entirely conventional story of a misunderstood fallen woman set during 1914–18. In *Mrs Miniver* (1942, directed by William Wyler), Greer Garson, English-born but Hollywood-based, is required to display the developing courage and resolve of a middle-class English housewife who nevertheless remains totally devoted to her husband and family. As film-makers had realised, traditional myths of the female would need reinforcement if they were to serve their patriotic purpose, whatever the social reality.

Later, in the 1940s and the 50s, it was as if the nation's spokesmen straightened their attire in an attempt to draw a line under what had gone on immediately before and to resume that idealised 'normality'. The Archbishop of Canterbury himself exhorted the British people in 1945 to 'reject "wartime morality" and to return to Christian lives!'[7] In addition the appeal to moral respectability was accompanied by the rise of gurus, of psychologists and sexologists, anxious to explain what exactly the 'normal' order should be. One of the most prominent was Eustace Chesser, author of *Love without Fear*, first published in 1940. Later editions still carried the story of an officer in the Royal Air Force, obliged to give evidence of his adultery to a divorce court judge, who confessed how

> he and the woman concerned found themselves 'emotionally aroused' at the time of the acute crisis which swept Europe in September 1938, and ended with the Munich Agreement. The judge commented upon this explanation of adultery, which probably struck him as being rather novel. But it is true that in time of crisis people are thus stirred. Similar confessions have come from both men and women.[8]

This is typical: the immediate past is explained and accepted, yet pronounced to be over. By the mid-1960s *Love without Fear* had sold some three million copies.

Richard Dyer is careful to insist that Laura in *Brief Encounter* isn't 'hysterical' because that would pathologise her; she is rather an 'ordinary' woman of her time attempting to live in a masculine world.[9] Dyer may well be right about Laura, but there was a great deal of pseudo-clinical language in the air nonetheless. Hester Collyer, for instance, was described very confidently as 'a pathological case' by at least one critic,[10] and it was, after all, a time when the term 'nymphomania' was still widely deployed. In a notorious review of *Deep Blue Sea*, the theatre critic Ivor Brown, a prominent journalist, could even comment about Hester Collyer that 'perhaps she just needs a good slap or a straight talk by a Marriage Guidance Expert'.[11] Brown was not only being crass and contemptuous, he may even have had in mind someone like Eustace Chesser.

It would be wrong, though, to think of Chesser's manuals and similar books as simply repressive. They stand somewhere between Victorian admonitory tracts and later 'liberated' guide books of *The Joy of Sex* type; they are strongly instructional and Chesser is actually very enthusiastic about heterosexual relations, although at the right time and in the right place. Rather more significantly, the general focus of his work was upon women rather than men. He even produced, in 1956, a thick volume called *The Sexual, Marital and Family Relationships of the English Woman*, based on massive statistical research and full of tables which demonstrated, for instance, such unsurprising facts as that 'women are more likely to think of sex with a man other than their husband if they have infrequent orgasm with their husband'.[12] Unsurprising perhaps, but pertinent to both *Deep Blue Sea* and *Brief Encounter*.

Not only was the contemporary stress upon the sexual problems of women rather than of men, it was invariably within a family situation. Another prominent psychologist, John Bowlby, regularly preached that the main function and duty of women remained motherhood, particularly when 'the break-up of society and of the greater family in western industrialized communities set grave problems'.[13] Bowlby, too, was extremely influential and his findings and recommendations were actually approved by the government. For there were, of course, political and economic reasons for this public emphasis on the family: the pressure of the war effort had meant that women had been needed as both workers (replacing absent men in the factories) and as mothers, producing the workers and the soldiers of the future. After the war, and despite the Welfare State, many women, as the feminist sociologist Elizabeth Wilson has explained, were expected to continue working, to bear children and to provide glamour, without the class or community structure that would support these multiple activities. The family often bore the brunt.[14]

Yet the wartime experience was by no means forgotten. In the words of one woman speaking in 1945:

We have known terror and heartbreak, frustration, strain, the unbearable joy which unexpected happiness amid war can mean, in all a world-wide testing of limb and spirit which has never been imposed on any earlier generation. We have matured more rapidly, emotionally, than any previous generation.[15]

For 'post-war woman' domestic and industrial centrality was accompanied by a contradictory and unsatisfying return to social marginality. Even though they are ostensibly about sexual mores, this is the deeper crisis that infuses both *Brief Encounter* and *Deep Blue Sea*. After all, it is noticeable that Hester never apologises for following her sexual impulses even if she finds them hard to explain, and Laura would surely have slept with her doctor companion if they hadn't been interrupted by the return of the friend who had lent them a flat.[16] Both women are isolated, already emotionally alienated from their formal male partners, their husbands. They are psychologically on their own – and in neither case are female friends or children much consolation. It is this solitariness that infuses their adulterous situations with anguish, which makes their stories far less complacent, either socially or sexually, than we may have been encouraged to think and turns them into the kind of role that any ambitious actress might well want to take on.

Isolation is even more destructive in another representative play: *Woman in a Dressing Gown* by Ted (later Lord) Willis, first seen as a fifty-five-minute TV drama in 1956, and made into a full-length feature film in the following year.[17] Amy, a wife and mother, neither renounces an illegitimate relationship nor forsakes her home. This time, more conventionally, it is the husband who is having the affair, partly because he can no longer tolerate living with someone so chaotically disorganised, so domestically incompetent, as his house-bound wife. On learning what is going on, Amy plans a three-way meeting over drinks with her husband and his mistress that is intended to clear the air, but which ends in humiliation when she gets appallingly drunk and collapses. This further confirmation of personal failure adds to a public shame which matters more to her than her jealousy on discovering that her husband is having sex with another woman. So pitiful is the spectacle she makes of herself – we also learn at this point (somewhat belatedly) that she lost her second baby – that her husband reluctantly, but inevitably, decides that he, too, must remain.

All three dramas were, of course, written by male playwrights, but that fact may even have contributed to the disturbingly emotional impact they had upon audiences: the writer sketches a sexual crisis in a seemingly controlled and objective way which the living actress then complicates and makes memorable with her subjective presence. And, in fact, in each case, the leading female role was played by an established performer with a relevant background.

Celia Johnson, whose performance in *Brief Encounter* was thought to define an era, came herself 'from a respectable middle-class family with none of the advantages such as titles, money and land',[18] the kind of upbringing assumed in many of the roles she undertook. By the early 1930s she was one of the brightest young stars on the London stage and in 1934 a critic enthused that 'Celia Johnson, with her tall and slender elegance, her lovely spaniel eyes, her quick sympathy, her lively intelligence, her humours and her wistfulness, is the Modern Girl at her most gracious.'[19] In 1935 she married the writer and traveller Peter Fleming and in 1936 she returned to the stage in a highly successful dramatisation of *Pride and Prejudice*. Marriage was to interrupt her professional career, but she made something of a comeback in 1954 when the stage magazine quoted at the start of this essay could still insist:

> Her love of domestic happiness dominates her life. In her work she expresses the feelings of an ordinary housewife with an effortless sincerity and a rich glowing sense of humour.
>
> This understanding and reality prevents her work from having the cloying sentimentality so often found in players of this type.
>
> Her large trusting eyes, her unglamourised face and rather flat voice are things which the ordinary woman in the audience can immediately identify in herself.[20]

Rather more challenging a personality, Peggy Ashcroft, who first created the role of Hester Collyer in *Deep Blue Sea*, was, in later years, to become celebrated for the ways in which, in the words of the director Peter Hall, her 'English containment and decency . . . contrasted with a wild passion'.[21] By the time she came to play Hester in 1952 she was forty-five years old with twenty-six years as a professional actress behind her and nearly forty years more to come (fig. 11). She had already played in Barrie and in Shaw. She had been Desdemona to Paul Robeson's Othello; she had played Juliet, Imogen, Rosalind, Portia, Perdita, Miranda, Viola, Ophelia and Cordelia; she had appeared as Nina in Chekhov's *Seagull* and as Irina in his *Three Sisters*. After *Deep Blue Sea* she was to star in 1953 as Shakespeare's Cleopatra and in 1954 as Hedda Gabler. And after that she was to take on ever more varied roles. As Michael Billington, the best of Ashcroft's several biographers, says, although 'from 1964 on she became a radical actress, exploring the desperation of women of violently different classes, cultures, temperaments and background', nevertheless 'before the war she epitomised the intelligent ingénue and immediately post-war conveyed better than anyone the ecstasy

Fig. 11. Peggy Ashcroft with Kenneth More in *The Deep Blue Sea*, 1952. (Mander and Mitchenson Theatre Collection.)

of desolation'.[22] There was an essential strength about Ashcroft's portrayals of women in love, in their 'ecstasy of desolation'; by refusing to submit to the very thing that possessed them they reached a higher level of self-awareness.

Yvonne Mitchell, who took the part of Amy in the film version of *Woman in a Dressing Gown*,[23] had, in many ways, a very different style from Ashcroft and Johnson. Nonetheless, it takes us close to the heart of the sexual impasses of the period, if by another route. Born in 1925, Mitchell trained at the Old Vic School in the 1940s under the French director, teacher and theoretician, Michel Saint-Denis, and then made her name in reps in Oxford, Birmingham and Bristol. She was a member of the Old Vic Company at the New Theatre in 1949–50, cast as Ophelia among other roles, and she spent the summer season of 1953 at Stratford playing Jessica in *The Merchant of Venice*, Katherine in *The Taming of the Shrew* and Cordelia to Michael Redgrave's Lear.

What remains impressive, even today through her filmed performances, is the way in which Mitchell expressed, with great technical precision and emotional power, another version of the feminine as it was felt at the time by her audiences and, very likely, by the actress herself. We can recognise it as a mixture of suffering and resistance, of heroic loyalty and great sympathy – in a word, of 'pathos', though that must not be confused with passivity.

In her greatest film performance, *The Divided Heart*, which is set in 1952 (1954, directed by Charles Crichton), Mitchell plays a Yugoslavian woman whose son has been adopted during the war by a German couple who at the time believed him to be an orphan (fig. 12). This means that Mitchell is required to act almost entirely in a foreign language, Slovene, a challenge that she meets with an astonishingly intense physical presence that at times recalls the acting styles of early silent film. When at the end of the story the woman regains her son, thanks to the intervention of a humane American judge, she is obliged to recognise that even Germans can be well-meaning and that, although she is 'someone for whom the clocks stopped ten years ago', she will have to earn the future love of her son. The film as a whole thereby makes a strong argument for post-war reconciliation without underestimating the legacy of loss.

There may, also, have been an autobiographical dimension to Mitchell's powerfully demonstrative interpretations. She came from a conservative Jewish background and had to fight hard to persuade her father to let her study as an actress. Indeed, her father told her that she would let down the family by entering the profession at all (allowing only, 'I wouldn't mind if I thought you'd be a Celia Johnson').[24] Mitchell, who was also an author of talent, again and again returns in her writings to the theme of a struggle for independence. It's at the heart of her play *The Same Sky* of 1950 (a Romeo and Juliet story set in the Blitz) as it is of her largely autobiographical book *Actress*, published in 1957.

No doubt significantly, one can find several instances of daughters at odds with their fathers among the parts in which Mitchell excelled, including those Shakespearean roles which seemed to offer her ideal opportunities: Jessica in

Fig. 12. Yvonne Mitchell in *The Divided Heart*, 1954. (British Film Institute and Canal Plus Image Ltd.)

The Merchant of Venice obviously, but also Cordelia. Surveying 'The Young Actresses' in 1953, the novelist and critic Caryl Brahms wrote:

> She is the only actress who has made Cordelia credible to me . . . And though it is the pace and spirit of her interpretations, the cataract of charm that she unleashes on to the stage, that have made her growing reputation, it is in her quieter moments that her work touches us to tears.[25]

This role obviously meant a good deal to Mitchell. She had named her own daughter after Lear's youngest, compared notes with Ashcroft who also played the part, and even thought of basing a play on *King Lear* because 'my own father had three daughters'. As the feminist writer and post-Freudian analyst Juliet Mitchell has stressed, though controversially, when thinking about the psychological development of women in general, 'there is an obvious link between the security of the Oedipal father-love and the happy hearth and home of later years'.[26] Whether consciously or not, the performances of Yvonne Mitchell acknowledged this theoretical link by registering the severe physical wrench felt when one kind of security breaks down, toppling the other as it does so – and yet she continued to search for sympathetic healing. Her Stratford Katherine was notable for the way in which towards the end, as she realised that she was in love with Petruchio, she, as one critic put it, 'gave him a smile which promised that the armistice, once signed, would be permanent'.[27] In other words, she found a way to welcome marriage and a general return to patriarchal discipline, to 'normality', whilst still registering the cost.

In the 1960s Mitchell's writing became increasingly ambitious, and she produced novels that were sometimes taken up with the pressures of trying to combine a professional life as an actress with a domestic life as wife and mother, a conflict that is complicated by her actress heroines' self-regarding habit of dramatising their situation, of living on several levels at the same time. Here is a passage of stream of consciousness from the novel *Martha on Sunday* published in 1970:

An actress are you? But you don't look like one. All actresses should be beautiful; and you don't seem like one, look at you brushing down the lavatory bowl, forgetting the Harpic; look at you tousled in bed in an unglamorous night-dress, without frills and unlipsticked. An actress should walk upon the stage in well chosen shoes, and eat at a restaurant with good-looking companions. An actress is an actress because she has a personality and wants to expose it to the onlooker. An actress is not a chameleon without any definite colour who exists only to take the shape of others and inhabit their egos. Perhaps she may dress in their clothes and talk in their voice for a few hours to delight us, but she is really that woman in the restaurant. I have dined there, I have nodded at her, I know.[28]

Clearly, for Mitchell, female dilemmas and career predicaments were enmeshed in one another. Perhaps, though, she personally managed to break free. In 1970 she left England to live in France, intending to combine her writing with her acting career. Because, sadly, she died from cancer in 1979 we don't know how she would have accommodated herself to later playwrights, to the National Theatre (though Peter Hall put her on the Board) or to the RSC (or, just as pertinent, how they would have adapted to her).

The post-war theatre critic Harold Hobson was fond of quoting the precept of the late nineteenth-century actress and Ibsen pioneer Elizabeth Robins that 'repose is nine tenths of acting',[29] but 'repose' is surely an inadequate term to describe the taut, unreliable feeling of willed restraint that characterises the best female acting of the post-war period. In Johnson, Ashcroft, Mitchell and their peers, we sense modes of performance that respond in dangerous ways to the dominant sexual ideologies of the time, to the constant if contradictory urge both to escape and yet stay put. It is this genteel yet powerful stoicism under threat, however 'ordinary', that gives the acting of the time its distinctive mood.

At the same time, it was because so much English acting was held to be rigidly circumspect and superficially decorous that the obvious exceptions were felt to be so disturbing, even when the attempt was made to put them to one side as 'melodramatic' and 'hysterical'. The truly 'hysterical' heroine, whose sexual nature is displaced, erupting in unexpected areas, was a largely cinematic phenomenon at this time and predominantly American, yet the woman who epitomised her above all others was English: Vivien Leigh.

When another, somewhat younger, actress, Claire Bloom, appeared with Leigh in 1958, she noted that at the first rehearsal the star arrived 'with every gesture, every nuance, as perfectly formed as it would be on the first and on the last night'. Bloom put this down to coaching by Laurence Olivier, Leigh's husband, while still wondering if 'her rigid self-control, her obsessive need for order and organization, was an effort to keep chaos and disorder at bay and counter the torrent of a mental illness that constantly threatened her fragile existence'.[30]

Leigh, as Claire Bloom had perceived, brought other, more frangible, qualities to her roles which, although theatrically effective, derived surely from her own bouts of manic depression: 'She was breakable, that was very much a part of her – that terror and anxiety and delicacy and fear.'[31] This, after all, was the actress whose Scarlett O'Hara had always commanded a vast female audience;[32] whose Blanche Dubois in A Streetcar Named Desire, on both stage (1949) and screen (1951), was a turning point in the history of post-war performance.

Confronted by Blanche in 1949, Harold Hobson chose to call her 'a rabidly sexual woman of good but decayed family',[33] a woman whose 'sexual nature' is 'rendered uncontrollable by circumstance'.[34] This was an extremely restricted way of putting it, since for many women, and for actresses in particular, Streetcar was a shattering breakthrough from a 'circumstance' that was seemingly universal in its oppressive effects. It is difficult to overestimate the importance that the role had for young women in the early 1950s. Elaine Dundy, later to become a successful novelist and to marry the critic Kenneth Tynan, but at the time an aspirant American actress living in Paris, speaks for many when she remembers auditioning for the part:

In the perfection of its creation I fused with Blanche du Bois; all her infirmities and debilities became my own. I was going through the same desperate actions as she was, and as each escape hatch was blocked for her, it was blocked for me. There is hardly a sentence Blanche utters that does not contain, along with a yearning for life as it should be, the frightened awareness of life as it is, lifting the play from a mere recitation of the pitiful adventures of its heroine to a universal level.[35]

In many ways Blanche Dubois continues the line of the 'hysteric' established in the late nineteenth century and described by Elaine Aston in this volume (see chapter 13) – which made it a superb, if initially unlikely, opportunity for Leigh, who knew those historical traditions well.[36] Despite, or because of, her failure to match her own aspirations, Blanche represented real needs. Indeed, it was not until Hester Collyer in 1952 that the English language theatre was to offer such a rewarding part for a mature actress. For all their cultural differences, both roles – Hester and Blanche – are to do with unacceptable desire, leading to attempted suicide in one case, madness in the other. Both spoke directly to audiences in a climate where the expression of female sexuality, though far from taboo, was authoritatively policed by the injunctions of the sexologists that it should remain within the family.

In every other respect, of course, the roles are quite distinct. The casting of the wildly glamorous Vivien Leigh as Hester for the film version of *Deep Blue Sea* was generally considered to be a great mistake, even 'absurd' in the words of Kenneth More, who played Freddie on stage and screen:

She was supposed to be an outwardly ordinary but secretly highly-sexed woman who meets a young pilot on the golf course and falls for him. My first lines on meeting her were to say: 'My God, Hes, you're beautiful.' She had never been told this before – and understandably it had a remarkable effect on her. But when the part is played by a woman generally held to be one of the most beautiful in the world, the whole meaning is lost.[37]

In any case, in the wider world of the post-war woman, the symptomatic 'female' condition was no longer identified as 'hysteria' (see chapter 13) so much as 'depression'. And the standard cure was far from Charcot's cold baths or the more searching enquiries of Freud: 'electroconvulsive therapy' (ECT), a treatment commonly prescribed for troubled women at this time, including Vivien Leigh herself.[38] Among others subjected to the indignity, the 'silent violence' of ECT[39] were the novelist Penelope Mortimer[40] and Elaine Dundy.[41] Today the treatment is perhaps best remembered in the context of Sylvia Plath's novel *The Bell Jar* (1963) but, reminded of what nervous collapse could actually lead to in the hands of male diagnosticians, one begins to grasp more fully the resistant power of these theatrical representations of the female condition and to speculate, perhaps, as to why Hester will not admit to breaking down (finding suicide an easier option than public explanation of her situation), why Laura opts for renunciation – and, conversely, why Blanche Dubois, who really does dissolve into 'madness', spoke so directly to actresses and to their female audiences.

The women who took on these roles, who came into their prime in the postwar years, needed a technical approach that would allow them to explore the social contradictions that drove the play in which they happened to be appearing. They had, of course, for the most part been through the mill of the drama schools and been 'trained' (see chapter 5). In some cases the methods were conventional; in others they were more innovative. Characterisation, for example, was treated in a variety of ways, which were either countered or reinforced later by the methods of working directors, though they invariably hinged on the traditionally vexed question of 'identification'.

The actresses themselves could be unexpected on the issue. Peggy Ashcroft is supposed to have said to her director, Frith Banbury, that playing Hester Collyer made her feel as if she were 'walking about with no clothes on'.[42] But Ashcroft also said that her initial feeling about the part was that Hester 'was terribly selfish and cowardly to try and commit suicide just because her lover left her or was being neglectful'.[43] There is a tough, possibly experienced, self-awareness here that goes beyond the mere embarrassment of sexual desire (which is effectively confessed by the character anyway) to touch upon the pain and uncertainty of living a sexual life condemned to unsatisfactory male partners. Ashcroft also referred to Ibsen's Hedda Gabler, a role in which she made a great impact, as if from a psychological distance. 'It's such a relief because there is absolutely nothing in Hedda at all,' she said. 'There is no feeling. She is woman of no feelings, everything is calculated. It makes no demands on me at all . . . I feel years younger doing it!'[44] It seems that her personal impatience with the some of the roles she played actually helped Ashcroft to realise them theatrically.

In contrast, Yvonne Mitchell, in all her comments about acting, was much more concerned with making contact with her emotional self through the role in hand. She insisted upon the principle that 'the actor [sic] must always live in the present, he mustn't foresee what he will do next, or what is going to happen to him.'[45] The actor mustn't anticipate; his or her expression mustn't assume what is to come. 'It is not a question of trying, or of doing a thing "right", or being word-perfect. It is a question of human reaction to the things that can happen; and it is not until a play is in its third act that one can take its pulse.'[46] This quality of the provisional, of the unknown, underwrites psychological validity. (Much of the 'business' of Woman in a Dressing Gown is said to have been improvised on set during filming.)

Nevertheless, in the case of Mitchell herself, as we have seen, the moments that counted, that were most spontaneous, where nothing of the future was known, often tended to involve disappointment, regret and breakdown. Her ability to cry was famous: 'The only time I cry when I come off the stage is when I haven't cried on it. You've got to get rid of your tears somehow', she told an interviewer in 1954.[47]

Once again, there would seem to be little or no room for Hobson's simple 'repose' here – indeed, self-control might, in Mitchell's view, imply having a premonition of the long-term forecast. It may well be that Mitchell learnt the principle of the unforeseen, or had her own inclinations reinforced, from her experience at drama school when she was taught by Michel Saint-Denis who believed that it was through improvisation, the 'art of the moment', that students learnt 'the relationship between the reality of his [sic] own inner life, both intellectual and emotional, and its physical expression, the means through which he can convey this reality to others . . . This means to give of himself totally.'[48]

Mitchell's mentor, Saint-Denis, was French, Ashcroft's early inspiration (though she, too, was directed by Saint-Denis) was Russian: Theodore Komisjarevky, the Chekovian director to whom she was briefly married, who, according to the actor Anthony Quayle, stressed above all else that 'everything was to do with reality and the truth of human relationships'.[49] The technique of clearing one's mind of prior knowledge, coupled with the search for human 'truth', enhanced the sense of the unknown that can be felt in all these English roles, a persistent apprehension of risk, of what it might cost to reach beyond oneself, beyond the boundaries prescribed by sexual and social conventions.

The rigidity of those conventions could be signalled by voice alone. To our ears most actresses of this generation possess piercingly middle-class accents, which does not *necessarily* mean that they recreated the way people actually sounded at the time – though, of course, they may have done so. Standard middle-class accents dominated the West End theatre because 'correct' enunciation was still one of the shibboleths of the drama schools, even if they were beginning to deny any class or regional bias. In his memoirs published in 1958 Kenneth Barnes, Principal of RADA, who had retired three years earlier, complains that

> Articles have sometimes appeared in the press impugning the RADA for cultivating a falsely refined method of speech, described as the 'Kensington' accent, and of imposing it on all students alike. There is no such tendency in our speech-training, and a school which has produced the widely varying voices of many of our leading players to-day cannot be accused of imposing uniformity.[50]

Nevertheless, Barnes goes on to stress the importance at the academy of training in both 'voice production and what is termed diction', which betrays a vestigial association between the ability to 'project', essential for stage work, and certain assumptions about the need to speak 'correctly' and to be heard by others that characterise a middle-class milieu.

Change was underway, though, as Barnes explicitly recognised. Even in Rattigan and Coward one class accent is frequently set against another. In *Brief Encounter*, restrained, but fundamentally assured, middle-class voices are contrasted with the flirtatious, even enviable, working-class banter of the station waiting room.[51] In *Deep Blue Sea*, Hester's firmly reproving tones are set against those of her garrulous, intrusive, but not entirely unsympathetic Cockney landlady. 'Correct' speech invariably goes with the 'correct' behaviour that is actually under scrutiny. Several actresses, Leigh and Ashcroft among them, were vilified by Kenneth Tynan for their Kensington vowels – though this may belong, in part, with Tynan's wish to see them display a greater degree of 'incorrect' sexuality. A move away from 'RP' (received pronunciation) is the single element that all the 'revolutionary' new plays of the 1950s were to share, whether Beckett or Osborne, Pinter or the proletarian drama championed by Joan Littlewood.[52]

A now dated clash of accents may also serve to remind us that in performance oppositions are never stable. Nor should we homogenise performances and performers into an historically convenient whole. When writing theatre history it is all too easy to rely on a mirroring model in which each interpretation is an exact reflection of its textual origin as well as of audience or cultural expectations. That is why it is always worth looking for variation. As it happens, the three actresses that this essay has concentrated upon deputised for one another, bringing their different qualities to the same play. Peggy Ashcroft and Yvonne Mitchell both played Ophelia and Cordelia; Ashcroft, Johnson and the Australian Googie Withers all played Hester.[53] Mitchell and Withers both played Amy in *Woman in a Dressing Gown*; Mitchell and Ashcroft both played Katherine in the *Shrew*, though only Ashcroft played Hedda Gabler. All were successful.

At the same time, the wrong performer in a central role can tell us as much about a shifting theatrical context as the most inspired stroke of casting. The very unsuitability of Vivien Leigh's febrile surface for the part of Hester may actually help us to appreciate what was so distinctive about the supposedly 'ordinary', and why, for other actresses, it could be so worthwhile. Certainly, the significance of these roles exceeded, though it may also have included, questions of sexual magnetism. When, in 1954, Kenneth Tynan wrote a piece under the title of 'Some Notes on Stage Sexuality',[54] he made reference to *Brief Encounter* ('thwarted love'), to *Deep Blue Sea* ('the penalty for extramarital pleasure was paid') and to *Streetcar* (likely to be dismissed, he says, by Englishmen as 'vulgar' or 'tasteless'). Complaining that British playwrights invariably created women characters in the spirit of 'why can't they be repressed like everyone else?', he protested at the lack of erotic roles for actresses between the ages of thirty and fifty, leaving a 'gap', a period of 'lost years', for which he blamed the prudery of playwrights. This may have been broadly true; yet the exceptional plays he criticised had provided expressive opportunities nonetheless. If, for a whole generation of theatre-goers, the post-war years were far from 'lost', it was largely thanks to the ability of some notably professional women to reveal the complex emotional truths that lay hidden behind the closed doors of ordinary life.

NOTES

1. *Plays and Players* 1.10 (July 1954), p. 4.
2. This is the preferred word of Richard Findlater in *The Unholy Trade* (London: Gollancz, 1952), p. 81.
3. Richard Dyer, *Brief Encounter* (London: BFI, 1993), p. 67. Also see Antonia Lant, *Blackout: Reinventing Women for Wartime British Cinema* (Princeton, NJ: Princeton University Press, 1991).
4. Produced on BBC TV in 1954 starring Googie Withers (when the *Radio Times* for 15 January described it as 'the best serious play written by an Englishman since the war'), and made into a feature film starring Vivien Leigh, released in 1955.
5. See Dan Rebellato, introduction to Terence Rattigan, *The Deep Blue Sea* (London: Nick Hern, 1999), pp. x–xxxvi.
6. Elizabeth Bowen, *The Heat of the Day* (London: Vintage, 1998), p. 100.
7. John Costello, *Love, Sex and War: Changing Values 1939–45* (London: Collins, 1985), p. 356.
8. Eustace Chesser, *Love without Fear: A Plain Guide to Sex Technique for Every Married Adult* (London: Rich and Cowan Medical Publications, 1951), p. 26.
9. Dyer, *Brief Encounter*, pp. 20–2.
10. A. V. Cookman, 'The Prose Drama', in J. C. Trewin, ed., *Theatre Programme* (London: Frederick Muller, 1954), p. 43.
11. Michael Billington, *Peggy Ashcroft* (London: John Murray, 1988), p. 141.
12. Eustace Chesser, *The Sexual, Marital and Family Relationships of the English Woman* (London: Hutchinson's Medical Publications Limited, 1956), p. 441.
13. *Child Care and the Growth of Love* (Harmondsworth: Penguin, 1953), p. 104.
14. See Elizabeth Wilson, *Only Halfway to Paradise: Women in Postwar Britain, 1945–1968* (London: Tavistock Publications, 1980).
15. John Costello, *Love, Sex and War: Changing Values 1939–45* (London: Collins, 1985), pp. 355–6.
16. For this topic, and for a comparison with the original play, see Peter Holland, 'A Class Act', in Joel Kaplan and Sheila Stowell, eds., *Look Back in Pleasure: Noel Coward Reconsidered* (London: Methuen, 2000), pp. 87–8.

17. See Ted Willis, *Woman in a Dressing Gown and Other TV Plays* (London: Barrie and Rockcliff, 1959).
18. Duff Hart-Davis, *Peter Fleming: A Biography* (Oxford: Oxford University Press, 1987), p. 131.
19. *Peter Fleming*, p. 131.
20. *Plays and Players* 1.10 (July 1954), p. 4.
21. Billington, *Peggy Ashcroft*, p. 140.
22. Ibid., p. 208.
23. There are suggestions that the play had, in fact, been written for Joan Miller, who played the part in the original TV broadcast. Miller's later career history was hindered by a falling out with Binkie Beaumont, the leading impresario of the day, and by the onset of illness.
24. Yvonne Mitchell, *Actress* (London: Routledge and Kegan Paul, 1957), p. 3.
25. Caryl Brahms, 'The Young Actresses', *Plays and Players* 1.1 (October 1953), p. 11.
26. Juliet Mitchell, *Psychoanalysis and Feminism* (Harmondsworth: Penguin, 1975), p. 11.
27. T. C. Kemp, 'Acting Shakespeare: Modern Tendencies in Playing and Production with Special Reference to Some Recent Productions', *Shakespeare Survey* 7 (1954), p. 127.
28. Yvonne Mitchell, *Martha on Sunday* (London: Anthony Blond, 1970), p. 18.
29. Harold Hobson, *Theatre* 2 (London: Longmans, Green and Co., 1950), p. 57.
30. Claire Bloom, *Leaving a Doll's House* (London: Virago, 1996), pp. 108–9.
31. Claire Bloom, *Limelight and After* (London: Weidenfeld and Nicolson, 1982), p. 150.
32. Helen Taylor, *Scarlett's Women:* Gone with the Wind *and its Female Fans* (London: Virago, 1989).
33. *Sunday Times*, 16 October 1949.
34. *Sunday Times*, 13 November 1949.
35. Elaine Dundy, *Life Itself* (London: Virago, 2001), p. 78. For American responses to Jessica Tandy, who premièred the role in New York, see Milly S. Barranger, *Jessica Tandy: A Bio-Bibliography* (New York: Greenwood Press, 1991). For surveys of later productions, see Philip C. Kolin, ed., *Confronting Tennessee Williams's* A Streetcar Named Desire: *Essays in Critical Pluralism* (Westport, CT: Greenwood Press, 1993), and Helen Taylor, *Circling Dixie: Southern Culture through a Transatlantic Lens* (New Brunswick, NJ: Rutgers University Press, 2001).
36. See John Stokes, *The French Actress and her English Audience* (Cambridge: Cambridge University Press, 2005), pp. 176–8.
37. Kenneth More, *More or Less* (London: Hodder and Stoughton, 1978), p. 163.
38. See Alexander Walker, *Vivien: The Life of Vivien Leigh* (London: Weidenfeld and Nicolson, 1987). For ECT also see Elaine Showalter, *The Female Malady: Women, Madness and English Culture, 1830–1980* (London: Virago, 1997).
39. Wilson, *Only Half Way to Paradise*, p. 113.
40. Penelope Mortimer, *About Time Too* (London: Weidenfeld and Nicolson, 1993), pp. 94, 100, 150, 154.
41. It should, however, be noted that Dundy believes that ECT 'did for me what years of therapy was not able to', Dundy, *Life Itself*, p. 339.

42. Charles Duff, *The Lost Summer: The Heyday of the West End Theatre* (London: Nick Hern, 1995), p. 131.
43. Billington, *Peggy Ashcroft*, p. 139.
44. Ibid., p. 155.
45. Mitchell, *Actress*, p. 18.
46. Ibid., p. 96.
47. London *Evening News*, 7 December 1954.
48. Michel Saint-Denis, ed. Suria Saint-Denis (London: Heinemann, 1982), p. 146.
49. Billington, *Peggy Ashcroft*, pp. 52–3.
50. Kenneth R. Barnes, *Welcome, Good Friends*, ed. Phyllis Hartnoll (London: Peter Davies, 1958), p. 153.
51. See Peter Holland, 'A Class Act', pp. 80–90.
52. See 'Goodbye, Voice Beautiful: Kate Parker Talks to Two of Britain's Leading Voice Trainers', *Plays and Players* 383 (July 1985), pp. 32–3.
53. Frith Banbury, who directed the play, 'says that they each took hold of the part in different ways; Peggy was the more tragic, and Celia the more pathetic. Whereas Celia brought tears to the eyes more readily, Peggy hit you in the stomach. Peggy's technique was the more assured. Celia "added a sense of utter desolation which tore at one's heart"': Kate Fleming, *Celia Johnson* (London: Weidenfeld and Nicolson, 1991), p. 169. Compare Kenneth More: 'Celia who is a doctor's daughter and a charming and competent housewife and mother, is a magnificent technician on the stage. Some parts of the play she did play better than Peggy. Others, Googie did better than Celia. And Vivien Leigh added to the part qualities not possessed by any of the other three. For my money, the best of the lot was Peggy . . . On the stage she is an actress of depth and brilliances, one of the greatest in Britain today. In my opinion she was the most suitable for Hester, both physically and mentally': Kenneth More, *Happy Go Lucky* (London: Robert Hale Ltd, 1959), p. 126.
54. Kenneth Tynan, *Tynan on Theatre* (Harmondsworth: Penguin, 1964), pp. 322–5.

FURTHER READING

Billington, Michael. *Peggy Ashcroft*. London: John Murray, 1988.
Bloom, Claire. *Leaving a Doll's House*. London: Virago, 1996.
   Limelight and After. London: Weidenfeld and Nicolson, 1982.
Duff, Charles. *The Lost Summer: The Heyday of the West End Theatre*. London: Nick Hern, 1995.
Dundy, Elaine. *Life Itself*. London: Virago, 2001.
Dyer, Richard. *Brief Encounter*. London: BFI, 1993.
Findlater, Richard. *The Unholy Trade*. London: Gollancz, 1952.
Fleming, Kate. *Celia Johnson*. London: Weidenfeld and Nicolson, 1991.
Lant, Antonia. *Blackout: Reinventing Women for Wartime British Cinema*. Princeton: Princeton University Press, 1991.
Mitchell, Yvonne. *Actress*. London: Routledge & Kegan Paul, 1957.
Tynan, Kenneth. *Tynan on Theatre*. Harmondsworth: Penguin, 1964.
Walker, Alexander. *Vivien: The Life of Vivien Leigh*. London: Weidenfeld and Nicolson, 1987.

7

TONY HOWARD

Icons and labourers: some political actresses

> Both [acting and politics] are about stripping things away. In their different
> ways, each is about trying to get to the truth.
> Glenda Jackson, London mayoral campaign, 2000

At the climax of István Szabó's film *Mephisto* the antihero, a careerist star who sells his soul to the Nazis, is trapped in a searchlight beam and cries, 'But I'm only an actor!' He is of course wrong. No one is *only* an actor, actress, baker or anything else; 'I,' said the Hollywood comedienne Judy Holliday during the McCarthy era, 'accept my responsibilities *as a citizen.*'[1] Everyone is caught in the choices of their time, and is accountable. Acting is a relatively, sometimes hugely, privileged profession and Simone Signoret, for example, criticised actors' general unwillingness to engage with politics.[2] Today when such figures as Jane Fonda and Vanessa Redgrave speak, angry websites demonise or dismiss them ('Who really cares anything what spews from Jane Fonda's mouth? . . . she is only an actress'),[3] with a frustration born of the fact that cinema (a key tool, Lenin said) made performers literally larger than life and television gained them access to the home. Yet throughout the twentieth century, stage and screen actresses, accepting their responsibilities as influential citizens, organised and spoke out. Two early performances, for example, mapped some possibilities.

Theatres of war and peace

In 1902, the Irish nationalist orator Maude Gonne took the title role in *Cathleen ni Houlihan* by W. B. Yeats and Augusta Gregory. She played an old woman who inspires peasants to fight the English. She is the spirit of Ireland, and when they rise she transforms into a young woman 'with the walk of a queen', but this metamorphosis was not shown on stage because it was unnecessary: the old lady Maude Gonne played was the flimsiest veil for her own unmistakable presence. A statuesque woman in her thirties, she physically dominated the other players and was photographed – her white hair blatantly false – gazing past them into the audience and the future. Born into an English military family, Gonne joined banned Irish organisations and founded the Daughters of Erin movement in 1900. The 'Irish Joan of Arc' led protests against rural evictions, campaigned against the Boer War, wrote revolutionary drama and, imprisoned in 1923, went on hunger strike. The tradition of personifying nations and ideologies in the female body is ancient; *Cathleen ni Houlihan* was an example of an activist using theatre to further her own mission. After the Easter Rising, Yeats asked, 'Did that play of mine send out/ Certain men the English shot?'[4] If so, it was the actress – whose husband was one of the executed rebels – as much as the text that drove them. Gonne – 'The very personification of the figure she portrayed on stage'[5] – saw heroism as the highest form of art. 'I am overwhelmed by the tragedy or the greatness of the sacrifice our friends have made,' she wrote in 1916. 'They have raised Ireland to tragic dignity.'[6]

In 1919 the pacifist Sybil Thorndike starred in an historic London production of *The Trojan Women* directed by her husband Lewis Casson. It celebrated the founding of the League of Nations Union and she later said, 'All the misery and awfulness of the 1914 war was symbolised in that play, and we all felt that here was the beginning of a new era of peace and brotherhood.'[7] Thorndike was the prototypical Fabian actress; her path towards political drama was the opposite of Maude Gonne's. She was a clergyman's daughter whose opportunities and experiences broadened unexpectedly as they did for many middle-class Edwardian women. As a child she saw the slums of Rochester: 'That was the beginning of my Socialist feelings, though I didn't know there were such people as Socialists.'[8] She trained as a musician but gravitated towards theatre and met a new radicalism there: 'Most of these highbrows are socialists,' she wrote, 'full of "the people".'[9] She assisted charities, heard Mrs Pankhurst, began to chair suffrage meetings, and she and Casson became increasingly involved with the pacifist movement and the Left. She supported the 1926 Great Strike (he chauffeured union leaders), and though Thorndike quickly became Britain's leading classical actress, she was only made a Dame in 1931 when Labour was in power. They staged Ernst Toller's work and – 'We were passionately concerned with the subject'[10] – *Six Men of Dorset* on the Tolpuddle Martyrs. Thorndike performed for mining communities; she was an internationalist, denounced during a 1930s Australian tour as 'under the thrall of the master-minds of Russia';[11] and in pre-war South Africa she refused to perform only for whites. Her career became iconic – a woman stepping outside her class and coming into contact not only with injustices but also with cultural and linguistic resources that enabled her to *articulate* those injustices. Through her acting she brought suffering to the attention of the privileged; off stage she campaigned for reform. Thorndike's idealism, stamina and sense of principle were the model for many later

West End actresses – from Peggy Ashcroft to the South African émigré Janet Suzman – who, invited into the Establishment because of their classical and Shakespearean work, sought to move opinion in liberal directions.

There were class issues, however. There were bitter disagreements in British and American actors' unions between those who wished to unite with workers in other industries and those who regarded themselves as a professional elite (many, as in the actor-managerial system, employers themselves). Sybil Thorndike was on the first elected council of British Equity (1931) and Casson became first president. His successor Beatrix Lehmann had been banned for pro-Soviet sympathies by the BBC. There were cyclical Equity clashes between Right and Left. In 1949 Lehmann, Casson and Ashcroft were voted off the council in an anti-Red campaign; during the 1970s, Workers' Revolutionary Party members including Vanessa and Corin Redgrave; Kika Markham and Frances de la Tour tried to radicalise the union; and a decade later Miriam Karlin and others fought the Thatcher government's attempt to break Equity's links with the TUC. Karlin, a lifelong campaigner, argued that many men in the arts avoided political involvement for career reasons: 'Women are far more prepared to stand up and be counted.'[12] Women were active in the international workers' theatre movement that grew up after the Russian Revolution; in 1931 the American academic Hallie Flanagan hailed 'men and women who work by day in shops, factories, or mines, and come together at night to make a theatre'. They rejected, she said, 'the art of illusion, for their object is to remain themselves – workers – expressing workers' problems' including 'wage cuts, unemployment, deportation, lynching, race prejudice, legal discrimination, war, and all oppression and injustice'.[13]

There is no space here even to begin to chart the political activities of twentieth-century actresses. Many were opponents of fascism and racism and were driven into exile (Spain: Margarita Xirgu; Germany: Helen Wiegel; Greece: Melina Mercouri; South Africa: Yvonne Bryceland). Some, supporters of the Soviet Union, died betrayed in Stalin's purges (Carola Neher, the Gulag; Zinaida Raikh, murdered and mutilated). Others fought totalitarianism with silence, as when Polish performers boycotted the media after martial law and exposed the false claim that 'normality' was restored. Few actresses identified themselves with the extreme Right – drama tends towards democracy, after all, based as it is on collaboration and contact with new thought – and those who did usually claimed they were not political at all, only espousing moral, 'patriotic' values (e.g. Leni Riefenstahl, Eva Peron and Brigitte Bardot who in 2003 attacked the 'Islamisation of France' – 'subterranean, dangerous, and uncontrolled infiltration').[14] Some actresses became working politicians (Mercouri, Minister of Culture; the Turkish film star Fatma Girik, a mayor of Istanbul; Bollywood's Shabani Azmi, aiding

136

slum dwellers). Perhaps the most powerful actress in history was Xiang Jing, Mme Mao, who secretly joined the Communists in 1933, only nine years after Chinese women were first allowed to act. At first Chinese propaganda theatre was a living revolution (it was 'a moving thing to see women with bound feet, who hitherto had not been allowed outside the home . . . acting out the part of an emancipated female'),[15] but in the 1960s Xiang Jing focused on censorship: 'It is inconceivable that, in our socialist country . . . the dominant position on the stage is not occupied by the workers, peasants and soldiers, who are the real creators of history.'[16] In 1964 she spearheaded the Cultural Revolution by approving eight 'model' heroic works including *Red Detachment of Women*, to which all theatre must conform. When Mao died she was one of the 'Gang of Four' who briefly controlled China, then fell. At the opposite extreme the American Judith Malina created the Living Theatre with her husband Julian Beck. From the late 1960s they toured the world as an anarchist commune, exploring how theatre might rehearse a revolution that would not betray itself: 'We were no longer playing characters, but ourselves.' Malina stressed both the eroticism and androgyny of acting; Beck's term 'the actressor' caught the rage she explored, as in her Vietnam War *Antigone* – so 'antigone's example/ after 2,500 years of failure/ might at last move/ an intellectual paying audience/ to take action/ before it is/ too late'.[17] In the 1970s they settled in Italy, where Franca Rame and Dario Fo were splitting from the Communist Party to create their own group La Comuna. Malina and Rame both identified radicalism with women's liberation; when Rame was kidnapped and sexually assaulted by fascists, she made it the subject of her solo piece *The Rape* – followed like all her work by intense audience discussions which made the performances themselves democratic events.

Amidst such diversity it was ironic that perhaps the fullest picture of actresses' day-to-day engagement with politics came in a period when radicalism became effectively a crime – during the anti-Communist hearings of the House Un-American Activities Committee: HUAC.

Witch-hunts

I am against censorship. I am against persecution of minority races and religions. I am against curtailment of civil liberties. Because of these beliefs I have on occasion allied myself with others I believed to feel the same way. Some of these groups are now cited as subversive.[18]

With the Depression and the rise of fascism, the causes Hallie Flanagan listed in 1931 became the concern of an entire generation. In 1950 nearly

150 artists – a third of them women, mainly actresses – were smeared as secret Reds planning a 'final upheaval and civil war' in *Red Channels*, a publication listing the causes they had supported. Many were summoned to testify before HUAC, most became unemployable.[19]

Alongside such figures as Einstein and Thomas Mann, actresses across a broad political spectrum had led or endorsed countless Left/liberal campaigns. *Red Channels* called them 'America's so-called "intelligentsia"'. Stella Adler, for example, was linked to twelve 'suspect' organisations (which included the Moscow Arts Theatre), and when China went Communist and the USSR developed nuclear weapons, this became 'subversive infiltration'. In 1947 HUAC subpoenaed leading left-wing artists to account for their activities, and in protest scores of cultural workers founded the Committee for the First Amendment to defend freedom of conscience and the 'Hollywood Ten'. The CFA backed the Ten in radio broadcasts featuring stars like Judy Garland and Lauren Bacall, who asked confidently, 'Have you seen *Crossfire* yet? Good picture. Against religious discrimination . . . The American people have awarded it four stars. The Un-American Committee [sic] gave the men who made it three subpoenas.'[20] A planeful of celebrities including Bacall and her husband Humphrey Bogart, Myrna Loy, John Huston, Marsha Hunt and Katharine Hepburn flew to Washington to denounce the hearings. They were, however, disconcerted by the committee's tactics; once the 'witnesses' cited the First Amendment (freedom of speech) they were shouted down, denied the right to speak, and jailed for contempt. After the press mentioned Katharine Hepburn's support for them, a Carolina audience stoned her onscreen. The alarmed studios blacklisted the Ten and put the liberals under pressure. Bogart apologised in a cowed *Photoplay* article, 'I'm No Communist', which Hunt called 'a body blow to our movement . . . Wow, if Bogart and Bacall are scared, maybe we'd better be.'[21] But the politics of conspiracy demanded more from these 'foolish exhibitionists'. 'Your wife, Lauren Bacall, is a beautiful young lady and you are a popular actor,' said the New York *Daily Mirror*. 'Somebody was using you. Who is that somebody?'[22] The pressure to indict others had begun. 'The liberals were not cowards,' the actress Karen Morley believed, 'they simply did not know what to do when their prestige had no appreciable effect on events. They were very naive.'[23] State paranoia and self-promoting politicians claimed Communism was undermining America, and required proof from famous faces. After the Ten – all unfamiliar writers and directors – HUAC preferred stars: Arthur Miller was told he need not answer questions if his wife Marilyn Monroe would pose for photos with the committee. Images were power.

The witch-hunts quickly shaded into xenophobia and anti-Semitism: 'I want to read you some of these names. One of the names is June Havoc. We found . . . that her real name is June Hovick . . . There is another who calls himself Edward Robinson. His real name is Emmanuel Goldenberg.'[24] Press attacks on black performers like Ruby Dee (blacklisted) and Lena Horne identified desegregation with 'racial agitation' and treason: Horne 'once acted as a speaker for the Civil Rights Congress, a red front'.[25] Some actresses persisted and later reconstructed their careers, especially theatre workers like Lee Grant and Uta Hagen (whose then husband José Ferrer humiliated himself before HUAC, pleading total political ignorance), but others could not. Mady Christians, heroine of *I Remember Mama*, had aided Spanish and German refugees; she was denounced and twice subpoenaed. Her health collapsed – victim, she said, of 'something unbelievable' – and she died in 1951. Dorothy Commingore (*Citizen Kane*) defended the rights of Mexican-Americans; her husband the writer Richard Collins gave names to the FBI. While their marriage collapsed in a bitter custody battle, HUAC interrogated Commingore; she was accused of being a Red, an alcoholic, an unfit mother and a prostitute. The blacklisted actress Frances Young committed suicide.[26] Yet this is not a mere chronicle of victimisation; these attacks must be read as an enraged response to the extraordinary energy of these and many other actresses over twenty years; and they discovered several ways to fight back.

The career of Karen Morley (*Scarface, Pride and Prejudice*) is representative. During the Depression 'I felt awash in a sea of unemployed. People came to my door all the time looking for odd jobs and meals. My fan mail was full of requests for assistance. And people constantly rooted around in the garbage cans behind our house.'[27] She worked in films exploring Roosevelt's New Deal, labour exploitation and (*Last Train from Madrid*) the fight against Franco; she worked on actors' committees campaigning for improved conditions and for progressive filmmaking – 'the better treatment of minorities in movies' and 'parts that showed the true relation that minorities bear to American life'.[28] And she temporarily abandoned acting to help organise exploited tobacco workers in the South. Morley married the Hungarian director Charles Vidor: 'Being married into a Jewish family during the 1930s, and . . . the growing terror against Jews in Europe, is what changed my whole attitude and my whole life.' The Spanish Civil War 'tipped the scales. After that I could be considered a radical.'[29] As a militant in the Screen Actors Guild she backed attempts to unite with the craft labour unions, which alarmed the studios and was seen by the Guild's conservative leaders as a threat to their status. In 1951 she and the actress

Georgia Backus went underground. HUAC subpoenaed them, but along with six writers and a director they chose to disappear, to test the legal position. Living undetected in Texas, Morley established that non-attendance was not a crime. But the Guild president Robert Taylor denounced her as a probable Communist, and though the actor Larry Parks broke down when pushed to name her ('I don't think this is really American justice to force me to do this'),[30] under compulsion Parks did name Morley and the actresses Gale Sondegaard, Anne Revere and Dorothy Tree. Though Morley made no films after 1951 and was reduced to theatre understudying, in 1954 she stood as Lieutenant Governor of New York State for the American Labour Party, 'on a totally feminist platform'.

Gale Sondegaard, who had won the first Supporting Actress Oscar, was one of HUAC's strongest opponents. She was a tireless activist (she and the German exile Luise Rainer were co-founders of the Joint Anti-Fascist Refugee Committee) and proud of her Party membership. Hollywood used her as a symbol of threatening exoticism – 'the Spider Woman'. When the Ten, including her husband the director Herbert Biberman, were imprisoned she narrated *The Hollywood 10* (1950), a documentary denouncing 'thought control' and the climate of fear. When the second wave of hearings began in 1951, Sondegaard pointed out in *Variety* that the Screen Actors' Guild was collaborating with the blacklists. Summoned by HUAC, she wrote to the Guild:

> I will appear next Wednesday. I would be naive if I did not recognize that there is a danger that by the following day I may have arrived at the end of my career as a motion picture actress . . . A blacklist already exists. It may now be widened. It may ultimately be extended to include any freedom-loving nonconformist or any member of a particular race or any member of a union; or anyone.

The Guild's board (president: Ronald Reagan) accused Sondegaard of trying 'to create disrespect for the American form of government' by publishing this letter: 'All participants in the international Communist Party conspiracy against our nation should be exposed for what they are – enemies of our country.' If any actor 'has so offended American public opinion that he has made himself unsaleable at the box office, the Guild cannot and would not want to force any employer to hire him'.[31] Sondegaard was one of the first to cite the Fifth Amendment ('a barrier to political and religious persecution'), declining to answer questions on the grounds of self-incrimination; the Supreme Court had ruled this was legitimate but her career was indeed over. Meanwhile Karen Morley, Marsha Hunt (not a Communist) and Anne Revere fought on within the Guild.

Lucille Ball acted tactically; before the war she signed petitions, backed Left causes and rallies, and supported persecuted workers on the radio. The Ten thanked her for aiding them; HUAC summoned her in 1952 and because she was America's leading television star leaked rumours to the press: 'LUCILLE BALL A RED'. Ball, however, bewildered her interrogators by appearing *in character*. Like the scatterbrain she always played, she explained she once registered to vote Communist to please her old socialist grandpa ('We thought we could make him happy'), and as for supporting the Committee for the First Amendment, she had no idea what it was: 'Refresh my memory on it. I can't ever imagine signing that. Did I sign that too? Was it under an assumed name? . . . In 1947? That certainly was not for grandpa. Grandpa was gone by then.'[32] Nonetheless her tactics required Ball – soon the most powerful businesswoman in Hollywood – to deny systematically the beliefs she once proclaimed. Others were more resilient: Judy Holliday ('Your real name . . . would be Oppenheim?')[33] defended her friends and pointed out that she had hardly been alone in her sympathies: '[General] Douglas MacArthur signed a big ad in the *New York Times* congratulating the Red Army. That was then, see?'[34] Her case typified the witch-hunters' misogyny: because 'the Holliday woman'[35] played dumb blondes, FBI investigators assumed this sophisticated artist was stupid: 'We won't pretend to know that Judy Holliday pretends to know a lot about Spain, peace, Africa, the Russian theatre, or intellectualism.'[36] When she proved otherwise, she fed paranoia: 'Judy only acts dumb. She's a smart cookie . . . The Commies got her a long time ago.'[37] In fact actresses were seen on all sides as publicity currency: if HUAC wanted to pose with Monroe, the Party refused membership to Betsy Blair because her husband Gene Kelly was a leading liberal. His campaign against HUAC would be devalued by marriage to a Communist.

Karen Morley said the witch-hunts crippled American cinema's ability to deal positively with social concerns: 'Now violence became an art, a cult, and with it came the passive women.'[38] Because the American Left failed to re-establish itself after the purges, activists, women and men, were henceforth more likely to speak individually – and were more exposed. Meanwhile the exposure of Stalin's crimes made it hard for radical artists elsewhere to speak with one voice except in such single-issue campaigns as CND or Anti-Apartheid. The next section of this chapter will examine examples.

The actress and the Party

It was impossible to have been twenty years old at the time of the Nazi occupation without being – whether one wanted to or not – involved in what some people call politics.[39]

Simone Kaminker adopted her mother's maiden name Signoret during the Nazi occupation of France. Her Jewish father was in London. Simone Signoret understood the role-play involved in life under totalitarianism: 'It was a game,' she wrote later, 'Nothing heroic.' She insisted on the difference between action and intention: 'I would be a liar if I told you that I was part of the Resistance . . . I did not perform a single heroic act.'[40] But as her film career grew she became prominent amongst the Parisian Left intelligentsia. She had a child by Trotsky's former secretary and formed a lifelong relationship with Yves Montand, the working-class actor-singer. She and Montand never joined the Party with its reductive cultural policies, but they became spokespersons for the French Left's conscience.

In the Cold War this placed Signoret as a critic of imperialism and America. She and Montand presented *The Crucible* in Paris. Signoret believed Arthur Miller had modelled the central characters on Julius and Ethel Rosenberg, the executed alleged 'atom spies'; before the last scene she read Ethel Rosenberg's prison letters, so 'I could with dignity temporarily transfer to Elizabeth Proctor the emotions they had evoked in me.'[41] Yet despite this political identification Signoret saw Elizabeth objectively, as an 'iceberg' in 'a marriage spoilt by their puritanism and her frustration'. Sartre adapted the play for a film made in Communist East Germany and Signoret approved his visual stress on economic factors – 'those huge estates, or those patches of land, depending on whether people were rich or poor'. The Church became a theatre of indoctrination where 'the rich had their pews and the poor had theirs – and the Negroes their designated places in the back, standing with the dogs'.[42] Sartre imposed a doctrinaire ending: the people rise against the corrupt Church and state in a finale that resonates with images of the Liberation. But Signoret more subtly made Elizabeth personify a community in transition. Buttoned-up, literally, suppressing all pleasure, she gradually realises she has denied her family's humanity. She directs the people against their true enemies and protects Abigail, a confused girl who at least admitted her own passion. Freedom demands tolerance based on self-respect. During the filming of this 'corrected' *Crucible*, however, Russia invaded Hungary. Signoret was due to travel to Moscow with Montand, who was on a singing tour; their dilemma – to denounce the invasion or publicly accept the fiction that the Hungarian people requested Soviet aid – dramatised the Left's confusion. They decided to use the opportunity and protested directly to Khrushchev after a concert. According to her, Khrushchev smiled unruffled; they were only actors.

Unlike many artists, Signoret kept away from the 1968 student uprising in Paris: 'I practically keeled over when I discovered that these middle-aged intellectuals had suddenly become revolutionaries.'[43] She felt her generation was on trial. The Soviet invasion of Czechoslovakia that year again forced her to a decision. She and Montand balanced their *Crucible* with *L'Aveu* (*The Confession*), 'an anti-Stalinist film', she said, dramatising Communist show-trials of the 1950s. The invasion stopped the planned French–Czech co-production but they made the film in 1972. As in *The Crucible*, Montand endures physical and mental torture while Signoret plays a wife trying to keep faith both in the system and in him. Signoret became a leading critic of state persecution in Czechoslovakia and Poland (travelling there during martial law); yet she remained firm in her socialist principles and distanced herself from Montand when he moved increasingly rightwards: 'Sometimes,' she said, 'Abbott appears without Costello.'[44] There was another battle coming, though. In 1976 she published an acclaimed autobiography, but there were sneers that she could not have written it herself. She sued. Though inseparable in the public mind from the Left intelligentsia, when the actress presented herself as a writer, when the figurehead laid claim to agency, she was slurred. Signoret won her case and went on to write a panoramic historical novel, *Adieu Volodya* (1986). Driving the narrative across Eastern and Western Europe and the century, she presented the *complexity* of political acts and ethnic identities, contradictions her tireless campaigns and petitions could not encompass.

Dreams and nightmares

I decided many years ago to invent myself. I had obviously been invented by someone else – by a whole society – and I didn't like their invention.[45]

Several actresses played a significant part in the American Civil Rights movement, including the writer Maya Angelou, who began as an actress and dancer. Angelou toured Europe and Africa in *Porgy and Bess*, created *Cabaret for Freedom* (1960) and was nominated for an Emmy in the historic television series *Roots*. She moved directly from running her *Cabaret* to becoming the Northern Co-ordinator ('a nice way of saying fund-raiser') for Martin Luther King's Southern Christian Leadership Conference. Although reluctant to appear in the US première of Genet's *The Blacks* (1960) because it 'says black people will act as cruel as whites',[46] Angelou relished the experience:

I used the White Queen to ridicule mean white women and brutal black men who had too often injured me and mine . . . Blacks should be used to play whites. For centuries we had probed their faces, the angles of their bodies . . . Often our survival depended upon the accurate reading of a white man's chuckle or the disdainful wave of a white woman's hand.[47]

After King's murder Angelou scheduled events for Malcolm X. She described her road from performer to activist in *The Heart of a Woman*. 'There was an incredible aura – air is better – of hope,' she said. 'There was a dream that we could change this country. I think that was a hope that died aborning.'[48] As racial violence intensified, many white liberals supported groups like the Black Panther Party. The FBI decided in 1970 to target 'Jean Seberg, well-known white movie actress', because 'she has been a financial supporter of the BPP and should be neutralized'. To 'tarnish her image', the FBI planted a false rumour in the *Los Angeles Times* about Seberg, who was married to the French novelist Romain Gary and was four months pregnant. 'She is beautiful and she is blonde', a columnist whispered, but 'Papa's said to be a rather prominent Black Panther.'[49] It led directly to Seberg's miscarriage, her breakdown, and the suicides of both herself and her husband. For conservatives the fantasy of a white actress consorting with black militants was abhorrent, and tempting. The Bureau considered similar tactics for Jane Fonda.

Evolving icon

Choosing what characters to play can reveal an aspiration on the part of an actor, not necessarily the actor's reality.[50]

Jane Fonda was deeply conscious of the symbolic power of acting. Her father Henry had represented the American liberal conscience onscreen since the 1930s: he 'was never vocal about race or class,' she said, 'yet the characters he played were the kinds of men he admired.'[51] Simone Signoret took her under her wing in 1960s Paris where Fonda became identified with the cinema of sexual liberation (*Barbarella*, etc.) and felt enfranchised by the intelligentsia: 'This long, up-close and personal (non-toxic) brush with European Communism is why, later, I didn't view it with the same phobic dread as did many other Americans.' Paris 1968 suggested to Fonda that radical change could be achieved through direct action, even in America where she (Miss Army Recruiter 1959) was drawn into a rejuvenated Hollywood circuit of intimate fund-raising evenings. Meeting army resisters politicised her: 'I had managed up until then to neatly compartmentalise my genuine, liberal opposition to war and avoid knowing more about the realities of this particular one' (fig. 13). Events, she said, made her 'a verb' ('Being a verb means being defined by action'). In 1970 she marched in support of Native Americans' land rights and spoke at anti-war rallies. Repeatedly stopped and questioned, Fonda realised that 'I had stepped across the line' separating

Fig. 13. Jane Fonda speaking to a rally of 2,000 students at the University of South Carolina in 1970. (Corbis.)

affluent WASPS ('especially celebrities') from others' daily realities. Nixon read regular transcripts of her tapped phone calls; she was arrested returning from Canada on bogus charges of drug smuggling and assault. Fonda suffered an identity crisis ('An actor? A mother? An activist?') but was persuaded not to retreat into grassroots anonymity. She began consciously 'using my celebrity'.

With Donald Sutherland, Fonda formed an anti-war theatre group. It launched with a conventional Hollywood gala but she quickly redesigned it as FTA (Fuck the Army), a satirical counterblast to Bob Hope's patriotic troop shows. She involved a broad alliance of Nixon's critics and gradually drew in more women including the director Frances Parker. Barred from South Vietnam, FTA toured the Pacific, performing sketches, poetry and songs outside US bases. Bootleg tapes reached Vietnam, and a film was made in 1972. That year Fonda was invited to Hanoi. She went to film evidence of the bombing of North Vietnam's dikes – a sub-nuclear strategy to force surrender, threatening the ecology and vast loss of life. 'I went alone. I'm not sure why.'[52] Appalled by the effects of air-raids and chemical attacks, Fonda volunteered to broadcast to US pilots, to bring home the reality of their missions:

Eighty per cent of the American people, according to a recent poll . . . think we should bring all you home. The people back home are crying for you . . . I believe that in the age of remote-controlled push-button war, we must all try very, very hard to remain human beings.[53]

There were demands that she be tried for treason.

She made a documentary revealing damage to the dikes; after two screenings the only copy vanished. However, the bombing of the dikes stopped. Fonda always insisted she was working *for* the troops and learned most from the veterans against the war who showed 'we may enter the heart of darkness' and survive.[54] With the paraplegic Ron Kovic and others, she developed *Coming Home*, a film about the treatment of Vietnam casualties but one which used the conventions of romantic melodrama and the consciousness-raising woman's picture. 'Empathy is the answer,' she wrote later; 'Once the war was over I returned to film-making.'[55] Fonda at last found a professional strategy to reconcile a wearied nation to her causes – 'I wanted to make films that were stylistically mainstream, films Middle America could relate to; about ordinary people going through personal transformation.' Moreover they did so from 'a perspective of gender'. Beginning with Ibsen's *A Doll's House* (1973), directed by the ex-blacklistee Joseph Losey – a deliberate alliance of radical generations – Jane Fonda reworked Ibsen's pattern. The films she originated tied polemics to the personal, showing a Stepford-Wives bride or an eye-candy newsgirl encountering militarism (*Coming Home*), the nuclear industry (*The China Syndrome*), employment inequality (*Nine to Five*) and, repeatedly, the distorting media. Fonda presented Everywoman's consciousness-raising and political dawn, but suggested that masculinity must be reassessed in the process: 'It is up to women – and men of conscience – to define a *democratic manhood*' not dependent on dominance.[56] Once dismissive of feminism as 'diversionary', Fonda relocated her politics within it.

Freeing speech

Motion: That this House applauds the courage and patriotism of GCHQ translator Katherine Gun who made public information about a memo from the US Government National Security Agency requesting UK assistance with a covert surveillance campaign of the United Nations Security Council members such as Mexico and Chile prior to voting on a resolution which would have endorsed the proposed invasion of Iraq.[57]

Fonda described the political pressure of voicing her own thoughts: 'I began to use radical jargon that rang shrill and fierce. You try to prove what you're not sure of.'[58] The case of Glenda Jackson was different. Jackson's career was shaped by her Northern working-class origins and she always defined herself as a socialist. In the 1960s she established herself on three fronts – in Peter Brook's Theatre of Cruelty, in films where her harsh depiction of sexuality broke boundaries, and on television as the power-figure Elizabeth I. All this work was distinguished by grit and caustic irony. Fonda's 'consciousness-raising' line did not fit Jackson, as was clear in the film *Giro City* (1982) where she played the 'Fonda' role of a film-maker discovering government corruption. After half an hour establishing her character's integrity, she is marginalised by a swashbuckling male journalist (cf. Michael Douglas in *China Syndrome*), almost vanishing except to offer him a bed. Jackson's acerbity exposed the token quality of her role. Soon after, she would move from dramatising issues of free speech to legislating for them: in Parliament in 2004 she called for reform of the Official Secrets Act, 'to afford whistle-blowers the defence of public interest'.

Jackson was a Labour Party member, supported Oxfam, UNICEF and Shelter, and campaigned for abortion rights and against persecution in Indonesia, South Africa and Czechoslovakia. But she often discussed a disparity between this and acting: 'I suppose it is true, this is a trivial profession.' She wondered if her 'energy' shouldn't 'be channelled into something more worthwhile'.[59] When planning *US* (1966), in which Jackson was the voice of contempt for liberal inaction, Brook wondered if it was possible for an actress to live a dual life, apportioning her time between rehearsals and signing petitions; when Thatcherism took root Jackson decided it was not. She retired from acting and was elected to Parliament in 1992. She refused to accept an arts brief, determined to be a working politician, not a pleader for special interests. In 1997 she became Parliamentary Under-Secretary of State for Transport. Yet photographs of Jackson at political events showed a strange embarrassment and many broadcasts sounded strained. She encountered parliamentary prejudice: 'Actors are presumed . . . to live outside what is deemed to be a real or ordinary life. And we're expected to be stupid.'[60] There was disproportionate criticism of her 'performance' as a minister: 'Why is she so much more interesting when she stops talking politics? Why does she leave her pale, brutally beautiful face so often unpainted?'[61] Actually Jackson was frustrated by her role, loyally reaffirming Blairite policies she often detested. It was when she stepped down from the ministry to seek the Labour candidacy for Mayor of London that Jackson finally found her voice. She had supported Neil Kinnock's fight against the hard Left in the 1980s because 'You have to be practical, have to know what will work. It's absurd to get stuck on abstract philosophies';[62] now, campaigning in the streets, she clashed with the party machine. Jackson became a leading critic of the invasion of Iraq – 'which will kill and maim innocent civilians and if, as has been predicted, it leads to an Iraq split into three states, there could be ethnic cleansing on a Balkan scale'. She called it blind vigilantism ('A world order based not on international law . . . is doomed to permanent conflict'),[63] and called in 'disgust' for Blair to resign over the death of David Kelly. The ex-actress demanded truthfulness from a media-obsessed administration that believed 'straight talk, verifiable facts, sharing the thinking behind policy announcements and acknowledging the responsibilities that power also brings, must be avoided, at all costs'. 'Poverty of aspiration', she insisted, was the most corrosive enemy of all.[64] Glenda Jackson became a significant politician when, years after entering Parliament, she stopped acting.

Materialising compassion

I would have felt ashamed if I hadn't made a protest.[65]

Accepting the 1978 Supporting Actress Oscar for *Julia*, set in Hitler's 1930s, Vanessa Redgrave honoured the Jewish people's 'great and heroic record of struggle against fascism and oppression'. As she spoke, Redgrave was being burned in effigy outside by what she called 'a small bunch of Zionist hoodlums', a phrase that would haunt her. Redgrave had replaced Fonda as a hate-figure in America because of her documentary *The Palestinians* (1977) showing conditions in refugee camps and under Israeli occupation. Once again, an actress was demonised for presenting fact not fiction, and accused of fabricating lies. Redgrave narrated and helped finance it after learning of the bombardment of Tal-al-Saatar, a refugee camp in Lebanon where 3,000 died. 'What had happened was so hideous that I immediately wanted to do something to assist the situation.'[66] She interviewed Yasser Aarafat along with doctors and refugees, and argued that the Palestinians' condition resembled Apartheid, 'with one essential difference: the Palestinians do not have the right to live in their own country'. Pressure groups claimed the film was a call to murder Israelis.

Vanessa Redgrave became a political figure at the very moment, the early 1960s, that she emerged as a classical star with the RSC. Like Thorndike she began as a pacifist – she was arrested at anti-nuclear demonstrations – and like Fonda she belonged to the acting aristocracy. However, her father Michael Redgrave had been on the BBC's blacklist and, bruised by the experience, he tried to persuade her that an actresses's responsibility is to her art and fellow actors. Instead she set out to gain a political education and eventually became the best-known member of the Workers' Revolutionary Party, standing in the 1974 General Election. Several things distinguished

Redgrave from other political stars. She identified herself with a Trotskyite faction; she became personally involved and was unafraid to support deeply unpopular causes, for instance standing bail for an alleged Chechen terrorist – an actor turned nationalist leader – detained in the UK. And she generally spoke impulsively rather than with prepared rhetoric, which left her open to charges that she distorted facts. Or lied.

Misrepresentation dogged her. When she was cast as the Holocaust survivor Fania Fenelon in Arthur Miller's *Playing for Time*, Fenelon protested that Redgrave was 'a known fanatic'. Yet it was here and in *Seven Sovereigns for Sarah*, a reinvestigation of the Salem trials from the women's perspective, that Redgrave showed most profoundly how her acting involved both immersion and conviction. Both were television films for the American mass audience, and each featured an extraordinary solo sequence condensing the character's experiences into one *gest*. In Auschwitz, Fania is offered a scrap of sausage by a friend who has prostituted herself. Redgrave/Fania refuses but, left with it, smells it, licks it, and finally cannot resist. She expects to vomit, expects her body to reject this tainted stuff. It does not. She is horrified by her capacity to survive. On trial for Satanism, Redgrave/Sarah is ordered to recite the Lord's Prayer, which no witch can do without error. She wrenches out every syllable, refusing to break, and defeats her accusers. They convict her anyway. Vocalising years of suffering, Redgrave's voice fades into a grinding whisper. Shaven-headed, starved and scarred in *Playing for Time*, her body absorbs the victims' anguish and her gaze drifts between bewilderment and defiance. Both films show her at a window, facing truths that most cannot, and end with the same image: the hollow face of a starved survivor, wrenched from appalling captivity but with eyes still open, studying the living and remembering the dead. Fonda wrote,

> Her grace seems to come from some deep place that knows all suffering and all secrets. Watching her work is like seeing through layers of glass, each layer painted in mythic watercolour images, layer after layer, until it becomes dark . . . she always seemed to be in another reality.[67]

After the rapturous reception of her early roles in Shakespeare, she reinterpreted Kate in the *Shrew* as a plutocrat's daughter emotionally deformed by wealth. She made *Antony and Cleopatra* first a cartoon of American imperialism (1972) and then (1995) a study of multi-cultural crisis and possibility: her Antony was black and the cast included Balkan refugees. Redgrave brought Jewish actors from Russia and Muslims from Palestine to state their case to British audiences without her mediation.

There were fascinating differences between the ways these actresses refashioned their personae through autobiography. Angelou used her experiences as raw material for many works of inspiration; Signoret wove a fluid web of public and private memories; Fonda gave firm shape to her experiences as a process of self-discovery; Jackson has not written her own story at all, but co-operated in 1999 with a biography by another Labour MP. Redgrave's *Autobiography* presents the conjunction of artistic and political activities most starkly: accounts of family life and key performances are broken by pages of European history, Marxist analysis and documented atrocities; less uncompromising than idealistic, Redgrave assumes the reader wants to follow her far from the safe havens of art.

Across the century, the move to militancy was always more startling when made by women; if actresses were socially suspect anyway in cultures where women belonged in the domestic sphere, making unpopular political statements was doubly provocative. They broke the fantasy-contract that states the performer's function is to please; they redirected public fascination with them towards divisive and confrontational ideas. But the contrast between Sybil Thorndike's 1919 *Trojan Women* and Redgrave's performance in Euripides' *Hecuba* (2005) registers an historical change. Thorndike used Hecuba's suffering to welcome 'a new age of peace and brotherhood'; Redgrave presented a victim of ethnic and territorial violence driven to commit her own atrocities. 'We have a very difficult situation in our world', and after 9/11 the major powers' growing violations of human rights, she told CNN, 'are a greater evil than terrorism': 'Even the lowly are allowed the law.'[68] The radical actress no longer operated within structures of solidarity or easy doctrine: postmodern violence and retaliation were now so fragmented and uncharted that it was Redgrave, the activist-actress most prepared to drive into contradiction, who came most to represent the committed conscience. Forever on the unacceptable margin – speaking for shadowy figures the Anglo-American mainstream feared, stepping onto a shifting political stage that always seemed threateningly unfamiliar – Redgrave was an actress who identified with those the audience would not, and struggled to crack the artifices of political communication that dictate how we understand our world. When the Iraq invasion began, the actress Janeane Garofolo was suspicious of the American media's eagerness to bring on performers like herself to attack the war: 'They have actors on so they can marginalise the movement. It's much easier to toss it off as some bizarre, unintelligent special-interest group . . . I'm being treated like a child, and that's how I think the American people are being treated by their media.'[69] Fonda, however, believed actors 'are attacked and infantalised by the Right' precisely because they 'command a wider audience when they speak'. In 2004 Redgrave co-founded the Peace and Progress party, to contest British elections on a human rights platform and provide an international debating forum. Losing contracts, perhaps blacklisted, Janeane Garofolo decided to work with new liberal talk-radio stations, contesting broadcasting's domination by the Right. In a culture of manipulated images, perhaps the actress might protect the word.

NOTES

1. Judy Holliday, personal statement, FBI file, Judy Holliday Resource Center, www.wtv-zone.com/lumina/statement.html.
2. See Simone Signoret, *Nostalgia Isn't What it Used to Be* (London: Weidenfeld and Nicolson, 1978).
3. Web responses by 'John Doe' to Fonda on Israeli policies: sf.indymedia.org/news/2002/12/1553029_comment.php.
4. Yeats, 'The Man and the Echo', in *The Poems, Revised*, ed. Richard J. Finneran (Basingstoke: Macmillan, 1993), p. 345.
5. Maire Nic Shiubhlaigh, *The Splendid Years* (Dublin: James Duffy and Co., 1955), p. 19.
6. Gonne in Janice and Richard Londraville, eds., *Too Long a Sacrifice: The Letters of Maud Gonne and John Quinn* (Selinsgrove, NJ: Susquehanna University Press, 1999), p. 168.
7. Sybil Thorndike, quoted in Euripides, *Hecuba*, trans. Tony Harrison (London: Faber and Faber, 2005), p. ix.
8. Thorndike in Elizabeth Sprigge, *Sybil Thorndike Casson* (London: Gollancz, 1971), p. 44.
9. Ibid., p. 73.
10. Ibid., p. 223.
11. Ibid., p. 207.
12. Miriam Karlin, interviewed on her work for the Anti-Nazi League by the women's paper of the Socialist Workers' Party, *Women's Voice*, February 1978. Karlin drew many actresses into the anti-racist movement. See Dave Renton, *When We Touched the Sky: The Anti-Nazi League 1977–1981* (Cheltenham: New Clarion Press, 2006). Years later she campaigned for pensioners' rights; in 2004 she renounced her Judaism in protest against Israeli policies.
13. Hallie Flanagan, 'A Theatre is Born', *Theatre Arts Monthly* (November 1931), p. 910.
14. In *Un Cri dans le silence* (Monaco: Rocher, 2003).
15. Jack Belden, 'China Shakes the World', quoted in Lois Wheeler Snow, *China on Stage: An American Actress in the People's Republic* (New York: Random House, 1972), p. 109. Snow, a blacklisted actress who appeared in Arthur Miller's *All My Sons*, emigrated to Switzerland.
16. See her manifesto, *On the Revolution of Peking Opera* (Peking: Foreign Languages Press, 1968).
17. Julian Beck, *The Life of the Theatre*, with a Foreword by Judith Malina (New York: Limelight Editions, 1986), pp. 64, 119.
18. Judy Holliday, sworn statement, 1952, FBI file, Judy Holliday Resource Center.
19. *Red Channels: The Report of Communist Influence in Radio and Television*, published by 'Counterattack', New York, 1950.

20. Extracts from CFA broadcast, included in *Hollywood on Trial*, BBC Radio 2, 9 August 2005.
21. *Photoplay*, March 1943, p. 53, cited in Larry Ceplair and Steve Englund, *The Inquisition in Hollywood: Politics in the Film Community 1930–1960* (Garden City, NY: Anchor Press/Doubleday, 1980), p. 291.
22. Victor S. Navasky, *Naming Names* (London: John Calder, 1982), p. 154.
23. Quoted in Ceplair and Englund, *The Inquisition in Hollywood*, p. 290.
24. John Rankin, politician, attacking the CFA. See Ceplair and Englund, *Inquisition in Hollywood*, p. 289.
25. *Hollywood Life*, 30 March 1951, quoted Eric Bentley, *Thirty Years of Treason: Excerpts from the Hearings Before the House Committee on Un-American Activities, 1938–1972* (London: Thames and Hudson, 1972), p. 305; Navasky, *Naming Names*, p. 192.
26. See Bentley, *Thirty Years of Treason*, p. xix.
27. Ceplair and Englund, *Inquisition in Hollywood*, p. 85.
28. Interviewed in Patrick McGilligan and Paul Buhle, eds., *Tender Comrades: A Backstory of the Hollywood Blacklist* (New York: St Martin's Press, 1999), p. 479.
29. McGilligan and Buhle, eds., *Tender Comrades*, p. 475.
30. See Bentley, *Thirty Years of Treason*, pp. 316, 322.
31. *Variety*, 16 and 21 March 1951.
32. See Joe Morella and Edward Z. Epstein, *Forever Lucy* (Oxford: Isis Large Print, 1986), pp. 117–20.
33. Senator Watkins at Holliday's HUAC hearing, Judy Holliday Resource Centre.
34. HUAC hearing, Judy Holliday Resource Centre.
35. Attorney-General memo, FBI file, Judy Holliday Resource Centre.
36. FBI Special Report, FBI file, Judy Holliday Resource Centre.
37. *Hollywood Life*, quoted in Bentley, *Thirty Years of Treason*, p. 306.
38. McGilligan and Buhle, eds., *Tender Comrades*, pp. 478–9.
39. Simone Signoret, *Nostalgia*, p. 311.
40. Ibid., p. 32.
41. Ibid., p. 145.
42. Ibid., p. 160. In East Germany she was also to have played Yvette in the film of *Mother Courage*.
43. See Catherine David, *Simone Signoret* (London: Bloomsbury, 1992), p. 136.
44. David, *Simone Signoret*, p. 155.
45. Maya Angelou in Jeffrey M. Elliot, *Conversations with Maya Angelou* (London: Virago, 1989), p. 88.
46. Maya Angelou, *The Heart of a Woman* (London: Virago, 1986), p. 175.
47. Ibid., p. 179.
48. Maya Angelou in 1977, in Elliot, *Conversations*, p. 72.
49. FBI documents released after Seberg's death. See *New York Times*, 15 September 1979.
50. Jane Fonda, *My Life So Far* (London: Ebury Press, 2005), p. 225.
51. Ibid., p. 68.
52. Ibid., p. 291.
53. Ibid., p. 305–6.
54. Ibid., p. viii.

55. Ibid., pp. 332, 359.
56. Ibid., p. 340.
57. Glenda Jackson, M. P., *Hansard*, 26 February 2004.
58. Fonda, *My Life So Far*, p. 227.
59. 'Glenda Jackson Talks to Margaret Hinxman', *Sunday Telegraph*, 8 April 1973, quoted in Christopher Bryant, *Glenda Jackson: The Biography* (London: HarperCollins, 1999), pp. 120–1.
60. Bryant, *Glenda Jackson*, p. 232.
61. *Guardian*, 25 January 2000.
62. Bryant, *Glenda Jackson*, p. 167.
63. Clive Soley and Glenda Jackson, 'Liberators or Vigilantes?' *Guardian*, 22 March 2003.
64. Glenda Jackson and Stephen Pound, 'Is it Time for Labour to Go?' *Guardian*, 26 July 2003.
65. Vanessa Redgrave quoting Soviet dissident (1968), CNN, 18 June 2005.
66. See Vanessa Redgrave, *An Autobiography* (London: Hutchinson, 1991).
67. Fonda, *My Life So Far*, p. 364.
68. CNN, 18 June 2005.
69. *Washington Post*, 27 January 2003.

FURTHER READING

Bardot, Brigitte. *Un Cri dans le silence*. Monaco: Rocher, 2003.

Beck, Julian. *The Life of the Theatre*, with a Foreword by Judith Malina. New York: Limelight Editions, 1986.

Bentley, Eric. *Thirty Years of Treason: Excerpts from the Hearings Before the House Committee on Un-American Activities, 1938–1972*. London: Thames and Hudson, 1972.

Bryant, Christopher. *Glenda Jackson: The Biography*. London: HarperCollins, 1999.

Ceplair, Larry, and Steve Englund. *The Inquisition in Hollywood: Politics in the Film Community 1930–1960*. Garden City, NY: Anchor Press/Doubleday, 1980.

David, Catherine. *Simone Signoret*. London: Bloomsbury, 1992.

Elliot, Jeffrey, M. *Conversations with Maya Angelou*. London: Virago, 1989.

Fonda, Jane. *My Life So Far*. London: Ebury Press, 2005.

Londraville, Janice, and Richard Londraville, eds. *Too Long a Sacrifice: The Letters of Maud Gonne and John Quinn*. Selinsgrove, NJ: Susquehanna University Press, 1999.

McGilligan, Patrick, and Paul Buhle, eds. *Tender Comrades: A Backstory of the Hollywood Blacklist*. New York: St Martin's Press, 1999.

Morella, Joe, and Edward Z. Epstein. *Forever Lucy*. Oxford: Isis Large Print, 1986.

Navasky, Victoir S. *Naming Names*. London: John Calder, 1982.

Nic Shiubhlaigh, Maire. *The Splendid Years*. Dublin: James Duffy and Co., 1955.

Redgrave, Vanessa. *An Autobiography*. London: Hutchinson, 1991.

Signoret, Simone. *Nostalgia Isn't What it Used to Be*. London: Weidenfeld and Nicolson, 1978.

Snow, Lois Wheeler. *China on Stage: An American Actress in the People's Republic*. New York: Random House, 1972.

Sprigge, Elizabeth. *Sybil Thorndike Casson*. London: Gollanz, 1971.

II

PROFESSIONAL OPPORTUNITIES

8

JO ROBINSON

The actress as manager

All the theatres then were either frankly commercial like the Adelphi, or commercial in disguise, and without exception were under the management of men chiefly in those days actor managers. Naturally the plays that were offered to them made the part the manager would play the chief figure in the scene.
Elizabeth Robins, 'Odd Bits'

We had begun by talking about going into Management as we might have talked about going to the moon.
Elizabeth Robins, 'Whither and How'

These are the later reflections of Elizabeth Robins who, along with her fellow actress Marion Lea, went into joint management in order to put on the first English production of Ibsen's *Hedda Gabler* at the Vaudeville Theatre in London in April 1891. Her memories of working within the actor-manager system provide a useful starting point, highlighting as they do the key challenges and rewards for the actress who took on this additional role.

Robins makes it clear that the dominant structures, within a theatre world that was resolutely commercial, were controlled by men, and she stresses their effects on the kind of theatre produced: writers had to offer plays with a star part for the actor-manager which meant in turn that 'men who wrote plays for women had long been seeing that they simply had little or no chance of being acted'.[1] Robins's own experiences in attempting to persuade actor-managers to stage *Hedda Gabler* had made this only too clear to her. In her talk on 'Ibsen and the Actress' given to the Royal Society of Arts in 1928 and published later the same year, she describes the process of going to see the managers to try to persuade them that 'their indifference and their loathing was equally mistaken'. She failed, meeting only such responses as: 'There's no part for *me*!' 'But this is *a woman's play*, and an uncommon bad one at that!'[2] Tracy C. Davis's recent work, which has revealed that women were, in fact, involved in all aspects of running theatres, has produced a much more nuanced sense of female involvement and power within the world of management and ownership, particularly in the provinces,[3] but it is nevertheless clear that from Robins's perspective in 1891, female managers were the exception rather than the rule.[4] Comparing the likelihood of going into management with that of going to the moon, Robins produces a powerful picture of the societal and cultural difficulties faced by women who tried to make the transition into management in the nineteenth century: the move required not just financial capital, but what we might term cultural and social capital as well. If, as the *Theatrical Times* of 1848 asserted, 'there can be no doubt' that 'a Manager should be a gentleman in all senses of the term', then it is obvious that actresses who aspired to become managers had to overcome cultural resistance within and without themselves.[5] Looking back to their earlier, unsuccessful plans for staging *Hedda Gabler*, Robins remembered that

> Marion Lea and I had no more capital in cash at that time than we had five months later when we took a London theatre. *We had to accumulate audacity* and that was what we had done by the end of the year.[6]

While it is true that the theatre, almost uniquely in the nineteenth century, offered a commercial environment in which women could on occasion compete equally with men, those women who did commit themselves in this way faced severe obstacles. By stepping even further into the public sphere they risked their reputations as well as their finances. Audacity was indeed still needed to take up the challenges.

Yet engagement with risk was nothing new (see chapter 1). Certainly the social and professional stigma attached to the Restoration actress-manager resonates with the experiences of British and many European women in the nineteenth and early twentieth centuries. According to Elizabeth Howe in *The First English Actresses*, success came at a cost:

> By assuming a public 'masculine' role in theatrical affairs [Elizabeth Barry] . . . exposed herself to fierce public ridicule and condemnation . . . Barry was pictured as a mercenary prostitute, unbounded in her lust for money, prepared to do anything for profit.[7]

The focus of this chapter is on the experiences of later actress-managers. Yet, while the language directed at them may not have been as lurid as that used in the seventeenth century to attack the reputation of Elizabeth Barry, any improvement in status could still bring with it an increase in unwelcome critical attention. Crossing from the feminine space of the actress to the 'gentleman's' role of manager – particularly when they did so as already established stars, in the glare of public attention – entailed a combination of femininity and business which had the potential to shake up existing theatrical and commercial practices.

The system

When we think of the never-ceasing, Sisyphus toil of the London actor-manager, when we realise how he has to be play-selector, rehearser, producer, and leading actor, besides giving 'an eye to the box-office', and an occasional hour to society and speech-making, we feel what an arduous existence is his.

Thus commented the editorial writer of the *Era* on 17 February 1906, describing the role of actor-manager that had grown throughout the nineteenth century to become the dominant form of theatrical management and which remained so in Britain at the start of the twentieth century, despite changes in theatrical ownership structures including increasing use of limited liability companies. The role of the manager – 'the apex of the Victorian theatrical hierarchy', according to Michael Booth – was for many years absolutely central to the running of the theatre: he (or she) was responsible not just for both the artistic and administrative sides, but for the economic as well.[8] When actors and actresses became managers, commercial success became even more closely linked to their particular star quality, and the choices made about repertoire reflected the need to place them centre stage.

The degree of financial risk undertaken in such ventures varied, however, according to the precise relationship between actor and theatre. Tracy C. Davis has drawn attention to the ubiquitous use of the term 'manager' to describe a whole range of activities from the involvement of individual entrepreneurs such as Henry Irving and Marie Bancroft running the Lyceum or the Prince of Wales's for many seasons to the shorter involvements of other lesser-known individuals, despite the variations in their actual commitments to the business of theatre, both artistic and financial.[9] As Davis makes clear, a distinction has to be made between those managers who also owned the theatres in which they worked, those who were lessees with responsibility for the upkeep and reputation of the premises and those who managed a company within a theatre or theatres owned and leased by someone else. Elizabeth Robins and Marion Lea, arranging to use the stage of the Vaudeville Theatre for five initial matinee performances of *Hedda Gabler* in 1891, are clearly engaged in a different level of enterprise from Marie Bancroft, who borrowed £1,000 to commence her management of the old Queen's Theatre in 1865 (although C. J. James remained as titular lessee for the first five years), or Sarah Bernhardt, who incurred a fine of 100,000 francs for breaking her contract with the Comédie Française in order to begin her independent career.

Davis is right to draw these distinctions, not least because she highlights the fact that for the majority of women, an entry into management tended not to entail any further involvement in the running or owning of the building. Lacking the capital to support the purchase or lease of a theatre, they were unable to tap into what Davis describes as 'the practices of "gentlemanly capitalism" [which] allowed men to raise money or rally guarantors from acquaintances in a wide occupational and social spectrum':

> Virtually no women overcame the prejudices of bankers to raise sufficient venture capital. However, being managers . . . was within the financial reach of many women: this meant renting rather than leasing real estate; hiring rather than making costumes, properties and sets . . . and paying copyright per performance rather than outright buying of untried scripts on speculation . . . The mobility patterns from performer to manager/impresario and thence to lessee/proprietor/entrepreneur are . . . bounded by gender.[10]

The experiences of Robins and Lea certainly bear Davis's argument out. Unable to persuade any manager to take on the production of *Hedda Gabler*, Robins went to see William Archer, who, initially at least, deluged her 'with reason and the cold water of his doubt. Archer [was] quite in favour of Langtry or Tree or some *accredited* and long *established* management.'[11] As a result, they decided to put on the play for themselves, as Robins recalls: 'Marion had a jewelled bracelet and I had a small treasure that I could throw in the pot.'[12] Their original commitment was for five afternoons' rent only, and although the success of the production meant that it continued for another five afternoons, and then transferred to the evening performances for the duration of May 1891, Robins and Lea were only ever paying a weekly rent to the manager of the Vaudeville. Their accounts also show that they hired the 'fireplace' and 'extra props'.[13]

While there are important distinctions to be drawn as to the economic positions of different kinds of management, there can be little disagreement that artistically the role was always a powerful one, an upwards step in the career path of any performer that outweighed any financial risks. As Booth makes clear,

> the actor-manager was entirely in control of his own parts; he could appear when he liked and how he liked, cast himself to the very best advantage in relation to a weaker company, or . . . build up a strong company with himself as the star. In fact, a West End actor-manager was automatically a star, and that in itself was a compelling motive for taking on the job.[14]

Not being a manager often meant not being able to control one's own artistic or commercial direction, and such frustrations are a common theme in the memoirs of nineteenth-century actresses. Marie Tempest claimed to an interviewer that she had 'never been allowed to play what I have wished. You don't seem to realise that actresses are the victims of managers',[15] while, later, Lena Ashwell, planning a move into management, also asserted that 'under the prevailing system I cannot get the characters I am ambitious to appear in'.[16] Elizabeth Robins again provides a forceful indictment of the system, reflecting on her return to being a mere actress forgoing the power of management:

> Events, after Hedda, emphasised for us the kind of life that stretched in front of the women condemned to the 'hack work' of the stage. That was what we called playing even the best parts in plays selected by the actor-manager. The important managers were actors then.[17]

One underlying reason, then, for an actress to take on management was that in so doing she might achieve greater control over her artistic development. But there were other factors as well: not least a desire to achieve commercial success, an ambition which was of course shared with male managers, but which had even greater importance to women as a means of obtaining some degree of financial independence. The motivations were various, the experiences too.

The names of many actress-managers have survived and will be familiar to any student of theatre history: Eliza Vestris and Marie Bancroft in nineteenth-century London and Sarah Bernhardt and Eleonora Duse in Europe took on established theatrical practices and traded on their names and notoriety as independent women of the theatre to further enhance their careers in management. More recent actress-managers such as Mrs Langtry, Violet Melnotte, Lena Ashwell and Gladys Cooper may be less well known, perhaps because the managerial ground of London theatre had been opened up by these famous forebears, and their later ventures into management provoked less noisy responses.

But while London provided a ready audience for these managerial ventures, and a critical fraternity ready to draw attention to the actresses's bravery or impudence in taking on the 'gentleman's' role, women who worked as managers in provincial theatre often went unremarked and have remained relatively unnoticed even by recent scholars.

Widows and daughters: the forgotten actress-managers

In 'Female Managers, Lessees and Proprietors of the British Stage (to 1914)', Tracy C. Davis lists the names of approximately 330 women involved in the administration of theatres and music halls in Britain prior to the First World War. Not all of these were actress-managers: many were proprietors of inherited property, or women who went into management without simultaneously pursuing a career as an actress. But one strand of a pattern emerging from recent research shows the frequency with which women took on the task of management as a result of family relationships, particularly in the provinces. From Mrs Stephen Kemble and Mrs DeCamp who ran the Theatre Royal, Newcastle during their husbands' absences in 1805 and 1823–4 respectively to Mrs Bateman, who picked up the lease of the Lyceum in London on her husband's death in 1875, through to Marie Saker, who took over management of the Alexandra Theatre, Liverpool on her husband's death in 1884, these women worked to secure the ongoing commercial existence of a family business, participating in what Davis sees 'emerging *as a tradition* of women taking charge – in various capacities – of this cultural industry, despite tremendous odds'.[18] Because little is recorded of these women, and much research remains to be done, they are often forgotten in the conventional histories and summaries of women's involvement with theatre. The Nottingham-based career of Marianne Saville – to take just one example – indicates an established and relatively unquestioned network of actresses in provincial management which, while complicating the unquestioning assertion of the *Theatrical Times* that managers must be 'gentlemen', extends our understanding of the responsibilities of women within the theatre of the past.

When the young actress Marianne Hobden married John Faucit Saville in November 1830, she joined an established theatrical family: John had first appeared on stage in May 1813 at the age of six, and he and his two brothers were to have long careers in British provincial theatres and the London minor theatres. After several seasons in the illegitimate London theatres, John moved into provincial management, involving all his family in the business: at the Theatre Royal Brighton 'his wife was the leading lady, and he himself took secondary parts; his uncle, Charles Diddear, was principal tragedian; his little daughters, Maria and Kate, appeared in pantomimes'.[19] Marianne was playing a full role in the stage business of the family from the outset; that she probably also had a role in managing its commercial business can be surmised by her involvement in management in later years when she proved herself to be financially astute and also able to manage a network of social connections within the provincial town in which she worked. This was Nottingham in the East Midlands of England, to where John moved in 1844, taking over the management of the Theatres Royal in Nottingham and its neighbouring town of Derby, with Marianne at his side. There, argues Carol J. Carlisle,

His family contributed heavily to his success: his wife was a versatile, highly competent actress, and their daughters were all useful – Maria, though not an actress, helped to operate the theatre; Kate was a much-applauded child actress who retained her popularity as she grew older; and Eliza Helena, the youngest, inherited some of Kate's earlier roles.[20]

As John took on other theatres (at Buxton, Chesterfield, Leicester and Sheffield) for varying lengths of time, so Marianne increasingly assumed responsibility for managing the Nottingham theatre on her own, being the effective manageress during most of 1851–2. In 1854 Saville successfully bid for the ownership of the Nottingham Theatre Royal, becoming proprietor as well as manager, and when he died unexpectedly at the end of 1855, Marianne took over both the ownership and management of the theatre, burdened as the role was with the debts of the purchase and a subsequent extensive refurbishment. She continued in this capacity until the old Theatre Royal closed in 1865, then joining the acting company of the New Theatre Royal which had opened in a much more central, prominent position above the town's marketplace. Her brother-in-law Henry F. Saville moved with her to become the acting manager at the new theatre under the management of Mr Walter Montgomery, but when Montgomery's short management was succeeded by the unsuccessful one of Mr G. F. Sinclair and members of the company began to leave, it was announced that the new managers would be Mrs Marianne Saville and her daughter Kate. Kathleen Barker argues that 'something had to be done to rally the loyalty of the Nottingham playgoing public' to the theatre: the appointment of a known and familiar actress as manager was clearly seen as a positive act.[21]

When the Savilles finally retired from involvement with Nottingham theatre in 1870, Marianne's farewell benefit took the form of a Grand Full Dress Masonic Bespeak attended by many figures of the town's establishment. She was presented with a silver tea and coffee service and salver, and made a grateful speech of acknowledgement to the people of Nottingham for their support throughout her management.[22] She was clearly a respected figure within the town.

Here then is an example of an actress as manager largely forgotten in the histories of British theatre but who was involved in the running of theatre in provincial Nottingham for nearly twenty years. Her quotidian life in provincial theatre may not have attracted the attention of critics and scholars, but she is representative of one kind of involvement of actresses in the ordinary running of the business of theatre, away from the headlines and what might be seen as the myth-making of Vestris or Bancroft, Bernhardt or Duse. Marianne Saville's successor at the Theatre Royal Nottingham was Lady Don, who had performed at the old Theatre Royal in November 1858 with her husband Sir William, and who took the title role in her first pantomime at the theatre, *Robinson Crusoe*. One actress-manager was succeeded by another actress-manager, without comment or concern within Nottingham as to their ability to run a theatre in an increasingly important provincial town.

Perhaps Marianne Saville and Lady Don were accepted within Nottingham and within the wider structures of nineteenth-century provincial theatre because they had both first been encountered there in the guise of wife, playing a supporting role. Davis argues that there may be another reason, noting that the lack of attention paid to provincial managers by both their contemporaries and later historians suggests 'a pattern of women's existence in business but exclusion from recognized art, with no consideration of the stakes in any of these operative categories'.[23] As theatre in the provinces has until relatively recently been neglected by historians, these women have been either ignored or characterised merely as businesswomen rather than as fully fledged actress-managers.

For those actresses who were not cloaked with the respectability of a supportive family, or who took on the business of theatre in the great cities of Europe, the move into management was much more remarked upon, and their motives for doing so perhaps more complex. Certainly they are better known to us through the accumulation of biographical material to which both their contemporary celebrity and their subsequent inclusion within the canon of theatre history have given rise.

Taking control

By the time that she took on the management of the illegitimate Olympic Theatre in December 1830, Eliza Vestris was an established theatrical star in burlesque. Marie Wilton (later Bancroft), too, was a burlesque star at the Strand Theatre when she assumed management of the old Queen's Theatre in Tottenham Street in 1865. Sarah Bernhardt had triumphed first in Paris, and then in London as a member of the Comédie Française during its 1879 visit, before she broke her contract with that theatre in April 1880 and embarked on an independent career which was to combine both tours and experiments in the management of various theatres in Paris. And Eleonora Duse was 'a major star in Italy, and a big box office attraction' as part of Rossi's company before she set up her own company, the *Compagnia drammatica della Città di Roma*, in 1887.[24] While Michael Booth suggests that entering management helped actors in their quest for stardom, it is clear that none of these four women needed to take the step just for that purpose.

Instead it seems that what management allowed them was the independence to exploit their stardom for their own benefit rather than for that of a male actor-manager or, in Bernhardt's case, for the organisation of the Comédie Française. That benefit can be seen to be operating in terms of increased artistic freedom – in just the same way as Robins and Lea went into management to put on the 'woman's play', *Hedda Gabler* – but also in terms of increased financial and business independence that enabled them to gain the commercial benefits of their hard-worked-for fame. All four seem to have made the move because of dissatisfaction with the repertoire offered them and its artistic interpretation, and because of their realisation that their value as performers could be better exploited for their own ends than for those of their existing employers. They were also unusual in that the level of their success enabled them to take on the financial risks (or to draw on an established network of financial support) that entry into management required.

Marie Wilton, working at the Strand Theatre and apparently 'doomed to appear in a long line of "burlesque boys" – which . . . "was none of my choosing"', found herself 'greatly exercised in my mind with regard to the future, anxious to better my prospects, and always desiring to act in comedy rather than burlesque'. 'In despair' and not knowing what to do, the suggestion of taking a theatre of her own was put to her and, with the help of a £1,000 loan from her brother-in-law, she took on the management (not, initially, the lesseeship, which remained with C. J. James) of the old Queen's Theatre in Tottenham Street.[25] In taking this step into management she has often been paired with and viewed as an heir to Madame Vestris, who also left behind a career in burlesque when she took on the lease and management of the Olympic Theatre in Wych Street, London in 1830. Vestris's own last engagement before moving to the Olympic had been a short season at the Tottenham Street Theatre – which was later to become the Queen's and then the Prince of Wales's. Unable to find a place at either of the major legitimate theatres, Covent Garden or Drury Lane, because 'from the manager's point of view, Madame Vestris was expensive and had become increasingly particular about the pieces she appeared in and the way they were presented', she signed a short but lucrative contract with the Tottenham Street management before making her own move into the management of a minor theatre in December 1830.[26]

Similar dissatisfaction with the roles being offered to them and with the lack of control over the rewards of their performances seem to have led to Bernhardt's and Duse's breaks with their established companies in 1880 and 1887 respectively. Bernhardt had experienced the acclaim of a London audience during a season in which she had triumphed as Phèdre, as Andromaque and as Doña Sol in Hugo's *Hernani*. The nineteenth-century English critic A. B. Walkley wrote of this visit, and Bernhardt's reception in England, that

It was the extraordinary, the exaggerated, the unreasoning fuss that we made over her in London in 1879 that suggested to her soul to become like a star and dwell apart. It was the Gaiety French Play season of 1879 that turned Sarah Bernhardt into Sarah Barnum.[27]

Leaving aside – for the moment – the implied criticism of the female actress's entry into commerce that comes with Walkley's employment of the familiar slur on Bernhardt as Barnum, Walkley's comments make it clear that Bernhardt's rapturous reception in London confirmed her view that she would be far better off outside the rigid structure of the Comédie Française. When in April 1880 she was asked to take on the disliked role of Clorinde in Emile Augier's drama *L'Aventurière*, without even being given sufficient time to study the part, Bernhardt severed relations with the company and in doing so broke the contract that had committed her for another fifteen years. She first transferred her talents to tours arranged by the impresario William Jarrett, but her ambitions to truly manage her own repertoire and the manner of her performances led her to investigate purchasing a number of Parisian theatres, the first of which she leased in her son's name in 1882.

As for the reasons behind Eleonora Duse's move into independent management and the creation of her own company, her own words perhaps speak clearest of all:

> My dream, my ideal is to realize in practical terms everything I think and feel about the moral advantage of the art form to which I belong.
>
> I want to set up a really large company with completely modern intentions and send back to the attic . . . all the old trickeries of our blessed organization.
>
> I want to bring a revolution (I do) in terms of staging as well, both in terms of setting up the stage and in terms of the final combination.[28]

These ideals are echoed again in Lena Ashwell's view in 1904 that 'my ambition will not be satisfied until I have a theatre in London at which I can produce serious works, and prove that there is as big a public for them, when they are of the right sort and properly presented, as for the lighter and more frivolous productions that have ruled so long'.[29]

However, writing of Duse, Susan Bassnett adds that 'as ever in [her] . . ., artistic ambition was fused with bourgeois social aspirations': 'she felt strongly that it was her duty as a mother to provide well' for her daughter.[30] Such social aspirations and desires for financial success seem to have coloured the schemes of all these women. Perhaps Marie Wilton, beginning with her loan of £1,000, can be judged to have best achieved them, as she and her husband retired from the Haymarket in 1885 with profits of £180,000 and some twelve years later were made Sir Squire and Lady Bancroft by Queen Victoria. But whether by touring, as with Bernhardt, Duse or Vestris, who recouped her losses on the lease of the Olympic with an American trip, or by establishing a close relationship with their audiences at the Prince of Wales's Theatre or the Haymarket for Marie Bancroft, or for Bernhardt at the Porte-St Martin, the Renaissance, and the Théâtre des Nations (renamed the Théâtre Sarah Bernhardt in her own honour), each of these women met with considerable financial and artistic success, and received critical attention from their own contemporaries which allows us to see them, in Davis's terms, as the women managers who 'most effectively broke through the green baize ceiling'.[31]

Encountering their critics

The criticism the actresses encountered when they dared to take on the management of the great theatres of Europe proves that this could be a contentious move, changing the terms by which their achievements were measured. As established stars they were already operating within the category of 'recognised art'; perhaps as a result, the reactions to their managerial activities was of a quite different order from the reactions of provincial critics in Nottingham to the businesses carried on by Marianne and Kate Saville, or by Lady Don.

First, there is recognition of their genuinely innovatory practices, both as businesswomen and as actresses. Vestris is credited with introducing payments to actors in advance, and rehearsing her company with care, while Bancroft, according to Davis, 'set up a company on economic principles of unprecedented elegance and efficiency', making changes in repertoire and length of run and – with the help of a feminisation of the auditorium – targeting a higher-paying audience.[32] When Bernhardt took on the Théâtre de la Renaissance in 1893 she, too, claimed for herself the role of theatrical innovator, forming the enterprise 'on the best English models', and while John Stokes's assessment is that 'not all of her grand claims were pursued', both in her acting and in her emphasis at this time on attention to detail in set and costume Bernhardt was seen as reflecting a changing theatrical atmosphere within Paris.[33] And we have already seen that Duse's ambitions for taking on her own company were charged with a desire to 'bring a revolution', which she did both by introducing Ibsen to the repertoire and by her development of a particular style of acting which contrasted strongly with the model provided by Bernhardt herself. Robins, too, took on management with Marion Lea in order to innovate, producing Ibsen on the English stage in a manner quite different to anything that had gone before:

To say the Hedda rehearsals were unique is to forget the rehearsals of no one play are like the rehearsals of any other. But I'll say the Hedda rehearsals were more unlike others than any I ever heard of . . . We ignored absolutely the usual stage device of 'introducing movement' by risings and crossings – unless these were indicated by Ibsen's sparse stage directions, or by implications in his text. We made a great merit of leaving a margin for the actors themselves to move freely in – just so they didn't contradict Ibsen.[34]

The second, most important, strand in the critical treatment of these actresses explicitly identifies them as feminine, and deals with them in those terms: perhaps not so surprising when one of the freedoms exploited by the actress-manager was to put on the 'women's plays' of Ibsen, as Robins and Duse were to do. The frustrations felt by actresses working under the control of male actor-managers were at least in part centred on the kinds of parts on offer; one legacy of the entry of women into management can be seen in the staging of plays about strong women characters, and the attraction of a new audience into the theatres as a result. Characters such as Hedda Gabler or Hilda Wangel in *The Master Builder* were introduced to London matinee audiences – predominantly made up of women – by Robins, while Duse brought Ibsen's Nora and Hedda and Sudermann's Magda to audiences in Italy and across the world in her extensive tours. Lena Ashwell's 1908 production of *Diana of Dobson's*, written by the suffrage writer Cicely Hamilton, brought questions of women's conditions of work before the fashionable audiences who came to enjoy the comfort and luxury of her Kingsway Theatre.

In addition to the opening up of repertoire – which in the case of Robins led to a more politicised sense of her female identity and to her joining the Actresses' Franchise League – some actress-managers actively utilised the perception that their femininity was being brought to the role. This was certainly an aspect that Vestris and Bancroft, in particular, made use of for themselves, stressing in the publicity for their new managerial enterprises the way in which they had transformed the surroundings in which they worked. Bancroft famously recalled of her renamed Prince of Wales's Theatre on its opening night that:

> The house looked very pretty, and, although everything was done inexpensively, had a bright and bonnie appearance, and I felt proud of it. The curtains and carpets were of a cheap kind, but in good taste. The stalls were light blue, with lace antimacassars over them; this was the first time such things had ever been seen in a theatre.[35]

Jim Davis and Victor Emeljanow have recently called into question the extent of the transformation of the Queen's Theatre 'dust-hole' claimed here by

Bancroft, but it remains clear that Bancroft herself wished to stress the feminisation – indeed civilisation – of the theatre of which her 'modest undertaking was the pioneer'.[36] Such language and imagery was taken up in respect of subsequent actress-managers: Mrs Langtry's 'exquisitely beautiful' refit of the Imperial Theatre in 1900 was described by the *Era* as having 'the stamp of the fair manageress's individuality', while Lena Ashwell's renamed and refitted Kingsway Theatre of 1907, 'fast assuming a very pretty appearance', was 'to cater for the matinee girl, [with] afternoon teas there for ladies'.[37] Viv Gardner has argued that 'paradoxically it is the very development of a more respectable, woman-friendly theatrical space that confirms the "private sphere" as the realm of the female within the public arena', and the very safety of the feminine certainly seems to have been exploited by Vestris and Bancroft, and perhaps later by the joint management of Gladys Cooper and Frank Curzon at the Playhouse Theatre in 1916.[38] Cooper's grandson Sheridan Morley writes that:

> Widely hailed as the most beautiful woman in London, G drew a large proportion of her audiences from the ranks of those who simply wanted to sit and stare at her . . . what [her audience] wanted was after-dinner entertainment and G had learnt the rules of that particular business better than most. Which, on balance, may well have been why Curzon took her into management at the Playhouse in the first place.[39]

A concept of feminisation as a civilising force may also have been at play when in 1892 Violet Melnotte built the Trafalgar Square Theatre (now the Duke of York's) in what the papers of the time described as 'practically a slum', but the double-edged nature of the discourse around femininity also saw her christened 'Mad Melnotte' for her enterprise in so doing.[40]

Indeed, the actual reception of actress-managers from Vestris to Bernhardt suggest that these individual entrepreneurs still represented a dangerous – and potentially 'mad' – breach in the line that separated private from public, feminine from masculine. Details of their private lives were discussed in print and in public, and on the occasion of their marriages remarkably similar satirical images of Vestris, Bancroft and Bernhardt depict them as monstrous women, towering over their midget husbands: Squire Bancroft is shown shrunken in a wheelchair, while Bernhardt's husband Jacques Damala is revealed as a tiny puppet, controlled by strings held firmly by his wife.[41] What these images – with their topsy-turvy rendering of gender and power – suggest is a real anxiety about the power of women usurping the traditional male power in theatrical business structures, a monstrous femininity which the step into management from out of the frame of the proscenium arch momentarily and disturbingly revealed to contemporary audiences.

Afterword

There were, then, a series of professional and economic motivations which led actresses into becoming managers: a desire for independence; financial ambition or security; control over artistic repertoire and staging; and control over reputation and representation. For those who took on the role of managers in the big cities and theatres of Europe, the move indeed required the accumulation of 'audacity' described by Elizabeth Robins, as attention focused not just on their business skills but on their personal and private lives. For the less-well-known (and as yet under-researched) actress-managers who took control of theatres in the provinces, away from the gaze of critical attention, management was – despite the claims of stardom and prestige associated with it – a practical, business role, with practical commercial and personal benefits.

Interviewed about her move into management in 1904, Lena Ashwell was asked if she enjoyed her new role. Her reply reminds us of both its artistic demands and its undoubted usefulness:

> I like it immensely. So far, it has been the most delightful experience of my life ... I love my work intensely, and am never so unhappy as when I have nothing to do. In fact, one of my chief reasons for going into management ... was my wish to avoid those long and weary periods of resting, from which I have suffered as badly as anybody. It seems to me that to be one's own manager is the only way to be constantly employed.[42]

NOTES

1. Elizabeth Robins, 'Odd Bits', MS, Fales Library, New York University, ch. 5, p. 8.
2. Elizabeth Robins, *Ibsen and the Actress* (London: Hogarth Press, 1928), p. 16.
3. Tracy C. Davis, 'Female Managers, Lessees and Proprietors of the British Stage (to 1914)', *Nineteenth Century Theatre* 28 (2000), pp. 115–44.
4. Kerry Powell's recent essay on 'Gendering Victorian Theatre' seems to share this view, stressing that 'it was *only* as actresses that Victorian women could realistically hope to succeed in the theatre'. In Joseph Donohue, ed., *The Cambridge History of British Theatre*, vol. 2, *1660 to 1895* (Cambridge: Cambridge University Press, 2004), pp. 342–68, p. 361.
5. 'Modern Guardians of the Drama, their Qualifications and Attainments', *Theatrical Times*, 25 July 1846, p. 51.
6. Elizabeth Robins, 'Whither and How', MS, Fales Library, New York University, ch. 5, p. 8. Emphasis added.
7. Elizabeth Howe, *The First English Actresses: Women and Drama 1660–1700* (Cambridge: Cambridge University Press, 1992), p. 30.
8. Michael Booth, *Theatre in the Victorian Age* (Cambridge: Cambridge University Press, 1991), p. 27.

9. Tracy C. Davis, 'Edwardian Management and the Structures of Industrial Capitalism', in Michael Booth and Joel Kaplan, eds., *The Edwardian Theatre: Essays on Performance and the Stage* (Cambridge: Cambridge University Press, 1996), pp. 111–29.

10. Ibid., pp. 113, 117.

11. Elizabeth Robins, transcript of diary entry, reproduced in 'Whither and How', ch. 8, p. 3.

12. Robins, *Ibsen and the Actress*, p. 16.

13. Elizabeth Robins, '*Hedda Gabler*: 5 Matinees Ending April 24th 1891', MS, Fales Library, New York University.

14. Booth, *Theatre in the Victorian Age*, p. 31.

15. Henry Hector Bolitho, *Marie Tempest* (Gloucester: Cobden-Sanderson, 1936), p. 33.

16. 'Miss Ashwell's New Departure', *Illustrated Sporting and Dramatic News*, 3 September 1904.

17. Robins, *Ibsen and the Actress*, p. 33.

18. Davis, 'Female Managers', p. 115. Examples taken from Davis's list, pp. 118–40.

19. Carol Jones Carlisle, 'The Faucit Saville Brothers: or, Theatre and Family', in Richard Foulkes, ed., *Scenes from Provincial Stages: Essays in Honour of Kathleen Barker* (London: Society for Theatre Research, 1994), pp. 114–26, p. 117.

20. Carlisle, 'The Faucit Saville Brothers', p. 118.

21. Kathleen Barker, 'The Performing Arts in Five Provincial Towns, 1840–1870' (PhD thesis, University of Leicester, 1982), p. 316.

22. *Nottingham and Midland Counties Daily Express*, 7 May 1870.

23. Tracy C. Davis, *The Economics of the British Stage, 1800–1914* (Cambridge: Cambridge University Press, 2000), p. 275.

24. Susan Bassnett, 'Eleonora Duse', in John Stokes, Michael Booth and Susan Bassnett, *Bernhardt, Terry, Duse: The Actress in her Time* (Cambridge: Cambridge University Press, 1988), pp. 119–70, p. 145.

25. Marie and Squire Bancroft, *The Bancrofts: Recollections of Sixty Years* (London: Nelson, 1911), pp. 30, 72. Bancroft initially went into joint management with the writer H. J. Byron, but took responsibility for the loan and for the business in his repeated absences.

26. John Williams Clifford, *Madame Vestris: A Theatrical Biography* (London: Sidgwick and Jackson, 1973), p. 86.

27. Quoted in Joanna Richardson, *Sarah Bernhardt and her World* (London: Weidenfeld and Nicolson, 1977), p. 88.

28. Olga Signorelli, *Vita di Eleonora Duse* (Bologna: Capelli, 1962), pp. 55–6. Quoted and translated in Bassnett, 'Eleonora Duse', p. 146.

29. 'Miss Ashwell's New Departure'.

30. Bassnett, 'Eleonora Duse', p. 146.

31. Davis, *The Economics of the British Stage*, p. 276. Davis's claim refers only to Vestris and Bancroft.

32. Ibid., p. 283.

33. John Stokes, 'Sarah Bernhardt', in Stokes, Booth and Bassnett, *Bernhardt, Terry, Duse*, pp. 13–63, p. 23.

34. Robins, 'Whither and How', ch. 14, pp. 8–9.

35. Marie and Squire Bancroft, *The Bancrofts*, p. 80.
36. Jim Davis and Victor Emeljanow, *Reflecting the Audience: London Theatregoing, 1840–1880* (Hatfield: University of Hertfordshire Press, 2001), ch. 5.
37. Langtry details quoted in Viv Gardner, 'The Invisible Spectatrice: Gender, Geography and Theatrical Space', in Maggie B. Gale and Viv Gardner, eds., *Women, Theatre and Performance* (Manchester: Manchester University Press, 2000), pp. 25–45, p. 39. For Ashwell information see *The Era*, 10 August 1907, and *The Star*, 3 October 1907.
38. Gardner, 'The Invisible Spectatrice', p. 38.
39. Sheridan Morley, *Gladys Cooper: A Biography* (London: Heinemann, 1979), p. 78.
40. 'Violet Melnotte Returns', unidentified clipping, March 1933. Mander and Mitchenson Theatre Collection.
41. 'Madame V—, and her Young Tiger'; 'Manageress and Manager', *Entr'Acte*, 23 November 1872; 'M. Damala', *Triboulet*, September 1882. For reproductions and fuller discussion of these images see Davis, *The Economics of the British Stage*, ch. 8, and Mary Louise Roberts, *Disruptive Acts: The New Woman in Fin-de-Siècle France* (Chicago: University of Chicago Press, 2002), ch. 6.
42. 'Our Latest Actress Manager: An Interview with Lena Ashwell', *Pall Mall Gazette*, 3 September 1904.

FURTHER READING

Bancroft, Marie, and Squire Bancroft. *The Bancrofts: Recollections of Sixty Years*. London: Nelson, 1911.

Bolitho, Henry. *Marie Tempest*. Gloucester: Cobden-Sanderson, 1936.

Booth, Michael. *Theatre in the Victorian Age*. Cambridge: Cambridge Press, 1991.

Carlisle, C. J. 'The Faucit Saville Brothers: or, Theatre and Family', in Richard Foulkes ed., *Scenes from Provincial Stages: Essays in Honour of Kathleen Barker*. London: Society for Theatre Research, 1994.

Davis, Jim, and Victor Emeljanow. *Reflecting the Audience: London Theatregoing, 1840–1880*. Hatfield: University of Hertfordshire Press, 2001.

Davis, Tracy. C. 'Edwardian Management and the Structures of Industrial Capitalism', in Michael Booth and Joel Kaplan, eds., *The Edwardian Theatre: Essays on Performance and the Stage*. Cambridge: Cambridge University Press, 1996.

Morley, Sheridan. *Gladys Cooper: A Biography*. London: Heinemann, 1979.

Richardson, J. *Sarah Bernhardt and her World*. London: Weidenfeld and Nicolson, 1977.

Roberts, Mary Louise. *Disruptive Acts: The New Woman in Fin-de-Siècle France*. Chicago: University of Chicago Press, 2002.

Robins, Elizabeth. *Ibsen and the Actress*. London: Hogarth Press, 1928.

Williams, Clifford John. *Madame Vestris: A Theatrical Biography*. London: Sidgwick and Jackson, 1973.

9

VIV GARDNER

By herself: the actress and autobiography, 1755–1939

> The autobiographical occasion (whether performance or text) becomes a
> site . . . ripe with diverse potentials . . . [and] can be productive
> in . . . articulating problems of identity and identification.
> Sidonie Smith and Julia Watson

Actresses' autobiographies and autobiographical performances[1] figure in several volumes on women and autobiography, but not in a number that reflects the ratio of actress-autobiography to other types of female life writing.[2] Part of the problem is that the actress in history has represented an atypical figure, one of the few examples of women with a public life. Actresses usurped the male right to a public persona both as individuals and as a class, but without losing their subordinate and domestic role as women: this dichotomy is inevitably manifest in the actress-autobiographer's writing.

This chapter offers both an overview of actresses' autobiography to 1939 and a model for reading these works for their 'diverse potentials'. It embraces the autobiographical work of performers from the 'beginnings' of the publication of actresses' autobiographies to the point in the 1930s where the 'autobiographical act' had stabilised as a commodity. The number of actress-autobiographers examined is inevitably limited by space, the range discussed intentionally diverse, situating the famous alongside the less well known, the Shakespearean alongside the musical comedy performer.

Diverse potentials

Dame Madge Kendal (1848–1935), writing towards the end of her life, prefaced her autobiography by saying,

> To speak one's part and, in doing so, to express one's personality is natural to all to whom, like me, 'the stage of life' has so largely been the stage, behind the footlights.[3]

The title page of her memoirs reads: *Dame Madge Kendal: By Herself* (1933). The frontispiece to the book shows the bespectacled actress in profile alone 'at her desk', unsmiling, pen poised over the papers on her desk – in a

Fig. 14. Dame Madge Kendal at her desk. (Author's collection.)

performance of authorship (fig. 14). The creation of the autobiography is represented here as the quintessential solo performance by an artist whose primary role is, or has been, 'behind the footlights' and whose reputation resides in the communal activity of stage performance. The autobiography offers its reader an apparently unique insight into the 'stage of life' of its author, *by* the author.

Ironically, Kendal was not acting 'by herself' in autobiography, any more than she had been on stage; as she herself acknowledges, she was 'relieve[d]' of the 'uncongenial labour of transcribing [her] reminiscences' by her friend, Mr Rudolph de Cordova.[4] She speaks her part and de Cordova records, advises and edits. The paradoxical image of the actor-author is at the heart of all performers' autobiography, raising as it does the issues of authenticity, individual agency and control common to all autobiography, to which must be added in the case of the actor, 'personality', celebrity – and by implication celebrity's inverse, the 'nobody'.[5] De Cordova alludes to this in his 'Editor's Note' when he expresses the hope that it has been possible for him 'to convey to the reader the full flavour of the inimitable personality whose memories and the record of whose life [is being] chronicled', that the reader would 'be afforded [the] feeling that Dame Madge is speaking to him [sic] as the spirit moves her although he is, unhappily, of necessity, divorced from the magic of the presence that held enthralled the English speaking theatre of two continents'.[6] For Kendal and de Cordova the purpose of autobiography is to make accessible not just the 'record of a life' but also the 'personality', the self, of someone whose personality has hitherto been available only through staged performance.

Kendal's autobiography comes towards the end of a period during which the volume of biographical and autobiographical material by stage actors[7] of both sexes had burgeoned and the popular 'memoir' (either an autobiography or a biography) had become 'not only a commonplace but a necessary adjunct to the role of theatre in society'.[8] These publications, whether in newspapers, journals, 'fanzines' or book form, attest to a public appetite for 'knowledge' of the private stories of the actors' lives which has not diminished. Reading these texts is problematic, particularly in the case of the actress. Jacky Bratton proposes that autobiographical material should be read 'as far as it is possible in its own terms, accepting the picture it paints as the intended activity of its authors'. Most importantly, the writers are 'intent on projecting an image of the world in which they are actors, those who do, not objects'.[9] This assertion of agency is particularly significant in reading autobiographies by women performers whose stories may have been either 'hidden from history' or appropriated by others (sensationalists, ghost writers, professional or life partners) who have consistently misrepresented the actress. Autobiography has often offered the actress an opportunity to articulate and negotiate, in Smith and Watson's words 'problems of identity and identification'. Whilst autobiography might be conceived as an act of individual self-representation, an assertion of individual identity, it is also part of 'a process of identity formation that extends beyond individuals to the group or community to which they belong'[10] or to which they want to belong. For the female performer, the group identity within which they wish to position themselves might be with their profession inside 'reputable' society mimicking the mores and attitudes of the bourgeois world or with other women within society – whether respectable or radical – or within their own working 'family' in one of the sectors of the profession.[11]

All this requires a 'polyfocal' reading of actress-autobiography, an alertness to both the social and theatrical context, to genre and to production (the market, the editorial and publication process etc), not all of which material is immediately accessible from the text itself, as well as to the 'voice' of the writer.

'To tell my story': gender and genres

Oh if I might write my own biography . . . without reservation or false colouring – it would be an invaluable document for my countrywomen in more than one particular – but *decency forbids!*   (Jane Welsh Carlyle, 1835)[12]

Histories of early women's autobiography expose the liminality of the actress-autobiographer. As Jane Carlyle's letter implies, the act of autobiography itself laid its female author open to charges of indecency, and unlike most of her contemporary female autobiographers whose domain was primarily domestic, the actress already commanded 'forbidden' space in the public domain. Her autobiography is usually situated alongside other 'odd' women 'writing about experiences not usually associated with their sex' – the female soldiers and adventurers, the businesswoman or the victim of shipwreck and pirates,[13] or other women whose experiences, both real and fictional,[14] were associated by society with their sex – the 'scandalous memoirists'.

The relationship of the fictional – often scandalous – memoir and the 'real' was very close in the eighteenth century – 'both media staked their claim to authenticity; [that] they were true to life'[15] – and this worked both for and against the actress-autobiographer. Charlotte Charke (1713–60) addresses this permeable boundary in one of the earliest actress-autobiographies, *A Narrative of the Life of Mrs Charlotte Charke* (1755): 'I have, I think, taken Care to make [my story] so interesting that every Person who reads my Volume may bear a Part in some Circumstances or other in the Perusal, as there is nothing inserted but what may daily happen to every Mortal breathing',[16] suggesting a common, ambiguous tension between entertaining her readers, and the authenticity of the events she is recording. Mindful of the association of the memoir with both real and fictional sexual scandal, Charke is, however, careful to pay 'due Regard to Decency wherever I have introduced the Passion of Love' to avoid 'fulsomely inflaming the Minds of my young Readers, or shamefully offending those of riper Years'.[17] Whilst Charke is cross-dressed for much of her 'picaresque' narrative, she is careful of both her own and her would-be lovers' reputations. Other eighteenth-century actress-autobiographers, whose circumstances – sometimes economic, sometimes erotic – had led them into 'notorious' ways, engaged directly with their standing as both actresses and women of 'publick fame'.

George Ann Bellamy (1731?–88) wrote her *Apology for the Life* (1785) to counter a previous mendacious and salacious account of her life promoted as autobiography, but 'confessed' to her own unconventional liaisons.[18] In contrast, Mary Robinson (1758–1800), in her posthumously published *Memoirs* (1801),[19] ended her life story at the point where she had established her reputation as a Shakespearean actress on the London stage, but before she is fully drawn into her notorious liaison with the Prince of Wales (see chapter 2). In doing so she implicitly positions herself as both a woman and an artist betrayed, first by her father who deserted and impoverished the family and then by her husband, who lived off her earnings and drove the family to debtor's prison. Her own daughter's introduction to the volume attempts to control its reception in the public domain, stating:

> the following brief Memoirs of a beautiful, engaging, and, in many respects, highly gifted woman require little in the way of introduction. While we may trace some little negative disingenuousness in the writer, in regard to a due admission of her own failings, sufficient of uncoloured matter of fact remains to show the exposed situation of an unprotected beauty . . . exposed to the gaze of libertine rank and fashion, under the mere nominal guardianship of a neglectful and profligate husband. Autobiography of this class is sometimes dangerous; not so that of Mrs. Robinson, who conceals not the thorns inherent in the paths along which vice externally scatters roses.[20]

In the context of the late eighteenth century, the assertion that the memoir was 'Written by Herself', as made by both Bellamy and Robinson, is both a convention and a claim to authenticity that was important for the actress-autobiographer in the face of the 'unauthorised' biography, and the 'admission of her own failings' a partial reclamation or renegotiation of her representation in the public domain.

While the tropes of normative femininity are threaded through both Bellamy and Robinson's autobiographies, and Robinson deals explicitly and unusually with pregnancy and breast-feeding, the memoirs of Sarah Siddons (1735–1831) 'perform' an apparently extraordinary act of female self-effacement for an actress so well established and well considered, and one who described herself as 'an ambitious candidate for fame'.[21] Her *Reminiscences* cover only the early part of her career and reveal little of either her private or her public life, the former being 'too painful to my feelings to dwell upon, too sacred and delicate for communication', the latter, since it would 'associate [her] with persons too August too noble, and too illustrious, for [her] to presume to mingle them with the private details of so inconsiderable so humble person as [herself]'. As a consequence she resorts to 'meer commonplace' and the retelling of 'events already partially known'.[22]

The pain of her experience of rejection by Drury Lane Theatre is framed as a model of female suffering and redemption. 'Who can conceive of this cruel disappointment,' she writes, 'the dreadful reverse of all my ambitious hopes . . . It was very near destroying me.' However, through 'indefatigueable' [sic] hard work and endurance 'for the sake of [her] poor babies' she recovers both her health and her fame.[23] While she is discreet about associating herself with persons 'too August too noble', she does include an account of George III's appreciation of her acting – 'the king was often moved to tears which he . . . vainly endeavoured to conceal behind his eye-glass, and her Majesty the Queen . . . told me in her gracious broken English that her only refuge from me was . . . to turn her back upon the stage'.[24]

In many respects Siddons's *Reminiscences* conform to the eighteenth-century norm for women's autobiography.[25] Siddons may have had 'prominence' but, as a woman, that position was vulnerable and, as told in her memoirs, was outweighed by the inequities and travails of her life. In contrast, the early nineteenth century was for women writers a period of growth and transition.[26] Women increasingly identified themselves as writers and readers, and this became the impetus for a greater confidence in all forms of writing by women including autobiography. If eighteenth-century autobiographical writing by actresses was written and read in the context of the 'scandalous memoir', then nineteenth-century autobiography is characterised by the variety and creativity of its generic models. The range of forms that emerge in the actresses' life writing in the nineteenth is wide. In addition to the traditional 'masculine' autobiography,[27] more 'feminine' modes – the diary, the journal, the populist memoir, autobiographical fiction and performance – find their way into print.[28]

Many nineteenth-century actresses kept journals, diaries, scrapbooks and copies of letters: these life writings often form the basis of the published autobiography. Fanny Kemble (1809–93), whose eight volumes of autobiography[29] were published between 1878 and 1890, uses the 'mass of letters' returned to her by her friend, Harriet St Leger, extensively in the two later autobiographical publications.[30] The resulting volumes are replete with detail, but lack the idiosyncratic narrative drive of the first volume on her childhood, intended as that was to 'amuse' the writer as she, 'having come to the garrulous time of life . . . have much leisure, and feel sure that it will amuse me to write my own reminiscences'.[31] But while the *Record of a Girlhood* provides entertaining portraits of her encounters with her aunt, Sarah Siddons, her schooldays and her reluctant entry on the stage, the letters reveal something of the 'constant present' of her later life, of people and views which, though not coherent, are immediate and apparently without artifice.

Ellen Terry (1848–1928) also uses the 'remnants of her life' in her autobiography (1908). She imagines the consternation of Mr Letts at the state of her diary, which 'neat little volume' is transformed into a 'sort of dustbin . . . swollen by newspaper cuttings, letters, dried flowers, recipes, telegrams, snapshots and what not!'[32] Terry uses her diaries (those she did not burn) and her letters strategically to reproduce relationships and praise for her performances at a remove, 'because things written at the time are considered by some people more reliable than those written years afterwards when memory calls imagination to her help'.[33] This self-portrait of a 'scatty' female, a 'womanly woman'[34] and amateur writer, belies the professionalism for which she was known on stage and the professionalism of her text. Gail Marshall describes Terry's memoir as a deliberate mimicking of her 'charming' stage persona which 'enables her to position her audience, characterising them in the role of the beloved, to be charmed, and wooed by her text, and subsequently to have their reactions influenced if not determined by the decisions that she as a writer is making'.[35] The personal documents are the key to Terry's negotiation of gender and professional image.

Other actress-autobiographers, from the eighteenth century onwards, used letters extensively in their memoirs. Mrs Patrick Campbell (1865–1940) goes so far as to call her autobiography *My Life and Some Letters* (1922). In the later part of the book, the letters take over the story-telling, giving at times a coherence, as in the chapter dealing with the experiences and death of her son, Beo, at the front in the First World War, and at times a sense of fragmentation, when letters from luminaries and lovers are mixed inchoately with thoughts on life and the work of the stage in what is perhaps an accidental reflection of a career-life trajectory.[36] The use of letters and diaries by the renowned Polish actress, Helena Modjeska (1840–1949), in her *Memories and Impressions*, is far more consistent than Campbell's and, like Terry's memoirs, skilfully uses letters to allow *others* to reflect on her successes, and selections from letters, diaries and scrapbooks (fig. 15) to express emotion more immediately and dramatically than the controlled and reflective narrative elsewhere allows. At one point, writing extravagantly to an unnamed friend, she portrays herself as a reluctant 'star': 'Ah! if I could be satisfied and contented in the midst of applause and flattery, and not desire anything more of myself! If I could enjoy the present moment sincerely, foolishly, gather the flowers I find on my path of life, bind them in a bouquet, drink in its perfume, and be glad and happy!'[37] Elsewhere she writes soberly of the 'unfortunate condition of the "star" system . . . [on] some young actors and actresses . . . raised suddenly to the dignity of a "star" before being quite ripe for the position'.[38] In contrast, the American Elizabeth Robins (1862–1952), in *Theatre and Friendship* (1932), reproduces letters to herself and Florence Bell from Henry

Fig. 15. 'The return from America': caricature by Paprocki soon after Modjeska's first appearance in America, 1876. (Author's collection.)

James[39] which allow her, indirectly, to record an account not just of her theatrical career in its most significant period (1891–1900), but of her own intellectual engagement with the art of theatre. Lena Ashwell (1872–1957) thanks her fellow artists for the use of *their* letters and diaries in the writing of *Modern Troubadours* (1922), without which the record of their, and her own, 'not altogether unimportant work in the Great War' could not have been completed.[40]

Not all actresses shared the view that the letter or diary had currency in the present. Looking back at her diary, Robins observes that

> I write about those days at a great distance – not only in terms of time. I cannot feel close to that young woman who went about in my name so long ago . . . She is often strange to me, sometimes antipathetic, now and then incredible, but for the self-conviction that stares me in the face from the scribbled page. There too I am at odds with her.[41]

But there are other issues with the publication of the diary. Few well-known performers in the nineteenth century were willing to embrace the exposure involved in the publication of a diary. The publication of a whole diary is rare, and it is significant that one of the notable stage examples, the *Diary of an Actress* (1885), is anonymous.[42] The author of the *Diary* in bringing 'the realities of stage life' to the knowledge of the public, also offers herself to '[o]utsiders' who she says, can have 'no possible opportunity of forming an opinion of . . . women, unknown beyond their immediate circle, their identity merged' – unlike that of her dedicatee, Mrs Kendal – 'in the characters they assume behind the footlights'.[43] The *Diary* shows not only 'much of the practical side of [the] profession . . . as [the author] was forced to realise it from day to day',[44] but also the exemplary personal journey of a new female entrant to the profession with an emphasis on its trials and temptations.

In this sense the *Diary of an Actress* is not untypical of the majority of mature autobiographies from the mid-nineteenth century onwards in that it reflects the 'mode of a *künstleroman* . . . works [that] feature the emergence and struggles of an artistic sensibility'.[45] Though many, like the anonymous diarist's, are stories of early struggles – from 'Perdita' Robinson's *Memoirs* (1801) to Robins's *Both Sides of the Curtain* (1940) – others written at the end of a professional life offer 'the "story of a calling" . . . a retrospective on a person's theatrical career, which has an arc towards success'.[46] Some, like Mrs Kendal, reflect with satisfaction on their careers and their eminence, others, like Mary Anderson, satisfaction that, despite a successful career, circumstances have enabled them to retire from 'the practice of [their] art . . . grown as time went on more and more distasteful' to them.[47] Or Lena Ashwell, writing as 'one who found the way of art stony and full of bitterness'.[48] Refreshingly, some 'comparatively unknown' actresses do not tell tales of struggle and failure, particularly as conditions in the theatre improved into the twentieth century. Maud Gill, who worked largely in the British provinces during the first half of the twentieth century, writes cheerfully in mid-career that despite her 'obscurity' she 'does not regret having entered "the profession." I could never,' she continues, 'feel that my life on the Stage has been a failure for I have enjoyed every minute of it . . . its glorious uncertainties, its "ups" and "downs".'[49]

Other actresses, looking back over a career, use their autobiographies to reposition their reputation, not as a defensive act, but, as Maggie B. Gale argues in relation to Lena Ashwell, in order to seize 'the opportunity to insert herself and her career into a history of English theatre, a history largely written and inhabited by men'. In four autobiographical works, Ashwell emphasises the 'professional over the personal', drawing attention to her managerial career, her war work and her pioneering leadership of the Lena Ashwell Players.[50] In a similar fashion, Cicely Hamilton (1872–1952), in her autobiography, *Life Errant* (1935), not only foregrounds 'the professional over the personal' but the 'political over the personal' in chapters on 'Women on the Warpath' – on her role in the women's suffrage movement – and 'Myth and Reality' – on her experiences in the First World War. She unapologetically expresses a political consciousness throughout her autobiography.[51]

Perhaps the most elusive of the autobiographical genres to emerge in the nineteenth century is the 'fictional work about the theatre written by someone whose career has been in theatre . . . which often displaces personal experiences and values into narrative'.[52] Thomas Postlewait cites the example of Elizabeth Robins's novels which can, he suggests 'offer some symbolic parallels to events in her acting career and life'.[53] Other novels are more specific. American-born 'unknown', Ina Rozant (1862–?) wrote two novels of the stage. The first, An Actress's Pilgrimage (1906), gives an engaging account of four months in a fit-up tour of The Days of Nero, very obviously a thinly disguised version of her own experience touring with Wilson Barrett's hugely popular The Sign of the Cross.[54] Florence Farr (1860–1917), perhaps disingenuously, perhaps mindful of possible legal action, prefaces her novel The Dancing Faun (1894) with a disclaimer: 'Owing to circumstances which have arisen since this story was written in the summer of 1893, it seems necessary to state that it is purely a work of imagination, and that none of the characters or events are taken from real life.'[55] The novel is a riposte to Shaw's rendition of their triangular relationship with Jenny Patterson in The Philanderer (1893). It was written 'more or less' as a joke'[56] and the 'hero', George Travers, is a satire on Shaw, the philanderer, himself. The reader of Farr's novel, especially those in their immediate circle, could not escape the autobiographical element, and this, with the frontispiece by Aubrey Beardsley, was undoubtedly responsible for the book's moderate success.

By the beginning of the twentieth century, the actress-autobiography was no longer characterised by the 'scandalous memoir' – though that did not disappear entirely – but more often than not by a narrative assertion of a professional self which mirrored the increased confidence, social and theatrical acceptability and education of the writers.

'See the players': towards a polyfocal reading

At its simplest, the actress advertises, like the now 'disappeared' actress, Elizabeth Macauley (1785?–1837),[57] that they are 'desirous . . . of being known and understood' in 'the most interesting species of biographical literature . . . because the most authentic'. Macauley writes:

> I write my life, because I wish it should be written; I send it to the world, because I wish it to be read; and above all, I send it forth because I desire to make advantage from its sale! This though a secondary motive, is nevertheless a very prominent one. The hey-day of my youth is past . . . I would not unwillingly eat the bread of dependence, or wait till the day of destitution comes, before I make one final effort to shield myself from the perils which have so often attended the declining years of talent and industry.[58]

Underlying this, however, is another, more political agenda. Macauley was writing from Marshalsea debtor's prison, and uses the autobiography to counter the 'innumerable . . . insults, degradations, and anxieties [she] had to encounter' in her career, and the '[m]any . . . petty efforts made to humble my pride'.[59] She states that she does not 'send forth these records as others have done, under the ambiguous title of *An Apology*. I am not disposed to apologize to my fellow beings on this earth for having been a sojourner amongst them.'[60] Few actresses take so uncompromising a stand.

The 'political' agenda in other actresses' autobiographies is more socially conventional and ameliorative, particularly from the mid-nineteenth century on. Adelaide Ristori (1822–1906) set out 'thinking it might not be unprofitable to those interested in art to follow the daily struggle of an artist . . . minimising [n]either its enthusiasms [n]or its disillusions'.[61] From a position of more modest attainment, the author of *The Diary of an Actress* writes: 'It has struck me that just now . . . a glimpse of the real life of a provincial actress might be of some interest, perhaps of some use.'[62] A similar exemplary purpose can be found in Madge Kendal's assertion that she will 'do what lies in her power to keep unblemished the best traditions of the stage' which she has 'protected by practice and precept' throughout her life, by 'omitting all reference to unsavoury details' in her reminiscences.[63] Clara Morris (1846/8–1925) writes one of her several autobiographies, *Stage Confidences* (1902), ostensibly in answer to those 'letters from young girls and women . . . [s]ome extravagant, some enthusiastic, some foolish, and some unutterably pathetic . . . [e]very actress of prominence receives', answering with 'brutal truthfulness' the question 'What chance has a girl in private life of getting on the stage?'[64] Mary Anderson (1859–1940), 'after five happy years of married life and retirement', is persuaded to write her 'few recollections' by similar motives: 'to show [young girls] that the glitter of the stage is not all gold, and thus to do a little towards making them realize how serious an undertaking it is to adopt a life so full of hardships, humiliations, and even dangers'.[65] While Eva Moore (1870–1925) 'thought that some day' her children, both actors, 'might like to know how different things were in the "old days"; like to know how one worked, and studied, and tried to save; might like to know something of the road over which their father and mother travelled . . . it might at least interest and amuse them'.[66]

Other actresses express more personal motives. Charlotte Charke, in an act of overt self-promotion, paradoxically dedicates her *Narrative* to herself in an attempt 'to illustrate those WONDERFUL QUALIFICATIONS by which you have so EMINENTLY DISTINGUISH'D YOURSELF'.[67] Whilst much of the book's purpose is to 'entertain my Friends', the book is also addressed to healing a 'BREACH BETWEEN A FATHER[68] AND A CHILD, who wanted only the Satisfaction of knowing her Name was no longer hateful to him.'[69] It is possible to see other autobiographical works, usually by less successful female performers, as attempts to insert themselves as 'somebodies' into the 'hierarchies and histories of the theatre',[70] or to retrieve a lost reputation. The actress and militant suffragist Kitty Marion (1871–1944) is just one example, who, writing in poverty in America, strove through her autobiography to recreate her 'glory days' when she was actively engaged, first in a modestly successful provincial stage career in Britain, and then notoriously with the women's movement in Britain and America. But her 'time had passed', and despite attracting the attention of the *New Yorker*'s 'Where Are They Now?' column,[71] her autobiography remains unpublished.[72]

Many actresses acknowledge and explore the multiple selves in their lives. It is not difficult to find examples across the period. Sarah Bernhardt's (1844–1923) memoirs are called *Ma Double Vie* (*My Double Life*, 1907).[73] Modjeska writes that she has 'two lives, and one is so different from the other that the transition oftentimes is puzzling, if not painful. My artificial life is too real at times and that is what makes the trouble'.[74] Tilly Wedekind (1886–1970) projects this ambiguous duality when she names her life story *Lulu: Die Rolle meines Lebens* (*Lulu: The Role of my Life*),[75] using the name of the character that had been so crucial to both her public and private life. In *To Tell My Story* (1948), Irene Vanbrugh (1872–1949) develops this problematic relationship further:

> Who and what is the person who spends most of his or her life impersonating other people, impersonating them strongly enough not only to convince themselves, but to convince thousands of others? . . . What then is the reality; how far has this constant re-creation of yourself obliterated the original? . . . [To be an actress] a sort of double life must be led.[76]

If the impersonation of others on stage created a double self, the stage character and the 'original', in creating the autobiographical 'character' actresses are often developing a 'third' self. Sometimes this is done with a specific object of undermining the character that has been created of them by others. George Ann Bellamy is not alone when, in her *Apology* she seeks to 'exert some control over the discourse of her "frailty" which had been used against her "in a wretched production, published in the year 1761" and full of "innumerable falsehoods"';[77] or Farr, in seeking to counter Shaw's portrait of her in *The Philanderer*. Bella Merlin argues that the reader can discern in Tilly Wedekind's autobiography an 'underlying desire to emerge from the often oppressive shadow of [her husband] Wedekind's fame and establish her own autonomous identity'.[78]

Autobiography is also used by the actress to negotiate her 'celebrity' self, yet another facet of the performer's public persona: the 'character' created at the intersection of 'individuals and institutions, markets and media'.[79] Some actresses sought to play down 'personality' in both their professional life and autobiography. Modjeska writes of the impossibility of 'leaving out entirely one's wretched "I"' in her autobiography, but vows to write 'discreetly' just as she seeks to eliminate 'self' in her performances.[80] She laments the impact of 'achieved' celebrity[81] on her life:

[A] woman who has dared to raise her head above the others, who has extended her eager hands for laurels, who has not hesitated to expose and throw to the crowd all that her soul possessed of love, despair, and passion, – that woman has given the right to the curious multitude to interfere in her private affairs, to rummage in the most secret recesses of her life . . . They censure her sadness, they make commentaries invariably false . . . they touch those who are dear to us.[82]

Other actresses embraced the 'public intimacy'[83] that inevitably attached itself to public success, but the autobiography became an important, but by no means consistent, tool for the 'committed self-publicist' to exploit 'the mechanisms available for creating and marketing a celebrity persona'.[84] Sos Eltis has examined the ways in which Bernhardt, Terry, Mrs Patrick Campbell and Lillie Langtry (1853–1929) each 'suppressed' or elided the 'facts' of their lives. She argues that while Bernhardt

appeared insouciant about her off-stage notoriety, even encouraged it as a complement to her on-stage roles of adulteress and courtesan, Terry, Langtry and Campbell sought to balance their commercial success with a degree of social respectability, not only through their memoirs, but also through their performances in the press and on stage.[85]

Langtry's autobiography, *The Days I Knew* (1925), fails to mention her affair with the Prince of Wales[86] and does not acknowledge her daughter, just as Bernhardt fails to refer to the illegitimacy of her son, Maurice, and Terry fails to refer to any details of her marriages and liaisons. The omissions made in actress-autobiographies are too many to list, but whilst most are examples of 'agency' or what Cicely Hamilton refers to as 'the Victorian tradition of reticence', [87] it is important to note at least one known example of coercion. It is not untypical of actress-autobiography of the period that Lillah McCarthy's (1875–1960) autobiography, *Myself and Friends* (1933),[88] refers to her marriage to Harley Granville Barker in just one line, but the censoring by Barker himself of all reference to her first husband is noteworthy. According to C. B. Purdom, Barker insisted on the removal of Shaw's

Foreword that discussed the divorce, and excised all allusion to himself in the book. The result is the omission not only of the eleven-year personal relationship between McCarthy and Barker, but also of the professional one.[89]

Some actress-autobiographers, rather than frustrating their public's 'prurient curiosity', market with relish their 'notoriety'. Like some of her eighteenth-century predecessors, Caroline – 'La Belle' – Otero (1868–1965), the Spanish music hall and operetta performer, 'wears her lovers like a coronet'[90] in her autobiography, and discusses at length the '[r]ough or tender seducers; ironic satyrs that look upon you hungrily; ingenious adorers, full of timid attentions; hard, complacent rich men who can pay for their pleasure and will take no refusal'.[91] Without flaunting her conquests as Otero does, the author of the *Diary of an Actress* does include details of both the unwanted advances made to her by men and her 'stupid' romantic 'adventures'.[92]

If the 'Victorian tradition of reticence' elides many close relationships, the autobiographies are often testimonies to friendships and networks. Dedications and guest introductions to autobiography can be illuminating. While the early autobiographies are usually dedicated to theatrical or social patrons, many in the nineteenth and twentieth centuries are to, or by, fellow members of the theatrical community who carry, in themselves, significant cachet. Thus, *An Actress's Pilgrimage* is dedicated to Rozant's 'hero', Ellen Terry, the *Diary of an Actress* to Mrs Kendal and Clare Morris's *Stage Confidences* to Mary Anderson. G. B. Shaw provides 'an aside' for Lillah McCarthy and a number of epistles for Elizabeth Robins's *Both Sides of the Curtain*. Noel Coward introduces Constance Collier's *Harlequinade* (1929) and Sir Cedric Hardwicke introduces Maud Gill's *See the Players* (1938). Though a large number of actress-autobiographies are dedicated with due thanks to supportive husbands, there are the occasional egotistical prefaces. Perhaps one the most self-promoting is that to Mrs Patrick Campbell's *My Life and Some Letters*:

> I came out by the stage-door of the Duke of York's Theatre at a quarter-past twelve on the first night of the production of *Madam Sand* . . . A girl of about fifteen, bare-headed, was standing against a wall, evidently waiting for someone. I said:
> 'What are you waiting for?'
> 'To see you . . . I walked here early this morning. I wanted to get a good place to see the play, and I did: and now I have been waiting to see *you*.'
> Then with a wild young look of ecstasy, she vanished into the night. To her I dedicate this book.[93]

Conclusion: by herself?

No autobiographical act is entirely singular: Rudolph de Cordova assisted Madge Kendal and Eva Moore dedicates *Exits and Entrances* (1932) to her husband, Harry V. Esmond, '[w]hose words head each chapter of what is really his book and mine'.[94] Many actress-autobiographers thank their husbands or the friends who have persuaded them to embark on the autobiographical journey, self-deprecatingly emphasising their own reluctance to undertake a task for which they are so unfitted, an act of 'little womanliness' that often sits ill with their life stories or professional achievements. Other partners (life, business and children) play a more significant role in the creative process. Few autobiographies that we know in the period are actually ghost-written, the notable exception being W. Macqueen Pope's role in writing Julia Neilson's (1868–1957) *This Time for Remembrance* (1940). It is possible that the Reverend H. C. Shuttleworth, the editor of the *Diary of an Actress*, was more than editor, but he claims to have 'left the writer to tell her own story, adding nothing, and curtailing little'.[95] Lillah McCarthy's second husband is credited with the re-creation of her autobiography after the destruction wreaked by Harley Granville Barker.[96] Christopher St John helped Ellen Terry in the editing of *The Story of My Life*, and both St John and Terry's daughter, Edith Craig, contributed significantly to the posthumous version published as *Ellen Terry's Memoirs* (1933) with 'preface, notes and additional biographical chapters', a similar role to that performed by Mary Robinson's daughter more than two hundred years earlier.

These types of knowledge, of processes, of social and theatrical contexts and of genre are all important in our reading of actress-autobiographies; they moderate and augment our understanding of the part that self-representation, identity and identification plays in the actress's life story; but ultimately, the autobiography has to be read as a kind of solo performance, 'By Herself', to get the 'full flavour of the inimitable personality whose memories and the record of whose life [is being] chronicled'.[97]

NOTES

1. I use the word 'autobiography' advisedly as an umbrella term to cover what is a highly contested lexicographical, historical and ontological terrain. See Sidonie Smith and Julia Watson, eds., *De/Colonizing the Subject: The Politics of Gender in Women's Autobiography* (Minneapolis: University of Minnesota Press, 1992).
2. Recent volumes on gender, auto/biography and performance include: Maggie B. Gale and Viv Gardner, eds., *Auto/biography and Identity: Women, Theatre and Performance* (Manchester: Manchester University Press, 2004); Lynn C. Miller, Jacqueline Taylor and M. Heather Carver, eds., *Voices Made Flesh: Performing*

Women's Autobiography (Madison: University of Wisconsin Press, 2003); Sidonie Smith and Julie Watson, eds., *Interfaces: Women/Autobiography/Image/ Performance* (Ann Arbor: University of Michigan Press, 2002).

3. Madge Kendal, *Dame Madge Kendal: By Herself* (London: John Murray, 1933), p. viii.

4. Ibid. Rudolph de Cordova (d. 1941), arts journalist, creator of scenarios for silent film (*Romeo and Juliet*, 1916) and biographer of a number of prominent actors.

5. See Viv Gardner, 'The Three Nobodies: Autobiographical Strategies in the Work of Alma Ellerslie, Kitty Marion and Ina Rozant', in Gale and Gardner, eds., *Auto/biography and Identity*, pp. 10–38.

6. Kendal, *Dame Madge Kendal*, p. ix.

7. Much of what is argued could be said of early screen actresses.

8. Thomas Postlewait, 'Autobiography and Theatre History', in Thomas Postlewait and Bruce A. McConachie, eds., *Interpreting the Theatrical Past: Essays in the Historiography of Performance* (Iowa City: University of Iowa Press, 1989), p. 249. See also Thomas Postlewait, 'Theatre Autobiographies: Some Preliminary Concerns for the Theatre Historian', *Assaph C* 16 (2000), pp. 157–72.

9. Jacky Bratton, *New Readings in Theatre History* (Cambridge: Cambridge University Press, 2003), p. 101.

10. Ibid.

11. See Mary Jean Corbett, *Representing Femininity: Middle Class Subjectivity in Victorian and Edwardian Women's Autobiography* (New York: Oxford University Press, 1992), p. 108; Gardner, 'The Three Nobodies'.

12. *I Too Am Here: Selections from the Letters of Jane Welsh Carlyle*, ed. Alan and Mary McQueen Simpson (Cambridge: Cambridge University Press, 1977), p. 74. The phrase quoted in the title to this section is taken from Irene Vanbrugh, *To Tell My Story* (London: Hutchinson and Co., 1948).

13. Estelle C. Jelinek, *The Tradition of Women's Autobiography: from Antiquity to the Present* (Philadelphia: Xlibris Corporation, 2003), p. 69.

14. Daniel Defoe's *Moll Flanders* and Samuel Richardson's *Pamela* and *Clarissa* are some of the most obvious examples of 'fictional memoirs'.

15. Lynda M. Thompson, *The Scandalous Memoirists: Constantia Phillips, Laetitia Pilkington and the Shame of 'Publick Fame'* (Manchester: Manchester University Press, 2000), p. 1.

16. Charlotte Charke, *A Narrative of the Life of Mrs Charlotte Charke, Daughter of Colley Cibber* (London: Constable and Co., 1929 [1755]), p. 16.

17. Ibid.

18. George Ann Bellamy, *An Apology for the Life of George Ann Bellamy, Late of Covent Garden, Written by Herself* (London: For the Author, 1785).

19. Mary Darby Robinson, *Memoirs of the late Mrs Mary Robinson, Written by Herself, with some Posthumous Pieces*, ed. and introduced by Mary Elizabeth Robinson (London: R. Phillips, 1801).

20. Ibid., pp. v–vi.

21. Sarah Siddons, *The Reminiscences of Sarah Kemble Siddons, 1773–1785*, ed. William Van Lennep (Cambridge, MA: Widener Library, 1942), p. 16.

22. Ibid., pp. 1–2.

23. Ibid., pp. 6–7.

24. Ibid., p. 13.

25. Valerie Sanders, *The Private Lives of Victorian Women* (New York: Harvester Wheatsheaf, 1989), p. 47.
26. See Jelinek, *The Tradition of Women's Autobiography*, p. 73.
27. Critics have argued that the 'male' autobiography is characterised as 'depicting the growth of a mind or the development of career', something that was 'alien and inappropriate for women [who] were not encouraged to think of themselves in those terms': Sanders, *The Private Lives of Victorian Women*, p. 11.
28. Autobiographical performance is rare before the twentieth century: for an exception see Helen Nicholson, 'Not Alone: Georgina Weldon's Dramatic Protest Against the Lunacy Laws', *Women and Theatre Occasional Papers* (1996), pp. 70–95.
29. Fanny Kemble, *Record of a Girlhood*, 3 vols. (London: Richard Bentley, 1878); *Records of Later Life*, 3 vols. (London: Richard Bentley, 1882); and *Further Records 1848–1883*, 2 vols. (London: Richard Bentley, 1890).
30. Kemble, *Further Records*, vol. 1, p. 145.
31. Kemble, *Record of a Girlhood*, vol. 1, p. 1.
32. Ellen Terry, *The Story of My Life* (London: Hutchinson and Co., 1908), p. vii.
33. Terry, *The Story of My Life*, p. 236.
34. Ibid., p. 211.
35. Gail Marshall, *Actresses on the Victorian Stage* (Cambridge: Cambridge University Press, 1998), p. 179.
36. Mrs Patrick Campbell, *My Life and Some Letters* (London: Hutchinson and Co., 1922).
37. Helena Modjeska, *Memories and Impressions* (New York: The Macmillan Company, 1910), p. 417.
38. Ibid., p. 521.
39. Elizabeth Robins, *Theatre and Friendship* (New York: G. P. Putnam's Sons, 1932).
40. Lena Ashwell, *Modern Troubadours* (London: Gyldendale, 1922), p. v.
41. Elizabeth Robins, *Both Sides of the Curtain* (London: William Heinemann Ltd., 1940), p. 18. See Mary Jean Corbett, 'Performing Identities: Actresses and Autobiography', in Kerry Powell, ed., *The Cambridge Companion to Victorian and Edwardian Theatre* (Cambridge: Cambridge University Press, 2004), and Marshall, *Actresses on the Victorian Stage*, pp. 174–7.
42. [Alma Ellerslie?], *Diary of an Actress, or the Realities of Stage Life*, ed. H. C. Shuttleworth (London: Griffin, Farran and Co., 1885), reprinted in *Nineteenth Century Theatre and Film* 32.1 (Summer 2005). Also see Gardner, 'The Three Nobodies'.
43. Ibid., pp. 159–60.
44. Ibid., p. 11.
45. Postlewait, 'Theatre Autobiographies', pp. 169–70.
46. Ibid.
47. Mary Anderson, *A Few Memories* (London: Osgood, McIlvaine and Co., 1896), p. 251.
48. Lena Ashwell, *Myself a Player* (London: Michael Joseph, 1936), p. 7.
49. Maud Gill, *See the Players* (London: Hutchinson and Co., 1938), p. 13.
50. Maggie B. Gale, 'Lena Ashwell and Auto/biographical Negotiations of the Professional Self', in Gale and Gardner, eds., *Auto/biography and Identity*, pp. 99–125.

51. Cicely Hamilton, *Life Errant* (London: J. M. Dent, 1935).
52. Postlewait, 'Theatrical Autobiographies', p. 167.
53. Ibid.
54. Ina Rozant, *An Actress's Pilgrimage* (London: T. Sealey Clark and Co. Ltd., 1906). Rozant's second, less obviously autobiographical stage novel was *Life's Understudies* (London: T. Sealey Clark and Co. Ltd., 1907).
55. Florence Farr, *The Dancing Faun* (London: Elkin Matthews and John Lane, 1894), Preface.
56. Cited in Josephine Johnson, *Florence Farr: Bernard Shaw's New Woman* (Totowa, NJ: Rowman and Littlefield, 1975), p. 64.
57. Elizabeth Wright Macauley, actress, solo performer, and Owenite lecturer, had some reputation on the Dublin and London stage until dismissed by Kean in 1818 as 'incapable'. See J. S. Bratton, 'Miss Scott and Miss Macauley: "Genius Comes in All Disguises"', *Theatre Survey* 37.1 (1996), pp. 59–74.
58. Elizabeth Wright Macauley, *Autobiographical Memoirs of Miss Macauley, Written under the Title of Elizabeth, or 'A Plain and Simple Tale of Truth'* (London: Charles Fox, 1835), pp. 10, 13. Cited in Jane Rendall, '"A Short Account of my Unprofitable Life": Autobiographies of Working Class Women', in Trev Lynn Broughton and Linda Anderson, eds., *Women's Lives/Women's Times: New Essays in Auto/biography* (New York: SUNY Press, 1997), pp. 31–50.
59. 'Statement of Miss Macauley's engagement at Drury Lane, in the Spring of 1818', *The Times*, 18 April 1819.
60. Cited in Bratton, 'Miss Scott and Miss Macauley', p. 63.
61. Adelaide Ristori, *Memoirs and Artistic Studies*, trans. G. Mantellini (New York: Benjamin Blom 1969 [1907]), p. ix.
62. [Alma Ellerslie?], *Diary of an Actress*, p. 11.
63. Kendal, *Dame Madge Kendal*, pp. ix–x.
64. Clara Morris, *Stage Confidences* (Boston: Lothrop Publishing Company, 1902), pp. 11–12. Canadian-born Morris wrote three autobiographical works.
65. Mary Anderson, *A Few Memories*, p. 1.
66. Eva Moore, *Exits and Entrances* (London: Chapman Hall, 1923), pp. 1–2.
67. Charke, *A Narrative of the Life of Mrs Charlotte Charke*, p. 13.
68. The Poet Laureate and actor Colley Cibber (1703–58).
69. Charke, *A Narrative of the Life of Mrs Charlotte Charke*, p. 220
70. See Gardner, 'The Three Nobodies'.
71. 'Where Are they Now? The Crusader', *New Yorker*, 4 July 1936, pp. 22–4.
72. Kitty Marion, 'Autobiography', unpublished manuscript, Museum of London. See Gardner, 'The Three Nobodies'.
73. Sarah Bernhardt, *Ma Double Vie* (Paris: Charpentier et Fasquelle, 1907).
74. Modjeska, *Memories and Impressions*, p. 418.
75. Tilly Wedekind, *Lulu: Das Rolle meines Lebens* (Munich: Rutten and Loening Verlag, 1969).
76. Vanbrugh, *To Tell My Story*, pp. 101–2.
77. Thompson, *The Scandalous Memoirists*, p. 180, citing Bellamy, *An Apology*, p. 3.
78. Bella Merlin, 'Tilly Wedekind', in Gale and Gardner eds., *Auto/biography and Identity*, p. 127.

79. Mary Luckhurst and Jane Moody, eds., *Theatre and Celebrity in Britain, 1660–2000* (Houndmills: Palgrave Macmillan, 2005), p. 1.
80. Modjeska, *Memories and Impressions*, pp. 15, 549–50.
81. Chris Rojek, *Celebrity* (London: Reaktion Books, 2001), pp. 17–18.
82. Modjeska, *Memories and Impressions*, p. 245.
83. Joseph Roach, 'Public Intimacy: The Prior History of "It"', in Mary Luckhurst and Jane Moody, eds., *Theatre and Celebrity in Britain, 1660–2000*, pp. 15–30.
84. Sos Eltis, 'Private Lives and Public Spaces: Reputation, Celebrity and the Late Victorian Actress', in Luckhurst and Moody, eds., *Theatre and Celebrity in Britain*, pp. 170–1.
85. Ibid., p. 171.
86. Ibid., p. 173.
87. Hamilton, *Life Errant*, p. 298.
88. Lillah McCarthy, *Myself and Friends* (London: Thornton Butterworth, Ltd., 1933).
89. See C. B. Purdom, *Harley Granville Barker: Man of the Theatre, Dramatist and Scholar* (London: Rockcliff, 1955), pp. 190–1.
90. Caroline Otero, *My Story* (London: A. M. Philpott, 1927), p. 10.
91. Ibid., p. 192.
92. [Alma Ellerslie], *Diary of an Actress*, p. 17.
93. Campbell, *My Life and Some Letters*, Preface.
94. Moore, *Exits and Entrances*, p. v.
95. [Alma Ellerslie], *Diary of an Actress*, p. 10.
96. See Purdom, *Harley Granville Barker*, p. 191.
97. Kendal, *Dame Madge Kendal*, p. ix.

FURTHER READING

Campbell, Mrs Patrick. *My Life and Some Letters*. London: Hutchinson and Co., 1922.

Corbett, Mary J. *Representing Femininity: Middle Class Subjectivity in Victorian and Edwardian Women's Autobiography*. New York: Oxford University Press, 1992.

Gale, Maggie B., and Viv Gardner, eds. *Auto/biography and Performance: Women, Theatre and Performance*. Manchester. Manchester University Press, 2004.

Gill, Maud. *See the Players*. London: Hutchinson and Co., 1938.

Hamilton, Cicely. *Life Errant*. London: J. M. Dent, 1935.

Kendal, Madge. *Dame Madge Kendal: By Herself*. London: John Murray, 1933.

Marshall, Gail. *Actresses on the Victorian Stage: Feminine Performance and the Galatea Myth*. Cambridge: Cambridge University Press, 1998.

McCarthy, Lillah. *Myself and Friends*. London: Thornton Butterworth, Ltd., 1933.

Miller, L. C., J. Taylor, J. Carver and M. Carver, eds. *Voices Made Flesh: Performing Women's Autobiography*. Madison: University of Wisconsin Press, 2003.

Moore, Eva. *Exits and Entrances*. London: Chapman Hall, 1923.

Morris, Clara. *Stage Confidences*. Boston: Lothrop Publishing Company, 1902.

Otero, Caroline. *My Story*. London: A. M. Philpott, 1927.

Ristori, Adelaide. *Memoirs and Artistic Studies*. trans. G. Mantellini. New York: Benjamin Blom, 1969 [1907].

Robins, Elizabeth. *Both Sides of the Curtain*. London: William Heinemann Ltd., 1940

Theatre and Friendship. New York: G. P. Putnam's Sons, 1932.

Stokes, John, Michael Booth and Susan Bassnett. *Bernhardt, Terry, Duse: The Actress in her Time*. Cambridge: Cambridge University Press, 1988.

Vanbrugh, Irene. *To Tell My Story*. London: Hutchinson and Co., 1948.

10

CHRISTINE GLEDHILL

The screen actress from silence to sound

> Who are these that come captivating us from the golden gates and cloudless
> skies of the Far West, this new generation of silent sirens, begotten by the
> swift magic of the camera, and who, though bereft of the old seductions of
> speech and song, do yet most potently enthral our multitudes in every town,
> ravishing and titillating the common imagination with allurements of dumb
> mimicry, and streaking the vast expanses of our drab modernity with ultra
> rainbow rays of romance?
> Henry Arthur Jones, *New York Times*, 1921

In the 1910s film acting was recognised in Britain and America as one among
a range of new professional opportunities for the modern girl. At the same
time players from legitimate theatre began to test cinema as an alternative
career outlet, while the trade, fan and journalistic press debated the impact
of filmmaking on the actor and the differences between the two forms. As
a powerful star system evolved in America, arguments began to distinguish
between stardom and acting. Much of this ferment turned on the pleasures
and anxieties aroused by new forms of public visibility centred on the film
actress. These debates are significant less for their outcomes – for there was
no decisive separation of screen from stage acting – but for the issues and
discursive constructions they put into play. Moreover, because cinema developed transnationally, these debates, albeit forced to engage with the dominant cinematic vernacular evolved by Hollywood, were crucially inflected
by local conditions.

Within a fluid context of international exchange, this chapter examines
the impact of film on the actress through the lens of three specific instances:
first, the curious career of Florence Turner, America's first 'real film star',
who switchbacked between America and Britain; second, the controversy
about the British film actress – contrasted with the American star – which
raged throughout the 1920s; and finally, the example of Madeleine Carroll,
who coming to prominence at the end of the 1920s in British cinema, made
the crossover not only into the talkies but into Hollywood, developing her
career as a transnational film actress to 1949.

Screen players

Initially, Richard deCordova argues, the figures who appeared in films were not discussed in terms of 'acting'.[1] Until 1902 what films showcased were the remarkable feats of the cinematic apparatus itself in reproducing the movement of things, the natural world and human beings, together with the fantastical properties of the technology. Before 1906 film catalogues are dominated by travelogues, topicals, sports films, newsreels, trick films and 'acts' (records of music hall and vaudeville turns). People were either caught about their routine work and leisure activities, or where short comic or story events (e.g. chase films) were involved, drawn from the film company's family or workforce. Such films depended, deCordova suggests, on physical action more allied to acrobatics than acting. Before this could be recognised, attention had to shift from the technology of film to the role of performers. Not least, the players had to be 'named'.

Much has been written about the anxiety of film companies at the prospect of losing control over players' conditions and salaries should they achieve public notoriety and about actors' unwillingness to expose their work in an upstart, disreputable form to their employers and audiences. However, more relevant, deCordova claims, was the emergence of mutually reinforcing economic and discursive conditions facilitating a product in which players could be central and acting practices defined and discussed. Economic growth required not only systematic production methods but social respectability, thereby attracting more inclusive audiences to fill the purpose-built cinemas appearing from 1909 onwards. To this end fiction proved a more predictable and controllable form than documentary.[2] The consequent shift towards drama and comedy put demands on the expressive powers of the performer, and now that players received more screen time and narrative prominence, reviewers and audiences began to isolate performance as part of cinema's aesthetic appeal. However, there were a variety of performance traditions on which film performers, critics and fans could draw, and considerable ambivalence about the status of the film player.

In America, writes Richard deCordova, a discourse of acting derived from legitimate theatre and focusing on the individual player not only led film narration in a particular direction – 'classic narrative cinema' – but fuelled a star phenomenon which, drawing on other media, reached beyond films to the player's life. The import in 1909 and imitation of French *Films d'art*, featuring famous stage actors and actresses, gave significant impetus to this process. Until now the main studios, although already employing stock companies of players, had not found it necessary to publicise their names. But the flurry of excitement around the appearance of theatrical 'greats' on film, together with clear evidence that audiences, with the help of reviewers, were identifying their favourite players by pet names – the 'Biograph Girl' (Florence Lawrence), the 'Vitagraph Girl' (Florence Turner), 'Little Mary' (Mary Pickford, so named after one of her film characters) – highlighted the promotional value of film players. The year 1909–10 became the year of the 'picture personality', floated on the strength of filmic rather than theatrical fame.

Although deCordova offers a convincing account of the emergence of the American star system, he confines 'acting' to psychological and narrative character development of classic cinema. This ignores performance traditions in which pictorial gesture, poses, bodily displays – in the popular theatre of melodrama and visual spectacle, fairground sideshows, magic lantern and picture postcard series – provided the centre of attraction. Such traditions were significant to the practice of Florence Turner and to the development of British cinema where she would flourish (fig. 16).

Florence Turner, from 'Vitagraph Girl' to 'Bernhardt of the Screen'

The career of Florence Turner, who vies with Florence Lawrence of Biograph as 'the first real film star', reveals some of the problems of the new medium. Turner began her career on the fringes of legitimate theatre, appearing in various child roles until packed off to school. However, in 1902, aged fifteen, her publicity says, she browbeat Henry Irving into letting her galvanise a lacklustre revolutionary mob in *Robespierre*.[3] While she went on to appear in musical comedy and Shakespeare, she made an independent name for herself in vaudeville as an impersonator. Like a number of celebrated female vaudeville performers of the time, her repertoire included imitations of well-known stage – and later film – professionals, alongside sketches that caricatured social types encountered in the workplaces and leisure venues of modern life. These were skills highly useful to the expanding film studios of 1907, needing to supply the nickelodeon boom with an increasingly fiction-driven but still largely action-based product confined to five or ten minutes. Thus persuading the Vitagraph studios of her talent as a *comédienne*, Turner appeared in a series of short comic and dramatic films. Her memory of her first, *How to Cure a Cold* (1907), suggests how narrative could be built on her skills. Playing a harassed wife responding to various relatives' remedies for her husband's cold, 'speed and action were the necessary requisites . . . I had to feel sorry, glad, disconsolate, weep, go mad, laugh hysterically and be tickled to death – all in the space of 60.'[4]

Fig. 16. Alma Taylor, Miss Gladys Cooper, Florence E. Turner, Miss Violet Hopson and Miss Betty Balfour – the last in *Squibs*. (Author's collection.)

The capacity for quick-change moods drew equally on the emotional swings of melodramatic performance and on the impersonator's art. Underpinning both was a fascination, now fuelled by cinematography, with the expressive power of the human body – particularly the face – which had generated the early film genre of the 'facial' from which Turner's practice clearly drew. Flourishing in America, Britain and France between 1897 and 1907, this popular genre exploited the capacity of the close-up to exhibit 'virtuoso display[s] of purely facial expressions'.[5] Such versatility was Turner's forte. A review of a 1911 vaudeville appearance declared: 'Few legitimate stars . . . can equal her marvellous facial expression changing from vacancy to intellectuality, from sunshine to storm. She runs the gamut, playing everything from a frowsy slum girl with distorted face to parts of emotional beauty.'[6]

In moving from vaudeville to film, narrative vehicles were developed to showcase her talents. Not only did she play across a wide range of genres from burlesque to Shakespearian drama, but her roles often involved doubling, disguise or shifts in age, class and even gender. However, while loving the variety of one-off performances for camera as opposed to the nightly repetition of theatre, she regretted the loss of the live audience, which contributed to timing, atmosphere and the personal following that ensured reliable box office.[7] Thus Turner never gave up theatrical performances of her famed impersonations. But beneath this artistic and economic good sense, something else was at work which both aided and eventually undermined her career in film – the gradual unfolding of the specific dynamics of film performance and its ultimate exploitation as film stardom.

Throughout the 1910s and 1920s film commentators and reviewers were drawn to a paradox of film versus stage acting. If the camera brought the public into closer intimacy than ever before with the bodies of players, promising access to piquant glimpses of apparently spontaneous being, the more evidently 'performing' actors of the stage offered 'flesh and blood' presences against the 'grey shadows' of absent actors on screen. Susan Glenn describes how celebrated theatrical female mimics of the period, avoiding costume and make-up changes and interacting with their audiences, asserted their own personality across impersonations.[8] Florence Turner's film career attempts to recreate this personal 'presence'. For despite the camera's capture of evanescent being, the projected personality – the 'Vitagraph Girl' – was only an image. Something had to fill the gap between image and actress, and between fleeting film appearances. Initially this was supplied by one of the many 'firsts' claimed by her publicity: the 'first picture tie-up' with another media form, the popular song, 'The Vitagraph Girl'. In April 1910 an enterprising Brooklyn showman arranged to have the song performed before screening one of her films. Out of curiosity about the song, so the story goes, she went along, only to find a large crowd already drummed up by the exhibitor. The success of this 'first' public appearance by a film actress led to the 'first' motion picture press agent arranging further appearances; while the song, accompanied by a series of slides for which she posed, frequently preceded her films.[9] Soon Turner received the 'first' billing of an actress in pre-film credits. Whether these 'firsts' actually hold up, building a living connection to her audience became central to her work as a performer and canny businesswoman. Richard deCordova quotes a report of 'Vitagraph Girl Night at the Academy':

Truly it was a revelation. That those who pose for the Silent Drama gain a tangible hold on their audiences we were aware. That the popularity of the Shadow Girl would cause a small riot by reason of the eagerness of those who knew only the 'shadow' to greet the reality was, to say the least, a surprise.[10]

When, in the spring of 1913, Turner moved to Britain to set up her own company with her director, Larry Trimble, she embarked on an ambitious tour round the country – visiting, Trimble claimed, 160 music halls in six weeks – a strategy for building on the popularity of her American films with British audiences and, as *The Era* commented, establishing her presence with both stage and cinema audiences.[11] James Anderson recounts: 'England, Wales and Scotland were all visited, "seeing my friends in person" . . . it was [the] party spirit which made her so loved. She stood in the foyer and shook hands with "her friends" as they passed out.'[12] Though supported by publicity outlets such as interviews and press releases, this was labour-intensive work, seeking to straddle both theatrical and filmic modes of public existence.

Reasons given for Turner's move to Britain are threefold. First, she longed to control her own production company and gain more profit from her work. In America the Motion Picture Patents Trust Company blocked independent producers. In fact this embargo would be broken shortly after she left. Secondly, competitors were on the horizon. In December 1911 she netted 225,000 votes to Mary Pickford's third place with 64,007 in a popularity contest run by the New Jersey *Morning Telegraph*.[13] By 1913 'Little Mary' was on the way to becoming the 'World's Sweetheart'. Finally Turner and Trimble were convinced that her popularity in Britain, even greater than in America, would reap reward. Turner made nearly thirty films in England between 1913 and 1916, many of them very successful. Distribution arrangements were made in America, while news of her professional activity was planted in the press. But when war undermined the viability of her company and she returned to America in November 1916, she found it impossible to relaunch her career. Sympathetic journalists explained that she had been absent from the fans too long. Paradoxically she had left just as the model of the successful film actress was shifting from 'picture personality' to 'film star', oriented to a different mode of filmic performance and public existence.

'Little Mary' versus 'India Rubber Gertie'

Florence Turner operated in the paradoxical crux of film acting, gaining a reputation for great emotional acting, the 'Bernhardt of the Screen', and

198

grotesque caricature.[14] The camera, however, moving in close to face and eyes, promised to reach beyond act and character to the inner essence of the performer. Many stage actors, subjected to the camera, warned that the smallest unpremeditated inflection or wandering thought would appear on screen, whereas the distanced and floodlit stage allowed such moments of inattention to pass unnoticed. At the same time the actor's body offered a human document open to audience reading and investment, as Louis Reeves Harrison discovered in Turner's solo and untitled role in *Jealousy: The Discarded Favourite* (1911):

> the inner emotions find wonderful expressions through the medium of their accomplished leading woman, Miss Turner . . . It gets close to pulsating life as we know it and feel it ourselves . . . a transmutation of life into pictorial art and back again to life as it pours through the channels of our being . . . The audience gazes into the mystery of the human soul. We sit entranced while this woman reveals one phase of emotion after another until she falls on the floor and writhes in a paroxysm of fierce passion.[15]

Here the gaze at the emoting film actress begins to elide character with a performer whose emotions pass directly to the spectator. In contrast to such transparency, Turner declared, 'I love caricature. The distortion of the human face is one of the most interesting studies to me.'[16] Her 1914 British film, *Daisy Doodad's Dial*, a late example of the facial genre in which Mr and Mrs Doodad take part in an amateur face-making competition, takes this predilection to extremes, with 'close-ups of Turner making hilariously horrifying faces' and 'mugging directly to the camera.'[17]

In contrast, Mary Pickford's meteoric rise shifts the core of stardom from 'acting' to 'being'. Like Florence Turner, Pickford made a childhood career in touring theatre (as 'Baby Gladys'), and similarly wanted to play vigorous roles, especially boys' parts. However, when two years behind Turner she moved into films, she came under the direction of D. W. Griffith, whose Pre-Raphaelite-tinged vision of girlhood, and growing ability to use composition and lighting to combine ethereal seductiveness with naturalistic detail, turned the blonde-haired, blue-eyed actress into an infectiously alluring persona – 'Little Mary'. This shift of focus – supported by intermedial texts, including publicity photographs, interviews, life stories – went beyond character and performance to generate a public icon, mixing spunky, somewhat androgynous girlishness with a touching innocence. Despite business acumen that enabled her to move from studio to studio on ever-higher salaries and eventually into independent production, and try as she might to say 'farewell to childhood on the screen', the public, she acknowledged, 'just refused to accept me in any role older than the gawky, fighting age of adolescent girlhood'.[18] In 1919 Pickford contributed to the (British) Standard Art Books series on film acting. The hagiographic introduction denies its own purpose in its commitment to a now fully articulated star discourse: 'Mary never acts – not even in films – ever natural, she is the same in her pictures as in her home life.'[19] She was born a star: 'Two beautiful blue eyes . . . [met] the glorious sunshine of a happy April morn – she smiled and in smiling she culled from the sunbeams all the happiness there is in sunlight and little Mary was born.'[20] Pickford's own text offers a fairly rigorous account of the labour of acting: preparing for a role, the demands of the studio, the techniques of what she calls 'action dialogue' (where gesture, supported by camera art, speaks) and above all, the discipline required by the director. Nevertheless, in her account actress absorbs character rather than the other way round: 'Try to think that the part you appear in is a leaf out of your own life. While the film is being taken live that part in your own life.'[21] In contrast, Turner was lost in her role: 'She can absolutely disguise her facade or obliterate her own charming personality.'[22] As the *Moving Picture Magazine* explains, 'Every character . . . [she] plays is a distinct creation . . . When Miss Turner is "The Dixie Mother" she is not Miss Turner at all. Miss Turner is forgotten.'[23] In England the *Bioscope* enthuses, 'She contains in her person the art of at least six widely different actresses.'[24] Self-disguise and multiple personality demonstrate insight into human character and versatility, but block access to the actress's person and the consistency across and beyond films necessary for stardom. This, suggests the *Motion Picture News*, explains Turner's displacement in American popularity: 'Past mistress of make-up and pantomime, she portrayed every sort of character . . . and thereby came misfortune . . . the public . . . began to decide that Florence Turner was getting old – that perhaps she was a "has been".'[25]

The genre of the 'facial', the revelations of the camera and the rise of psychoanalysis all suggest modernity's intense focus on the nature of identity, secreted behind the facades of public roles, staged performances and the evasions of verbal language. Film stardom, Richard Dyer argues, comes to enact just this crux, oscillating between the hype of extra-filmic publicity and the apparent transparency of filmic presence, each feeding off the other to promise revelation of the true person.[26] Turner's delight in impersonation refuses such revelation. Moreover, her skills at face-pulling – earning her the soubriquet, 'India Rubber Gertie'[27] – challenged an increasingly intense emphasis on female youth and beauty, which, begun on the stage, would become the sine qua non of female stardom.[28] As one journal commented on her return to America in 1917, 'her vogue was held to be out of date. Artistry gave way to prettiness.'[29]

Alma Taylor: 'Our English Mary Pickford'?

Paradoxically, just as Florence Turner abandoned the industry that would produce film stardom to set up her production base in Cecil Hepworth's Walton-on-Thames studios, Hepworth himself was promoting the career of his most popular film player, Alma Taylor, later to be dubbed 'Our English Mary Pickford' (fig. 16). Although Britain's apparent inability to produce film stars was frequently blamed on the lack of imagination, financial outlay and enterprise of its film companies, Jon Burrows has shown how fully cognisant Hepworth was of publicity techniques to establish the public identity of players, linking screen image to personality and life story.[30] Taylor, like 'Little Mary', was promoted as a child natural, initially gaining popularity in the Tilly Girls series in which she and Chrissie White starred as a pair of mischievous tomboys. Like Pickford's, her publicity claimed she was not acting, but simply being her own natural self.

Working against this understanding of stardom, Burrows suggests, was Hepworth's concern to raise the status of film as an art form that could claim national distinctiveness and prestige. For his female stars this meant developing a nationally iconic English femininity distinct from foreign players. Consequently, in the mid-teens, Hepworth cast Taylor in stage adaptations for which some critics felt she lacked dramatic gravitas and skill. Nevertheless she was voted favourite British film actress in 1915, continuing to appear in popularity polls into the 1920s, and critics remained strikingly respectful. *The Bioscope* even distances itself from its house reviewer when confronted by a letter from the playwright A. W. Pinero to Taylor, declaring that in *Iris* (1915), 'So eloquent and expressive is your performance that it came to me as a piece of real life, and enabled me to forget that I had ever had a hand in fashioning the story.'[31]

If this 'star' quality survives its theatrical context, it is due, perhaps, to Hepworth's practice as a highly pictorial director and cinematographer, combined with Taylor's reserved but pliant personality. Unlike Florence Turner, the mature Alma Taylor is not predominantly a mobile presence on screen. The harum-scarum energy of her Tilly Girl matures into a capacity for stillness and contemplative poses that meld into pictorialised landscapes which were Hepworth's forte, lending human significance to the scene. As a poem published in *Pictures and the Picturegoer* intones:

> Those placid brows and peaceful eyes
> 'Mind me of lakes 'neath summer skies:
> The sweet half-smile, tip-tilted nose,
> A certain look of wistfulness,
> Your girlish grace and form, no less
> Of some wild wind-kissed English rose.[32]

This association with the English landscape constitutes Taylor's gravitas. In a 1921 interview she rejects the star-making mechanisms of the public appearance – she prefers 'to be enshrined in the hearts of picturegoers as a favourite character' – and personal revelations – she's married to her work and the studio, so no gossip there.[33] It is the pastoral quietude of her photographic image, attuned to wartime nostalgia – 'faithful, modest English girl with big, gentle eyes and quiet ways'[34] – which critics and fans can claim as 'English' when they have little to say about her acting.

'The "IT-less" British Girl'

Although the search for cultural respectability led film companies to seek associations with legitimate theatre (while also drawing on music hall and vaudeville), cinema continued to develop as a mass medium. On 'Vitagraph nights' Florence Turner was introduced as 'a person very much like ourselves – just an ordinary, everyday young lady, with extraordinary talent'.[35] Film stardom represented an egalitarian route to success irrespective of social background. This offered an enormously attractive model to British audiences, experiencing increasing liberalisation of social and gender relations accelerated by the war. However, as the example of Alma Taylor suggests, American stardom could not be seamlessly reproduced within British culture. British cinema started from a different place, initially drawing on those theatrical and performance traditions evolved to manage rather than dissolve social stratification as in the 'melting pot' of American egalitarianism. For the sake of audience recognition, the boundaries of representation were expanding, but 'acting', role-playing and character typage remained central to a cultural aesthetics based on the visibility of social difference. This both impacted on British approaches to naturalism and worked against the ethos of film stardom which denied such constructions.

In this context two traditions were central to British discourses of film acting: restraint and underplaying reserved for 'straight' – largely middle-class – roles, and character acting, associated with a diversity of comic, social and media types, whose function in making social difference visible contributed to processes of cultural definition and contest. It was to the latter that Florence Turner owed her success in Britain, her egalitarian spirit and skills of impersonation taking her further than many British actors towards unpatronising characterisations of regional, class and gender types, while her penchant for character switches enabled her not only to present social differences in pointed juxtaposition but to stage the possibility of social mobility.[36] However, by the time of her second attempt on the British film scene in the early 1920s, Hollywood's emphasis on female youth and beauty had moved towards openly sexual display, and this neither Turner nor the British film actresses of the time offered. Significantly, the performance arena from which Turner had come – vaudeville, music hall and variety – had generated a type of female performer – the showgirl – who, though largely suppressed in critical discussion, represented a third performance practice more supportive of female film stardom.

It is no accident that the first picture players to achieve public notoriety were young girls, for 'the girl' dominated melodramas and musical comedies, popular songs and fictions from the end of the nineteenth century into the 1920s. At once rebellious and dutiful, androgynous and girlishly feminine, the figure of the girl on the cusp of change provided a focus for modernising gender roles which interacted with the spread of mass education and the growth of consumer industries, advertising and new forms of mass entertainment such as cinema. Under cover of the innocence of adolescence, the figure of the girl chipped away at gender and class taboos. While, as Jon Burrows suggests, the 'showgirl' in British musical theatre hinted though innuendo or bold outrageousness at a freer sexuality,[37] it was Hollywood that put her on screen. Nowhere, it was complained, could she be found in British films, for she conflicted with culturally legitimate conceptions of femininity distinguishing British from American cinema. The British film actress, then, was trapped in a double bind. By 1923 the problem was urgent, for the industry's renaissance promised by the Michael Balcon/Graham Cutts hit, *Woman to Woman*, established the practice of employing American actresses as leads.

Reiterated complaints declared that British film actresses were neither young nor attractive. Counter-arguments blamed directors and cameramen for their inability to handle lighting and camera position to bring out the actress's 'screen values'. Employment of well-known and therefore older stage actresses in order to pre-sell films kept out the 'beautiful and talented actresses . . . who would be the world's sweethearts if only given the opportunity'.[38] Equally undermining was the assertion that British actresses lacked 'screen temperament' and were devoid of 'personality'. Shifting the notion of 'type' from character to star, an indignant Mabel Poulton challenged the British director: 'Does he study the girl? . . . does he . . . experiment with her . . . until she learns her own power and develops her own "type", as American directors study stars?'[39]

Most problematic, however, was the supposed ingrained dominant of national character: reserve, translated in acting terms as 'restraint' and 'underplaying'. As a performance aesthetic, 'restraint' had developed from the reform of melodrama in line with middle-class codes of verisimilitude. Its advocates argued that emotion held back was aesthetically more powerful.

Nevertheless, 'restraint' exercised over bodily gesture and personal expression, thereby splitting public from private, self from role, distinguished the well-bred from the proletarian, easing encounters between socially differentiated protagonists. By the 1920s the gender implications of 'our national social system, directed to repressing the exhibition of real emotion' were becoming apparent.[40] While male restraint enhanced 'manliness' of a kind unavailable to Americans, the British film actress was simply 'repressed'. In 1926 playwright and theatre critic St John Ervine declared in the *Morning Post* that the failure of English women to become successful film actresses was due to

> the immobility of feature so fashionable among nicely-bred girls. The practice of what is called 'good form' has resulted in a host of persons from whose faces expression has almost been eliminated . . . what was formerly an exercise in self-control has become a standardised and an empty appearance. Our young ladies betray so few of their feelings in their faces that one is tempted to believe they are wearing masks.[41]

Ervine in replying to one of his correspondents makes the class dimension of his position explicit: 'When we invite . . . [our young actresses] to be vivacious in their manner, we are not asking them to behave like low-class barmaids: we are asking them not to look like mummies or funeral mutes.'[42] Both social and representational systems depended on a middle-class femininity to hold the line between private and public spheres, between the actress and the performed role, between performer and audience. It was precisely this gap that the American star overcame.

Writers in the trade and fan press frequently advised that the film industry should look beyond the stage to a different class of girl for star material. Ervine himself is quoted by *The Bioscope* as saying 'it may be . . . that the English film-actress will come from the working class, where immobility of expression is not practised'.[43] But, while suggesting that the showgirls of variety and cabaret make good film performers because they can 'get over' to an audience, Manning Haynes reassures *Picturegoer*'s readers that they are often also 'cultured and well bred'.[44] In fact, Betty Balfour, the one actress who could claim stardom in the 1920s, consistently topping popularity polls and nicknamed 'Britain's Queen of Happiness', began her career in variety and derived her screen persona from a music-hall song, *Squibs* (fig. 16). Balfour had been fortunate in her director, George Pearson, who combined an appreciation for the art of acting and cinema as visual storytelling with a feel for popular culture. Drawing on Balfour's comic gifts, Pearson had seen in the title, 'Squibs', the potential for 'fireworks', infusing the stereotype of the Cockney skivvy with a sense of irreverent fun, laced with a pathos generating empathy for others capable of cross-class appeal.[45] For Balfour as Squibs he devised a narrative structure of episodic 'turns' with a capacity for generating a music hall rapport with her invisible audience, which proved so successful that four Squibs films were made before director and actress wearied of her. Betty Balfour's popularity, then, traded on skills of characterisation and performance similar to those of Florence Turner. Unlike Turner, however, Balfour solved the problem of consistency through the repeated character. She retained her place in the polls in part because she supplied a popular yearning for a recognisably British star to which she loyally adhered. But hers was a stardom locked into a cultural type that could not grow with the times, and increasingly beside the American star had the appearance of fancy dress. There was a vital element missing.

Reviews and fan magazines, with an eye on the American actress, frequently referred to this as 'pep' and 'vim', denoting spontaneity rather than the sincerity which sank personality in a character. But a more suggestive tag was found in Elinor Glyn's response to Clara Bow: 'It'. As British films increasingly risked cabaret and showgirl scenes involving the 'undress habit', 'It' was acknowledged as 'sex appeal', that mysteriously charged connection between film actress and fans that fuelled female stardom. In December 1928 *Film Weekly* published a report from Hollywood by May Edginton on 'The "IT-less British Girl': 'English girls are considered in Hollywood to be at a discount because of their lack of emotion . . . On the screen they are cool; they are chaste; there are no sirens . . . they photograph coldly.'[46] Mabel Poulton, the rising star of *The Constant Nymph* (1928), addressed a furious diatribe to British filmmakers on behalf of British girlhood yearning for stardom, citing the musical stage as evidence of a feminine allure.[47]

'The movie world is searching for its voice'

The arrival of the talkie added further fuel to these debates. The impact of sound is well known through Hollywood's self-parody, *Singin' in the Rain* (1952). Notably its hilarious object of satire is the unfortunate actress with the nasal accent who, when required to speak into a concealed microphone, proves to be a 'dumb blonde' without an ounce of acting ability.

For the film actress, the talkie was a threat on three counts. First was the assumption, initially proved correct, that production companies would turn not only to stage plays as ready-made material, but to stage actresses for competence in speaking dialogue. Consequently many film actresses rushed for voice training. Second, anxiety emerged about voice quality and accent. Clara Novello-Davis (Ivor Novello's mother), who offered voice training to film actors in New York and London, commented on her trainees' desire for 'the best English accent . . . [which] is, of course, no particular accent at all'.[48] Many believed that with the 'best speaking voices in the world', British actors had the advantage over Hollywood, and were caustic at the expense of American accents: 'Mabel Poulton and Lilian Hall-Davies . . . [have] voices that are much easier listened to than the shrill shrieks of Clara Bow and Alice White.'[49] Third, and more significant, the voice introduced a new dimension that threatened the persona established by the actor's bodily appearance. *Film Weekly*'s American correspondent wrote up Garbo's first words in *Anna Christie* as a moment of fateful suspense:

> From a few hundred hearts goes up the sigh which will be echoed, in a few weeks' time, by thousands, a sigh first of relief and then of delight, for we are listening to perhaps the most thrilling of all talkie voices. Very low and somewhat husky it is, musical and enticing with its Swedish hardening of consonants. It is a voice which grips you with its infinite expression, its range, its subtle modulation.[50]

Clearly, the foreign accent is part of the appeal. More significant is the implied power of the voice to leave the screen, crossing the gap between film and audience: 'All through this magnificent outburst the voice weaves its spell about us.'[51]

Returning the English voice to the British actress, however, served to exacerbate arguments about 'the "IT-less" British Girl'. May Edginton warned: 'It is not wise to imagine that because of their educated diction English actresses will triumph over the world. Pure English is not always wanted in film stories. Nor are educated voices.'[52] Nerina Shute, the twenty-year-old *enfant terrible* employed as columnist by *Film Weekly*, warned off aging theatrical actresses, taking Isabel Jeans to task for her 'stagey' microphone voice, while instructing aspirant flappers they must cultivate 'sex appeal'.[53] Meanwhile, she noted, 'sad little Mabel Poulton' was waiting anxiously the outcome of a proposal to cast her in a talkie. She would, Mabel said, play the part of a 'Cockney'.

Mabel Poulton's attempt to move beyond her working-class origins into film stardom demonstrates all too painfully the problems for the actress in British culture. Paradoxically, the occasion of her 'discovery' required her to impersonate Lillian Gish in a live-action prologue for the première of *Broken Blossoms* (1919). Her surviving silent films – for example *Palais de Danse* (1928) and the film that clinched her star potential, *The Constant Nymph* – do indeed suggest a Gish-like screen presence. She offers to the camera an almost transparent performance, the luminosity of which lacks any protective shell, whether from the control of middle-class underplaying or the abrasive direct address of music hall tradition. What seems like spontaneous investment in the feelings of her character, together with a paradoxical combination of disregard for social protocols and deference to admired superiors, produces a complicated mix of vulnerability, charm and gaucherie. While this cinematic presence served the fantasies of British cinema at the end of its silent era and is probably the closest it came to producing star performance on American lines, British cinema could not sustain her once sound arrived. Given the continuing dominance of middle-class characters in straight parts and the drive to shape the star actress within a nationalised femininity as distinct from the Hollywood star, her ineradicable Cockney accent, as she herself saw, would limit her to character parts, which in turn would require a mode of impersonation alien to her.

The fate of Poulton and Betty Balfour suggests that return of the actress's voice clinched the push towards modernising femininity at work in the debate about British actresses. Despite still being voted favourite British actress in 1929 and claims that she had a good speaking and singing voice, Balfour's career also petered out in the sound era. Sharing predilections with Florence Turner, but unable to repeat her diversity, Balfour's stardom became entangled with her character. Like Mary Pickford seeking to move beyond Little Mary, she and her directors could not escape Squibs. But whereas Mary simply wanted to grow up, Betty, in order to play more serious roles, had to cross a class line in which her critics and fans did not recognise her.

A report from Hollywood on Pickford's first all-talking picture, *Coquette* (1929), declares it 'proves she has a voice, and that she can use it to good effect . . . but the day of such mushy sentiment as goes to make up this story is over. The film is too remote from real life to please the majority of modern audiences.'[54] The technology of sound, itself another triumph of modernity, also ratcheted up the stakes of representation. The actress who would step into this new medium needed writers to provide new roles, accompanied by words a modern woman could speak. Betty Balfour's demise in the wake of Gracie Field's rise suggests that both she and Mabel Poulton were caught in a set of contradictions around modernising femininity as it intersected with class. But equally crucial was cinema's relation to sex. For if the vaudeville entertainer promoted a personal relationship with her audience and the showgirl exuded sex appeal, the absent presence of the film star, making body and personality available to the viewer via a camera, crossed the barrier between the performer's exhibitionism and the voyeurism haunting spectatorship. On film, the performance antics of Turner and Balfour got in the way of eroticism – the female star's ultimate allure.

Fig. 17. Madeleine Carroll. (British Film Institute.)

'From "iceberg" to "volcano"'

Madeleine Carroll's achievement was to grasp the conditions of film stardom and turn her initial production as an icon of chilly British femininity into a Hollywood-made star of international standing (fig. 17). After escaping an oppressive future as a French teacher in a Brighton girls' school for the stage, Carroll took a screen test that promoted her blonde elegance to the role of upper-class heroine in *The Guns at Loos* (1928). Her university degree, society marriage, a castle in Spain and encounters with royalty, combined with what one reviewer later called her 'Bond Street sheen'[55] to represent an upper-class national femininity, while exhibiting the British equivalent to the trappings of Hollywood stardom. But her persona and performance style were far removed from the showgirl's sex appeal needed to compete with the American actress. Reviews of her films invariably noted her charm, restraint and competence, but increasingly complained of a coldness, often blamed on 'colourless' parts offering little opportunity for acting.

Having continued stage appearances, Carroll was well placed when sound arrived in Britain. In 1929 Nerina Shute identified her as 'The Girl with a Future'. 'Here is a stage girl, more lovely than any girl I have met in the film world, who speaks in cultured accents . . . Probably she is the most valuable British actress in our talkie studios.'[56] Carroll certainly believed in her advantage:

> Talkies are creating a demand for a class of actress of somewhat higher qualifications than were necessary in the silent films. Jazzy flappers were made to be seen and not heard. The talkie heroine must speak her lines intelligently . . . English actresses are especially well suited to portray the finer kind of heroine that the talkies need and justice to screen womanhood demands.[57]

'Screen womanhood' is Carroll's theme. Inspired by Dorothy Arzner's film *Sarah and Son* (1930), this article is a proto-feminist polemic against cinema's misplaced idealisation and misrepresentation of women. While noting that, Arzner aside, 'talkies are almost exclusively a man-made entertainment' and that 'women today are something more important than objects of sex interest', Carroll demands that actresses be given 'roles worthy of their mental qualities'. In the 1930s she writes regular articles in *Film Weekly*, frankly explaining her thoughts about acting and career moves. Thus in 1932, announcing her new contract with Gaumont British, she lays out her conditions and programme of work. She is, she says, 'determined not to be a type' and to this end she has won choice of stories, director and writer.[58] The following year she writes a more explicit diatribe against 'Mr. British Producer' for his use of female stereotypes who 'must remain simple and sugary, and as a rule, just a little dumb'.[59]

In this respect she and her publicists use magazine journalism as a less exhausting and self-exposing means than public appearances to cement her relationship with her audience, while examining how, as a highly ambitious actress, she can make stardom work to her advantage. In 1933–4 she put her toe in Hollywood's water as 'the first British actor in the new reciprocal "charm exchange"' between Gaumont British and Fox, taking a one-off role in John Ford's anti-war epic, *The World Moves On* (1934). Her publicist, Iris Foster, works hard in the American *Photoplay* to build up Carroll's star credentials with details of her British social standing, romantic marriage and size of salary, while also mediating between her 'high-hat' class background and American egalitarianism (she and her husband take infinite pains to look after the welfare of estate workers and servants).[60]

Back in England, two films with Hitchcock expanded her skills, while also undermining her upper-crust image. Stories already circulated about her difficulty relaxing during bedroom or kissing scenes, and how Hitchcock, when asked in relation to a Titanic project whether he knew anything about icebergs, had declared he ought to – he'd directed Madeleine Carroll.[61] In 'De-bunking My Serenity' Carroll takes control of this story, recounting how Hitchcock persuaded her to take the 'screen comedy plunge' in *The 39 Steps* (1935): '"You won't recognise yourself when I've finished with you!" he warned me' and she proceeds to detail the indignities to which she and Robert Donat were subjected, including being locked handcuffed together in a room with a double bed.[62] By the time she explains 'Why I am Going to Hollywood' she expresses regret that she has been 'typed in so many "cold and severe" parts' and writes enthusiastically about her current role in *The Secret Agent* (1937) – one that works against the grain of British feminine reserve.[63]

The move to America represented a bid for 'international stardom' which only Hollywood's opportunity for consistent work and star-building machinery could support. Thus despite her desire to avoid typecasting, she recognises the need for a transnational niche she might occupy, a new persona neither confined to her particular cultural inheritance nor pretending to pass as an all-American heroine:

> I have . . . become too closely associated with the serene, dignified and rather cool English girl. She can become a very tiresome person. In America she may even appear quite unreal . . . I recognise the necessity to 'break down' a little. I must be prepared to broaden my style before I can hope to broaden my appeal.[64]

According to Walter Wanger, her American producer, there are five or so 'classes of film star for which an international following can be created and maintained'. Garbo, Hepburn, Colbert and Dietrich have each defined a particular type of femininity, but Carroll has identified a gap: the 'travelled, cultured, and sophisticated woman' of indeterminate nationality, 'who might be a somewhat hard bachelor girl or an experienced young matron'. This figure is both a construction, a persona or mask, *and* someone Carroll might plausibly be. It requires the production of behaviour, gesture, vocal intonation capable of marrying Carroll's own physical type, personal beliefs and culturally informed performance habits to what she calls her 'screen character'. She gives some idea of the transformation required of her English girl persona in her description of her next role:

> As 'Hope Ames' I portray the young wife who having married a young man against the wishes of his mother . . . finds herself accused of his murder. The young woman is not of the clinging vine type. She is well able to take care of her own affairs . . . Tense action breaks up all serenity and there is little or no time for nice English manners.[65]

Madeleine Carroll's 'transnational' stardom is based on lessons that eluded Florence Turner and Betty Balfour. She, her directors and her publicists constructed a film persona out of the culturally given performance traditions she brought with her, deploying character-acting skills to play on the very split between self and role instituted by restraint, the suturing of which was the promise of the Hollywood star. Just as Turner in her most successful films found scenarios that enabled her to switch from one impersonation to another, crossing class, age and even gender roles, Carroll's two Hitchcock films played the perfected surface of her high-toned English persona against more ambivalent but repressed emotional undercurrents of plot situation, offering her acting opportunities outside the constraints of the image. While Hitchcock never directed her in Hollywood, he had arguably revealed the piquantly dramatic possibilities of British feminine restraint, which contained the depths of what was held back rather than 'IT-lessness'. The *New York Post* reported, under the heading 'From "iceberg" to "volcano"', a rather more American approach by E. H. Griffith, tasked with directing the 'blonde Briton' in *Café Society* (1939):

> He has swept away the austerity and severity distinguishing the actress's style and intends to bring out a warmth, sparkle and spontaneity of which few suspect she is capable . . . [by] having her engage in a siphon water battle, jump in a lake with her clothes on and perform other hoydenish capers . . .
> [He says] 'I am bringing Miss Carroll down-to-earth, releasing her from the ethereal pedestal to which previous pictures had confined her.'[66]

If nothing else, Madeleine Carroll's breakthrough into Hollywood stardom demonstrates the potential exchange value of national character types and performance modes, and the discursive clashes and shifts around gender roles and definitions of femininity that take place in the process.

NOTES

1. Richard deCordova, *Picture Personalities: The Emergence of the Star System in America* (Urbana: University of Illinois Press, 1990).
2. Ibid., p. 28.
3. Elisabeth Peltret, 'The Return of Florence Turner', *Motion Picture Classic*, February 1919, pp. 72–3, and *Motion Picture News*, 24 May 1924, p. 2431. See also 'The Girl on Film, No. 9: Florence Turner', in *Pictures and Picturegoer*, 6 June 1914, 359–60, for a slightly different version of her beginnings.
4. *Pictures and the Picturegoer*, 8 December 1917, p. 610.
5. Joe Kember, 'Face-to-Face: The Facial Expressions Genre in Early British Films', in A. Burton and L. Porter, eds., *The Showman, the Spectacle and the Two-Minute Silence: Performing British Cinema before 1930* (Trowbridge: Flicks Books, 2001).
6. Unidentified clipping, 1911, in Florence Turner's scrapbook, Seaver Center for Western History Research, Los Angeles.
7. *New York Dramatic Mirror*, 30 October 1912, p. 28.
8. Susan A. Glenn, *Female Spectacle: The Theatrical Roots of Modern Feminism* (Cambridge, MA: Harvard University Press, 2000), pp. 76–7.
9. *Motion Picture News*, 24 May 1924, p. 2433.
10. DeCordova, *Picture Personalities*, p. 66.
11. *Moving Picture World*, 19 August 1916, p. 1223; *The Era*, 6 August 1913, p. 29.
12. James Anderson MS, Special Collections, British Film Institute.
13. *New Jersey Morning Telegraph*, 17 December 1911, cutting in Robinson Locke Collection, Series 2, New York Public Library.
14. *Moving Picture World*, 21 October 1916, Robinson Locke Collection.
15. *Moving Picture World*, ca. 1911, Turner's scrapbook, Seaver Center.
16. *Moving Picture World*, 18 May 1912, p. 622.
17. Ann-Marie Cook, 'The Adventures of the "Vitagraph Girl" in England', in A. Burton and Laraine Porter, eds., *Pimple, Pranks and Pratfalls* (Trowbridge: Flicks Books, 2000), pp. 33–41, p. 34.
18. Mary Pickford, *Sunshine and Shadow: The Autobiography of Mary Pickford* (London: William Heineman, 1956), pp. 252, 255.
19. Mary Pickford, *How to Act for the Screen*, Lesson One of *Cinema: Practical Course in Cinema Acting in Ten Complete Lessons* (London: Standard Art Books, 1919), p. 4.
20. Ibid., p. 3.
21. Ibid., p. 18.
22. *Motion Picture World*, ca. October 1910, Turner's scrapbook, Seaver Center.
23. *Moving Picture Magazine*, October 1912, Robinson Locke Collection.
24. *The Bioscope*, 26 November 1914, p. 913.
25. *Motion Picture News*, 24 May 1924, pp. 2430–1.
26. Richard Dyer, '*A Star is Born* and the Construction of Authenticity', in Christine Gledhill, ed., *Stardom: Industry of Desire* (London: Routledge, 1991), pp. 132–40.
27. Peltret, 'The Return of Florence Turner', p. 28.
28. Glenn, *Female Spectacle*, p. 47.
29. Unattributed cutting in Turner's scrapbook, Seaver Center.

30. Jon Burrows, '"Our English Mary Pickford": Alma Taylor and Ambivalent British Stardom in the 1910s', in Bruce Babington, ed., *British Stars and Stardom* (Manchester: Manchester University Press, 2001), p. 29.
31. *The Bioscope*, 11 November 1915, p. 685.
32. May Herschal-Clark, 'Alma', *Pictures and the Picturegoer*, 2 May 1917, p. 1134.
33. *The Picturegoer*, March 1921, pp. 41–4.
34. *The Bioscope*, 5 October 1916, p. 109.
35. Unattributed cutting, ca. 1910, Turner's scrapbook, Seaver Center.
36. See Cook, 'Adventures of the "Vitagraph Girl"', p. 38.
37. Jon Burrows, 'Girls on Film: The Musical Matrices of Film Stardom in Early British Cinema', *Screen* 44.3 (Autumn 2003), pp. 314–25.
38. *Motion Picture Studio*, 21 October 1922, p. 11.
39. *Film Weekly*, 31 December 1928, p. 12.
40. *Motion Picture Studio*, 24 February 1922, p. 7.
41. *Morning Post*, 29 June 1926, clipping in Sidney Carroll scrapbook, Special Collections, British Film Institute.
42. Ibid.
43. *The Bioscope*, 8 July 1926, p. 49.
44. *The Picturegoer*, June 1927, p. 9.
45. George Pearson, *Flashback: An Autobiography Of A British Filmmaker* (London: George Allen and Unwin, 1957), p. 95.
46. *Film Weekly*, 17 December 1928, p. 9.
47. Ibid., 31 December 1928, p. 12.
48. Ibid., 27 May 1930, p. 13.
49. Ibid., 5 April 1930, p. 18.
50. Ibid., 12 April 1930, p. 4.
51. Ibid.
52. Ibid., 17 December 1928, p. 9
53. Ibid., 17 June 1929, p. 12.
54. Ibid., 15 April 1929, p. 6.
55. *Kinematograph Weekly*, 15 October 1936, p. 34.
56. *Film Weekly*, 24 June 1929, p. 13.
57. Ibid., 31 January 1931, p. 9.
58. Ibid., 4 November 1932, p. 7.
59. Ibid., 26 May 1933, p. 25.
60. *Photoplay* 46.2 (July 1934), pp. 32, 112–13.
61. See *St Louis Post Dispatch*, 20 March 1941; *New York Post*, 28 July 1936.
62. *Film Weekly*, 7 June 1935, pp. 8–9.
63. Ibid., 30 November 1935, p. 9.
64. Ibid., 30 May 1936, p. 7.
65. Ibid.
66. *New York Post*, 14 November 1938.

FURTHER READING

Burton, A., and L. Porter, eds. *The Showman, the Spectacle and the Two-Minute Silence: Performing British Cinema before 1930.* Trowbridge: Flicks Books, 2001.

Cook, Ann-Marie. 'The Adventures of the "Vitagraph Girl" in England', in A. Burton and Laraine Porter, eds., *Pimple, Pranks and Pratfalls*, pp. 33–41. Trowbridge: Flicks Books, 2000.

deCordova, Richard. *Picture Personalities: The Emergence of the Star System in America*. Urban: University of Illinois Press, 1990.

Dyer, Richard. '*A Star is Born* and the Construction of Authenticity', in Christine Gledhill, ed., *Stardom: Industry of Desire*, pp. 132–40. London: Routledge, 1991.

Gledhill, Christine. *Reframing British Cinema: 1918–1928*. London: British Film Institute, 2003.

Glenn, Susan A. *Female Spectacle: The Theatrical Roots of Modern Feminism*. Cambridge, MA: Harvard University Press, 2000.

Kember, Joe. 'Face-to-Face: The Facial Expressions Genre in Early British Films', in A. Burton and L. Porter, eds., *The Showman, the Spectacle, and the Two-Minute Silence: Performing British Cinema before 1930*. Trowbridge: Flicks Books, 2001.

Pearson, George. *Flashback: An Autobiography of a British Filmmaker*. London: George Allen and Unwin, 1957.

Pickford, Mary. *How to Act for the Screen*, Lesson One of *Cinema: Practical Course in Cinema Acting in Ten Complete Lessons*. London: Standard Art Books, 1919.

Sunshine and Shadow: The Autobiography of Mary Pickford. London: William Heinemann, 1956.

11

LYNETTE GODDARD

Side doors and service elevators: racial constraints for actresses of colour

> This moment is so much bigger than me. This moment is for Dorothy
> Dandridge, Lena Horne, Diahann Carroll. It's for the women that stand
> beside me – Jada Pinkett, Angela Bassett, Vivica Fox – and it's for every
> nameless, faceless woman of color that now has a chance because this door
> tonight has been opened.
> Halle Berry, Oscar acceptance speech, 2002

When Halle Berry won the Best Actress in a Leading Role Academy Award for *Monster's Ball* (2001), she dedicated her Oscar to the African American actresses who had come before her, whose struggles, activism and perseverance had helped to pave the way for her own success. Berry's award (the first given to a leading black woman in the seventy-four-year history of the Oscar)[1] was held to be deeply significant in marking a professional development for black actresses and a progressive narrative of racial discourses. Almost fifty years earlier, Dorothy Dandridge had been the first black woman to be nominated in the Best Actress category for the role of Carmen in Otto Preminger's film version of Bizet's opera *Carmen Jones* (1954). But whereas Dandridge's success had been against the odds – a 'Negro' woman in a white man's world – Berry belongs to a supposedly integrated society where black women are said to have the same opportunities as everyone else. Berry's Oscar seemed to mark a progression from times past, when black actresses were either absent from stage and screen or played minor or racially typecast supporting parts as mammies, matriarchs, Jezebels or tragic mulattoes. In the 1940s, 1950s and 1960s Louise Beavers, Hattie McDaniel and Ethel Waters were subjected to the wrath of the National Association for the Advancement of Colored People (NAACP – founded 1910) for accepting roles as maids and servants that were thought to perpetuate racial stereotypes of black women, whereas Berry appears to be part of a generation where casting is no longer based primarily on associations with a particular skin colour, but is made on the basis of acting 'talent'.

Black theatre histories have shown how Berry's predecessors endured the effects of Jim Crow segregation laws from the end of the Civil War in the 1860s until desegregation and the development of the modern Civil Rights movement in the late 1950s and 1960s. Until the 1930s, black performers were denied union rights, which left them subject to being mistreated with poor pay and working conditions. Black shows had to have white sponsors and were often staged during the summer 'dark' season with inadequate facilities.[2] Black performers had to use side doors or service elevators and, in some venues, were not allowed to use the rest rooms. Finding places to stay on tour was difficult and they sometimes slept outside or in tour vehicles when there were no 'coloured only' guest houses available. Black people were not even allowed as audience members in many venues and, even after desegregation, were still often separated into the least-sought-after seats. Arguably, such difficult times have since passed and contemporary celebrity culture seems to afford 'A-lister' Halle Berry the same possibilities and privileges as any other big (white) Hollywood star. Yet, Berry still felt it necessary to acknowledge that although she was born in the late 1960s and her career has been easier to establish than those of her predecessors, it was still difficult for a black actress to succeed in a white-centred Hollywood system that, even today, rarely casts female black performers in leading roles.

Jo A. Tanner's 1992 genealogy of early black dramatic actresses identifies the first black woman character on the American stage as 'a comic servant in William Milns's *All in a Bustle; or, The New House*, on 29 January 1798 at the Park Theatre in New York'.[3] The role was played by a white woman, however, because 'at the time, black women were not allowed to perform on the professional stage'.[4] According to Tanner, black women first started performing on stage in minstrel shows in the 1850s, becoming professional in the 1860s, before gaining real prominence in black musical shows in the 1890s.[5] From these early roots onwards, black actresses' careers have been controlled by the effects of race discrimination and gender politics on the ethics of performance. The few existing analyses of their achievements tend toward celebration, signalling archetypal strong black women who persist and thrive in difficult circumstances. Tanner's tribute to black women on the US stage in the early 1900s declares that in 'the spirit of keeping on, they not only survived, but flourished'.[6] Glenda E. Gill hails the accomplishments of performers in the Federal Theatre Project (1935–9) with the proclamation, 'In spite of Herculean obstacles, black actors had a prodigious output in the Thirties.'[7] Donald Bogle commemorates black women 'divas' (mostly singers) – from Ma Rainey to Diana Ross – who were known to the mainstream between the 1920s and the 1980s, but he does confess that his aim is to 'concentrate on the important figures – those women who captured the imagination of millions and became *bona fide* legends'.[8]

Few black British actresses have gained esteem comparable with high-profile African American women, whose status is accorded through the star system at the centre of the popular music and Hollywood film industries. Oscar nominations brought some international acclaim for Marianne Jean-Baptiste (*Secrets and Lies*, 1996) and Sophie Okonedo (*Hotel Rwanda*, 2004), and Cathy Tyson was praised for her performance in *Mona Lisa* (1986), but most jobbing black British actresses, who have focused more on stage rather than screen careers, have not had lasting international recognition nor the concomitant biographical attention and critical analysis.

Biographies of individual actresses of colour focus on those who are well known from film and television, especially Hollywood, providing a record of their achievements for fans and general readers.[9] They highlight tales of personal turmoil and resistance, where offstage difficulties (absent fathers, abusive relationships, marriages, divorces and family rifts) are central to narratives of success in the face of adversity. While these make compelling reading, in the end they tell us little about the conditions of the actresses' professional lives. Their successes are related as personal triumphs by determined and tenacious women who overcome individual difficulties, rather than considered in relation to either their roles as advocates for their profession or the broader contexts in which they worked. The actresses themselves often see their struggle as attributable to factors beyond their personal control; they are actresses of colour working in a predominantly white industry. Berry made this clear in her acceptance speech by taking an unusually long time to thank those who supported her throughout numerous rejections, and Dandridge describes resisting racist pigeonholing by refusing to take on roles that she found racially belittling.[10]

The obviousness of the claim that black actresses have encountered difficulties because of the effects of racism and sexism might explain the tendency to dwell not on constraints so much as on commemorating their achievements. However, black actresses do work within different social and professional limits, and their lack of power within a predominantly white industry both in Britain and the USA warrants further exploration.[11] Narratives of success, of flourishing employment and of historical progress obscure the pernicious ways in which racism and sexism still negatively impinge on black actresses' careers, where typecasting and professional disadvantage are compounded by Eurocentric ideals about black womanhood.

The Harlem Renaissance to the contemporary British stage: an overview

The Harlem Renaissance marked a momentous turning point for black stage performers in North America. Between 1910 and the Great Depression of the 1930s, black stage artists emerged in force on the professional stage. Actresses Inez Clough, Evelyn Ellis, Alberta Hunter, Florence Mills and Ethel

Waters starred in black musical shows such as *Blackbirds* (1926), *Plantation Revue* (1922), and *Shuffle Along* (1921), while dancer Aida Overton Walker and the huge success of Josephine Baker testified to the possibilities for black women performers on the popular stage. Black women sang, danced and performed cabaret and vaudeville, but what was really significant about the Harlem Renaissance was that it was during this period that black performers started to move away from the stereotypes associated with minstrelsy traditions and to initiate possibilities for a genuinely black aesthetics of performance.

Several black theatre sources attribute the development of significant roles for black actresses to Ridgeley Torrence's landmark production *Three Plays for a Negro Theatre* (1917), which Tanner cites as 'the first *dramatic* presentation on the Broadway stage in which black actresses appeared'.[12] Opening at the Garden Theatre in Madison Square Gardens on 5 April to high acclaim, *The Rider of Dreams*, with Blanche Deas as Lucy Sparrow, *Granny Maumee*, an all-female show with Marie Jackson-Stuart in the title role, and *Simon the Cyrenian*, with Inez Clough as Procula, were notable because they were dramatic representations of ordinary black people in plays without singing or dancing. A white playwright, Ridgeley Torrence, had started a trend whereby black performers played serious dramatic characters on stage, which heralded further opportunities arising throughout the 1920s in productions of Eugene O'Neill's *All God's Chillun Got Wings* (1924) and *The Emperor Jones* (1920). Equally, plays by black male playwrights such as Langston Hughes and Willis Richardson, and black women playwrights such as Marita Bonner, Georgia Douglas Johnson, Alice Dunbar-Nelson, May Miller, Eulalie Spence and Angelina Weld Grimke, provided substantial stage roles for black actresses in the USA.

This may all seem cause for celebration, but black theatre histories show that black performers encountered some of the worst effects of racism during this era. Black performers were confined to work organised through the Theatre Owners' Booking Association (TOBA), run predominantly by white people and then colloquially known as Tough On Black Actors, which restricted them to a particular circuit of venues. Segregated theatres meant that black performers had to decide whether they should perform in spaces from which black audiences were barred. David Krasner highlights the fact that practitioners and critics questioned whether black theatre should be trying to appeal primarily to either black or white audiences, or both, raising the connected issue of whether black theatres should stay in separate communities or seek mainstream recognition and success.[13] Though segregation was not as integral to British policies as those in America, British black performers still found their opportunities for performance limited and touring troupes could not use the front door in some venues.

Such blatant racism is no longer the case, but black actresses are still faced with the decision of whether to limit their opportunities for work by building their careers within the black theatre sector, or whether to aim for the mainstream where exposure is granted in 'white' plays. Racial politics and solidarity can be accentuated by segregated working conditions, which mean that discussions of 'black' aesthetics tend to foreground race and exclude the issues of sex and gender that specifically affect black women. There is a current consensus of opinion among many black theatre practitioners that racism has determined their position in British theatre, but the problem is accentuated for women who also experience the effects of sexism. The particular issues faced by black actresses tend to be obscured by an industry that foregrounds either race *or* gender as sites for discussion. DuBois's oft-quoted principle of the 'double-consciousness'[14] of the black psyche has another dimension for black women in a white- and male-dominated industry, where Euro-American discourses of race and sexuality, vis à vis beauty and femininity, underscore their capacity for success as actresses and determine the types of roles that they tend to play.

In the 1930s, the establishment of the Negro units within the Federal Theatre Projects (FTP) in major cities such as Chicago, Los Angeles, New York and Seattle were fundamental to providing opportunities for black actresses. Before the advent of the FTP they performed mainly in minstrel shows, vaudeville and pantomime acts, but Gill argues that the projects 'led to visibility that led to roles on Broadway and in Hollywood'.[15] Moves towards greater integration were signalled by black performers being admitted into theatre unions beyond TOBA and getting opportunities to take on classical and non-stereotypical parts. Edna Thomas played Lady Macbeth at Harlem's Lafayette Theatre in 1936 in Orson Welles's 'voodoo' *Macbeth*, set on the West Indian island of Haiti with the witches as voodoo women. The production was panned by white critics, but the unprecedented attention it received made it a significant step towards black actresses performing in classical plays. Moreover, developments in black aesthetics encouraged black actresses to perform in plays that dealt explicitly with black social issues.[16]

The politically heightened Civil Rights and Black Power decades in the 1950s, 1960s and 1970s gave rise to questions about whether black actresses should accept stereotypical parts as servants and maids in Hollywood films. The black theatre sector continued to debate the issues of a separatist and oppositional black aesthetic and plays by black women, including Alice Childress's *Florence* (1950), Lorraine Hansberry's *A Raisin in the Sun* (1959), Adrienne Kennedy's *Funnyhouse of Negro* (1962) and Childress's *Wine in the Wilderness* (1969), all provided black actresses with opportunities to play prominent roles that coupled racial with gender-specific concerns. In Britain, this era also saw the concerted emergence of first-generation black actresses onto the theatre scene.[17] The experiences of some of these women are well documented in Jim Pines's *Black and White in Colour* and Stephen Bourne's *Black in the British Frame*. Interviews and discussions with black women practitioners, including Pearl Connor, Mona Hammond, Pauline Henriques, Joan Hooley, Carmen Munroe, Cleo Sylvestre and Elisabeth Welch, tell recurrent stories of the difficulties of trying to establish careers as black actresses in theatre.[18] Pauline Henriques explains that 'It was hard breaking into the theatre and I found myself playing a variety of American coloured maids',[19] while the tendency to cast black actresses as exotic background characters, nameless and silent, in someone else's scene is captured in Carmen Munroe's account of her early career:

> I might have been asked to play a role where the character was just described as 'exotic'. She wouldn't have a character name or title, and she wouldn't have much to do – she would just be exotic. You know, 'enter exotic nurse'.[20]

As these actresses had not trained in Britain they were not given recognition by British theatre institutions, a situation exacerbated by the theatre establishment's relatively closed shop, where entrance was achieved either through a friend already in the business or through contacts made from a shared university education, neither of which would have been very likely for the newly arrived black female immigrant. Established theatres rarely employed black artists and, despite the growing number of black people in Britain, few dramatists wrote black British parts. American images dominated the stage and screen and touring shows brought over African American star performers to play the key roles, with black British performers as understudies or supporting parts.[21] The Royal Court's 1958 production of Errol John's *Observer* prize-winning play *Moon on a Rainbow Shawl* (1956) cast three of the lead roles with American performers, and its production of Barry Reckord's *Skyvers* (1963) is renowned for justifying the use of white actors in black roles with the claim that suitable actors of colour could not be found. Peter Nichols's *The National Health or Nurse Norton's Affair* (National Theatre, 1969) cast Cleo Sylvestre as a central character – Nurse – but black actresses were more likely to be cast as background maids and servants. The actresses's dilemma was to either play a stereotypical role, or forgo her career; when Pauline Henriques got fed up with predictable parts she retrained as a social worker.

By the 1970s, when it was clear that British performers of colour were still not getting opportunities comparable with their white counterparts and as the critical mass of black practitioners increased, a few specialist black theatre companies were formed, including the Dark and Light Theatre Company, later called the Black Theatre of Brixton (founded 1974; folded 1977), Black Theatre Co-operative (now Nitro; founded 1979), and Temba (1972–92). These foreshadowed a boom in the 1980s, with the formation of Black Mime Theatre (1984–98), Double Edge (founded 1984), Talawa (founded 1986) and the Theatre of Black Women (1982–8), to name a few. The formation of black theatre companies brought debates about appropriate roles for black actresses to the fore, debates which were heightened by the emergence of British-born second-generation black women onto the theatre scene. Black theatre companies staged productions of classical plays, as well as plays by black playwrights, but second-generation black actresses, such as Josette Bushell-Mingo, Josette Simon and Cathy Tyson, asserted their right to parts on mainstream British stages.[22] Mainstream recognition is sometimes used as a cultural marker of the extent to which a black actress can be said to have 'made it' professionally, and the detrimental effects of racism are often seen to have been overcome as a result. Integrated/colour-blind casting initiatives soon led to black actresses being cast in non-racially specific ('white') roles in the Royal Shakespeare Company (RSC) and the National Theatre (fig. 18).

Since the 1990s, British black theatre practitioners have persistently debated whether there is, in fact, still a need for specialist subsidised companies which seem to delimit the possibilities for integration so heavily pursued in political rhetoric in general and by many British actresses of colour in particular. The closing of several specialist black theatre companies throughout the 1990s, and consequent dispersal of black practitioners throughout the industry, coincided with the Arts Council of England (ACE) 'Cultural Diversity' initiatives to redress the imbalance of roles for actors of colour. Recommendations such as those in *The Eclipse Report: Strategies to Combat Institutional Racism in the Theatre* (2002) advocate a return to a type of quota system that requires all theatres to create opportunities for cultural diversity in their programming, casting and administration. The aim is to bring the theatre closer to reflecting multi-racial British culture, both through the types of plays that are presented and in terms of colour-blind casting and employment.

The Eclipse Theatre Company was established in January 2002 as a direct result of the recommendations of the *Eclipse* report. They have toured black and multi-racial plays, including a revival of Errol John's *Moon on a Rainbow Shawl* (Nottingham Playhouse in collaboration with the New Wolsey Theatre, Ipswich and the Bristol Old Vic, 2002), Dipo Agboluaje's West African version of Bertolt Brecht's *Mother Courage and*

Fig. 18. Sophie Okonedo as Cressida in *Troilus and Cressida*, The National Theatre, 1999.
(Photo: Catherine Ashmore.)

her Children (Nottingham Playhouse with the New Wolsey Theatre, Ipswich and Birmingham Repertory Theatre, 2003) and Roy Williams's *Little Sweet Thing* (New Wolsey Theatre, Ipswich in association with Nottingham Playhouse and Birmingham Repertory Theatre, 2004) set in a contemporary multi-racial urban community. The West End transfers of Paul Sirett's *The Big Life* (2004) and Kwame Kwei-Armah's *Elmina's Kitchen* (2003) (the first non-musical black British play to make such a move) are undoubtedly significant effects of cultural diversity initiatives. These achievements appear to signal progress, as all of these productions have prominent parts for black actresses, until we note that in fact Williams's and Kwei-Armah's plays present critiques of male 'black on black' gun violence, with black women as archetypal bad girl bullies or sexually licentious women, and *The Big Life* is a Windrush-inspired Ska musical based on *Love's Labour's Lost*, that once again sees black actresses in popular performance where singing and dancing are central.

Stereotyping: singers, showgirls and sepia sex objects

Black women performers are well known as singers and sportswomen and a list of prominent African American actresses of earlier decades (Lena Horne, Eartha Kitt and Ethel Waters) also sounds remarkably like a roll call of famous blues and jazz singers. Black women often started out as singers or dancers before moving into dramatic careers. Lena Horne mostly appeared in films as herself, performing musical numbers in segregated scenes that could easily be cut when shown in the Deep South. Dorothy Dandridge wanted to be a 'serious' actress, but her most prominent roles were those that involved singing.

Career prospects for black actresses are often limited to racially typecast roles in popular entertainment that require singing and dancing, or dramatic roles as delinquents, maids and prostitutes. The difficulty today is that employment opportunities are even more limited once such parts are removed from the equation. It may be better to *play* a maid than to *be* one, and black women often take on demeaning roles in order to stay in the industry, hoping that things might eventually give way to a system where casting really is based on acting capability and not on fixed assumptions of race and gender. Some critics argue that actresses of colour have developed ways to play against the grain of certain roles. Bogle claims that Louise Beavers used subtle looks to undermine seemingly obedient and stoic characters,[23] and Carlton Jackson argues that the controversy surrounding Hattie McDaniel's Beulah role was unfounded because her refusal to speak in dialect 'diminished some of the "stereotypical" image of black subservience with which the NAACP had charged her'.[24] Some black actresses maintain the view that accepting negative roles endorses black women's denigration and runs the risk of upsetting black audiences, and Dandridge, Horne, Munroe, Corinne Skinner and Cathy Tyson have all taken the more radical step of turning down parts that they found racially demeaning to draw the attention of producers to the fact that the parts were stereotyped.

Questions surrounding stereotyped roles are a key concern for black actresses, particularly those relating to sexuality and sexual objectification on stage. Representations of black women on stage and film are often located within certain prescriptions of identity that are sustained by neocolonial

Anglo-American tendencies to devalue black womanhood. 1920s showgirl Josephine Baker was one of the most well-known black women stage performers in history, but Andrea Stuart argues that her success was premised on her constructing herself as a sexual object which played into racial fantasies of the hypersexual black woman. Stuart argues that the black showgirl's appeal can be linked to neocolonial fascinations with erotic black women and attendant concepts of beauty. Most of the 1920s black chorus line girls fitted Eurocentric perceptions of beauty and eroticism, and were usually light-skinned 'sepia . . . "high yaller" female dancers who were under the age of twenty one and over five foot six in height',[25] with straight hair and Europeanised features. However, Baker was darker-skinned than the typical chorus line girl and Stuart attributes her huge star status in Paris to the way she reproduced the age-old archetype of the sexually predatory, dangerous and vulgar black woman, likening the preoccupation with Baker's bottom to the objectification of Saartje Baartman (the Hottentot Venus), the Dutch slave who was displayed in Paris freakshows in the nineteenth century.[26] The need to remain young, beautiful and sexually erotic is illustrated by Baker's failure to successfully relaunch her career in the 1970s when she 'looked fat, [and] puffy, a diva who had lost her physical appeal'.[27]

Issues of skin colour stretched far beyond these dancing 'black beauties' and into the careers of black dramatic actresses in the post-war years, where shadist discourses (those which discussed the varying shades of black actresses' skin) determined the types of roles that they played. Dark-skinned black women are not deemed beautiful in Eurocentric terms and they have typically played roles as desexualised mammies and maids, epitomised in Louise Beavers's and Hattie McDaniel's portrayals in Hollywood cinema. Lighter-skinned black women sit opposite the mammies as glamorous sex objects or Jezebels, and very light-skinned black actresses, such as Fredi Washington, were typically cast as the archetypal tragic mulatto whose 'one drop' of black blood would cause her downfall, exemplified by the character Peola in Douglas Sirk's 1959 film *Imitation of Life*. A third category of black actresses struggled to find roles because they were too light to play black parts and too dark to play white. Dandridge recounts that she 'wasn't fully accepted in either world, black or white [because she] was too light to satisfy Negroes, not light enough to secure the screen work, the role, the marriage status available to a white woman'.[28] If a role required a light-skinned black woman, a white woman could just as easily darken her skin to play the part, as was often the case when 'Hollywood used white women in more respectable roles by using "Light Egyptian" skincream in order not to use black women.'[29] Black women were expected to look black on stage, and lighter-skinned actresses sometimes had to apply make-up to darken their skin for roles so as to keep the stage free from possible hints of miscegenation when playing against black men.

Contemporary British actresses have not so obviously been affected by discourses of shadism. Where dark-skinned actresses in earlier eras were precluded from leading roles, Marianne Jean Baptiste, Josette Bushell-Mingo, Carmen Munroe, Corinne Skinner-Carter and Josette Simon are all of dark complexions and have all played prominent parts on the British stage. There is less need for black British actresses to conform to Eurocentric ideals of beauty because their careers are not so grounded within the American star system and the requirement to fulfil conventional perceptions of beauty are not as pressing. Mammies, matriarchs and tragic mulattoes are film roles that are not as apparent in stage representations of black British cultural experiences. Black British actresses encounter different stereotypical assumptions within black theatre companies, most notably appertaining to expectations of race and accent. Many contemporary black British plays, and black parts in sitcoms and soap operas, require the ability to perform in Caribbean accents or speak a slang that captures the sound of urban dialects and street culture. Cultural diversity quotas are often met with productions by African American playwrights, and the occasional importation of black American actresses to play lead roles further limits prospects for black British women.[30] Thus black actresses may lose roles because of race or complexion, but equally because their accent does not fit with expectations.

Career prospects: integrated casting and cultural diversity

Most productions on the professional British stage are not productions of black plays, so integrated casting is one way that black actresses can secure a visibility in roles granted on the basis of talent rather than racial specificity. Integrated/colour-blind casting has been welcomed in Britain as a way of achieving equal opportunities that also helps the stage to reflect contemporary multi-racial demographics and acts as an incentive for black attendance at the theatre. Until the 1960s it was an accepted convention for white performers to black up to play black parts, but black actresses playing 'white' parts is a more recent phenomenon that, until quite recently, would always raise comment and debate in the press and within the profession. Errol Hill locates integrated casting measures in the USA as being prompted by the US Supreme Court's 1954 *Brown v. Board of Education* ruling that segregation in education maintained inequality. This paved the way for discussions of racial discrimination in theatre: black performers 'sought entrance into the professional theatre and clamored for roles in nonblack plays, requiring a more venturesome policy in casting Shakespearean productions'.[31] In Britain, integrated casting initiatives were undoubtedly heightened by the boom in black theatre production in the 1980s, which saw companies such as Talawa and Temba mounting 'Binglish'[32] revivals of canonical plays with black casts.[33]

During the early 1980s, Equity and the Independent Theatre Council (ITC) promoted the idea of 'casting irrespective of skin colour or disability',[34] and the main producing companies developed strategies for employing black performers. The RSC started employing a few black performers for each season at Stratford-upon-Avon, and the National Theatre used predominantly black companies for entire seasons (such as the NT Ensemble, 1999) which allowed for casting across the full range of roles in plays such as *Troilus and Cressida*.[35] These interventions were premised on race, however, and they primarily benefited black male actors such as Ray Fearon, Adrian Lester, Dhobi Oparei and Hugh Quarshie; there was no special provision for gender, and few black women were cast in leading roles (fig. 18).

Josette Simon is one of the few black British actresses to have been cast in a range of lead roles usually played by white women. These include Rosaline in *Love's Labour's Lost* (RSC, 1984), Isabella in *Measure for Measure* (RSC, 1988) and Vittoria Corombona in John Webster's *The White Devil* (RSC, 1991), as well as more contemporary parts including Maggie in Arthur Miller's *After the Fall* (National Theatre, 1990), Ellida Wangel in Ibsen's *The Lady from the Sea* (Lyric Hammersmith and West Yorkshire Playhouse, 1994) and Madame in Genet's *The Maids* (Donmar Warehouse, 1997).[36] Reviews of her performances establish the extent to which perceptions of integrated/colour-blind casting and attitudes towards black actresses in the mainstream have changed since she first appeared in 1984.

Critics of Simon's early appearances at the RSC invariably question the director's reasons for casting a black actress, which it is thought must have been motivated by a specific, racially determined purpose. Putting multiracial casts in plays from the classical repertoire with no amendment and no overt statement was viewed suspiciously as a way of avoiding issues of race and identity that needed urgently to be addressed. Reviews looked for reasons to justify the casting choice, reconciling Simon's casting as Rosaline in *Love's Labour's Lost* as a literal embodiment of the text's 'By Heaven thy love is black as ebony.' Reviews of *After the Fall* saw the casting of a black actress as a useful way to distance the character from associations with Marilyn Monroe. Philip Prowse's production of *The White Devil* cast the entire Corombona family with black performers, thus making questions about associations between race and casting choice inevitable, and almost all the reviews of the production considered the effect of this decision on the audiences' understanding of the play. Several reviews suggested that Nicholas Hynter's casting of Simon in *Measure for Measure* rendered the play racist and added nuances that would not otherwise have been there. Jim Hiley remarked, 'When Isabella wonders, "Did I tell this, who would love me?", she clearly expects to be dismissed because of her race, as well as her gender and status,'[37] and Milton Shulman claimed that 'Being a black girl in a white court, her problems are intensified.'[38] These responses highlight what Celia R. Daileader terms the 'Catch-22 of colour blind casting: even when the director is "blind" to "colour", the audience often will not be.'[39] Yet, the more well known Simon became, the less compelled reviewers felt to mention race. Although most of the critics discuss the issue in reviews of *Love's Labour's Lost*, by the early 1990s it had become less prominent in their comments on Ibsen's *The Lady from the Sea* (where the actress is mostly referred to as Miss Simon or Josette Simon) – a shift in attitude that may well also be an effect of a 'nineties sensitivity'[40] when they tended politely to ignore race so as not to appear racist.

One danger with colour-blind casting is that a lack of awareness about the ways in which race signifies in performance means that unwitting connotations between racial stereotype and role can be prolonged. Daileader refers to the association between black male virility and casting choices exemplified by plays that insinuate 'Othellophilia . . . [through] the fascination with this theatrical fable of "black on white" sex'.[41] Similarly, casting Josette Simon as Vittoria Corombona in *The White Devil* could imply the sexually licentious black woman, as would the innumerable black Biancas in productions of *Othello*. Or we can look to such ambiguous castings as Katie Mitchell's 1997 production of Edward Kemp's *The Mysteries* for the RSC where Josette Bushell-Mingo played both Mary, mother of Jesus, and Eve, the cause of the fall of mankind.

Integrated casting is usually premised on putting black actresses into 'white' parts, opening up possibilities for crossover into the mainstream at the cost of fewer parts that deal with the specificities of black women's lives. Fundamentally, this means that black women are integrating into systems that marginalise their identities. At the same time the closure of black theatre companies has seen the British theatre industry gradually return to a system that is integrated and culturally diverse in principle, but not in fact – black actresses remain marginal because so few black women's parts are written for the professional stage and casting is still mostly aligned to the race of a character. During the Harlem Renaissance, Dubois sanctioned the idea of theatre about, by, for and near black people.[42] Continuing to produce plays *about* black women, *by* black writers *for* black audiences is crucial to creating spaces for black actresses to be cast in key roles that address issues of invisibility and identity.

Oscars and out

Halle Berry's Oscar acceptance speech caused much controversy, with many people feeling that it was unnecessary for her to frame her personal victory within the historical experience of black actresses. Critics world-wide felt that she had gone overboard in her histrionics, in harking back to times long past and in raising issues that bore little relevance to her winning the award or to race relations in the contemporary world. In a public debate on BBC News Online, for example, it was said that because race is no longer an 'issue' Berry was wrong to mention it. Her admirers, though, insisted that she was right to introduce the subject, especially as she had had to fend off stiff competition from top white nominees – Nicole Kidman (*Moulin Rouge*), Sissy Spacek (*In the Bedroom*), Renée Zellweger (*Bridget Jones's Diary*) and Judi Dench (*Iris*) – to secure the award. The significance of the occasion should not be underestimated because clearly Berry had achieved what most black women nominees before and since have failed to do.[43] History was being made.

But let us not forget the role for which Berry's Oscar was awarded. Leticia Musgrove is a single black mother who tyrannises her comfort-eating obese child before unknowingly starting an affair and falling in love with the benevolent recovering racist white man who had executed her husband on Death Row. The film ends just as she has discovered his identity, but she leaves the issue unchallenged as they share chocolate ice cream and stare into the moonlight. The role resonates with archetypes of bad black mothers, hard-nosed matriarchs whom black men find difficult to love and who can only be rescued by the good deeds of a heroic white male. The Academy Awards recognition of a black woman for this type of role signals that things may not have come so very far in the years since Hattie McDaniel's Best Supporting Actress award for playing Mammy in *Gone with the Wind* (1939), or Whoopi Goldberg's for playing a fraudulent soothsayer in *Ghost* (1990). Hattie McDaniel had been barred from *Gone with the Wind*'s Atlanta première in 1939, and, even now, black women continue to face discrimination. British actress Marianne Jean-Baptiste recalls not being invited to the 1997 Cannes film festival launch party for Mike Leigh's *Secrets and Lies* even though she was nominated for an Oscar for her part: 'There was only one Oscar-nominated actor who wasn't there, and that was me.'[44]

Clearly, there have been significant strides in the professional possibilities for black actresses since their early appearances in the mid-nineteenth century. But there is still a very long way to go to achieve anything near equality with their white counterparts. While the so-called 'race year' at the 2002 Oscars (Denzel Washington won Best Actor in a Leading Role and Sidney Poitier was honoured with a Lifetime Achievement Award) may have helped Halle Berry's individual career, there has not been the significant impact in the career prospects for black actresses that her acceptance speech hoped for. Empowerment narratives that play down the working conditions that prevail for black actresses and foreground black women's resilience are invariably flawed. Black women may well require resilience to maintain careers in racist and sexist discourses, but many leave the profession altogether and retrain in alternative careers. Tanner's survey of early black dramatic actresses (published in 1992) concludes:

> The legacy of the early Black actress, like her life, was severely impacted by racism. Historically, some of the problems of race relations in America have been demonstrated by the roles Black women are forced to play on the professional stage. Faced with double discrimination, that of race and sex, Black actresses have been generally restricted to performing within a prescribed framework that permitted limited opportunity.[45]

That this statement still obtains today is testimony to the difficulties that black actresses continue to face when establishing and maintaining their careers. Racism has gone underground, implicit in the types of roles in which black actresses are still often cast, if not in the explicit segregations and blatant mistreatment that had shaped previous decades. Looking at success only in terms of star status and mainstream visibility leads to the assumption that things have vastly improved, but if we study the careers of black actresses as a whole we can see that, while there has been some improvement, all out celebrations are somewhat premature.

NOTES

1. Hattie McDaniel was the first black woman ever to receive an Academy Award for Best Supporting Actress for her part as Mammy in *Gone with the Wind* (1939); Whoopi Goldberg also received a Best Supporting Actress Oscar for playing Oda Mae Brown in *Ghost* (1990).
2. See Errol G. Hill and James V. Hatch, *A History of African American Theatre* (Cambridge: Cambridge University Press, 2003), for considerable discussion of the conditions within which black performers worked.
3. Jo A. Tanner, *Dusky Maidens: The Odyssey of the Early Black Dramatic Actress* (London: Greenwood, 1992), p. 8.
4. Ibid.

5. Ibid.
6. Ibid., p. 132.
7. Glenda E. Gill, *White Grease Paint on Black Performers: A Study of the Federal Theatre, 1935–1939* (New York: Peter Lang, 1988), p. 74.
8. Donald Bogle, *Brown Sugar: Eighty Years of America's Black Female Superstars* (New York: Harmony Books, 1980), p. 11.
9. See, for example, Donald Bogle, *Dorothy Dandridge: A Biography* (New York: Amistad, 1997); Christopher John Farley, *Introducing Halle Berry: A Biography* (New York: Pocket Books, 2002); Brett Howard, *Lena Horne: Singer and Actress* (Los Angeles: Melrose Square Publishing Company, 1991); Carlton Jackson, *Hattie: The Life of Hattie McDaniel* (Lanham, MD: Madison Books, 1990); and Frank Sanello, *Halle Berry: A Stormy Life – The Unauthorised Biography* (London: Virgin Books, 2003).
10. Dorothy Dandridge and Earl Conrad, *Everything and Nothing: The Dorothy Dandridge Tragedy* (New York: Abelard Schuman, 1970).
11. This chapter draws on interviews with black British actresses in Stephen Bourne, *Black in the British Frame: The Black Experience in British Film and Television* (London: Continuum, 2001); Jim Pines, ed., *Black and White in Colour: Black People in British Television since 1936* (London: BFI Publishing, 1992); Alison Oddey, ed., *Performing Women: Stand-ups, Strumpets and Itinerants* (Basingstoke: Macmillan, 1999); Roland Rees, *Fringe First: Pioneers of Fringe Theatre on Record* (London: Oberon Books, 1992); and Carole Woddis, ed., *Sheer Bloody Magic: Conversations with Actresses* (London: Virago, 1991).
12. Tanner, *Dusky Maidens*, p. xii.
13. David Krasner, *A Beautiful Pageant: African American Theatre Drama and Performance in the Harlem Renaissance 1910–1927* (Basingstoke: Palgrave Macmillan, 2002), p. 5.
14. W. E. B. DuBois, *The Souls of Black Folk*, ed. Henry Louis Gates, Jr. and Terri Hume Oliver, Norton Critical Edition (New York: W. W. Norton and Company, 1999), p. 11.
15. Gill, *White Grease Paint*, p. 2.
16. Such plays included Langston Hughes's *Mulatto: A Tragedy of the Deep South* (1935), Frank Wilson's *Walk Together Chillun* (Harlem: FTP, 1936), and Theodore Ward's *Big White Fog* (Chicago: FTP, 1938).
17. Black actresses had performed in Britain before the 1940s, particularly in touring shows from the USA. See Susan Croft, ed., *Black and Asian Performance at the Theatre Museum: A User's Guide* (London: Theatre Museum, 2003), for a list of key productions between 1825 and 2000.
18. Black actresses of this era also included Nina Baden-Semper, Nadia Cattouse and Corinne Skinner-Carter.
19. Pines, *Black and White in Colour*, p. 26.
20. Ibid., p. 61.
21. Pauline Henriques was understudy for Georgia Burke in the American Negro Theatre's touring production of *Anna Lucasta* (1944) at His Majesty's Theatre (1947); she was instrumental in setting up the understudy company to mount their own productions.
22. Second- and third-generation actresses include Mojisola Adebayo, Adjoa Andoh, Doreene Blackstock, Lorna Brown, Antonia Coker, Judith Jacob, Jenny Jules,

Nadine Marshall, Josephine Melville, Ashley Miller, Tanya Moodie, Cecilia Noble, Sarah Powell, Susan Salmon, Ellen Thomas and Angela Wynter.

23. Bogle, *Brown Sugar*, p. 73.
24. Jackson, *Hattie*, p. xii.
25. Andrea Stuart, *Showgirls* (London: Jonathan Cape, 1996), p. 80.
26. Steven Watson, *The Harlem Renaissance: Hub of African-American Culture, 1920–1930* (New York: Pantheon Books, 1995), p. 126.
27. Bogle, *Brown Sugar*, p. 191.
28. Dandridge and Conrad, *Everything and Nothing*, pp. 154–5.
29. Bruce M. Tyler, *From Harlem to Hollywood: The Struggle for Racial and Cultural Democracy, 1920–1943* (New York: Garland Press Inc., 1992), p. 129.
30. David Lan's production of Lorraine Hansberry's *A Raisin in the Sun* (Young Vic 2001; revived 2004 for Young Vic on Walkabout) cast African American actress Novella Nelson as Lena Younger.
31. Errol Hill, *Shakespeare in Sable: A History of Black Shakespearean Actors* (Amherst: University of Massachusetts Press, 1984), p. 143.
32. Jatinder Verma, 'The Challenge of Binglish: Analysing Multi-Cultural Productions', in Patrick Campbell, ed., *Analysing Performance: A Critical Reader* (Manchester: Manchester University Press, 1996), pp. 193–202, p. 193.
33. Talawa have produced Oscar Wilde's *The Importance of Being Earnest* (Bloomsbury Theatre, 1989), *Antony and Cleopatra* (Liverpool Everyman and Bloomsbury Theatre, 1991), *King Lear* (Oxford Playhouse and Cochrane Theatre, 1994) and a multi-racial *Othello* (Drill Hall, 1997). Temba's productions include *Romeo and Juliet* and Ibsen's *Ghosts*.
34. Delia Jarrett-Macauley, *Equal Opportunities: Policy into Practice: Race* (London: Independent Theatre Council, 1988), p. 18.
35. Members of the NT Ensemble 99 also performed in *The Merchant of Venice*, John Caird's version of Voltaire's *Candide*, Nick Dear's version of Maxim Gorky's *Summerfolk*, Rita Dove's *The Darker Face of the Earth*, Anthony Drewe's *Honk! The Ugly Duckling* and Edward Lyttleton's *Money*.
36. Claire Benedict, Josette Bushell-Mingo, Nadine Marshall, Jo Martin, Cathy Tyson and Marianne Jean-Baptiste are among others who have acted at the RSC and/or National Theatre.
37. *Listener*, 19 November 1987, repr. in *London Theatre Record* 7.23 (5–18 November 1987), p. 1496.
38. *Evening Standard*, 11 October 1988, repr. in *London Theatre Record* 8.21 (7–20 October 1988), p. 1418.
39. Celia R. Daileader, 'Casting Black Actors: Beyond Othellophilia', Catherine M. S. Alexander and Stanley Wells, eds., *Shakespeare and Race* (Cambridge: Cambridge University Press, 2000), pp. 177–202, p. 183.
40. Daileader, 'Beyond Othellophilia', p. 189.
41. Ibid., p. 178.
42. Errol Hill, ed., *The Theatre of Black Americans: A Collection of Critical Essays* (New York: Applause, 1987), p. 4.
43. Failed black women Oscar nominees in the Best Supporting Actress (BSA) and Best Actress (BA) categories are Ethel Waters BSA (*Pinky*, 1949); Dorothy Dandridge BA (*Carmen Jones*, 1954); Diana Ross BA (*Lady Sings The Blues*, 1972); Cicely Tyson BA (*Sounder*, 1972); Diahann Carroll BA (*Claudine*, 1974);

Whoopi Goldberg BA (*The Color Purple*, 1985); Angela Bassett BA (*What's Love Got to Do with It*, 1993); Marianne Jean-Baptiste BSA (*Secrets and Lies*, 1997); and Sophie Okonedo BSA (*Hotel Rwanda*, 2005).

44. Oddey, *Performing Women*, p. 97.
45. Tanner, *Dusky Maidens*, pp. 132–3.

FURTHER READING

Bogle, Donald. *Brown Sugar: Eighty Years of America's Black Female Superstars*. New York: Harmony Books, 1980.

Dorothy Dandridge: A Biography. New York: Amistad, 1997.

Boume, Stephan. *Black in the British Frame: The Black Experience in British Film and Television*. London: Continuum, 2001.

Curtis, Susan. *The First Black Actors on the Great White Way*. Columbia: University of Missouri Press, 1998.

Dandridge Dorothy, and Earl Conrad. *Everything and Nothing: The Dorothy Dandridge Tragedy*. New York: Abelard-Schuman, 1970.

Gill, Glenda E. *White Grease Paint on Black Performers: A Study of the Federal Theatre, 1935–1939*. New York: Peter Lang, 1988.

Hill, Errol G. *Shakespeare in Sable: A History of Black Shakespearean Actors*. Amherst: University of Massachusetts Press, 1984.

Hill, Errol G., and James V. Hatch. *A History of African American Theatre*. Cambridge: Cambridge University Press, 2003.

Jackson, Carlton. *The Life of Hattie McDaniel*. Lanham, MD: Madison Books, 1990.

Pines, Jim, ed. *Black and White in Colour: Black People in British Television Since 1936*. London: BFI Publishing, 1992.

Sanello, Frank. *Halle Berry: A Stormy Life – The Unauthorised Biography*. London: Virgin Books, 2003.

Stuart, Andrea. *Showgirls*. London: Jonathan Cape, 1996.

Tanner, Jo A. *Dusky Maidens: The Odyssey of the Early Black Dramatic Actress*. London: Greenwood Press, 1992.

III

GENRE, FORM AND TRADITION

12

JACKY BRATTON

Mirroring men: the actress in drag

When seeing a man cross-dress we may read the construction of 'woman'.
When we see a woman cross-dress as a man, the 'real' in our culture, what
do we see? We may read power. But if we read (a construction of) a man, that
which is supposedly not constructed, faith in the real may begin to break down.

Elizabeth Drorbaugh

Since the development of a discourse of sexual identity in western culture, a great deal of academic attention has focused upon cross-dressing on stage; less than half of it, however, has been upon the actress who dresses and performs a masculine role. And yet, as Drorbaugh and others have suggested,[1] the woman's act in dressing up as a man may be far more transgressive, challenging and disturbing than the opposite transformation. Butler formulates it as 'a monstrous ascent into phallicism'.[2] It cannot be read, like male cross-dressing, simply as defining and playing with the womanly other; it challenges not only the way we read the hierarchy, but also the ontology, of the male. There are further ways in which the two acts of cross-dressing are deeply dissimilar. It is at least arguable that male cross-dressing has always contributed in similar ways over many centuries to the philosophical and ritual underpinning of the patriarchal societies;[3] but the material culture goes its own way, and the enactment of the male by women seems to me to be always specific to the immediate, historical negotiations of interpersonal power through gender. Women, in other words, perform on stage in male clothes, or parts or versions of male clothing, for various reasons and with extremely different effects at different points in the history of the actress.

In the simplest and most enduring case, as soon as there were actresses on the British public stage they began to wear breeches or trousers to show their legs while dancing, and dramatic roles were very soon written in which they could make a similar display for the sexualised enjoyment of the spectator, and, in some cases, could make fun of male appearance and self-regard in the process.[4] For as long as female clothing concealed the lower body and the legs in drapery, garments which are more like male ones – bifurcated, tighter and more revealing – have continued to be used on stage for this reason. One might well add that stage dress for this kind of display soon became very unlike the street wear of either sex, and had a separate developmental line involving thinner fabrics, brighter colours and even some specific garments – tights, abbreviated shorts, the 'body,' shining or spangled surfaces, tassels, tight-waisted corsets – which had more to do with dressing up the stage itself as a zone of sensation and physical excitement than with mixing the signs of gender. It is also true, however, that this stage sign system was constantly enlivened by playful reference to the worlds of fashion and of everyday life, and carnival appropriation of, for example, the sparkling midshipman's uniform, the jockey's cap and whip, or the sailor's tight-thighed, wide-bottomed trousers added piquancy to the sexual display. This version of 'cross-dressing' is scarcely more or less than a display of the female body, and as time went on a performance tradition developed that executed this 'impersonation' in an increasingly inflated, exaggerated and overt manner in no way intended to confuse reception of the sexual identity of the performer.

From the first some complexities of reading did begin to enter, as evidenced by the widely repeated anecdote about Margaret Woffington's Harry Wildair, in the early eighteenth century, which she averred made half the men in the audience think she was a man, to which a rival actress is supposed to have responded that the other half could easily put them right on that score. It was, however, in the nineteenth century, after the birth of the concept of 'psychology' in the Romantic melting-pot but before the new analyses of the late nineteenth-century sexologists became common knowledge, that the most interesting male impersonations occurred. The use of tights, breeches or trousers to expose and emphasise a female body was still a keenly enjoyed performance. Kirsten Pullen, in her recent study of the actress/whore trope, points out that in this, the period of the 'cult of true womanhood', 'the prostitute, like the female burlesquer, used male attire to highlight her sexuality and project an aura of domination', offering a sexuality that was 'thrillingly masculinized'[5] because it was available for money, and suggested a woman prepared to take the sexual initiative. I would add that within this period, the relatively straightforward hypersexuality (to use Pullen's term) of the actress performing in revealing pseudo-masculine attire went through a series of robust manifestations, which may reward further exploration in the British context; but cross-dressing was also complicated by and intertwined with a different aesthetic objective, possibly not without sexual meanings of its own. There were, I would suggest, historical reasons why female to male cross-dressing became important in offering an on-stage exploration of the meanings not of being a man or a woman, but of being a boy. This impersonation branched off from the simpler mode; it was not simply the 'legitimate' stage's version of what in the world of the illegitimate remained a titillating entertainment, but was, rather, a pointed, not necessarily conscious but always emotionally charged, response to particular constraints upon the performance of sexuality; and it occurred both in the music hall and on the dramatic stage. The rest of this essay will consider the work of certain individuals in both the hypersexual and the 'boy' impersonations through the century in the light of this suggestion.

Burlesque and the body: Vestris and her heirs

Lucia Elizabeth Bartolozzi, later Vestris, then Mathews, known profession-ally as Madame Vestris (1797–1856), is an instructive instance of the mal-leability of the reputation of the actress in the hands of theatre history. She became a celebrity when she returned alone to London after an operatic training and a brief marriage into a famous dancing family in Paris. Her starring solo career began in 1820 under Elliston's management at Drury Lane, where she cross-played as Don Juan and as Macheath in *The Beggar's Opera*, and became famous in the title role of Moncrieff's *Giovanni in London*, a romp which combined burlesque, cross-dressing and topical jokes about the Town. Contemporary journalism instantly gave her a lucrative but potentially awkward reputation: pornographic pamphlets and broad-side cod-biographies exploited her racy private life, and described with relish her beauty, her voice and, especially, her legs. Soon after her death, how-ever, a Victorian lady biographer managed to represent the hard-working and sensational theatrical entrepreneur as a domestic goddess and a duti-ful wife, and by 1930 she was, even less excitingly, being credited with the invention of the box set.[6] Recently she has been celebrated by Elizabeth Schafer for her pioneering revivals and productions of Shakespeare: Schafer shows convincingly that in the early 1840s at Covent Garden Vestris's managerial decisions combined the practical and the innovative in ways no Victorian male actor-manager ever achieved.[7] Trevor Griffiths has also claimed Vestris's *Midsummer Night's Dream*, in which she played Oberon and cast women in all the fairy characters, including Puck, while restoring Shakespeare's version of the text to the stage for the first time in 200 years, as a massive achievement thoroughly undervalued by theatre history ever since.[8] And finally in the late twentieth century Kathy Fletcher, inspired by Nina Auerbach's influential revisiting of the Victorian woman and her power, has rediscovered Vestris's cross-dressed performances at the Olympic, where she was lessee and manager in the 1830s, and reads them as a sign of the 'challenges which she faced as a manager in a male-dominated, male-oriented commercial theatre'.[9]

At the Olympic Vestris built a modern, 'tasteful' and commercially suc-cessful theatre for the middle classes upon her earlier career as a celebrity, a beauty and, specifically, upon her earnings and reputation as a cross-dressed performer and a fast woman. Leigh Hunt in *The Examiner* said she was 'an actress who contrived to be at once so very much of a gentleman and yet so entire and unaltered a woman',[10] and she hired a gentlemanly writer of extravaganza and burlesque, J. R. Planché, to create vehicles for her appearances in 'male' roles with spectacular costumes and exotic settings. The extravagant display of good taste and the much-insisted-upon domestic charm and beauty of the little theatre were nevertheless settings within which, essentially, Vestris and a succession of other beautiful women offered their bodies in striking but scant costumes for the visual delight of fashionable audiences. Perhaps the pseudo-masculinity of her roles emblematised her controlling position, but contemporary accounts stress how much her 'lusciousness' of voice, her 'accustomed grace' of movement and her 'archness' of manner engaged the audience in a conspiracy with her which telegraphed female availability.[11]

George Cruickshank depicted Vestris dressed as Giovanni as one of the illustrations in a best-selling serial story, *Life in London* (1821), with text by Pierce Egan. In this episode Egan has his heroes, three fashionable young men about town, stroll into the greenroom at Drury Lane. They are bored by actors grumbling about management; they leave, commenting that they don't like cross-dressing on stage, because they cannot believe 'that the females who are engaged in the same piece can act their parts with such spirit and feeling as when a man is their hero'.[12] One might hear in this put-down something of the sexual anxiety that can attend male response to usurpation by an attractive female in masculine dress. But Cruickshank produces a portrait of Vestris that lacks any such edge. In the picture (fig. 19) the three gentlemen stand round in their evening finery of opera hats, high neck-cloths and skin-tight buckskins displaying a clearly marked masculinity, while in their midst the woman, a head shorter and standing in a regressive, self-deprecating way with her head on one side, wears a pretty compromise of a costume. Its high waist and V-necked bodice belong to very fashionable (female) walking-dress, but it terminates at midthigh to reveal shapely legs in white tights – not the whole lower body as displayed by the men. She carries a cane in her white-gloved right hand, but the left is raised towards her face to ward off compliment and the gaze of her nearest admirer. Stage costume is obvious in the large crucifix round her neck, indicating Giovanni's Catholic foreignness, and in the stage-hero's feather on the head that she wears, not in the masculine hat or helm, but in her uncovered hair, like a lady at an evening engagement.

Planché's extravaganzas, written as a vehicle for Vestris's personal style, build upon the tradition of travesty in stage burlesque: they take heroic

Fig. 19. Madame Vestris, 'The Green Room at Drury Lane Theatre: Tom and Jerry Introduced to the Characters in Don Giovanni'. Illustration to Pierce Egan, *Life in London*, London: Sherwood, Neeley and Jones, 1821, drawn and engraved by I. R. and G. Cruikshank. (Author's collection.)

subjects and characters, especially from classical antiquity, and make fun by inversion, dropping them into incongruously modern, domestic situations and plots. Later he added fairy-tale and romance subjects, but the point was still the mixing of incongruous elements, the cross-dressing of ordinary life and language in elaborate costume and settings. This procedure is the taproot of the British pantomime tradition: it laces homely comedy into a display of glitteringly revealed female bodies, headed by a cross-dressed leading lady. David Mayer, in his seminal psychoanalytic examination of British pantomime, has pinpointed the 'principal boy' as originating in Vestris's time, and traces the figure onwards through the century.[13] It is worth adding that burlesque travesty as developed at the Olympic also continued in more exclusively adult musical entertainment, flourishing for example at the Gaiety Theatre in London's West End and being exported, with explosive results, to America. In 1868 Lydia Thompson and her troupe of British Blondes were widely attacked and frequently banned from performing the classical burlesque *Ixion* in the major cities of the USA. Their costume as well as their material reached back to the Olympic over thirty years before. Kirsten Pullen argues that the outrage they caused was not simply at their hypersexuality, but also their 'attempts to claim male privilege' by their gender-bending.[14] In Britain burlesque was always a very feminised form, so it was only in the USA that the British Blondes seemed to aspire to a revolutionary take-over of the genre. Pullen is persuasive in her demonstration that the US press could not handle Thompson's assertiveness – the fact that she 'talked like a man but walked like a woman'.[15]

The Olympic was by no means the only London West End theatre to stage gender play in the 1830s, before the onset of Victorian proprieties and strict role-definition, and it is arguable that there were other strands of representation that interlaced with the hypersexual pantomime version of cross-dressing in the ensuing decades. In many farces and short comedies women played men, or girls who dressed as men for part of the action; and some went further than a mere leg-show, and began to test the assumptions of the binary they crossed. Farces like Collier's *Is She a Woman?* (Queen's, 1835), in which the dashing and hearty Louisa Nisbett played a woman given to hunting and shooting who has changed social roles with her delicate brother, were openly exploring and, eventually, tightly resetting the boundaries of acceptably gendered behaviour. Nisbett's costuming in this role would have reflected the playful experimentation of women's street dress at the time; but in *The Rifle Brigade* at the Adelphi in 1838 she donned full-dress uniform and wooed and kissed a jealous husband's wife before his face; the audience, of course, were aware not only of her femininity but also of the 'real' gender of the character she was playing.[16] At a less fashionable theatrical level melodrama also probed some of the same ground. Marcia Macarthy (1808–70) made a solid career in the London minor theatres, where by 1838 she was joint manager of Sadler's Wells with her husband Robert Honner. A small, slight woman with a big voice,[17] Mrs Honner's personal speciality was in energetic boy roles or as women in masculine disguise; one of the more remarkable of the latter was her creation of Margaret Catchpole, in a play by Edward Stirling (Surrey 1845) based on the true story of a working-class Suffolk woman whose cross-dressed criminal career included being condemned to death and then transported for horse-theft but culminated in her becoming a wealthy and respectable Australian matron. The topic of gender was primarily, however, a middle-class preoccupation. The 1830s saw the beginning of the career of Mary Ann Hehl, a.k.a. Fanny Clifton, who married Edward Stirling and became a redoubtably respectable Victorian theatre manager. At the New Strand in 1837–8 she played a girl called Arabella who dresses up as a 'handsome officer' in a piece called *Venus in Arms*, which was apparently the sole dramatic effort of Vestris's future biographer, Mrs Baron Wilson. Arabella's cousin is doubtful of the success of the proposed disguise – which is simply intended to facilitate their travelling – saying she has not much of the air of a military man, but she exclaims, 'never fear – I'll soon acquire it! A well-cut coat . . . a good crop of mustachoes, and a little blustering – if these don't make a fashionable fellow, may I die an old maid.'[18] Mrs Stirling won journalistic approval in this role, and then delighted *The Idler* even further when her husband wrote her a play, *Batchelor's Buttons*, to display her versatility: she appeared as a romping schoolgirl, a jockey, a maid-of-all-work and a 'sport', 'all blood and no bone', which the journal declared she played with 'a sprightliness and "*je ne-se-quoi*," original as it was delightful'.[19]

In the following decades, leading ladies and/or female managers in theatres in London and across the country sometimes chose to play masculine parts, at every level from the penny gaff to the West End; Macheath, the ubiquitous midshipman, even certain Shakespearean roles were often chosen by women who had sufficient power in the theatres where they appeared sometimes to please themselves about what role they played. Virtuoso costume-changing by young stars and playful self-assertion by sometimes large and always heavily corseted ladies playing Richard III or Hamlet on their benefit nights remained an understood phenomenon through the middle of the century. Then, as the music hall began to acquire a separate performance tradition and distinct audiences, serio-comic singers took over the (often hypersexual) cross-dressed performance as one of their possible guises. Many, regardless of their build or of verisimilitude, did quick-change impersonations like Mrs Stirling's that included male characters. Others made a deliberate character and costume mix in order to create a stage persona that combined the female with a sexual assertiveness and awareness that was progressively being appropriated exclusively to the male. Annie Adams, for example, a substantially built singer of ballads and comic songs, is pictured wearing a masculine coat and tie with a full crinoline, cinching in her waist to emphasise her swelling bosom under the male accoutrements, and singing of being 'the merriest girl that's out'.[20] Many female performers explored such ways of temporarily entering the culture of physical enjoyment and relative sexual freedom that characterised the fantasy world of the halls, which was otherwise off limits for women.

The boy in the ballet: from the Elsler sisters to Peter Pan

But proxy participation in the masculine world of sexual fun and games was not the only reason for actresses to cross-dress. Some performers found roles in which to explore a more subtle vein of gender uncertainty: they were playing 'boy'. Eva Le Gallienne defended her 1936 performance of the role of Hamlet thus:

It is possible for an actress at the height of her powers to give the impression of being a boy, while having at her command all the craft, range, force, and subtlety which such great roles require. This has always been true of Rostand's *L'Aiglon* ... De Musset's Lorenzaccio, and – in a very different mood – Barrie's Peter Pan.[21]

I would argue that the fascination of a woman playing 'boy' is more complicated than the combination of smallness with acting experience. The pantomime 'principal boy', like the British Blondes in the burlesque, wore tights to flaunt female curves and indeed often padded her thighs to ensure the proper effect, as the serious actress Olive Logan pointed out with quivering distaste in her attacks upon the British Blondes;[22] but others dressed and played a slender, diminutive boyishness with less obvious sexual responses in mind; and they sometimes delighted audiences, but they also ran into other kinds of disapprobation and disquiet. Perhaps the archetype here is Dorothy Jordan as Little Pickle in *The Spoil'd Child*, first performed for her benefit in March 1790. 'Little Pickle' is a mischievous adolescent full of 'animal spirits', who plays physical tricks – tying lovers' clothes together, serving up a pet parrot for dinner – and then dresses up to impersonate a sailor boy. The play was so tailored to Jordan's personal performance that one published edition is attributed to her as author. The printed text attributed to Bickerstaffe concludes with a duet on the theme of leniency, ending

> Then censure not a school boy's faults
> But laugh at and excuse 'em,

but Jordan's version ends with a speech to the audience in which she excuses herself for transgressing – only to amuse.

Dorothy Jordan was greatly loved by the public, both as performer and as the long-time partner of the future William IV. In that generation the actress and her many-faceted sexuality were widely understood and tolerated, even admired; but such openness to experiment did not continue, and the actresses had to occlude and indeed close down their explorations. Priscilla Horton, for example, was a child star who in 1834 made the transition from second string in Vestris's extravaganzas to Shakespeare by becoming the first performer to undertake the role of the Fool in *King Lear* for over 200 years. She was then nineteen, and played him according to Macready's conception as a 'fragile, hectic, beautiful-faced, half-idiot-looking boy', wearing a knee-length tunic, long curly hair and a cockscomb cap. She went on to play the ambiguously sexed Ariel for the same manager, with what Forster described as 'submissive animal spirits'.[23] She had been preceded in this role by other girls with gauzy wings and thigh-revealing skirts, and was followed in Charles Kean's 1857 production by a thirteen-year-old Kate Terry. Christine Dymkowski argues persuasively that Ariel was being conceived, at this point, within a gender pattern that makes her a clearly female fairy; but in the Fool, Horton was thinking of herself as a boy.[24] But times changed, such theatrical experiments ceased to be acceptable, and as Horton put on seniority and weight she transformed herself into Mrs German Reed, and cultivated the fiction that she was not appearing in dramas, but rather acting the hostess, welcoming the serious-minded to evenings of music and 'Illustrations' of modern life at her Gallery in Regent Street.

Similarly, Ellen Tree, who managed to disguise her managerial powers and yet continue to appear on stage after 1842 by becoming firmly *Mrs Charles Kean*, had included 'boy' amongst the early work that established her fortune. She was 'broad-shouldered as well as tall, and her long limbs had the fine proportions of the huntress Diana', so that Fanny Kemble, who wrote this appreciative description, found her 'a very pretty fellow' as Romeo to her own Juliet – it was, she said, '[t]he only occasion on which I ever acted Juliet to a Romeo who looked the part'.[25] Tree made a sensation in the title role of Telfourd's classic drama *Ion* at the Haymarket in 1836, playing a saintly boy philosopher who, when he unexpectedly inherits the throne, sacrifices his own life in order to bring about republican rule – an interesting message for the year leading up to the young Victoria's accession. Macready, however, annoyed that the role had been taken out of his hands, and that Tree had succeeded so sensationally where he had not, wrote in his diary that she 'is no more like a young man than a coat and waistcoat are', and moreover she made the role a 'nasty sort of epicene animal'.[26] She backed away from such suspicions, and soon married and 'submerged her individuality completely' in her husband's.[27]

In setting up females in the peacock military uniforms of the period, and even preferring female impersonations of Romeo, the dramatic stage in the 1830s and 1840s was echoing a very striking development in the Romantic ballet. During, as Lynn Garafola has it,

> a twenty-year golden age stretching from the July Revolution to about 1850, the *danseuse en travesti* usurped the position of the male *danseur* in the corps de ballet and as a partner to the ballerina . . . [s]tepping into roles previously filled by men, women now impersonated the sailor boys, hussars, and toreadors . . . of the corps de ballet, even as they displaced real men as romantic leads.[28]

Her argument is that this displacement was a direct response to changing market forces, when the entrepreneurs who took over the opera houses from state control across Europe and Britain began to cater directly to the tastes of their bourgeois subscribers, who made the ballet serve their own sexual pleasure on stage and off. These men did not want the competition of male dancers in their backstage forays, and they found, she suggests, that on stage the 'choreographic play of female bodies' dancing both genders whetted jaded appetites. The travesty dancer stripped the male role of power and mirrored the ethereal ballerina, suggesting moreover further sexual satisfactions on top of her idealisation of femininity; but 'the travesty dancers of the nineteenth-century ballet offered no meditation on the usages of gender, no critical perspective on the sexual politics that ruled their lives, no revelation of the ways masculine and feminine were imaged on the ballet stage'.[29] This remained, perhaps, for the cross-dressing actress to do; and such responses as Macready's, quoted above, suggest that for at least some interested spectators such a challenge – or delight – could indeed sometimes be present in their work.

Consider, for example, the painter Walter Goodman's rather curious book *The Keeleys on Stage and at Home*, inspired, as is clear from the outset, by his unbounded admiration for the actress Mary Anne Goward, Mrs Keeley (1806–99), and especially her execution of 'boy' roles. He opens by stating that 'the very first drama that profoundly interested me was "Jack Sheppard"'.[30] Jack was one of several boy roles that were very important to mid-century actresses. Mrs Honner, mentioned above, was in management at Sadler's Wells in 1839 when the theatres rushed to stage versions of Ainsworth's novel; she played the 'impudent boy of thirteen' in the first act of their version, and her husband took over in act 2 to play the adult Sheppard.[31] There were many more female interpreters of Jack, as well as of several other boys from novels – especially Dickens's Smike and Joe the crossing sweeper from *Bleak House* – who made the names of their female impersonators, and were enshrined as moving miracles of emotional effect in the memories of playgoers. Goodman boasts that his first theatrical portrait was of 'the actress who created the principal character' of Jack in the Adelphi version, with whom, moreover, he claims to be 'intimately acquainted'.[32] But this is 1895, and the book is hagiography rather than pornography; he offers a reverential account of Mrs Keeley's boy impersonations, quoting newspaper critics who admired 'the naiveté, the assurance, the humour and the boldness' of her first, 1839, Jack, and her rendering of the 'audacious, spirited, spoiled, daring young criminal'[33] in the revival at the Haymarket in 1852, by which stage the criminality of the hero at least in the text had been considerably toned down. Every detail of Keeley's performance is clearly engraved in Goodman's memory, which he actually derived from the next revival, at Sadler's Wells in 1855; he saw it all thirteen times and could, he claims, recite all the parts.[34]

Goodman devotes a whole chapter of his book to a loving appreciation of what thrilled him in Keeley's Jack. What he stresses most is her authenticity: she really planes a plank of wood, really puts up her fists to box, really wore and slipped out of genuine metal handcuffs securely locked, really studied picking pockets until the 'actor of Jonathan Wild seldom, if ever, felt the small, flexible hand of Mrs Keeley as it dived neatly into his pocket'.[35] He values the fact that all these accomplishments were the subject of meticulous study, just like her singing and her mimicry of the voices of the other actors in the piece. Her costume as Jack, opening 'in his shirt-sleeves, with a carpenter's apron rolled up to his waist, a long drab waistcoat, knee-breeches, high-heeled shoes, and a red handkerchief tied loosely round his neck' is also lovingly described; it was completed with a George II coat and 'a three-cornered hat, cocked carelessly over his short-cropped hair'.[36] In the rest of his book Goodman touches, rather incoherently, upon many aspects of Mrs Keeley's very substantial theatrical career: her partnership with her husband in management, the family of successful performers she headed, her serious and comic parts, her curtain speeches, her meetings with the great and the good from Queen Victoria downwards; but the heart of his appreciation is her embodiment, for him, of the boy, of animal spirits. That often-repeated, somewhat oxymoronic phrase expresses, I think, appreciation of the volatile and brief human combination of the material and the metaphysical. Goodman fleshes out his response as admiration for authentic bodily skills and for the actress's acute observation and, more importantly, her daring and energy in stepping beyond the limits of the feminine. The painter is fascinated by her capabilities, because they go beyond his conception of what women are and can be; his sense of her superiority is embodied in her moving picture of the young male – or rather, of boy. Her Jack Sheppard impersonation has for him a kind of idealised realism, a vision of humanity that surpasses both male and female, and is simultaneously masculine and innocent, feminine and knowing.

The real boy – Vesta Tilley, the London Idol

I would argue that just such a phenomenon is at work in the widespread idolisation of the next generation of male impersonators, whose stamping ground was not the theatre but the music halls. I have described elsewhere the rising tide of this performance, which began early in the history of the halls within the varied acts of such first-generation stars as Jenny Hill, but soon had many dedicated exponents in the 1880s and 1890s;[37] I would like here to focus on the star male impersonator whose name has survived in

245

show-biz memory: Mrs Matilda Powles, later Lady De Frece – Vesta Tilley (1864–1952). Alfred Butts, an impresario of the grandiose days of the halls and a friend of the actress, insisted that she was 'a frail simple little thing, just radiating the joy of life . . . as light and graceful as a child' whose songs were 'a sincere expression of all the simple emotions of life'[38] – a judgement which, if it is not simply a whitewash, suggests profound self-delusion on the part of the old man. Tilley was, by her own account, a life-long professional with an athlete's understanding of her body and its capabilities, and a complex attitude to the materials of her unique act. Other commentators have come a little nearer to seeing how she worked. Willson Disher's account of Tilley's genius stresses that she developed an understanding of the young men she impersonated gradually, as she 'found herself' as well as them. Before she 'became the London Idol', he says, she understood and sympathised with the 'victims' in her mildly mocking songs, because she had a 'frank admiration of the young male, no matter how rowdy'. But later, when she had the 'full assurance of the public's loyalty', she gave them 'something more than entertainment – something that has a direct bearing on life'. Enacting the young man, 'she brought her wits to bear upon him critically', showing us these rather pitiful creatures 'not as we would see them in real life but viewed through a clever woman's eyes'. Here, at last, is male impersonation that offers a vision of its subject rather than simply a leg-show. Disher, writing in 1938, can only approach the articulation of what he learns about masculinity from Tilley by couching it in terms of military heroism. He castigates the older generation of pre-First World War clubmen, 'crochety veterans', as he calls them, who never grasped the truth about the lanky youths and weedy shopmen of Edwardian England, and were finally responsible for sending those boys to the trenches to die in their tens of thousands. Tilley, he insists, 'knew the heart of the junior clerk', and when she impersonated him as a recruit, a 'meagre figure in khaki' swaggering pathetically across the stage in boots too heavy for him, the mixture of pluck and pathos was comically heartrending.[39]

It is necessary to look to Disher for this description because there is a remarkable absence of press reports describing Tilley's act itself. Most reports simply say it was of course marvellous, and rush on to describe her reception, often in terms of the female fans, hordes of whom she excited to an enthusiasm not matched until the days of the Beatles. She arrived in Oldham, for example, at Christmas 1911, to be 'met by several hundred mill girls . . . They escorted her to the theatre, and then the "spokesgirl" of the crowd intimated that they had arranged to visit the theatre *en masse* every evening of that week.'[40] Some of her cuttings books have survived, and offer remarkable evidence of the devotion she inspired. They include many fan letters, some from young men asking who her tailor is, or requesting autographs for their collection, but mostly from adoring girls:

Dear Miss Tilley
Please forgive a poor girl for writing to such a great actress and so beautiful a lady as yourself. But I feel I must write and tell you how much I love you and admire you. I should love to be with you always and to be a great actress like you is my greatest ambition. Please would you mind telling me how much you charge for bringing little girls out like me.

My darling 'Dick',
Please pardon my presumption in writing to you, but I simply can't help it. I'm so hopelessly in love with you, tho' only a girl.

Dear Miss Vesta Tilley
I want to ask you a favour Vesta I want to see if you will take me as one of your own I am between 16 and 17 years of age don't refuse me Vesta because I love you I love you with all my heart Vesta ever since I saw you at the theatre royal. If you will only take me I will be your slave I will die for you Vesta you do not know how I love you I will do anything for you only take me If it is only to love you I know I am doing wrong but I would give the world to see you Vesta . . . I am not a rich girl I am just a poor girl but as poor as I am I love you the more Vesta my heart is broke for fear you refuse me
From your girl lover
Maggie Arnotte
18 Buxton Street
May I send a kiss for love's sake?[41]

And so on, and on, all from desperately enamoured girls aged from thirteen up. The sweep across class and situation, from the verbal struggles of near-illiteracy to little dignified attempts by young ladies to make small jokes to veil their emotions, is one striking aspect of these missives; another is that Tilley saw fit to preserve them.

The scrapbooks suggest that Tilley hoarded everything about herself, as if the collection provided a mirror of her public face that was important down to the last inch. Even here, however, there is a curious shortage of British press notices that say anything substantive; but on her American tours she was widely reported and interviewed. The columns and features she collected stress, more than anything else, her immaculate, novel and ultra-fashionable dress. Reporters marvel over her ability to do quick changes from Eton suit to flannels to army uniform to white dress tie without the use of anything fake or specially made. This means, as the writers soon begin to point out, that her stage costume is, actually, real menswear, and so might escape from its theatrical frame. The headlines show varying degrees of uneasy consciousness of the pitfalls here. It is one thing to note the imitation of life by art: 'Her Way of Wearing Men's Clothes Shows Careful Study from the Originals', but features begin to move on to the other transition, from stage to street, and there the issue of gender becomes important: 'This Actress Sets Style For Fads in Men's Attire.' Here the word 'fads' puts down those men who are silly enough to copy how a woman dresses; but the largest spreads the scrapbooks preserve face up to her challenge to men more directly, if, apparently, still in jest: 'It Takes a Woman To Show a Man How to Wear His Clothes' and, finally, the bottom line: 'How to be a Successful Man. By . . . Vesta Tilley' (ellipsis original). Figure 20, a publicity poster that still to a modern eye radiates sexuality, suggests how striking 'The London Idol' must have been. There is an unease here that Tilley herself points out when, interviewed about her work, she stressed her physical fitness, her need to stay slim and active by healthy eating, because she had to look more perfect than a man. She said that when a woman goes 'out of her province' into male dress 'audiences – especially the masculine portions thereof – are then more critical, not to say a little jealous, and inclined to make caustic comparisons'.[42] Such awareness of the challenge she presented to the masculine takes us right back to Pierce Egan's worried sneers at Madame Vestris; but no one could say Tilley did not inspire females with 'spirit and feeling'.

The absence of British reviews, the disclaimers Tilley herself became more and more keen to voice as her career climaxed and closed, as well as her eagerness to issue publicity pictures of herself in elaborate female clothes 'in real life', all underline that, as she produced him, 'boy' is uneasy territory. After the popularisation of the new science of sexology and of Freudian notions in the early twentieth century, it became virtually a no-go area for the actress. The perfect imitation of the transient, imperfect creature that is 'boy' was troubling in several ways. A woman cross-dressed as a man, as Drorbaugh suggested in the remarks with which this essay began, may challenge masculine power, and that is in itself transgressive; but there is more to 'boy' than that. If the actress has learnt to plane a plank, pick a pocket, tie a perfect cravat and sit astride a chair smoking a cigarette with an opera hat on the back of her head, and the audience loves and desires that construction of a male/female reality, then she has, indeed, challenged something deeper: the gender division itself, and so the pre-existence of man. She is showing up the constructedness not only of the signs, but also of the 'real', which the whole polarised system of signification is supposed to represent.

248

Fig. 20. Vesta Tilley: a handbill advertising Vesta Tilley's music hall act ca. 1894–5. (Reproduced by courtesy of the Worcestershire Record Office, ref. BA 13801/6/1, b899.)

NOTES

1. Elizabeth Drorbaugh, 'Sliding Scales: Notes on Stormé Delarverié and the Jewel Box Revue', in Lesley Ferris, ed., *Crossing the Stage: Controversies on Cross-dressing* (London: Routledge, 1993), pp. 120–43.
2. Judith Butler, *Bodies that Matter: On the Discursive Limits of 'Sex'* (London: Routledge, 1993), p. 103.

3. See Laurence Senelick, *The Changing Room: Sex, Drag and Theatre* (London: Routledge, 2000).
4. See Gilli Bush-Bailey, *Treading the Bawds* (Manchester: Manchester University Press, 2006), pp. 112–13, 114–17.
5. Kirsten Pullen, *Actresses and Whores on Stage and in Society* (Cambridge: Cambridge University Press, 2005), p. 120.
6. See Allardyce Nicoll, *A History of Early Nineteenth Century Drama, 1800–1850*, 2 vols. (Cambridge: Cambridge University Press, 1930), vol. 1, p. 38; more detail is given in C. J. Williams, *Madame Vestris: A Theatrical Biography* (London: Sidgwick and Jackson, 1973), p. 124.
7. Elizabeth Schafer, *Ms-Directing Shakespeare: Women Direct Shakespeare* (London: The Women's Press, 1998), pp. 196–9.
8. Trevor Griffiths, 'A Neglected Pioneer Production: Madame Vestris' *A Midsummer Night's Dream* at Covent Garden, 1840', *Shakespeare Quarterly* 30 (1979), pp. 386–96, quoted in Elizabeth Schafer, *Ms-Directing*, p. 199.
9. Kathy Fletcher, 'Planché, Vestris, and the Transvestite Role: Sexuality and Gender in Victorian Popular Theatre', *Nineteenth Century Theatre* 15 (1987), pp. 9–33, p. 32.
10. *Examiner*, 30 July 1820, quoted Fletcher, 'Planché, Vestris', p. 22.
11. Press comments quoted in Fletcher, 'Planché, Vestris', p. 17.
12. *Life in London, or, the Day and Night Scenes of Jerry Hawthorn, Esq. . . .* (London: Sherwood, Neely and Jones, 1821, repr. London: Methuen and Co., 1904), pp. 258–9.
13. David Mayer, 'The Sexuality of Pantomime', *Theatre Quarterly* 4.3 (1974), pp. 55–64.
14. Pullen, *Actresses and Whores*, p. 98.
15. Ibid., p. 95.
16. See Jacky Bratton, 'Irrational Dress', in Viv Gardner and Susan Rutherford, eds., *The New Woman and her Sisters: Feminism and Theatre 1850–1914* (London: Harvester Wheatsheaf, 1992), pp. 77–91, pp. 83–4.
17. See Allan Stuart Jackson, *The Standard Theatre of Victorian England* (London: Associated University Presses, 1993), pp. 72–5.
18. *Venus in Arms* (London: Cumberland, 1837), p. 15.
19. Percy Allen, *The Stage Life of Mrs Stirling* (London: T. Fisher Unwin, 1922), p. 44, quoting *The Idler*.
20. See Bratton, 'Irrational Dress', p. 84.
21. Quoted in Ferris, *Crossing the Stage*, p. 2.
22. In both *Apropos of Women and the Theatre* (1869) and *Before the Footlights and Behind the Scenes* (1870), quoted in Pullen, *Actresses and Whores*, pp. 104 and 116.
23. Quoted in Shakespeare, *The Tempest*, ed. Christine Dymkowski (Cambridge: Cambridge University Press 2000), p. 37.
24. Kathy Fletcher in 'Planché, Vestris', 'stresses her dash and vivacity as smart young gentlemen in Planché pieces, and her manipulation of innuendo about spanking'; see p. 25.
25. Frances Ann Kemble, *Records of a Girlhood* (New York: Henry Holt, 1883), p. 200.

26. *The Journal of William Charles Macready*, ed. J. C. Trewin (London: Longmans, 1967), pp. 74–5.
27. J. M. D. Harwick, *Emigrant in Motley: The Journey of Charles and Ellen Kean in Quest of a Theatrical Fortune* (London: Rockliff, 1954), p. 10.
28. 'The Travesty Dancer in Nineteenth-century Ballet', in Ferris, *Crossing the Stage*, pp. 96–106, p. 96.
29. Ibid., p. 104.
30. Walter Goodman, *The Keeleys on the Stage and at Home* (London: Richard Bentley and Son, 1895), p. 1.
31. Dennis Arundell, *The Story of Sadler's Wells* (Newton Abbot: David and Charles, 1978), p. 126.
32. Goodman, *The Keeleys*, pp. 1–2.
33. Ibid., pp. 5, 10.
34. Ibid., p. 12.
35. Ibid., p. 20.
36. Ibid., p. 14.
37. See Bratton 'Irrational Dress', and also J. S. Bratton, 'Beating the Bounds: Gender Play and Role Reversal in the Edwardian Music Hall', in Michael R Booth and Joel H. Kaplan, eds., *The Edwardian Theatre* (Cambridge: Cambridge University Press, 1996), pp. 86–110.
38. From 'An Appreciation', quoted in Sara Maitland, *Vesta Tilley* (London: Virago, 1986), p. 110.
39. In his foundational twentieth-century study of the halls, *Winkles and Champagne* (London: Library Association, 1974 [1938]), pp. 78–80.
40. *The Era*, 23 December 1911.
41. Scrap books in Worcester County Record Office, The Vesta Tilley Collection, accession no. 13081.
42. Headlines from cuttings from unidentified newspaper, date-stamped 7 April 1909; a second unidentified paper; an unnamed Chicago Sunday magazine, 4 October 1903; and the *Weekly Dispatch*, 3 July 1904; the interview quoted is in the Chicago magazine of 1903.

FURTHER READING

Allen, Percy. *The Stage Life of Mrs Stirling*. London: T. Fisher Unwin, 1922.
Butler, Judith. *Bodies that Matter: On the Discursive Limits of 'Sex'*. London: Routledge, 1993.
Discher, Willson. *Winkles and Champagne* (1938). Repr. London: Library Association, 1974.
Ferris, Lesley, ed. *Crossing the Stage: Controversies on Cross-dressing*. London: Routledge, 1993.
Goodman, Walter. *The Keeleys on the Stage and at Home*. London: Richard Bentley and Son, 1895.
Kemble, Frances Ann. *Records of a Girlhood*. New York: Henry Holt, 1883.
Macready, William Charles. *The Journal of William Charles Macready*, ed. J. C. Trewin. London: Longmans, 1967.
Maitland, Sara. *Vesta Tilley*. London: Virago, 1986.

Schafer, Elizabeth. *Ms-Directing Shakespeare: Women Direct Shakespeare*. London: The Women's Press, 1998.

Senelick, Laurence. *The Changing Room: Sex, Drag and Theatre*. London: Routledge, 2000.

Williams, Clifford. *Madame Vestris: A Theatrical Biography*. London: Sidgwick and Jackson, 1973.

13

ELAINE ASTON

'Studies in hysteria': actress and courtesan, Sarah Bernhardt and Mrs Patrick Campbell

In the second half of the nineteenth century, new spectacles of feminine suffering began to appear on the fashionable French and English stages as audiences were mesmerised by the figure of the fallen woman and the actresses who played her. The French actress who took the role of courtesan, or the English actress who played a disgraced wife or prostitute, risked the stigma of their own profession and that of the fallen woman. 'For a large section of society,' writes Tracy C. Davis on the employment of actresses in the nineteenth century, 'the similarities between the actress's life and the prostitute's or *demi-mondaine's* were unforgettable and overruled all other evidence about respectability. She was "no better than she should be".'[1]

Juxtaposed with the risk to the actress of being seen as 'no better than she should be' was the 'redemption' of star actress through her celebrity status. It is a condition of celebrity-making that a star's aura, her charisma, can overcome these kinds of tensions and conflicts. This goes some way to explaining why, for example, Ellen Terry was fêted as 'an icon of Victorian femininity' despite being a mother of two illegitimate children. The two actresses focused on in this chapter, Sarah Bernhardt and Mrs Patrick Campbell, both had illegitimate children, numerous affairs and failed marriages, but both achieved international stardom, and in Bernhardt's case especially, cult status.

It is further the case that a star-celebrity can help to endorse or promote a difficult or controversial 'product'. Playing her 'double', the star actress could potentially, by means of playing and producing the 'feminine', effect a rescue or redemption of the fallen woman, who was otherwise left to the mercy of male playwrights whose plot lines, dramatic action and dialogue did little to save the 'disgraced' heroine from the conservative views of and judgements on 'womanly' and 'unwomanly' behaviour. Radical, transgressive possibilities are demonstrated in two mainstream courtesan performances: Sarah Bernhardt and her interpretation of the *première courtisane* role

Marguerite Gautier in *La Dame aux camélias* by Dumas *fils*, and Mrs Patrick Campbell as Paula Tanqueray in Arthur Wing Pinero's *The Second Mrs Tanqueray*.

Like the hysteric confined to couch or clinic whose 'stories' were interpreted by husbands and medics, on stage the courtesan/fallen woman roles were not portrayed from a woman's point of view, but were scripted by male playwrights, whose ideas, even when more outspoken or daring about the 'rescue' of a 'disgraced' heroine, ultimately tended to uphold dominant views of womanly behaviour. Given these various social, cultural and theatrical constraints, a question arises as to how the actress found the occasion to radicalise this mainstream tradition of actress/courtesan or actress/fallen woman. Theatre history has taught us to look for signs of rebellion in the 'new drama' and the 'new actress', but what were the chances for the star actress of the late nineteenth century?

Actress and courtesan

The courtesan was an object of fatal attraction: a 'brilliant, exotic bird that flourished in the days of a permissive Imperial Court, of widespread social licence and political irresponsibility'.[2] The French Second Empire, as Elizabeth Wilson explains, was based on 'speculation and on the Stock Exchange' and courtesans promoted themselves as commodities of exchange, bartering sex for money on an unprecedented scale.[3] Transactions were public rather than private and the theatre was used interchangeably by actresses who abandoned their acting careers for a lucrative life of courtesan luxury,[4] or by courtesans who used the theatre to showcase their 'profession'. The courtesan also began to figure in a number of plays, notably by the prominent playwrights Emile Augier and Alexandre Dumas *fils*. Augier's verse drama *L'Aventurière*, which premièred at the Comédie Française in 1848, features a fortune-seeking adventuress, an actress with a dubious past. Unsympathetic as a role, it was overshadowed a few years later by the most successful courtesan role on the nineteenth-century stage: Dumas's Marguerite Gautier in *La Dame aux camélias* (Vaudeville, February 1852), inspired by real-life courtesan Marie Duplessis (1824–47).

Bernhardt and *La Dame aux camélias*

Gold-digging courtesans (they earned the nickname *mangeuses d'or*) and their willingness to risk the financial ruin of their lovers and their homes, families and wives from which they had strayed, increasingly provoked bourgeois anxiety and censorship. In the face of mounting criticism, a sympathetic stage representation of the courtesan required careful treatment. Dumas's compassionate representation was dependent on the play's romantic transfiguration of Marguerite from high-class prostitute into a 'chaste' young woman. Briefly, Marguerite's courtesan existence undergoes a transformation when she meets and falls in love with the young, handsome, but financially constrained Armand Duval. The couple escape 'courtesan city' for a romantic life in the country closely followed, however, by Armand's irate father who comes in secret to persuade Marguerite of the necessity of sacrificing her happiness for the good of Duval's bourgeois family. Not knowing of his father's intervention, Armand believes himself betrayed and turns against Marguerite. Finally, when he learns the truth of her sacrifice, Armand hurries back to her side, just in time for her to die a consumptive death in his arms.

Within the play's heightened melodramatic style is couched an important issue: the degree to which it is possible for an unmarried woman with sexual knowledge to regain her 'innocence'. Marguerite tragically aspires to such innocence. 'One has always had a childhood, whatever may have occurred,' she argues, and her reminiscence of a past 'purity' is the foundation on which she builds her future love for Armand.[5] Except that, like the hysteric, she is condemned to acting out, repeating her desire for that which, ultimately, she knows she cannot have, or, more significantly, *society will not allow her to have*. The constant melodramatic twists and turns of Dumas's plot through which Marguerite repeats her desire, only to suffer its reversal or denial, mirrors the hysterical seizure in which female suffering is played out over and over again, until the final attack – death.

As a mid-century courtesan figure, Marguerite is an exotic antecedent of the woman-with-a-past of the social problem play of the late nineteenth- and early twentieth-century European theatre. The anachronistic gap between the play's 1845 Parisian *demi-monde* setting and its moment of theatrical production in 1881 was arguably beneficial to finally getting the play past the English censor.[6] The passage of time, however, merely served to heighten audience curiosity about the courtesan lifestyle. As John Stokes argues, '[sexual] inquisitiveness only increased as the play's subject matter became more and more anachronistic'.[7] The illegitimate daughter of a courtesan, and herself the mother of an illegitimate son, Maurice, Sarah Bernhardt had intimate knowledge of the ways of the *demi-monde*.[8] However, by the time she played Marguerite, a courtesan shadow of her former self, she was married to the Greek actor, Jacques Damala: husband and wife were now playing lover and courtesan (fig. 21).[9]

Given the weaknesses inherent in Dumas's melodramatic script, Marguerite's transformation is heavily dependent on the skill of the actress.

PUNCH'S FANCY PORTRAITS.—No. 79.

THE TRANSIT OF THE CONSTELLATION SARA.

BRILLIANT SCENE IN A CIRCLE, OR "RAPID ACT," WITH WHICH THIS
VARIOUSLY GIFTED *ARTISTE* HAS SUCCESSFULLY TERMINATED HER
LATEST, SHORTEST, AND MOST IMPORTANT ENGAGEMENT, WHEN SHE
TEMPORARILY QUITTED THE STAGE FOR THE SAKE OF THE MASTER OF
THE RING. THIS SEASON WE SHALL WELCOME *LA DAME*,—NO, *LA
DAMALA AUX CAMÉLIAS!* OR THEY MIGHT APPEAR IN A FRENCH
VERSION OF *THE HAPPY PAIR* AND THE OLD FARCE OF *SARAH'S
YOUNG MAN.*

Fig. 21. A *Punch* cartoon (15 April 1882) showing Sarah Bernhardt at the time of her
marriage to Jacques Damala as a shooting star captured in a wedding ring.

256

The original Marguerite was the boulevard actress, Marie Doche, who was as successful in this popular tradition of theatre as Rachel, Bernhardt's predecessor at the Comédie Française, was in her classical repertoire. Although critically acclaimed, Doche's performance, unlike Bernhardt's, did not manage to elevate Marguerite above the status of her courtesan existence. Questions of talent aside, where Bernhardt had the advantage over Doche was in her training, a composite of both classical and boulevard stages.

An anatomisation of Bernhardt's craft is to be found in Gerda Taranow's meticulous dissection of the actress's voice, visual acting style, costume and orchestration of the stage ensemble and aesthetic.[10] In particular, Taranow draws attention to ways in which Bernhardt's method synthesised opposite types of training: 'her vocal acting remained classical, her visual acting subsequently reflected the combination of classical and popular traditions'. The consequence of mixing two systems, classical and popular, was that a melodrama like *La Dame* was 'endowed with an unprecedented tragic dimension'.[11] An infusion of the tragic into the melodramatic was undoubtedly beneficial to the transformative playing of Marguerite: it helped to effect her metamorphosis from courtesan to *jeune fille* through the tragic suffering and ennoblement of the figure.

Hysterics and histrionics

Fundamental to Bernhardt's success as Marguerite was her histrionic, visual 'acting-out' of extreme feminine suffering that bore a close resemblance to the female patient as hysteric. Bernhardt is thought to have attended the famous and fashionable *leçons du mardi*: the Tuesday afternoon demonstrations by the celebrated theorist of hysteria Jean-Martin Charcot at his Salpêtrière clinic in Paris. Whatever the veracity of this, the female hysteric was a much publicised and scrutinised figure in medical, social and cultural media,[12] and the visual choreographies of female suffering on the histrionic stage and the *attitudes passionelles* of Charcot's patients in the clinic are indeed striking.

To give an example: one of Charcot's 'star' hysterics was Augustine, who entered the clinic in the mid-1870s, while Bernhardt was essaying classical drama at the Comédie Française. Augustine was a victim of repeated sexual abuse: from the age of thirteen she was violated by her employer, also her mother's lover.[13] The surviving photographs of her 'performances' show an affinity with the gesturing and posing of the histrionic style.[14] They also attest to her youth (Augustine was fifteen when she first entered the clinic), to her femininity (she has long, flowing hair, pleasant features, an air of childlike innocence) and to her desire to please: to rehearse and stage, tableau by tableau, scene by scene, her emotional seizures for her 'master', Charcot.[15] These seizures were orchestrations of events from the patient's life: in Augustine's case the story set against the appearance of childlike innocence is one of violent sexual knowledge. Embodied in the spectacle of Augustine's body taken up in hysterical crisis is the memory of her 'fall': child and woman in one body.

Bernhardt's playing of Marguerite as 'saintly sinner' is not dissimilar. Like the hysteric, she played, overplayed, female suffering through facial and corporeal acting: emotions were conveyed through the physical text of the body, making words virtually redundant. The mesmeric effect she had on her audiences was achieved through the playing of opposites in a style of 'nervous power', replete with hysterical symptoms (suppressed cries, breathless agitation, outbursts of sudden laugher). In particular, reviews attest to the way in which her histrionic/hysteric style drew the focus of attention away from the action of the stage to the emotional drama located in the body of the actress, convulsed, contorted and traumatised, like that of the show girl hysteric before her audience of medical men. The death scene in act 5 provides an apposite illustration.

Bernhardt's death scenes were much admired by her international audiences. These were highly visual and carefully choreographed. Taranow's frame-by-frame reproduction of the death scene in *La Dame* (taken from a 1911–12 silent film recording of the play)[16] shows, for instance, the manner of Bernhardt's dying: from a standing position draped around the actor playing Armand, into a semi-circular fall, with Armand scooping up her body, breaking her fall and gently laying the 'corpse' to rest on the floor. Some critics questioned the realism or the 'physiological authority' of this,[17] while on the other hand, May Agate, an acting pupil of Bernhardt's, describes how her old family doctor, who saw the death scene performed as a single act some years later at the Manchester Hippodrome, was struck by Bernhardt's medical precision.[18] In his observations on death and the 'collapse of the spinal column', the doctor estimated that it 'would take about thirty seconds from the moment the heart stopped beating before the spinal cord ceased to support [the body]' and that Bernhardt 'had allowed for this with perfect accuracy'.[19] Medical observations aside, the various details of the death scene highlight the foregrounding of the actress's body as the spectacular site of feminine suffering. Significant also is the way in which the ultimate fatal feminine spiral recalls the body of the hysteric, arched in full grand seizure. Into the death of Bernhardt's Marguerite, collapsed against Armand's body, spirals the famous lithograph of Charcot adjacent to the swooning body of the hysteric held by his *chef de clinique* Joseph

Babinski, while he lectures to an attentive male audience. In both the medical and cinematic frames the attention is on the swoon/spiral of the female body.[20]

The radical possibilities of Bernhardt's performance 'text'

At this point, however, I come back to the question of radical possibilities. As French theorists Catherine Clément and Hélène Cixous argue, the hysteric is an ambiguous figure: radical in the sense that hysteria is a mark of rebellion; conservative given that ultimately she is confined to couch or clinic.[21] Given her performative association with the hysteric, an issue that arises is to what extent Bernhardt, as an actress trained in histrionic technique, mobilises radical possibilities through her performance 'texts'? To pursue this I combine further detail of *La Dame* with three more general observations about Bernhardt's work as an actress: her acting method and her relationship to audiences; her approach to the writer's text; and her realisation of a 'universal feminine'.

Fuelled by Denis Diderot's *Le Paradoxe sur le comédien* (published posthumously in 1830, with an English translation appearing in 1883, a couple of years after Bernhardt's London performance of Marguerite), acting methods were a controversial nineteenth-century topic, particularly, as Gail Marshall notes, in the context of the morality of the stage and the actress.[22] Briefly, such controversy centred on the idea devolved from Diderot's paradox that a performer might remain in control of their emotions, whilst producing emotions in an audience. If this situation were to obtain in the case of the actress, then it suggests that she would be 'capable of manipulating her audiences, controlling rather than being subject to their desire, and hence wresting the power of dramatic determination from them and the playwright. Such a possibility was strongly resisted.'[23] As something of an aside, but by way of further illustration on this point, there was a comparable 'acting' controversy emerging in the context of Charcot's clinic: were performances in hysteria 'authentic' or were, as many suspected, the women being coached in their roles?[24] If the latter, aside from challenging Charcot's methods and reputation, it also raised questions about a female patient's capacity to manipulate 'audience' emotions.

Bernhardt always identified herself with an emotionalist, rather than Diderot's anti-emotionalist, school of acting and theatre critics mostly endorsed this view. In respect of *La Dame*, for example, Bernhardt's identification with her character was a subject of much discussion. Typical are these comments extracted from the *Morning Post*'s review of her Marguerite: 'an instance of complete interpretation', or 'absolute identification', in which 'an actress enters within the body, so to speak, of an imaginary conception which she animates and informs', and 'when there is not an intonation of voice or a movement of limb that is not characteristic of the adopted individuality'.[25] However, there is also evidence that she relied on technique and distance from character. Her own comments explain how technical training could help to conserve energy in demanding emotional roles and Agate, among others, testifies to her use of technique as essential to surviving the rigours of touring and long runs. Agate deals with this contradiction by arguing that while Bernhardt did not always feel the emotion she was playing, the 'work was *conceived* in sincerity'.[26]

At the close of her career Bernhardt wrote a treatise on acting, *L'Art du théâtre* (1923), in which, looking to posterity, she fostered her own legend: as an actress unparalleled in the emotionalist, histrionic method. By masking anti-emotionalist technique her power to captivate is attributed to her ability to live in the emotional moment and not as a matter of premeditation. Yet her careful choreography of *La Dame*'s death scene, and countless other examples of her attention to performance detail, such as her meticulous management of the overall stage aesthetic,[27] testify to her ability and desire to calculate the effect she would have on her audiences.

Such calculations also entered into her choice of roles. In addition to her repertoire of classical and *travesti* roles,[28] Bernhardt preferred roles that were either written especially for her (notably those by Victorien Sardou), or those, like Marguerite in *La Dame*, that she could adapt to her particular style. As critic William Archer somewhat crossly observed, 'she does not dream of taking a great piece of literature and bending her genius to its interpretation. It is the playwright's business to interpret *her*.'[29]

Moreover, in performance the authority of the playwright was constantly undermined by interventions of Bernhardt's own devising. For instance, act 3 of *La Dame* dramatically represents Marguerite in conflict with paternal authority: a scene 'with all those waves and currents and *changes of conflicting emotion* of which Sarah Bernhardt is such a complete mistress' (my emphasis).[30] While Dumas's dramatic focus is on the conflict between Duval and Marguerite, Bernhardt deflects from this with her visual acting out of the emotional shifts occurring within Marguerite. Methodologically her approach to character 'authors' Marguerite in a Racinian style of emotional, passionate inner turmoil (reinforced by her classical delivery) rather than Dumas's melodramatic heroine. Her irreverence for the writer is compounded by the substitution of lines of her own which she felt more effective than those of the dramatist, or her interruption and upstaging of Duval's delivery with effective hysterical outbursts.[31]

When Eleonora Duse, the Italian star actress and Bernhardt's stage rival, played Marguerite in a London revival in 1900, one critic insightfully observed that Duse's performance suffered by comparison to Bernhardt's because she remained faithful to the dramatist's character, whereas the French actress triumphed in her creation of 'the universal feminine'.[32] Essentialist as this is in current feminist terms, in the moment of its cultural production Bernhardt's 'universal feminine' was arguably her most transgressive achievement as an actress. The paradox of Bernhardt's 'universal feminine' was that, like the courtesan doubling of innocence and sexual knowledge, it fused femininity and sexuality. Agate objected to the term 'sex appeal',[33] but reviews testify to Bernhardt's irresistibility as dependent on a sexually charged feminine. French critic Jules Lemaître claimed that her originality as an actress came from her willingness to play 'avec tout son corps', 'tout son sexe'. This would be shocking in any other actress, he argues, but in Bernhardt's case, for those that felt her attraction, femininity conspired to make her sexual audacity an 'exquisite' experience.[34]

'The new drama', 'the new actress'

In the first half of the twentieth century the courtesan role of Marguerite was played by many international actresses, among them Eleonora Duse, Sada Yacco, Cécile Sorel, Ida Rubinstein, Blanche Dufrène, Ludmilla Pitoëff and Edwige Feuillère. On the contemporary stage, modern dramatists have tried to give the play a social-realist makeover, as, for example in Pam Gems's *Camille* (with Frances Barber as Marguerite, 1984), or more recently still, Neil Bartlett's *Camille* (with Daniela Nardini, 2003). Such endeavours achieve only a qualified success: the romance and the sentimentality of Dumas's original, which argue in favour of Marguerite's transformation and critique the bourgeois values of Armand's world, make the drama ideologically resistant to this kind of serious social treatment.

The late nineteenth-century stage experienced its own culture clashes between the kind of Dumas–Bernhardt histrionics on the one hand, and, on the other, the 'new drama', characterised by a greater attention to social realism, and the 'new actress', identified with a quieter, more subdued acting style appropriate to psychological, rather than histrionic, representation. Ibsen was the pioneer of the 'new' and, for a moral conservative majority, 'unpleasant' drama; Janet Achurch, Florence Farr, Elizabeth Robins were among those actresses who appeared in the 'new drama'. Where the figure of the fallen woman and 'her sisters' was formerly drawn from a recognisable set of histrionic conventions, the 'New Woman' roles created the opportunity for psychologically drawn portraits of social and sexual female discontent. As Elin Diamond explains:

> the conventionalised fallen woman became more than automatic sinner. Her social position, her desires, her confusion, most of all her secret sexual past, were a problem, *the* problem or enigma, that has to be solved. Like Freud's case histories, the new realism progresses by going backward, revealing the psychobiography of nervous women.[35]

In 1889 the English theatre hosted the landmark production of Ibsen's *A Doll's House* (with Janet Achurch as Nora at the Novelty Theatre), heralding the 1890s arrival of several more of Ibsen's 'women' on the English stage. In April 1893 an account of Freud and Breuer's preliminary findings for *Studies on Hysteria* (published in full in 1909) was delivered to a meeting of the Society for Psychical Research in London,[36] while the following month, British playwright Arthur W. Pinero premièred his dramatic study in female hysteria or 'psychobiography', *The Second Mrs Tanqueray*, with Mrs Patrick Campbell in the title role.

The Second Mrs Tanqueray

Pinero's *The Second Mrs Tanqueray* relocates from Dumas's French courtesan *demi-monde* to respectable English society, where Aubrey Tanqueray, a widower, is about to remarry. His choice of partner, *Miss* Paula Ray, also known as Mrs Dartry and Mrs Jarman, is an unmarried woman with a succession of former lovers.[37] At a mid-point in Dumas's drama, Marguerite has the opportunity to confess her sexual past to a paternal authority, thus effecting her transformation from 'sinner' to 'saint'. Pinero, however, refuses Paula an early opportunity of sexual confession: in the opening act Tanqueray declines to read the letter she offers him that contains a list of ex-lovers and burns it on the fire.[38] With the list destroyed, Paula's confession remains unread, unheard. Without absolution she finds it impossible to escape her 'past' and to keep up her masquerade as a respectable married woman. In consequence, her sexual history is the 'subject' on which the play turns, made visible through a range of hysterical symptoms – tears, tantrums, sighs, laughter, stifled speech – and displays of 'common', 'vulgar' behaviour that will not be repressed.

Where *La Dame* used paternal interference to break up the romance between Marguerite and Armand, *The Second Mrs Tanqueray* figures Aubrey's virtuous daughter, Ellean, from his first marriage. When Ellean falls in love with a young man who turns out to be an ex-lover of Paula's, the hopelessness of Paula's social situation reaches a crisis point. In a more melodramatic turn of events (for which Pinero was criticised), Paula commits suicide.

Pinero, as Clayton Hamilton's introduction to a 1917 collected edition of Pinero's drama suggests and this brief account indicates, was influenced both by the dramatic conventions of the popular, mainstream drama and the serious, social concerns of the Ibsen 'alternative': a combination of Dumas's 'technique' and Ibsen's 'social intention'.[39] In a modern analysis, Catherine Wiley proposes a political sliding scale for the 'New Woman' drama from conservative to feminist, positioning *The Second Mrs Tanquerary*, as a 'liberal' play.[40] The drama is neither, therefore, accorded the status of 'great literature', nor remembered for its radicalism (even though it was regarded as daring for its time). Rather the play is significant for marking an emergent shift in English drama towards social realism and, like Dumas's *La Dame*, for the opportunity it afforded the actress.

'Looking' for Paula

Turned down by John Hare of the Garrick Theatre, who had previously staged his drama *The Profligate* (1889), Pinero persuaded George Alexander, actor-manager of the fashionable West End St James's Theatre, to risk his new play, *The Second Mrs Tanqueray*. Playwright and actor-manager realised they had then to find an actress willing to take on the part of Paula. Actresses they considered included Janet Achurch, Olga Nethersole, Winifred Emery, Lily Hanbury, Julia Neilson, Lena Ashwell, Maude Millet, Marion Terry and Elizabeth Robins, who at one point was contracted for the part.[41] Accounts of their deliberations stress looks and acting method as the two criteria informing their search: a shared concern that the actress should *look* the part and *be* the part.

In 'looking' for 'Paula', actor-manager and playwright were searching for an actress whose physique and appearance would signify a 'neurotic', troubled female sexuality. At this time, Campbell was recovering from a near-fatal episode of typhoid fever. Emaciated, fragile, deathly white and anxious, her hair thinned by poor health, the actress typified an anorexic style of nervous illness,[42] one associated with discursive representations of the 'New Woman'. Her height and thin frame (captured by Aubrey Beardsley in his black-and-white illustration for the *Yellow Book*, April 1894) were accentuated by a style of dress that left her throat bare: an expanse of whiteness that emphasised her lack of colour (health) and figured, by association, the choked-off speech of suffering hysteric.

The 'look' of the actress was particularly significant in the light of the play's compositional shift away from the visual, histrionic registers (the melodrama of Paula's suicide not withstanding) that, for example, Dumas's writing encouraged and Bernhardt capitalised upon, and its greater reliance on a kind of 'inner' acting appropriate to the play's realism. Mrs Patrick Campbell as Paula signalled a rather different connection to hysteria and to the histrionic than Bernhardt as Marguerite. If Bernhardt's histrionic performance style can be compared to the full grand hysterical seizure of the Charcot patient, then Mrs Patrick Campbell is arguably more akin to a kind of English nervous femininity stretched to breaking point on the late Victorian couch. 'Her fit of crying is quite the best of its kind,' wrote Kate Terry Gielgud of her Paula, noting also the 'nervous, characteristic hands' of the actress and the 'tinge of commonness about' her that Gielgud argued were of benefit to the part.[43]

While the list of 'possibles' for Paula suggests that the new style of intellectual actress was important to the deliberations of playwright and actor-manager, when Pinero and Alexander eventually 'found' their actress[44] she was not, in point of fact, playing one of Ibsen's 'New Women'. Rather, she was appearing in a melodrama at the Adelphi in the role of rejected lover in R. Sims and R. Buchanan's *The Black Domino*, a part which William Archer opined she 'played with an effectively undulant and Bernhardtesque languor'.[45] Reviews of her early acting suggest an emergent emotionalist style of feminine playing with descriptions, for instance, of a 'nervous frame' that 'vibrate[s] with emotion',[46] but also a sense that she played more complexly, more intelligently than the conventions of melodrama allowed for. Just as Pinero's play mixed strains of the popular with social purpose, the acting style that Mrs Patrick Campbell brought to *The Second Mrs Tanquerary* was one that fused emotionalism (melodrama) with a quieter mode of reflexivity (realism): an exotic doubling of the 'new actress'.[47]

In brief, looking back to Bernhardt's unsurpassed reputation as an actress of the histrionic in the nineteenth century and forward to the 'new drama' and the 'new actress', Mrs Patrick Campbell arguably occupies a position in between the two: fuses the 'old' emotionalist, visual style and the 'new' realism. As a study in hysteria, her Paula Tanqueray marks a shift away from melodrama to the new social drama: from the body of actress, the role of fallen woman and the female hysteric of Charcot's clinic, to the 'talking cure' of Freud's consulting room.

An absence of training and the 'method' of absorption

As Paula, Mrs Patrick Campbell may have displayed a more muted, emotionalist style than Bernhardt, but it is detectable nonetheless, despite the widely acclaimed 'realistic strength' of her delivery.[48] Moreover, it was not just repertoire that 'schooled' Mrs Patrick Campbell in emotionalism: her lack of formal training is also an important factor.

Unlike the nineteenth-century French stage, the English theatre had no Conservatoire, and Mrs Patrick Campbell had none of the advantages of being born into and brought up in a theatrical family. Like so many other women of her class and (embarrassed) financial circumstances, Mrs Patrick Campbell took to the stage as the only means of earning a living. A brief burst of amateur dramatics convinced her she might manage an acting career, while appearance and an ability to pay for her own dresses were her only qualifications for turning professional.[49] Consequent upon this lack of formal training, Mrs Patrick Campbell relied on her *feeling* for and identification with a character. Her desire to win over an audience formed 'the instinctive principle' of her acting.[50]

Of her profession as an actress, Mrs Patrick Campbell would further observe that her 'method' of absorption was also a cause of her disordered nerves. After one of her many breakdowns, she speculates on whether formal training might have helped 'to spare [her] emotional temperament'.[51] There is something of a paradox, or an irony, here in that the untrained English actress, resorting to the stage as her only means of becoming an independent woman, risked a collapse into the nervous, hysteric condition of the frustrated, domesticated, dependent middle-class woman – the very position from which she sought a way out. Except that generally this 'circle' of events was broken by one crucial difference: becoming an actress generally meant there was no going back, no social redemption, after taking up the acting profession. In the popular imagination the actress was, to borrow the words of her 'fallen' stage 'double', 'tainted through and through'.[52]

The idea of the 'difficult' actress

Playing Paula Tanqueray was Mrs Patrick Campbell's professional breakthrough. Previously she had come to some critical attention and was earning an acceptable salary of eight pounds a week, but her engagement as Paula almost doubled her wage to a substantial fifteen pounds a week. Success in the role would certainly assure her more profitable engagements in the future. Despite being fully aware of all that was at stake, Mrs Patrick Campbell was, as she always would be, a 'difficult' actress. Star actresses were notoriously wilful – Bernhardt being a case in point – and Mrs Patrick Campbell was no exception to this. Yet it is worth noting that some of this 'difficult' behaviour may be attributed to the position of the actress and the gender hierarchy and power relations of professional theatre. The role of hysteric Mrs Patrick Campbell played off stage was arguably more rebellious and radical than the one she was hired to perform on stage.

Where Bernhardt gained financial and artistic independence following her break from the Comédie, Mrs Patrick Campbell, at this stage in her career, had terms, artistic decisions and direction dictated to her by management and playwright. On matters of dramatic interpretation Alexander and Pinero led and she was required to follow. As an actress, even an actress in a leading role, she was not given the space for autonomous, intelligent thinking. Mrs Patrick Campbell rebelled against these constraints. Various accounts of the rehearsal process testify to her 'asserting her individuality'.[53] Her behaviour was stormy, rebellious and tearful, particularly in relation to George Alexander's reserve and formality which 'brought out the devil in her'.[54] Her insubordination reached a crisis and turning point over the matter of piano playing. Discovering that contrary to expectation she was indeed an accomplished pianist (she had held, though had also abandoned, a scholarship at the Guildhall School of Music), Pinero especially and Alexander more reservedly were inclined to revise their gendered assumptions and attitudes towards their actress, acknowledging, finally, that she might indeed have an intelligent contribution to make.[55]

While on stage Mrs Patrick Campbell was necessarily constrained by the conservatism of the role, off stage she repeatedly refused to 'behave'. As a sign of Mrs Patrick Campbell's radicalism, I would argue the conservatism of her autobiographical writing – the retrospective account, for example, that she gives of her life in the aftermath of *The Second Mrs Tanqueray*, undoubtedly fuelled by the idea that actress and role were one and the same:

> For a long while I thought it comic that many people held the attitude – 'she could not play "Mrs Tanqueray" as she does if she did not know something of that kind of life' – and 'Which is the real acting, Paula Tanqueray on the stage, or the unworldly creature she appears off?'[56]

Consequently, whereas on stage her method of performing had suggested her identification with the role, off stage she was concerned with representational strategies that might put distance between herself and the woman with a sexual past.

In truth, Mrs Patrick Campbell had a sexual past to conceal. Pregnant at nineteen, she had married in secret. Her husband was constantly abroad and variously out of touch, attempting, unsuccessfully, to make money out in the colonies. After the production, Mrs Patrick Campbell[57] contrived to be back in touch with her errant husband and provided the financial means to bring him home. Her autobiography fictionalises a romantic interest in her marriage. Moreover, a letter from an aristocratic friend, Lord Pembroke, strategically inserted into the autobiographical narrative at this point, alludes to the difficulty of her being 'unprotected' and in a 'state of siege' from male advances.[58] While Tracy C. Davis has persuasively argued the realities of sexual harassment that an actress faced,[59] it is hard to reconcile Mrs Patrick Campbell's self-representation as vulnerable victim, given other accounts of her spirited conduct, which gave *men* plenty to complain about.[60] Her autobiographical 'performance' as victim, wife and sexual innocent makes sense, however, given her desire for respectability and her investment in aristocratic friendships. Her deception masks the reality of her irregular domestic and social situation: a 'single' mother with two children to provide for in an employment where she was public, sexual property.[61] This autobiographical deceit connects to the marital masquerades of the 'second' Mrs Tanquerary: in pleading Paula's case – as *Mrs* Patrick Campbell determined to do[62] – she was also in some sense pleading her own.

As actresses, Mrs Patrick Campbell and Sarah Bernhardt 'trespassed against' their sex. As star actresses they were objects of a highly gendered theatrical and media gaze. Like their hysterical 'doubles' Paula and Marguerite, they were viewed with (sexual) fascination and terror. Constrained by the roles and conventions of the mainstream, both stars knew, however, how to 'play' the system. Variously rebellious, 'difficult', sexually audacious, or fatally attractive, they created opportunities of their own to gaze back, to answer back and to effect their own actress transformations from 'women no better than they should be' into spectacles of 'irresistible' femininity.

NOTES

1. Tracy C. Davis, *Actresses as Working Women: Their Social Identity in Victorian Culture* (London: Routledge, 1991), p. 69. See also Nina Auerbach, *Woman and the Demon: The Life of a Victorian Myth* (Cambridge, MA: Harvard University Press, 1982).
2. Joanna Richardson, *The Courtesans* (London: Weidenfeld and Nicolson, 1967), p. 3.
3. Elizabeth Wilson, 'Bohemians, Grisettes and Demi-mondaines', in Nicholas John, ed., *Violetta and her Sisters: The Lady of the Camellias, Responses to the Myth* (London: Faber and Faber, 1994), pp. 21–9, p. 28.
4. Examples of actresses who turned courtesan include, for instance, Alice Orzy (1820–93), Mlle Maximum (1842–94) or Caroline Letessier (dates unknown, fl. 1870s).
5. Quotation is from Bernhardt's edition of *La Dame* (New York: F. Rullman, 1880), Act 2, p. 12.
6. Although performed in Paris in 1852, *La Dame* was banned in England on moral grounds until Bernhardt acquired permission to present it on the London stage in 1881. Previously English audiences had only experienced the play either in

a more palatable adaptation, *Heartsease* by James Mortimer, or in the operatic form of Verdi's *La Traviata*.

7. John Stokes, 'Sarah Bernhardt', in John Stokes, Michael R. Booth and Susan Bassnett, *Bernhardt, Terry, Duse: The Actress in her Time* (Cambridge: Cambridge University Press, 1988), pp. 13–63, p. 53.

8. The courtesan 'connections' of Bernhardt's mother were instrumental in launching Sarah's career at the Conservatoire.

9. In the early 1880s audiences were especially curious about Sarah's marriage to Damala: '*La Dame aux camélias* might offer, it was thought, insights into a much publicized relationship' (Stokes, 'Sarah Bernhardt', p. 53).

10. Gerda Taranow, *Sarah Bernhardt: The Art within the Legend* (Princeton, NJ: Princeton University Press, 1972).

11. Ibid., p. xiii.

12. Reports are both claimed and disputed. See Christopher G. Goetz, Michel Bonduelle and Toby Gelfand, *Charcot: Constructing Neurology* (Oxford: Oxford University Press, 1995).

13. See Elaine Showalter, *The Female Malady: Women, Madness and English Culture, 1830–1980* (London: Virago, 1987), p. 152

14. Photographs are reproduced in Showalter, *The Female Malady*, ch. 6, 'Feminism and Hysteria', pp. 145–64. See also Anna Furse, *Augustine (Big Hysteria)* (Amsterdam: Harwood Academic Publishers, 1997), and Georges Didi-Huberman, *Invention of Hysteria* (Cambridge, MA: MIT Press, 2003).

15. Watching the repetition of Augustine's suffering did nothing to address its cause and over time, the trauma of the 'sexual trespass' takes its toll on Augustine's body and her behaviour. Her desire to please is overturned by her distress, anger and revolt. Finally, she escapes the clinic in male disguise.

16. Taranow, *Sarah Bernhardt*, pp. 108–9.

17. *The Times*, 13 June 1881, p. 11.

18. May Agate, *Madame Sarah* (London: Home and Van Thal, 1946), p. 131.

19. Ibid., pp. 131–2.

20. Spirals were a characteristic of Bernhardt's style: 'the effectiveness of her spiral pantomime was based upon the amplification of her slim and flexible body in appropriately manipulated costume' (Taranow, *Sarah Bernhardt*, p. 105).

21. Hélène Cixous and Catherine Clément, *The Newly Born Woman* (Manchester: Manchester University Press, 1987). See specifically Clément's analysis of 'Sorceress and Hysteric' in part 1.

22. Gail Marshall, *Actresses on the Victorian Stage: Feminine Performance and the Galatea Myth* (Cambridge: Cambridge University Press, 1998), p. 123.

23. Ibid.

24. Showalter, *The Female Malady*, p. 150.

25. *Morning Post*, 13 June 1881, p. 3.

26. Agate, *Madame Sarah*, p. 129, Agate's emphasis.

27. See Taranow's analysis of Bernhardt's grouping of characters in pictorial arrangements for her production of *Adrienne Lecouvreur*: Tanarow, *Sarah Bernhardt*, pp. 150–1.

28. See Elaine Aston, *Sarah Bernhardt: A French Actress on the English Stage* (Oxford: Berg, 1989), ch. 7, 'Male Guises', pp. 113–30.

29. William Archer, *The Theatrical World of 1895* (London: Scott, 1896), p. 205.

30. *Daily Telegraph*, 13 June 1881, p. 3.

31. May Agate's retrospect description of Bernhardt's playing of this scene provides the detail: 'Her mind not being able to grasp such a thing as parting from Armand *altogether*, she used to shake her head, looking quite vacant for a moment, and here she usually slipped in a line, "Alors je ne vois pas" . . . instead of the pretentious, "What more can you ask of me?" of the text . . . He starts to explain, and here Madame Sarah never listened to what he was saying – she who was such a perfect listener – but went on trying to puzzle it out, racking her brains until suddenly it flashed across her, and she cut in with an intake of breath which left Papa Duval high and dry in the middle of a ponderous sentence' (May Agate, *Madame Sarah*, p. 127).

32. *Speaker*, 16 June 1900, p. 299.

33. Agate, *Madame Sarah*, p. 159.

34. Jules Lemaître, *Les Contemporains: Etudes et portraits*, 2nd ser. (Paris: Société française d'imprimerie et de librairie, 1902), pp. 205–6.

35. Elin Diamond, *Unmaking Mimesis* (London: Routledge, 1997), p. 18.

36. Ibid., p. 21.

37. See Arthur W. Pinero, *The Second Mrs Tanquerary* (London: Samuel French, 1964), Act 1, p. 16.

38. Ibid.

39. Clayton Hamilton, ed., *The Social Plays of Pinero*, vol. 1 (New York: E. P. Dutton and Co., 1917), Introduction, p. 20.

40. Wiley's scale is as follows: Henry Arthur Jones's *Mrs Dane's Defence* (conservative); Pinero's *The Second Mrs Tanqueray* (liberal); G. B. Shaw's *Mrs Warren's Profession* (radical); and Elizabeth Robins's *Votes for Women* (feminist). See Wiley, 'The Matter with Manners: The New Woman and the Problem Play', in *Women in Theatre*, Themes in Drama, vol. 11 (Cambridge: Cambridge University Press, 1989), pp. 109–27, p. 111.

41. Having been interviewed and engaged by Pinero and Alexander for *The Second Mrs Tanquerary*, Mrs Patrick Campbell discovered that her managers at the Adelphi were suddenly unwilling to let her go. The part of Paula was then offered to Elizabeth Robins who accepted. When Mrs Patrick Campbell was later released from the Adelphi, Robins graciously conceded the role back to Campbell.

42. See Showalter's quotation from Dr George Savage recounting a neurasthenic type, which includes this kind of detail, and might equally well be describing Mrs Patrick Campbell at the point of recovering from her illness: 'The body wastes, and the face has a thin anxious look, not unlike that represented by Rossetti in many of his pictures of women. There is a hungry look about them which is striking' (quoted in Showalter, *The Female Malady*, p. 134).

43. Kate Terry Gielgud, *A Victorian Playgoer* (London: Heinemann, 1980), p. 11.

44. Mrs Alexander and Graham Robertson, who went to see her playing at the Adelphi, first discovered Mrs Patrick Campbell. They then reported back to Pinero and Alexander.

45. Archer, quoted in Alan Dent, *Mrs Patrick Campbell* (London: Museum Press, 1961), p. 53.

46. See review details of Mrs Patrick Campbell in Sims and Buchanan's *The Lights Home*, reproduced in W. Macqueen-Pope, *St James's, Theatre of Distinction* (London: W. H. Allen, 1958), p. 128.

47. Tracy C. Davis argues that while the new style of Ibsen performer aimed to restrict the 'excesses of external acting', the most successful performances in the 'new drama' were those which struck a 'balance between truthful embodiment and theatricalized effect': 'Acting in Ibsen', *Theatre Notebook* 39.3 (1985), pp. 113–23, p. 113. On these grounds Mrs Patrick Campbell's emergent performance style has more in common with the 'new actress' than might first be supposed.

48. See review of *The Second Mrs Tanqueray* in the *Daily Telegraph*, 29 May 1893, p. 6.

49. Mrs Patrick Campbell gives an account of her dealings with an agent who, for a one-guinea fee, secured her a professional engagement at £2 10s a week with the actress to supply her own costumes. Mrs Patrick Campbell, *My Life and Some Letters* (London: Hutchinson, 1922), p. 37.

50. Ibid., p. 39.

51. Ibid., p. 120.

52. Arthur Wing Pinero, *The Second Mrs Tanqueray*, Act 4, p. 70.

53. Dent, *Mrs Patrick Campbell*, p. 58.

54. Ibid.

55. In the play itself, the piano and Paula's playing symbolise her frustration with her social and marital circumstances. In Act 2 she withdraws to the piano, alienated from the paternal exchange between Aubrey and his daughter (p. 26), and in Act 3, visited by 'friends' from her 'past' life, she refuses a request for 'comic songs' and retreats from their company to play a piece of Schubert, while her husband, outside the window, observes 'how ill and wretched she looks' (p. 43). Significant also is the way in which the piano in the morning room in Act 2 is replaced by the grand piano in the drawing room in Act 3, emblematic of Paula's mounting frustration and alienation.

56. Campbell, *My Life and Some Letters*, p. 82.

57. As an assertion of her respectability, Mrs Patrick Campbell took her husband's name for her stage name, even though this convention was more widely adopted by women whose husband and/or families were in the theatre business.

58. Campbell, *My Life and Some Letters*, p. 84.

59. See Davis, *Actresses as Working Women*, pp. 86–97.

60. There is a delightful anecdote concerning Alexander's attempts to control Mrs Patrick Campbell's behaviour during the Tanqueray production. He wrote a note requesting her not to laugh at him on stage. The reply came back: 'Mrs Patrick Campbell presents her compliments to Mr George Alexander and begs to inform him that she does *not* laugh at him on stage . . . she waits until she gets home' (quoted in Dent, *Mrs Patrick Campbell*, p. 135). Her treatment of Alexander was not an isolated case. Throughout her career, Mrs Patrick Campbell would give actor-managers and playwrights much to complain of – most significantly in later life G. B. Shaw, whom she drove to artistic and romantic distraction.

61. See also biographer Margot Peters's account of Mrs Patrick Campbell's 'romantic' characterisation of herself in *Mrs Pat: The Life of Mrs Patrick Campbell* (London: Bodley Head, 1984), p. 84.

62. Campbell, *My Life and Some Letters*, p. 70.

FURTHER READING

Agate, May. *Madame Sarah*. London: Home and Van Thal, 1946.

Aston, Elaine. *Sarah Bernhardt: A French Actress on the English Stage*. Oxford: Berg, 1989.

Auerbach, Nina. *Woman and the Demon: The Life of a Victorian Myth*. Cambridge, MA: Harvard University Press, 1982.

Campbell, Mrs Patrick. *My Life and Some Letters*. London: Hutchinson, 1922.

Cixous, Hélène, and Catherine Clément. *The Newly Born Woman*. Manchester: Manchester University Press, 1987.

Dent, Alan. *Mrs Patrick Campbell*. London: Museum Press, 1961.

Diamond, Elin. *Unmaking Mimesis*. London: Routledge, 1997.

Garelick, Rhonda K. *Rising Star: Dandyism, Gender and Performance in the Fin de Siècle*. Princeton, NJ: Princeton University Press, 1998.

Gielgud, Kate Terry. *A Victorian Playgoer*. London: Heinemann, 1980.

Kaplan, Joel H. 'Pineroticism and the Problem Play: Mrs Tanqueray, Mrs Ebbsmith and "Mrs Pat"', in Richard Foulkes, ed., *British Theatre and the 1890s*, pp. 38–58. Cambridge: Cambridge University Press, 1992.

Macqueen-Pope, W. *St James's, Theatre of Distinction*. London: W. H. Allen, 1958.

Peters, Margot. *Mrs Pat: The Life of Mrs Patrick Campbell*. London: Bodley Head, 1984.

Richardson, Joanna. *The Courtesans*. London: Weidenfeld and Nicolson, 1967.

Showalter, Elaine. *The Female Malady: Women, Madness and English Culture, 1830–1980*. London: Virago, 1987.

Taranow, Gerda. *Sarah Bernhardt: The Art within the Legend*. Princeton, NJ: Princeton University Press, 1972.

14

MARIA M. DELGADO

Beyond the muse: the Spanish actress as collaborator

When examining the modes in which the working relationships between actresses and playwrights have been documented, what becomes immediately apparent is the dominance of the term *muse* as the filter through which these collaborations are read. The association of Harriet Bose with Strindberg, Olga Knipper with Chekhov, Eleonora Duse with D'Annunzio, and more recently Billie Whitelaw with Beckett, invariably prioritises the playwright. The problem stems from the model that has been used to analyse and document achievement in theatre: it is derived from literary studies and consequently seeks to locate creativity in the figure of the author. Although twentieth-century theatre historians have moved from the exclusive study of playwrights to take account of other aspects of the performance event, the authorial model has not been easily replaced. Directors, designers, architects, etc. have come to be treated as *auteurs* in their own right, with the result that their work is now subject to as much scrutiny as that of playwrights. The prioritising of authorship as a singular (habitually male) entity, however, has too often reduced collaborative relationships between writers and actresses to the all too familiar packaging of the mentor–muse paradigm. The construction of a theatrical hierarchy that places individual authorship at its pinnacle is problematic. It negates the concerted creative work that underpins theatre-making and in so doing provides a historiographical focus where craft, endeavour and labour occupy a secondary position to the celebration of the literary and the connotations of genius that often accompany it.

In mapping out the collaborative networks that actresses have instigated, this chapter takes up the 'archaeological' schema of feminist theatre historians who have documented the working lives of 'lost' or 'forgotten' stage women whose histories offer alternative routes to comprehending the theatrical culture of their times. Crucially, however, this particular act of retrieval focuses on actresses outside the Anglo-American world – beyond the 'mainstream', to examine collaborations in Spain that, in discursively constituting wider demographics of feminist performance, question historical process, challenge the stereotypic and present examples of the manifold contributions of women to onstage performance.

Creator and/or object of the gaze: creative actresses

Recent years have witnessed an interrogation of the paradigm of actress as muse across archival, critical and performative idioms. When female performers are positioned as inspirations to male agency, so that they function as largely passive beings rather than creators or connoisseurs, restrictions are obviously placed on female creativity and authority. In opposition to this, Susan Rutherford's work on the nineteenth-century German soprano Wilhemine Schröder-Devrient challenges the more traditionally 'patronising and antipathetic' views of the singer and looks at how and why she made such an impact on the composer and why Hector Berlioz and H. F. Chorley may have found her performances so contrary to their tastes and to the pre-eminent female voices at the time. The concern with delineating the specifics of Schröder-Devrient's acting counters the generalised terms in which the muse as sexual object and sign is so often presented.[1]

An extensive range of plays have looked to demonstrate the ways in which women sought to assert their rights in a profession where they have habitually been denied agency and where their worth has been defined solely through their bodies and the potential for exhibitionism. While the best known of these are those that have been written and presented in English (e.g. Ronald Hayman's *Playing the Wife* (1995), Adrienne Kennedy's *A Movie Star Has to Star in Black and White* (1976), Terrence McNally's *Master Class* (1996), Sharon Pollock's *Blood Relations* (1980), Stephen Sondheim's *Follies* (1971) and Marvin Hamlisch and Edward Kleban's *A Chorus Line* (1975)), it is probably those whose point of origin lies outside the English-speaking world that have provided the most potent questioning of assumptions around authorship, the act of reading, interpretation, criticism, ideology and meaning. These have often revolved around modes of encountering a classic text, as with Maria Irene Fornes's *The Summer in Gossensass* (1998), a dramatisation of the attempts by nineteenth-century American actresses Elizabeth Robins and Marion Lea to stage *Hedda Gabler*. The actresses are shown grappling with textual intricacies and making measured guesses, careful deductions and investigative leaps in preparing their production. This is the actress as analyst and inquirer, translator and interpreter, providing interpretations that recognise the weight of previous practice without slavishly adhering to its vocabularies.

Another legendary actress's relationship within the dramatic output of a turn-of-the-century playwright has also been subject to dramatic reassessment in Peter Brook's staging of Carol Rocamora's adaptation of the letters of Olga Knipper and Anton Chekhov, *Ta Main dans la mienne* (*I Take your Hand in Mine*) (2003). This ninety-minute two-hander created for Brook's wife Natasha Parry and veteran French actor Michel Piccoli provides astute observations on the Knipper–Chekhov working partnership. Much taken with her Arkadina in *The Seagull* (1899) and Elena in *Uncle Vanya* (1899), Chekhov went on to write Masha in *The Three Sisters* (1901) and Ranevskaya in *The Cherry Orchard* (1904) for her. What *Ta Main dans la mienne* demonstrates is that this convenient positioning of Knipper as pliant muse to the 'active' writer occludes her considerable input into the process of realising his works in stage terms. Illness meant that Chekhov was not able to travel to rehearsals in the capital and only saw one of the four openings of his works at the Moscow Arts Theatre. Isolated from the process of production, he desperately relied on Knipper to inform him of what was happening in the rehearsal room. As such, her comments serve as valuable observations on Stanislavski's methodologies and on the particulars of his work with actors. Equally, Knipper's anecdotes wove their way into the plays – as with the cure for baldness that is recycled from a letter into *The Three Sisters*. As Piccoli/Chekhov's final question 'What does it all mean?' suggests, the production knowingly investigates the 'sealing-off' of the Chekhov–Knipper relationship into a fixed past tense where the latter's hedonism and late-night drinking with friends and associates led to all too familiar associations with immorality and impropriety – the familiar actress/whore trope – that threatened to override her substantial artistic contributions.

It is worth noting that *Ta Main dans la mienne* was premièred and co-produced by the Fundación de la Comunidad Valenciana Ciudad de las Artes Escénicas and opened at Valencia's Micalet Theatre on 25 June before transferring to Paris. The end of Francisco Franco's dictatorship in 1975 has witnessed an extraordinary growth in Spain's cultural production, matched by a process of historical reconstruction that has generated the rehabilitation of cultural figures whose work did not fit into Franco's homogenous vision of Spain that 'tried to unify the nation by projecting difference outside its borders, or confining it to internal exclusion zones, in the form of otherness: *la anti-España*'.[2] Actresses have played a conspicuous role in this process of rehabilitation, evident in the staging of numerous works that have sought to provide revisionist views of female performers and their relationship to a male canon. One of the most resonant early critical successes of the transition to democracy was Fabià Puigserver's staging of Per Olov Enquist's 1975 play *The Night of the Tribades* for Barcelona's Teatre Lliure in 1978 (revived in 1999). *La nit de les tríbades* proved an investigative deconstruction of misogynistic myths of creative genius. Centring on Strindberg's relationship with his ex-wife Siri von Essen as the couple rehearse *The Stronger*, the presence of Danish lesbian writer Maria Carolina David decisively questions the problematic assumptions that govern understanding of Strindberg's behaviour. Its resonance in a year when adultery and homosexuality were decriminalised, but when divorce and abortion were still illegal, was not lost on reviewers. The casting of Anna Lizaran, one of the founder members of the Lliure co-operative in the role of Maria Carolina David – a role she was to reprise in 1999 – pointed to the moves towards accelerated female agency both in the private and public spheres: the repealing of articles of the civil code that insisted on male permission for affairs relating to family finances was pushed through in 1981; the Instituto de la Mujer (Institute for Women's Affairs) was set up as part of the Ministry of Culture in 1983; the 1985 abortion law saw a limited legalisation of abortion.[3]

For a generation of dramatists whose work was censored during the Franco regime (1939–75) too, the female performer has offered a potent symbol through which to enact the trauma of a nation silenced by the mechanisms of dictatorship. In Catalonia the reconstruction of national identity in the aftermath of the Franco era was linked to the cultural sphere – Franco's prohibition of 'dialects' in 1941 effectively meant that it was not until 1946 that theatrical productions were partly permitted in Catalan. The figure of the actress thus served to reinforce the double institutionalised marginalisation – of language and gender – that functioned under the Franco regime.[4]

Josep Benet i Jornet, in his 1994 play *ER*,[5] uses a fictional actress, Empar Ribera, to deconstruct the gendered historicisation of the recent past. Benet's structuring of the play like an investigative essay – with a young female theatre student preparing to audition for the role of Ribera by interviewing three actresses who trained with her – is symptomatic. The process of historical recovery is shown to be fraught with conflicting views as the three elder actresses all provide differing opinions on the legendary performer. The casting of Nuria Espert (b. 1945), Rosa Maria Sardà (b. 1941) and Anna Lizaran (b. 1944) in Ventura Pons's film adaptation of the play, *Actrius* (1996), was a further homage to female performers whose careers had played a seminal role in shaping the theatrical culture of the Franco years and its immediate aftermath. And indeed it is significant that actresses have been noteworthy protagonists in the oeuvre of the most influential cultural export of the post-Franco era, Pedro Almodóvar. Roles that dramatised the modes in which women were breaking out of the shackles of Francoism were exemplified by the 'new woman' – increasingly defiant, independent and assertive – embodied by Carmen Maura in *Mujeres al borde de un ataque de nervios/Women on the Verge of a Nervous Breakdown* (1988). It was to Maura that Carlos

Saura was to turn when casting the film version of José Sanchis Sinisterra's 1987 play ¡Ay, Carmela! in 1990, a study of itinerant Republican vaudeville artists trapped behind enemy lines during the Spanish Civil War. The play's huge success in Spain is indelibly linked to the ways in which it retells both political and theatrical history from the point of view of the vanquished – an itinerant female performer functioning on the bounds of legitimacy: a subject Sanchis Sinisterra was to return to in his 1994 play El cerco de Leningrado (The Leningrad Siege).

The period between the Spanish revolution of 1868 and the outbreak of the Civil War in 1936 saw the nation's theatrical culture flourish. It is to this period that dramatists have returned in attempting to interrogate the past and reconstruct a history neglected, erased or repackaged by Francoism, participating in what Jo Labanyi terms 'something approximating . . . a "recuperation industry"'.[6] This reassessment of the past has led to a creative retrieval of cultural symbols misappropriated through the dictatorship years and a tracing of theatrical movements through the twentieth century and into the new millennium. Perhaps the most emblematic of these is playwright Enrique Lenza González's La amarga soledad[7] (Bitter Solitude), a staged encounter between Spain's most important actress-managers of the early twentieth century, María Guerrero and Margarita Xirgu. For the purposes of this chapter, the choice of Guerrero and Xirgu as case studies affords an opportunity to map out collaborative contributions that go beyond virtuoso performances to the tracing of advocacy and agency in the financial and artistic processes that govern theatre-making.

By the latter end of the nineteenth century there was, in Spain, a new acceptance of women playwrights which evidently had implications for the kinds of roles that were emerging for actresses.[8] And yet, it is the male playwrights of this era whose work forms the backbone of published histories of the period.[9] As Gale and Gardner remind us, 'absence from the histories is not an indication of absence from history'.[10] What is often obliterated from histories or overviews of this particular period is the fact that these male dramatists were encouraged, nurtured and promoted by actress-managers whose companies dominated the Spanish stage in the latter years of the nineteenth century and the period up to the outbreak of the Civil War.

María Guerrero: actress and impresario (1867–1928)

The deaths of the two most celebrated male performers of late nineteenth-century Spain, Rafael Calvo in 1888 and Antonio Vico in 1902, had effectively marked the symbolic transition of power to a triptych of actress-impresarios: Rosario Pino (1871–1933), María Tubau (1854–1914) and María Guerrero. While the emotive, populist Pino was a muse to Benavente, both she and Tubau proved to have a more limited performative range than Guerrero. If Benavente was to refer to Guerrero as the finest actress he had seen, superior to Duse and Bernhardt,[11] it was to do with the extraordinary breadth of her repertoire that far exceeded the thirty-something plays in which Duse was to perform or Bernhardt's more tailored catalogue. From her debut in 1885 to her death in 1928 Guerrero performed in close to 300 works varying from Golden Age classics to fashionable comedies, from nineteenth-century neo-romanticist plays to naturalist dramas. However, her importance lies in the role she played in *cultivating* a significant proportion of that repertoire.

The daughter of a wealthy, well-connected businessman, Guerrero had enjoyed private lessons with Teodora Lamadrid (1821–96) before making her debut with Emilio Mario's company at Madrid's Princesa Theatre in Miguel Echegaray's *Sin familia* (*Without a Family*) on 28 October 1885. Mario, arguably Spain's first significant stage director, sought out plays that embodied something of the spirit of innovation sweeping through northern Europe. Guerrero came into contact with the key literary figures of the day and with them orchestrated a renewal of the capital's theatrical scene.

She first met José Echegaray on 27 March 1890. Throughout the 1890s and into the twentieth century, first at the Comedia and then with the companies she set up at the Español and the Princesa, Guerrero offered Echegaray a bridge to new theatrical developments. She encouraged him to attend rehearsals. Knowing of his admiration for Ibsen and his liberal positions on clerical influence and social emancipation, she oversaw his burgeoning friendship with the novelist-turned-dramatist Benito Pérez Galdós (viewed as the Ibsen of Spain).[12] Indeed, the palpable shift in Echegaray's writing from 1890 is evident in the move from neo-romantic melodrama and dramatic models from the Golden Age canon dominated by a range of tormented male protagonists torn between conflicting desires, to a more symbolic naturalism marked by a range of forceful female characters that he was to shape around Guerrero's ability to convey subtle transitions of mood. While her performance as Luisita in *Siempre en ridículo* (*Always Ridiculous*) (1890) had failed to impress the critics, Echegaray persisted in tailoring his works to what her biographer, the critic Felipe Sassone, termed her fierce and intelligent resolve.[13]

A tall, imposing figure with a handsome rather than beautiful face, what Benavente referred to as her 'low, contraltified register'[14] allowed her to support herself on the most intimate essence of poetic thought, her guide, her reason, her *leitmotif*. It sheltered her for a moment, and she sang without droning, with such a richness of texture in her voice and with such control of accentual perception that far from impeding each other, meaning and music, logical and poetical sense, all melded into one.[15]

A canny mimic, Guerrero varied her verse declamation with vocal modulations that moved across the emotional range[16] in ways that encouraged dramatists to compose works that transcended caricature. The critic Eduardo Zamacois referred to an aquiline nose and harsh irascible profile. Her voice, marked by short energetic breaths, suggested a tinge of reproach and a style of delivery defined by the somewhat threatening 'solemn slowness of her gestures . . . her melodic voice' and 'her pallid cheeks that arose', in Zamacois's view, 'from the constant autosuggestion that great dramatic frenzies require'.[17]

Guerrero denied an interest in politics or feminism,[18] nevertheless, the collaborations with Echegaray betray a placing centre-stage of the feminist polemics of the day. The no-nonsense peasant Pacorra in *Sic vos non vobis* (1892), the single girl prey to the wealthy older man with social standing, in *Mariana* (1892) and *El poder de la impotencia* (*The Power of Impotence*) (1893), and the feisty independent widow, Fuensanta, of *El loco dios* (*The Mad God*) (1900) were all written with Guerrero in mind. *Sic vos non vobis* is dedicated to her and *Mariana* dedicated to Emilio Mario's company of which she was then the *primera actriz*.

Echegaray's affected manner was vehemently rejected by the forward-looking writers who classified themselves as the Generation of '98.[19] Guerrero, however, continued championing his work even though critics felt that his mannered dramaturgy had hardened her style.[20] She encouraged him to move into translation, commissioning from him versions of Àngel Guimerà's *María Rosa* (1894) and *Terra baixa* (*Marta of the Lowlands*) (1898) and Calderón's *Semíramis o La hija del aire* (*The Daughter of the Air*) (1896). Not insignificantly he was awarded the Nobel Prize in 1904, after an intense period of collaboration that had seen Guerrero première four of his works within a three-year span.

Guerrero was also to play a seminal part in encouraging Benito Pérez Galdós, Spain's foremost late nineteenth-century novelist, to return to the stage. He had first seen Guerrero at the Comedia in *Felipe Derblay* in 1892 and his memoirs testify to the impression that her voice, manner and distinguished stage presence had on him.[21] Mario's company were preparing to stage Pérez Galdós's adaptation of his 1889 novel *Realidad* (*Reality*).[22] In *Realidad* Guerrero demonstrated how acting was, to appropriate Ellen

Donkin's terms, 'seen to be a production of the actress and not coextensive with the actress'.[23] *Realidad* ran for twenty-two performances – a significant production run in a theatrical culture used to comparatively short runs – mobilising critical opinion and shifting modes of production firmly towards naturalist paradigms. He may have crafted the role of Clotilde in *Realidad* for his mistress Concha-Ruth Morell, but it was Guerrero who came to embody 'the new woman' that Pérez Galdós promoted in the twenty-two plays he wrote between 1892 and 1918.[24]

The prolific correspondence between Guerrero and Pérez Galdós provides evidence of the ways in which she transformed rehearsals from merely a blocking exercise to a space for research and discussion. From Pérez Galdós's memoirs we know that Guerrero made dramaturgical suggestions about revising the ending of *La loca de la casa* (*The Mad Woman of the House*) during rehearsals in 1893, where she rehearsed the final scene 200 times in a single morning.[25] Guerrero was prepared to confront Mario when she didn't agree with his directorial approach or suggestions and refused to compliantly accept his familiar retort that he was older (and therefore inevitably wiser) than her.[26] For Guerrero plays necessitated analysis, what she called 'judgement' rather than simple acceptance.[27] Rehearsing *La de San Quintín* (*The Duchess of St Quintín*) (1894), she argued over the qualitative weight of characters, refusing to accept that *significance* was rendered through the counting of lines allocated.[28] She resented the fact that Mario's lack of direct engagement with the company involved her having to find out what was going on in the press.[29] When she inevitably left Mario's company to form her own at the Español (with her father's considerable financial backing), Pérez Galdós considered the move to be madness but was unable to persuade her to return to the Comedia. Indeed, Guerrero exerted a far more palpable influence over the writer than he ever did over her. She encouraged him to write for the theatre when other constraints impinged on his time, and kept him informed on the progress of his works on tour.[30] Following the split with Mario she pressured Pérez Galdós to provide work for her new company. The result, *Voluntad* (*Willpower*) (1894), can now be seen as much as a comment on Guerrero's escalating dominance of Madrid's commercialised theatre as a character study of Isadora's entry into the closed, male, mercantile world of business.

Whereas Guerrero's presence in Echegaray's texts is perhaps more obviously discernible in the repeated plot device of the older respectable middle-class gentleman pursuing a girl half his age, the Guerrero–Pérez Galdós partnership staged the dilemmas of the age. From *La loca de la casa*'s advocation of a greater degree of class mobility to *Mariucha*'s (1903) championing of a more egalitarian society where class and gender were no longer impediments to social progress, from *El abuelo*'s (*The Grandfather*'s) (1904) treatment of heredity to *Alceste*'s (1914) rewriting of mythology, they offered a space for the incursions of women into a public space that had all too often either negated or wilfully packaged their visibility.

Whereas popular opinion of the time pitted Benavente's work as a rebellion against Echegaray's, she was quick to see Benavente as his heir.[31] While Benavente felt threatened by Guerrero's creative influence and often felt more comfortable with actresses who were more pliant and less insistent on directorial control – like Carmen Cobeña (1869–1963), who had launched him onto Madrid's theatrical landscape with *El nido ajeno* (*The Intruder*) in 1894, and comic specialist Rosario Pino – he was to write three of his most accomplished works for her. Their most fertile period of collaboration between 1913 and 1924, initiated by *La malquerida* (*The passion flower*), concurred with the award of the Nobel Prize in 1922.

Guerrero never perceived herself as the 'property' of a single dramatist. Rather she juggled professional associations with a range of diverse writers embodying divergent dramatic trends. Her cultivation of Eduardo Marquina and Luis Fernández Ardavín's historical verse dramas at the Princesa shrewdly turned back to Spain's 'glorious' imperial past as a way of forgetting its crumbling decadent present, symbolised by the defeat at US hands that had brought the loss of the final outposts of its colonial empire: Cuba, Puerto Rico and the Philippines. A substantial proportion of the plays may now be perceived as outdated literary relics,[32] but their palpable impact can be traced to these early productions in which she performed and which she also produced, and the attention they generated in the press and with the intelligentsia who were to shape Spanish politics during the Second Republic.[33]

Industrious, ambitious, opinionated, self-critical and able, Guerrero revolutionised the Spanish stage because she realised more than any of her predecessors that theatre was a collaborative art that required disciplined preparation. Her marriage to the aristocratic Fernando Díaz de Mendoza in 1896 marked his transition from a limited actor to an influential director and indispensable accomplice. From Emilio Mario she learned of the benefits of more extensive rehearsal periods and the possibilities of a *régisseur* to orchestrate proceedings from the 'other side of the curtains'. As early as 1895 Díaz de Mendoza had showed tendencies towards dramaturgical shaping. Like Guerrero, he paid close attention to diet. Both collaborated on all aspects of production from stage design to translation and were known to be fiercely hardworking and controlling in rehearsals.[34] Their fastidious work on diction, the undertaking of meticulous historical research on all productions and the supervision of decor to ensure consistency allowed for the development of a directorial approach that tried to adapt Antoine's attention to naturalistic detail to the demands of a larger proscenium arch venue – what Rodríguez Mendez refers to as 'Spanish-style naturalism'.[35]

Reading widely in French, German and later English, Guerrero soon demonstrated herself a shrewd programmer, balancing the writers of the day with Golden Age classics and the introduction of new international dramatists (Oscar Wilde, Edmond Rostand, Gaston Leroux, Rabindranath Tagore, Arthur Wing Pinero). Touring the Americas over twenty-five times between 1897 and 1928, as Margarita Xirgu was later to do, she recognised the importance, post-1898, of building up touring networks that went beyond the 'exporting' of European models of assumed excellence.

Her purposeful attitude to self-improvement garnered resentment from certain quarters. The writer Felipe Sassone referred to her as 'more craft than inspiration'.[36] Nathalie Cañizares Bundorf collects views of detractors who saw her as mannered, cold and opportunistic, and resented ways in which she had made the most of her father's lucrative business contacts in the profession.[37] A Francophile, she spent time in Paris training with Constant Coquelin in 1891 and was supposedly then offered a place with the Comédie Française.[38] Her admiration of Bernhardt, with whom she performed in 1895 at the Princesa, her tours to Paris in 1898 and 1900 and her programming of significant international companies that allowed Madrid audiences to see the work of Aurélien Lugné-Poe and Dario Niccodemi positioned her within an exclusive touring circuit that further underlined her associations with a European theatrical royalty.[39]

Socially, her marriage to Díaz de Mendoza served further to disassociate her from the actress/prostitute paradigm. Their philanthropic exercises and soirées at the Princesa, where the family lived post-1916, further served to consolidate her position as the ultimate professional, the *grande dame* whose life was her art. She challenged assumptions that performers who were paid to exhibit themselves in public were virtually indistinguishable from common prostitutes by publicising her literary and managerial abilities. The matronly Guerrero embodied decency, respectability and social acceptability in ways that the divorced Duse and Bernhardt were never quite able to do. She was linked to the upper echelons of Spanish society, fêted at bullfights as a fellow celebrity, and the patronage by royalty reinforced the associations with the ruling class.

Aware of the fickle nature of the press, she won journalists over with charm offensives that ensured that her husband's dalliances (and illegitimate son) remained well-kept secrets.[40] Guerrero's funeral on 24 January 1928 attracted the crowds habitually reserved for bullfighters and monarchs, with eulogies situating her alongside El Cid, St Teresa and Isabel of Castile as a component of the national fabric, a *reconquistadora* of the Spanish theatre.[41]

281

Less than a month later the Princesa was renamed María Guerrero. It is now the home of the Centro Dramático Nacional, effectively Spain's National Theatre.

Margarita Xirgu (1888–1969): politics, national identity and the institutionalisation of Federico García Lorca

While popular discourse often pits actresses against each other, María Guerrero loaned the young Catalan actress Margarita Xirgu the Princesa when she made her Madrid debut in 1914. Correspondingly, Xirgu recognised Guerrero as her most conspicuous Spanish role model. As Jesús Rubio Jiménez has indicated, both performers can be viewed as indicative of facets of the two Spains that were to implode in 1936.[42] Guerrero relied on the patronage of the aristocracy and mercantile middle classes, Xirgu's appeal lay within both the intelligentsia and the proletariat and her political allegiances were to differ from the more conservative leanings of Guerrero.

Xirgu often surfaces as a supporting player in the trajectory of Federico García Lorca's evolution from poet to dramatist. His own comments on their relationship, his dedication of a poem to her, as well as interviews given by both practitioners during the period between 1927 and 1936, indicate that Xirgu shaped the Granadine's theatrical vision in ways which are too rarely acknowledged.

In contrast to the Italian *grande dames* Ristori and Duse or her French contemporary, Bernhardt, Xirgu – like Guerrero – has never really permeated the consciousness of the English-speaking world.[43] This may certainly have been due, in part, to the fact that she never toured outside the Hispanic domains, but it may also have resulted from her exile (1936–69) in the Americas, far from the dominant theatrical infrastructure of Western Europe.

Born in Molins del Rei (Barcelona) on 18 July 1888 to a working-class family, Xirgu made her theatrical debut at an early age in the amateur theatres of Barcelona. Joining the Romea's Catalan-language company in 1906, she made her first appearance with them in leading Catalan dramatist Àngel Guimerà's *Mar i cel* (*Sea and Sky*) that same year. Here she came into contact with the key Catalan dramatists of the time, continuing to promote their work long after leaving the Romea.

Xirgu was always attracted to dramatists who sought to re-envisage the conceptual possibilities of the stage. As such, the company she set up at the suggestion of the actor Miguel Ortín, later to become her second husband, showed decidedly international leanings, promoting dramatists such as Wilde, D'Annunzio, Shaw and Lenormand. It is, however, in her work in nurturing and endorsing Spanish-language drama that her most lasting influence lies. Post-1914, moving her theatrical base to Madrid, she was to collaborate with living writers from both the generations of 1898 and 1927, many of whom were to perish or escape into exile during the Spanish Civil War and the dictatorship which followed. With them she played a significant role in rethinking ways in which theatre might be harnessed towards the reconception of a national identity. The modernisation of the theatrical landscape that she fostered in the 1930s in her association with director Cipriano de Rivas Cherif cultivated a dramatic renaissance in the 1920s and 1930s not seen since the Golden Age.

By the time Xirgu first met García Lorca, she was a significant star and he an aspiring playwright with only a published collection of poems to his name and a rather inauspicious debut play, *El maleficio de la mariposa (The Butterfly's Evil Spell)*, which had been shouted down by the audience when first produced in 1920. García Lorca struggled to find a producer for his 1924 play *Mariana Pineda*, a romantic treatment of the nineteenth-century Granadine martyr during a time when military insurrections threatened Primo de Rivera's tight grip on power. When García Lorca first met Xirgu in the summer of 1926, he was sure that when she realised how many others had turned the play down, she would lose interest in the project, but Xirgu remained firm that if she liked the piece she would stage it.[44] Directed by García Lorca (who subsequently dedicated the play to her), the production opened at Barcelona's Goya Theatre on 24 June 1927. Now perhaps best remembered for Salvador Dalí's warped curving set, it crucially marked the beginning of a theatrical relationship that was to witness five further collaborations: *La zapatera prodigiosa (The Shoemaker's Prodigious Wife)* in 1930, *Bodas de sangre (Blood Wedding)* (1935), *Yerma* (1934), *Doña Rosita la soltera (Doña Rosita the Spinster)* (1935) and the posthumous *La casa de Bernarda Alba (The House of Bernarda Alba)* (1945).

However, *Mariana Pineda* also played a significant role in consolidating the actress's political affiliations. As early as 1911 the manifestations of a social consciousness in Xirgu were visible in her socially aware choice of Catalan plays.[45] Following her move to Madrid in 1914 she became intrinsically linked with the reinvigoration of the Spanish stage articulated by such philosophers as José Ortega y Gasset and Miguel de Unamuno and realised in the plasticity of the theatrical models put forward by Ramón Gómez de la Serna and Ramón del Valle-Inclán. During the Primo de Rivera dictatorship the identification between Xirgu and the emblematic heroine was to shape an increasing perception of Xirgu as a markedly politicised figure and powerful social icon, carrying the ideological values of artists censored by the regime.[46]

There are enough comments made by García Lorca during the period between the première of *Mariana Pineda* and his death nine years later to affirm Xirgu's importance in shaping his theatrical career.[47] At a banquet in 1935 he stated emphatically that he owed her everything that he had achieved in the theatre.[48] At the time of his death he had published only two dramatic works, *Mariana Pineda* in 1928 and *Bodas de sangre* in 1936: his reputation lay in the staged productions and not the printed word which has now reclaimed him. Certainly, the texts of García Lorca's plays that have reached us in published form have been indelibly marked by his collaborative work with Xirgu. As assistant director to the innovative Rivas Cherif on *La zapatera prodigiosa*, he added the prologue to the play during rehearsals and was to perform it himself in the production that opened in Madrid on 24 December 1930 with Xirgu in the title role. Indeed Xirgu's support of García Lorca's involvement in rehearsals may well have been a factor in encouraging 'the poet to continue writing for the theatre'.[49] Gibson states that *Bodas de sangre*, drafted in less than four weeks, was written 'almost certainly'[50] for Xirgu, although she was not to present the play until November 1935, two years after its initial première.

With *Yerma*, too, he appears to have had Xirgu in mind. Its opening on 29 December 1934 was marked by heckling, and reviews were split along predictably polarised lines, testifying to the political tensions that were soon to erupt in civil war. *Yerma* was seen as a defiant expression of cultural dissent, denaturalising and subverting dominant gender roles and overtly indicating the ideological struggles of the time. The production and play came to be identified with Xirgu – indeed García Lorca referred to her as 'creator of the role'.[51] Her enactment of an increasingly rebellious female sexuality served alongside her interpretation of the bayonet-wielding Virgin in Alberti's *Fermín Galán* in 1931 and the wayward Mari-Gaila in Valle-Inclán's *Divinas palabras (Divine Words)* in 1933 to associate her with female insurgency.

Doña Rosita la soltera, the last of García Lorca's works premièred during his lifetime, opened in Barcelona on 12 December 1935. As with his previous collaborations with Xirgu, the piece reinscribed the absence of women as subjects by placing on stage female cultures. *Mariana Pineda* had explored allegorical uses of the female as an emblematic image of liberty. *Bodas de sangre* had foregrounded the isolation faced by rural women drawn into arranged marriages. *La zapatera prodigiosa* and *Yerma* had explored marital incompatibility and the problems of childlessness in a society where women are defined by their ability to procreate. Now *Doña Rosita* mapped out the emotional geography of middle-class women who are unable, or choose not, to marry. While critics have often problematically perceived García Lorca's defiant female protagonists as a veiled displacement of the dramatist's homosexuality,[52] the plethora of these roles has more to do with what García Lorca himself recognised as 'an appalling lack of actors, of good actors'.[53]

In January 1936 Xirgu left for Latin America for a planned six-month tour. García Lorca was due to join her there in February, but postponed his visit to finish *La casa de Bernarda Alba* so Xirgu could open it in Argentina before the company returned to Spain. Political events were to intervene and García Lorca was shot soon after the outbreak of the Civil War in Granada in 1936. His fate convinced Xirgu that she should stay in the Americas, and after moving from Cuba to Mexico, Argentina and Chile, she finally settled in Uruguay where she was to remain until her death in 1969. Although the Argentine actress Lola Membrives (1888–1969) had staged *Bodas de sangre*, *La zapatera prodigiosa* and *Mariana Pineda* in Buenos Aires in 1933–4, it was Xirgu who was seen as the faithful cultivator and promoter of García Lorca's legacy in the Americas. The institutionalisation of the dramatist was undertaken not merely through the programming of the García Lorca repertoire that she had premièred in Spain or her opening of *La casa de Bernarda Alba* at Buenos Aires's Avenida Theatre on 8 March 1945, but also through the numerous reformulations of the dramatist's work with which she was to become involved. Hers was not a folkloric appropriation of the dramatist and his plays. On the contrary, she seems to have been willing to associate herself with projects that sought to re-envisage the works within different media. In 1937 she performed extracts from the plays on the radio. In 1938 she was involved in a film version of *Bodas de sangre*. The following year, in Montevideo, she directed a musical reworking of the play by Juan José Castro. In 1949 she staged an opera of *La zapatera prodigiosa* by the same composer in Buenos Aires.[54]

During the difficult post-Civil War years when García Lorca's work was decisively absent from the Spanish stage, Xirgu forged his reputation through productions.[55] In 1963 Xirgu joined forces with the Paris-based actress and fellow exile, María Casares, to direct her in Buenos Aires in her first Spanish-language production, *Yerma*.

The longevity of Xirgu's association with García Lorca's work and the close nature of their collaboration certainly attest to a relationship that moved beyond the parameters of author and muse. Xirgu cites the death of García Lorca as one of the reasons she began teaching, and he was to remain a palpable presence in the repertory to which students were introduced in the various theatre schools with which she was associated.[56] Significantly, the only one of her productions seen in the English-speaking world was *Yerma*, presented in 1967 at Smith College in Massachusetts. This was her final García Lorca project, for she died in Montevideo on 25 April 1969.

A potent symbol of the Republic in exile, in death as much as during her years in the Americas, she had functioned as an emblematic reminder of all that had been lost with Franco's victory in 1939. Her career trajectory both in Spain and in exile was marked by a choice of works that overtly tackled the corrupt political body, social discontent and government injustice. Her performances in the mid-1940s evoked a phantom presence haunting the regime with works that could not be presented within Francoist Spain. In 1943, her decision to stage Alberti's reworking of Cervantes's *Numancia* – where she took on the symbolic role of Spain itself – was a brutal reminder of the illegitimacy of a regime that had usurped a democratically elected government on whose behalf she had campaigned and whose cultural programmes she had been part of. Journalistic tirades accompanied news of her possible return to Spain and, as late as 1966, plans for a Madrid theatre to be renamed in her honour were thwarted by the authorities for whom she remained a political pariah tainted by Catalanism.[57]

It is not surprising, therefore, that the period since 1975 has witnessed such a reappropriation of Xirgu. On the centenary of her birth the Catalan government, the Generalitat, oversaw the return of her remains to the town where she was born. Her promotion of a theatrical revolution in Spain, assisted by a strategy of state intervention in cultural funding, was continued by Felipe González's socialist government in the 1980s. Public squares, theatrical venues and schools now bear her name; her theatrical legacy has spawned revisionist monographs[58] and playtexts – in Alberto Miralles's *Okupes al Museu del Prado* (*Squatters at the Prado Museum*) (2000) she is positioned alongside Rafael Alberti, Picasso, Ortega y Gasset, García Lorca and Luis Buñuel as a mythical icon defending the emblematic museum against a possible sale to the Guggenheim – and a recent opera – Osvaldo Golijov's *Ainadamar*, directed by Peter Sellars for Santa Fe Opera in 2005, configures the Xirgu/García Lorca relationship in ways that recognise her symbolic importance as a pedagogue in the Americas promoting the cultural legacy of the Second Republic (1931–6). Reassessing Xirgu's importance, it is clear that if Spanish dramatists like Casona, Valle-Inclán and García Lorca are often credited for having composed plays around the dichotomies of female subjectivity, then Xirgu's characterisation of these roles played a major role in canonising the works. Ramón Pérez de Ayala's review of Benavente's *El mal que nos hacen* (*The Evil they Do Us*), crafted for her in 1917, makes a case for the importance of her performance in clarifying the more opaque and listless facets of Benavente's dramaturgy.[59] Indeed, in Benavente's own view, she 'discovered beauty in the works that authors were unable to make out'.[60] This was because she recognised the importance of bringing together a team of collaborators, an ensemble of sorts, who were able to engage in extensive script reading, methodical training and extended rehearsal periods.[61] Dispensing with the prompt box, she joined forces with adventurous designers (such as Dalí, Santiago Ontañón and Siegfried Burmann) who were pursuing conceptual scenic environments, incorporating them into all preparatory work and encouraging their dialogue with dramatists and performers. Indeed her production of *Los fracasados* (1928), a version of Lenormand's *Les Ratés*, saw the introduction of a moving set for the first time on a Spanish stage. With Rivas Cherif at the Español between 1930 and 1935 she established a working partnership that actively sought out texts from poets and politicians, even attempting to persuade celebrated medic Gregorio Marañón to write for the stage.[62]

Indeed, Xirgu and Guerrero's importance as actresses lies far beyond their conspicuous roles as the grand *tragédiennes* of the day, displaying in the public arena 'what was publicly disallowed' and allowing the 'representation of suffering and of desire' to function as 'the first signs of resistance'.[63] Rather, as instigators, facilitators, cultivators and promoters they definitively shaped a theatrical culture that is too often reduced to its dramaturgical traces. The career trajectories of Xirgu and Guerrero call for a rethinking of the boundaries of investigation beyond the geographical dominance of the English-speaking world, but also exemplify the many ways in which actresses have functioned as artistic collaborators across time and across continents.[64]

NOTES

1. Susan Rutherford, 'Wilhemine Schröder-Devrient: Wagner's Theatrical Muse', in Maggie Gale and Viv Gardner, eds., *Women, Theatre and Performance: New Histories, New Historiographies* (Manchester: Manchester University Press, 2000), pp. 60–80.

2. Jo Labanyi, 'Conclusion: Modernity and Cultural Pluralism', in Helen Graham and Jo Labanyi, eds., *Spanish Cultural Studies: An Introduction* (Oxford: Oxford University Press, 1995), pp. 396–406, p. 397.

3. See John Hooper, *The New Spaniards* (Harmondsworth: Penguin, 1995), pp. 46, 157–61, 164–75, 182–5.

4. Ibid., pp. 166–8, for information on gender bias in legislation.

5. Benet i Jornet, *ER*, Els llibres de l'Escorpi Teatre / El Galliner (Barcelona: Edicions 62), 1997.

6. Labanyi, 'Conclusion', p. 402.

7. Published with *Nubes de verano* in Coleción texto teatral, no. 102 (Madrid: La Avispa, 2002).

8. See David Thatcher Gies, *Theatre and Politics in Nineteenth-Century Spain: Juan de Grimaldi as Impresario and Government Agent* (Cambridge: Cambridge University Press, 1988) and *The Theatre in Nineteenth-Century Spain* (Cambridge: Cambridge University Press, 1994), pp. 191–230.

9. See, for example, Francisco Ruiz Ramón, *Historia del teatro español (desde sus orígines hasta 1900)* (Madrid: Catedra, 1986) and *Historia del teatro español. Siglo XX* (Madrid: Catedra, 1984).

10. 'Introduction', in Gale and Gardner, eds., *Women, Theatre and Performance*, pp. 1–6, p. 5.

11. Ismael Sánchez Estevan, *María Guerrero* (Barcelona: Iberia/Joaquín Gil, 1946), p. 9.
12. Rafael Altamira y Crevea, *De historia y arte* (Madrid: Suárez, 1898), p. 281.
13. Felipe Sassone, *Maria Guerrero (la grande): Primera actriz de los teatros de todas las Españas* (Madrid: Escelicer, 1943), pp. 114, 123.
14. 'Plan de estudios para una escuela de arte escénico', *Obras completas*, vol. 7 (Madrid: Aguilar, 1953), pp. 1191–1206, p. 1195.
15. Sassone, *María Guerrero*, p. 113.
16. Ibid., pp. 113–14.
17. Eduardo Zamacois, *Desde mi butaca: Apuntes para una psicología de nuestros actores*, 2nd edn. (Barcelona: Maucci, 1911), pp. 14, 20.
18. Luis Antón del Olmet and José de Torres Bernal, *Los grandes españoles: Maria Guerrero* (Madrid: Renacimiento, 1920), p. 123.
19. See Joseph Harrison and Alan Hoyle, eds., *Spain's 1898 Crisis: Regeneration, Modernism, Post-Colonialism* (Manchester: Manchester University Press, 2000).
20. Zamacois, *Desde mi butaca*, p. 20.
21. Pérez Galdós, *Memorias*, ed. Alberto Ghiraldo (Madrid: Renacimiento, 1930), p. 17.
22. See Pérez Galdós, *Memorias*, pp. 17–18, and Carmen Menéndez Onrubia, *El dramaturgo y los actores: Epistolario de Benito Pérez Galdós, María Guerrero y Fernándo Díaz de Mendoza*, Anejos de la Revista 'Segismundo' 10 (Madrid: Consejo Superior de Investigaciones Científicas, 1984).
23. Ellen Donkin, 'Mrs Siddons Looks Back in Anger', in Janelle G. Reinelt and Joseph R. Roach, eds., *Critical Theory and Performance* (Ann Arbor: University of Michigan Press, 1992), pp. 276–90, p. 285.
24. See Lisa Pauline Condé, 'Galdós and his Leading Ladies', *Bulletin of Hispanic Studies* 75 (1998), 79–91.
25. Pérez Galdós, *Memorias*, p. 177.
26. Menéndez Onrubia, *El dramaturgo y los actores*, pp. 56–7.
27. Ibid., p. 57.
28. Ibid., pp. 59–60.
29. Ibid., p. 62.
30. Ibid., pp. 40–2.
31. Sánchez Estevan, *María Guerrero*, p. 247.
32. See, for example, Gwynne Edwards, *Dramatists in Perspective: Spanish Theatre in the Twentieth Century* (Cardiff: University of Wales Press, 1985), pp. 1–35.
33. See Sandie Holguin, *Creating Spaniards: Culture and National Identity in Republican Spain* (Madison: University of Wisconsin Press, 2002), pp. 1–46.
34. Sánchez Estevan, *María Guerrero*, pp. 230–1, and José María Carretero, 'El Caballero Audaz', in *Galería: Más de cien vidas extraordinarias contadas por sus protagonistas*, 2 vols. (Madrid: ECA, 1943), vol. 1, pp. 111–19.
35. José María Rodríguez Méndez, *Comentarios impertinentes sobre el teatro español* (Barcelona: Ediciones Península, 1972), p. 112, cited in Nathalie Cañizares Bundorf, *Memoria de un escenario: Teatro María Guerrero 1885–2000* (Madrid: INAEM, 2000), pp. 158–9. See also Luis Araquistáin, *La batalla teatral* (Madrid: Compañía Iberoamericana de Publicaciones/Mundo Latino, 1930); and Cañizares Bundorf, *Memoria de un escenario*, p. 158.

36. Felipe Sassone, *Maria Guerrero*, p. 119.
37. Felipe Sassone, 'María Guerrero: La buena estrella', *ADE teatro* 77 (October 1999), pp. 234–6.
38. Classes with Bernhardt are mentioned by Sánchez Estevan, *María Guerrero*, p. 87, but there appears little evidence to substantiate these claims.
39. Ibid., pp. 168–75.
40. See Cañizares Bundorf, *Memoria de un escenario*, p. 154 and Menéndez Onrubia, *El dramaturgo y los actores*, p. 212.
41. See Benavente, 'María Guerrero', in *Obras completas*, vol. 11 (Madrid: Aguilar, 1958), pp. 88–90, and Sassone, *María Guerrero*, p. 222.
42. Jesús Rubio Jiménez, 'Margarita Xirgu (1888–1969): Una actriz comprometida', in Luciano García Lorenzo, ed., *Autoras y actrices en la historia del teatro español* (Murcia: Universidad de Murcia, Servicio de Publicaciones, 2000), pp. 179–200, p. 189.
43. See Maria M. Delgado, *'Other' Spanish Theatres: Erasure and Inscription on the Twentieth-century Spanish Stage* (Manchester: Manchester University Press, 2003), pp. 21–66.
44. See Antonina Rodrigo, *Margarita Xirgu: Una biografía* (Barcelona: Flor del Viento Ediciones, 2005), pp. 137–50.
45. See Delgado, *'Other' Spanish Theatres*, pp. 24–32.
46. García Lorca's *Amor de don Perlimplín con Belisa en su jardín* (*The Love of Don Perlimplín with Belisa in his Garden*), rehearsed at Rivas Cherif's El Caracol, was closed down by the authorities in February 1929. For further details, see Leslie Stainton, *Lorca: A Dream of Life* (New York: Farrar, Straus & Giroux, 1999), 200–5.
47. See, for example, Federico García Lorca, *Obras completas*, vol. 2, *Teatro*, ed. Miguel García-Posada (Barcelona: Galaxia Gutenburg/Círculo de Lectores, 1996), p. 82; García Lorca, *Obras completas*, vol. 3, *Prosa*, ed. Miguel García-Posada (Barcelona: Galaxia Gutenburg/Círculo de Lectores, 1996), pp. 194–7, 269, 547–9, 577, 617–18, 622–4, 632; Rodrigo, *Margarita Xirgu*, pp. 137–50, 269–71, 275.
48. Rodrigo, *Margarita Xirgu*, p. 284.
49. Ian Gibson, *Federico García Lorca: A Life* (New York: Pantheon Books, 1989), p. 307.
50. Ibid., pp. 314–15.
51. Alberto M. Oteiza, *Margarita Xirgu: En el entorno de Federico García Lorca* (Buenos Aires: Ediciones Olimpo, 1990), p. 135.
52. See, for example, Paul Binding, *Lorca: The Gay Imagination* (London: GMP, 1985), p. 189, and Gwynne Edwards, 'Introduction' to *Lorca: Three Plays* (London, Methuen, 1987), pp. 11–30, p. 14.
53. Cited in Gibson, *Lorca*, p. 378. See also Miguel García-Posada, 'García Lorca en Uruguay', *Triunfo* 21–2 (July–August 1982), pp. 82–8.
54. See Rodrigo, *Margarita Xirgu*, pp. 373–6; Oteiza, *Margarita Xirgu*, pp. 149–92; María Esther Burgueño and Roger Mirza, 'Margarita en América: Una pasión inextinguible', in *Cuadernos 'El público'* 36 (1988), pp. 21–7.
55. See Rodrigo, *Margarita Xirgu*, pp. 338–42.
56. Ibid., pp. 309–11.
57. Delgado, *'Other' Spanish Theatres*, pp. 56–66.

58. See Francesc Foguet i Boreu, *Margarida Xirgu: Una vocació indomable* (Barcelona: Pòrtic, 2002), and María del Carmen Gil Fombellida, *Rivas Cherif, Margarita Xirgu y el teatro de la II República* (Madrid: Editorial Fundamentos, 2003).
59. Ramón Pérez de Ayala, *Las máscaras*, vol. 1 (Madrid: Renacimiento, 1924), p. 141.
60. Cited in Rodrigo, *Margarita Xirgu*, p. 387.
61. See Oteiza, *Margarita Xirgu*, pp. 117, 121–2, and Delgado, *'Other' Spanish Theatres*, pp. 56–66.
62. Domènec Guansé, 'Toda una vida', in *Margarita Xirgu: Crónica de una pasión, Cuadernos 'El público'* 36 (1988), pp. 29–63, pp. 49–50.
63. Michael R. Booth, John Stokes and Susan Bassnett, *Three Tragic Actresses: Siddons, Rachel, Ristori* (Cambridge: Cambridge University Press, 1996), p. 9.
64. This chapter was completed with assistance from an Arts and Humanities Research Council Research Leave award.

FURTHER READING

Burgueño, María Esther, and Roger Mirza. 'Margarita en América: Una pasión inextinguible', in *Cuadernos 'El público'* 36 (1988), pp. 21–7.
Delgado, Maria M. *'Other' Spanish Theatres: Erasure and Inscription on the Twentieth-century Spanish Stage*. Manchester: Manchester University Press, 2003.
Foguet i Boreu, Francesc. *Margarida Xirgu: Una vocació indomable*. Barcelona: Pòrtic, 2002.
García Lorenzo, Luciano, ed. *Autoras y actrices en la historia del teatro español*. Murcia: Universidad de Murcia, Servicio de Publicaciones, 2000.
George, David. *The Theatre in Madrid and Barcelona, 1892–1936: Rivals or Collaborators?* Cardiff: University of Wales Press, 2002.
Gibson, Ian. *Federico García Lorca: A Life*. London: Faber, 1989.
Gil Fombellida, María del Carmen. *Rivas Cherif, Margarita Xirgu y el teatro de la II República*. Madrid: Editorial Fundamentos, 2003.
Menéndez Onrubia, Carmen. *El dramaturgo y los actores: Epistolario de Benito Pérez Galdós, María Guerrero y Fernándo Díaz de Mendoza*, Anejos de la Revista 'Segismundo' 10. Madrid: Consejo Superior de Investigaciones Científicas, 1984.
Olmet, Luis Anton del, and José de Torres Bernal. *Los grandes españoles: Maria Guerrero*. Madrid: Renacimiento, 1920.
Oteiza, Alberto M. *Margarita Xirgu: En el entorno de Federico García Lorca*. Buenos Aires: Ediciones Olimpo, 1990.
Rodrigo, Antonina. *Margarita Xirgu, una biografía*. Barcelona: Flor del Viento Ediciones, 2005.
Sánchez Estevan, Ismael. *María Guerrero*. Barcelona: Iberia/Joaquín Gil, 1946.
Sassone, Felipe. *Maria Guerrero la grande: Primera actriz de los teatros de todas las Españas*. Madrid: Escelicer, 1943.
Zamacois, Eduardo. *Desde mi butaca: Apuntes para una psicología de nuestros actores*, 2nd edn. Barcelona: Maucci, 1911.

15

MAGGIE B. GALE

Going solo: an historical perspective on the actress and the monologue

Julia Varley's solo performance *Dõna Musica's Butterflies* (1997) is one of the many performance pieces made by contemporary actresses which play with ideas of 'self' and 'character' (fig. 22). The performance, still on tour in 2005, is centred on Varley's Dõna Musica, an old, white-haired woman, standing alone in a circle of white roses, questioning her relationship to the actress who performs her.

> Did the actress give me life? . . . Did the actress mould her energy so as to transform it into Dõna Musica? Or did I, Dõna Musica, modulate the actress's energy?[1]

Dõna Musica/Julia Varley[2] brings into focus one of the fundamental characteristics of solo performance, namely, the centrality of the relationship between text and performer. Varley interlaces an autobiographical perspective with an on-stage investigation into the creation of characters who originate in processes of improvisation and devising, giving the actress the dual role of actress and *auteur*. Thus *Doña Musica's Butterflies* engages with the complex matrix of relationships between the actress/performer, the performed 'self', the context and content of performance and the audience for whom the performance is being made. Although many of the earlier solo performances by women examined in this chapter do not engage so self-consciously with these issues, there is a consistent awareness of the fluidity of the monologue as a form, and a deliberate professional strategising and theatrical self-reflection which reverberates in the work of actresses using the monologue from Fanny Kelly in the mid-nineteenth century, through to Joyce Grenfell in the 1950s.

Working on their own: early actress/monologists and professional reinvention

Responding to the implicit accusation that the monologue is somehow a hybrid and bastardised form, a *'genre* . . . a familiar form easily understood

Photo Jan Rüsz

Fig. 22.   Julia Varley as Dõna Musica in *Dõna Musica's Butterflies*, Odinteatret, 1997.
(Photo: Jan Rüsz.)

because it has appropriated several characteristics of related types', many literary critics, whilst observing the importance of spoken delivery in the emerging 'monodramatic poetry' of the nineteenth century, have defined the monologue predominantly in literary terms.[3] Such critics often fail to foreground in their analyses the fact that the monologue developed into a theatrical form and so compare it to poetic readings and platform performances – the materials for which were often prose or poetry. Equally, there is a critical tendency not to locate the monologue in 'socio-political terms' – yet the growth in the popularity of monologue performance is directly linked to the changing cultural contexts in which it takes place.[4] There is a general agreement that the burgeoning of the monologue during the nineteenth century was connected to a number of social factors: the development of the 'new' sciences such as sociology, and a gradual process of individuation and democratisation.[5] A. Dwight Culler also points to the blurred lines of definition in the early nineteenth century, where public stage readings were sometimes called 'monodramas'.[6] The ever-changing process of naming and defining this type of performance could be seen as a reflection of the fact that the monologue has consistently been transformed through practice: the form was often adapted according to the performance context. Thus, many women performers used monologue in their music hall performances during the nineteenth and early twentieth centuries, often alternating with song and speaking to music. A broader study would encompass such mixed acts, but for the purposes of this chapter, although many of the solo actress performers under examination crossed easily between 'illegitimate theatre' – music hall and variety – and 'legitimate' theatre, it is the creation, performance, distribution and currency of the monologue and its performance by actresses which is under investigation.

For many actresses working in the commercial theatre industries of the mid- to late nineteenth century, the solo form provided the opportunity to develop outside the remit of a mixed-gender company. It became a means to an end and gave leading actresses such as Fanny Kelly (1790–1882), Fanny Kemble (1809–93) and Charlotte Cushman (1816–76) a chance to revitalise and reshape their careers at a point when they might have been considered too old for the leading roles and too experienced for the minor ones. In a culture where women were stigmatised as the 'weaker' sex, the actress, standing on stage alone, without the comfort of scenery or fellow actors, carried a different set of social and theatrical signifiers to the male actor engaged in the same activity. Such signifiers are culturally determined and specific and are moulded by the social, economic and political position of women in any given culture at any given time. Thus an actress working alone on either a small makeshift or a more formal stage in the mid-nineteenth century carried with her performance work associations of impropriety, whereas by the mid-1950s such associations had largely disappeared. In contrast, in part because of the focus of the texts and in part because of the context of the struggle for the vote on both sides of the Atlantic, by the 1920s and 1930s, critics identified a strong link between political emancipation and the proliferation of actresses finding success with the solo form whether on popular stages or in other more intimate performance contexts.

Early solo performance in America can be divided into two strands, public, and later platform, 'readings', which moved onto the Chautauqua public entertainments circuits by the early twentieth century; the Chautauqua circuits were a development of the Chautauqua Assemblies in New York which had originally been set up as large public religious and educational open-air meetings. In such contexts established actresses such as Fanny Kemble and Charlotte Cushman, following the example of Anna Cora Mowett (1819–70) in the early 1840s, revitalised their careers by performing, for example, readings from Shakespeare, 'in character'. Solo performance gave Cushman the possibility of the '"reinvention" of her public persona',[7] and it is the notion of 'public persona' that enabled many of the early actress/monologists to market their work within a growing industry of popular performance. The Chautauqua performance circuits were largely formulated around the idea that cultural expression had a clearly educative and religious function;[8] actresses who performed solo work in these contexts were using a theatrical form in a context which, although highly theatrical, did not always frame itself as such. John S. Gentile notes that the Chautauquas distinguished themselves from the vaudeville theatres, which were considered socially and morally disreputable.[9] However, the theatrical and the theatrical potential of imitating celebrity personalities lay at the heart of Helen Potter's solo performances in the 1870s and 1880s. Touring on the public entertainment circuits, Potter became well known for her impersonations of actors and lecturers, 'giving extracts from their principle plays or lectures': Ellen Terry as Portia, Sarah Bernhardt as Dõna Sol, or a version of the political activist Susan B. Anthony giving her 'On Trial for Voting' speech.[10] Beginning as platform readings, Potter's work became more and more defined by a combination of the monologue and impersonation, which allowed her to take advantage of an audience's already existing knowledge of celebrity actors and political speakers. This was a strategy picked up by later solo vaudeville performers in the early years of the twentieth century.

Already in 1833, in England, Fanny Kelly had created a substantial solo performance, *Dramatic Recollections and Studies of Character*, at the Strand Theatre. Kelly was a celebrated actress who had built up a faithful audience while she was working at the patent Drury Lane Theatre. She created

Dramatic Recollections in part as a means of funding her own drama school, and Jacky Bratton now sees Kelly as an actress whose solo performance experiments were pitted against the dominance of the legitimate theatres in London.[11] The performance, which lasted some two hours, included texts written by others, but also what one of her biographers, Basil Francis, describes as 'pure Kellyana'.[12] One of the celebrated characters she created was Mrs Parthian, reportedly written for her by Charles Lamb (fig. 23).[13] Mrs Parthian is a kind of performing 'theatre historian' who tells her own 'history' rather than having it told for her.[14] Basil Francis describes Mrs Parthian's stage entrance thus:

> she walked slowly on to the stage, leaning on her ebony stick . . . She would then lean forward and in a vague, confidential manner gossip to her audience of her recollections of bygone actors and personalities and events of her own youth as a travelling actress.[15]

Francis's biography of Kelly only hints at the fact that she wrote and adapted much of the performance material herself; such removal of Kelly's agency as author/performer is questioned by more recent theatre histories, thus Bratton points to the fact that a substantial amount of the performance, the 'Kellyana', was in fact autobiographical. Kelly capitalised on her celebrity status and the audiences' knowledge of her career to create solo work which was marketable. Francis implies that audiences lost interest in her show after a while, but there is no statistical evidence to suggest that it was not a continuing success. When the show closed in London, in March 1833, the books were balanced, and it successfully toured the provinces and was revamped in the early 1840s.

Kemble, Cushman and Kelly all attained both theatrical and celebrity status and needed late in their careers to reinvent themselves professionally. The solo/monologue performance form gave them a discernible level of control over what they performed and how they performed it. By the 1870s the same could also be said for Helen Potter, mistress of observation and imitation, who through her solo work became a well-known cultural figure at a time when performance and issues of social identity in America were becoming ever more closely linked.

Imitation, identity and character: the *fin de siècle* and a changing social climate

The solo performer often played with imitation on stage, but the whole process and social function of imitation as performance shifted in significance

Fig. 23. Miss Kelly in the character of Mrs Parthian, by F. W. Wilkin. (From the collection of Basil Francis.)

during the latter part of the nineteenth and into the twentieth century, as Susan B. Glenn has pointed out:

> The dynamic interplay between theatrical and non-theatrical concepts of imitation in this period was fuelled by contemporary fascination with mass production, the role of the artist as critical observer and debate about the significance of imitation for the constitution of the self.[16]

In turn, monologues by such popular actresses as May Isabel Fisk, performing in the late nineteenth and early twentieth centuries,[17] and Beatrice Herford (1868–1952) move towards investigation of identity and observation of social types; this at a time when the acceleration of urban industrialisation meant that individuality and social identity were becoming an issue in the popular press. Moving into the twentieth century, Warren Susman points to the fact that sociologists and psychologists were making strong assertions in their social analyses of a newly perceived crowd mentality, the crowd from which the individual was becoming less distinguishable.[18] Susman notes that 'self-help' texts published in the United States around the early years of the twentieth century foregrounded the idea that one could 'construct' a self differentiated from the crowd, that personality and character were socially constructed and could be individually formulated; there was in fact a paradigm shift toward the idea that 'character', one's 'self', could be constructed and improved for the benefit of the individual as well as society at large. 'Self-help' was in part framed by the idea that one could improve one's social position and find ways of designing one's individual personality and identity within a culture where immigration and cultural assimilation were key social and economic issues. This has a specific significance for women in general and for the actress in particular. If personality and character can be constructed, then the idea of 'natural' and gender-specific characteristics begins to be undermined. Thus the range of supposedly female personality characteristics can be expanded.

Fisk and Herford capitalised on such a possibility, publishing numerous volumes of their monologues, which had a cultural currency beyond the professional theatre industry in the fast-growing amateur market. Just as the growth in popularity of female solo performers and monologists in the late Victorian period has been associated in part with changes in women's social status, so too some social historians have identified the increasing numbers of solo women performers with the general cultural shift around notions of the 'self', 'identity' and 'personality'. It was within this context that actresses such as Fisk and Herford developed the monologue as a popular form that experimented with staged observations of the social context of characters, social types and personalities.

Susan B. Glenn suggests that, by the early twentieth century, there was a clear trend of women performers who capitalised on their imitative performance skills in a culture where the idea of personality reigned supreme.[19] Such performers often worked as actresses outside the vaudeville context but, both within and without, they were keen to assert the fact that imitative performance, and monologues in turn, were as 'dramatic' and theatrical as anything likely to be offered by the production of a play. Thus for

Cornelia Otis Skinner (1901–79), writing in 1931, the monologue was more than a 'left branch of the concert stage', and its performers had helped to develop the form and expand the possibilities of the theatrical event. Skinner recognised that a great deal of monologue performance had grown out of the amateur platform stages of the nineteenth century, but saw it as an experimental and fluid form, which had by the 1930s become far removed from the 'fusty tradition of the dramatic recitation' – it had become a viable entertainment form in both middle-class and popular performance contexts.[20]

May Isabel Fisk and Beatrice Herford also took the monologue out of platform staging, in part by writing their own work, but also by consciously using the monologue to play out *versions* of female character and women's lives – not always uncritically. Both came out of a tradition where many had seen the monologue performance as recalling 'an army of artistically inclined ladies calling themselves "readers" . . . who present on the stage of their local parish house a program of school-of-expression recitations'.[21] To some extent it is this 'army of artistically inclined ladies' of whom they make fun in much of their work, both playing with the 'fourth wall' convention – their monologues often offer the opportunity for direct address – and playing on the audiences' ability to recognise and critique social types.

The actress as *auteur* and social commentator

Fisk and Herford tapped in to a market in which social and economic development meant that identification of and identity within certain social groups was paramount. They equally developed performative skills which can be connected historically with late twentieth-century solo performers and writers such as Victoria Wood and Lily Tomlin. Fisk and Herford's work contains a strong anthropological perspective, the ability to create a dramatic scene with few or no props, the ability to story-tell from the first-person perspective and to move between depictions of different imaginary stage characters simultaneously. Both commented in the press on their need to connect directly with an audience, to have an up-to-date quality and social relevance in their work.

May Isabel Fisk created and performed numerous monologues about society women, whose regard for their servants, their children and those who surrounded them in their everyday lives was less than considerate (fig. 24). These characters are often lacking in any self-awareness and, bored with their lives, find ways of distracting those whose services they require. Thus in 'Calling on the Doctor', the woman, played by Fisk, insists that there is something wrong with her, only to be met with comments which make her respond, 'Well, I shouldn't call it normal – it's much more *ab*normal all the

Fig. 24. May Isabel Fisk. (Photo: Aimé Dupont, New York.)

time – that's what I should call it. There I've forgotten something! . . . No, not a symptom – it's my umbrella.'[22] Similarly, in Beatrice Herford's 'Telephoning the Doctor', the character complains to her doctor that her young son is not 'as lively as I'd like to have him', that she is unsure of whether to let him wear the bonnet her mother-in-law gave him, that she wonders if the clothing he is wearing will be too cold for the weather the next day, and so on. She keeps the doctor on the telephone line and shouts at the nanny to look after the needs of the child about whom she claims to be so concerned herself.[23] Such monologues provide an implied social commentary on women whose lives are bound by the constraints of middle- and upper-middle-class lifestyles; they spend their time with children and servants and often don't have the wherewithal to communicate with 'ordinary people'. Both Herford and Fisk also played with stereotypes of the working classes, creating servants and shopkeepers such as in Herford's 'The Country Store'.[24] However, the majority of their monologues depict upper-middle-class women who are self-obsessed. These women are located in domestic spaces but also public spaces such as grocery shops or markets, where the women rarely have any idea how to look after children or even how to purchase basic foodstuffs:

> What are these? . . . Chops? Well, I never saw chops growing in bunches before . . . I don't care – when I was at home we often had chops, but they weren't like that, but sort of one and one, with little bits of parsley around them.[25]

The monologues often portray women and their children on an outing, without the support of their regular nanny. There is chaos as the women realise how hard it is to complete a task with a child competing for one's attention. Herford and Fisk also make consistent reference to 'Society' women reading theories of childcare in the latest manuals for women of their class, and failing to put the theories successfully into practice; similarly they ridicule the obsession with faddish diets or 'life management' strategies, such as in Fisk's hilarious 'Mrs Meekey Explains the Higher Thought'.[26] Mrs Meekey, surprised by a visit from a friend, bustles about the house, shouting at the servant, telling her friend that she really doesn't have time for a visit as she has so much to do, but that she has been 'saved' by the 'atmosphere of the higher thought'. This she learnt about at Mud Pond where they teach all the new 'isms', and 'while not really the thing, like going to the Continent . . . it was not *common*'. Her friend Ada, laughs at her and suggests that she has been fooled by 'cranks', but Mrs Meekey goes on wildly to insist that she has discovered a new equilibrium and inner peacefulness in her everyday life; this is completely contradicted by the way she behaves in the monologue.

One of the principal things they teach you is modesty and humility of the spirit! That was the first thing *I* learned and I can tell you I wasn't there ten days before I could beat them all at it – there wasn't one could touch me at it – not *one* – not even the teachers themselves! . . . I'm going to be a healer . . . No, no; not a h-e-e-l-e-r – A h-e-a-l-e-r. It's all done with thought . . . Thought concentration – that's it. You just sit in silence and think what you want.[27]

Mrs Meekey continues to explain her new philosophy of life whilst shouting at the maid to stop the dog licking the newly painted woodwork.

Fisk and Herford both found ways of depicting different classes of women on stage; that many of the characters they wrote to some extent played into social stereotypes is less important than the fact that they wanted to present and play with a *range* of dramatised female types, as actresses authoring their own performances. Thus as 'social commentators' both Fisk and Herford worked with the 'typical cultural scene' of their audiences – often middle-class women – both 'exaggerate and distort' what Stephanie Koziski calls the 'socially enacted' behaviour of their *own* society *to* their own society.[28] Of equal importance to what they did is an investigation of how they did it. This path of enquiry was often taken by the press with both Fisk and Herford but also later with Ruth Draper (1884–1956), who became the most celebrated of monologue writer/performers in the 1920s and 1930s.

Refining the form: the technique of monologue performance

Beatrice Herford, who was born in Manchester but moved to America after marriage, had worked as an actress before becoming a monologist, but it was through her solo work that she gained notoriety. Aware of the social composition of her audiences, she commented that women 'don't ever seem to get offended because no woman ever sees herself in my types'.[29] One reviewer characterised her audience as that 'prosperous middle class which has made its fight in the world and is not ignorant of it, but is tranquil enough now for contemplative enjoyment'.[30] In reference to the extant recordings of Herford, Linda Sue Long suggests that 'she used dialect, and spoke rapidly without lengthy pauses for the other character dialogues'. For Herford, the solo form was an art form but also 'a game'.[31] She did not rehearse in front of a mirror because it made her self-conscious; rather, she wanted her performances to be spontaneous.[32] Implicit in such an approach is the desire to create an immediacy with an audience, to work from a structured framework, such as a script, but to be allowed performative freedom within it. Fisk recognised the fact that 'every motion and gesture, every glance of the eye and turn of the head, must be replete with meaning'[33] and that the monologist had to remember that to 'act *at* a character is hopeless – one must *be* it, divested of ego, and casting aside any personal inclination to mannerisms. Anything consciously artificial . . . puts to flight that essential and subtle element of success termed magnetism.'[34] Thus for Herford and Fisk the monologue required a different preparation and style from stage acting which involved other actors and scripts usually created by non-performers.

Similarly, the Glasgow-born Cissie Loftus (1876–1943), who worked with Herford in 1924, talked of her own solo performances in terms of what Linda Sue Long calls 'non-cognitive transactions', using words such as 'absorption', 'self-mesmerism' and 'self-hypnotism' to describe what happened to her on stage.[35] Loftus, who came from a family of popular music hall performers and became famous for her impersonations of celebrity performers, but who also worked with the monologue, pointed to the fact that solo performing involved high levels of observational skills and the ability to 'isolate' and assimilate observed gestures and vocal intonation.[36] Her notes on performance technique show an awareness and application of a type of acting technique that was still in the experimental stages for many stage actors of her generation. Between them, Fisk, Herford and Loftus, who worked across the late nineteenth century and into the early decades of the twentieth century, took the actress as solo performer more firmly towards *auteur*/performer status. Each theorised their performance technique and the complexities of the relationship between the solo actress and her audience. All three, on different occasions, noted that the solo actress needed to be able to combine an absorption in character with a heightened level of spontaneity and an ability to respond to the performance space and the audience within it. These actresses weren't just pandering to a performance craze; they were consciously analysing how monologue performance operated and developing technique directly out of their experiences of playing with the form.

The new generation: Ruth Draper and her 'company of characters'

The curtained stage was empty save for a few pieces of essential furniture: a sofa, a couple of chairs, and perhaps a table. Ruth Draper walked on, a tall, dark-eyed lady, elegant in her simple brown dress, beautifully cut, and looked out over the auditorium with grave composure. Her authority and her concentration were absolute. How swiftly she transformed that stage into her own extraordinary world, transporting us at her immediate bidding to other places, other countries . . . creating in each of those imagined settings a single dominant personality, and then seeming to surround herself . . . with an attendant crowd of minor characters, children, animals, servants, husbands, lovers . . . so marvellously observed and minutely executed . . . How did she rehearse and develop them over the years? She once told me that . . . she could shorten or lengthen them while she was playing as she felt the reactions of her audience demanded. (John Gielgud)[37]

I want to declare Miss Draper open to the new generation of playgoers, and to trample on their suspicions, which I once shared, that she might turn out to be a museum piece, ripe for the dust-sheet and oblivion. She is, on the contrary, about as old fashioned and mummified as spring, and as I watched her perform her thronging monologues . . . I could only conclude that this was the best and most modern group acting I had ever seen . . . She worked her miracle benignly and unfussed . . . with the accuracy, tact and wisdom of her technique. (Kenneth Tynan)[38]

Ruth Draper, who originated from the American upper classes, worked professionally from the late 1910s through to her death in 1956. Her performances translated across continents and language divides, and she was unique in both the length of her stage career and in the range of performance materials she developed over almost fifty years. One attempt was made, late in her career, to televise her performances but the recordings did not get her approval, were never broadcast and were then lost, and so there remain only written testimonies to her work, late recordings and the scripts which she wrote down almost at the end of career.[39] She impressed many, amongst them Eleonora Duse, J. M. Barrie and Henry James (who wrote a monologue for her which she declined), performed on numerous occasions for royalty and even caught the attention of Virginia Woolf.[40] Her performances were recirculated by other female solo performers of the day through on-stage imitation.[41] Draper knew Beatrice Herford's repertoire and there are reverberations of the kinds of monologue developed by both Herford and Fisk in her own work. However, Draper took the monologue form further into the realms of 'drama', creating programmes of performances that were longer and more complex than those of her forebears; by mid-career a Draper performance involved a number of pieces, some lasting more than thirty minutes, played in sequence.

Morton D. Zabel points to the fact that Draper 'never analysed her art' but that her art was 'inevitably much more calculated and complex than she allowed'.[42] In one interview, made late in her career, she suggested that she never rehearsed and that she didn't know what she was going to perform until the producer told her just before she went on stage.[43] Later in her life there was a sense in which the 'myth' of Ruth Draper had overtaken the reality of the depth of her working method; Zabel frequently uses words like 'spell', 'sorcery' and 'magic' in reference to her work, and other critiques and testimonies seem split between presenting Draper as some kind of stage trickster and as a performer who had developed a complex and layered technique. Thus, Iris Origo notes that Draper 'laboriously worked out for herself her own technique, alone . . . she lived herself into her subject, she worked before the mirror, experimenting with facial expressions and gestures. Sometimes the preparation of a sketch . . . took eight or ten years.'[44] Draper, much like Cissie Loftus, stressed the ways in which one had to *become* the person one was playing.[45] She noted the importance of working with the audience's imagination, and believed that monologue performance is a live and fluid form; Origo suggests that Draper used the scripts, all of which existed only in her head until late in her career, as 'frameworks' for performance.

David Kaplan and Patricia Norcia compare Draper's stage persona, a reverberative and extended vocal range matched by a chameleon-like physique, to that of Bernhardt and Duse. They suggest that there was, compositionally speaking, a musical structure to her performances – she used the sonata or allegro form, or created pieces with three movements such as 'Three Generations in a Court of Domestic Relations' and 'Three Women and Mr Clifford'.[46] Draper's collected letters reveal that she trained with a voice coach in the 1920s and that she regularly targeted her charity and leisure visits whilst on tour so as to listen to accents and observe behavioural mannerisms.[47] Draper had only on a limited number of occasions worked as an 'actress', but embraced and applied the technical skills an actress requires to enhance her ability as a monologist.

She began developing and performing her monologues in an amateur context in the 1910s; it was friends of her parents as well as artist admirers such as Henry James who encouraged her to turn professional. Her first professional performance in England took place at the Aeolian Hall in London in 1920. Here she was received by critics in positive terms and this kind of reception continued throughout her performing career, despite the break created by the Second World War. The critic for *The Times* noted in 1920 that in 'her swift and lively dramatic portraits of types in England . . . America and . . . France . . . there is no caricature; it is all faithful portraiture, but mighty shrewd'.[48] Later, in 1947, another critic comments on the 'credible' and 'almost palpable . . . exhilarating company' she bought to the stage. He also makes reference to her technique:

> Miss Draper's great reputation as a creator almost blinds one to the fact that she is, first of all, an actress, that the miracle is at least partly to be explained by uninterrupted superlative technique, and that the sheer virtuosity of some two hours' unbroken speaking and acting would by itself be impressive.[49]

Draper was admired as *the* queen of the monologue, and unlike many of the actresses mentioned previously, apart from a short foray into script writing, it was the only form with which she worked. Despite giving the impression later in life that she did not have control of programming and tour management, there is every indication that she was a savvy manager of her own work. Her programmes varied from night to night on tour, such that on one evening, for example, she might perform 'The Italian Lesson' and 'In County Kerry 1919', followed by a musical interval provided by her brother Paul, an accomplished pianist, followed by 'Doctors and Diets', 'Showing the Garden' and 'A Scottish Immigrant at Ellis Island'. The next evening the programme would change to 'Opening a Bazaar' followed by 'Doctors and Diets', her brother's concert and then 'An Exhibition in Boston', another piano recital and 'The Actress'. This last piece, featuring an actress of East European origins, who speaks in accented English, French and a fabricated East European dialect, is both a homage to and a humorous take on the great 'star' actresses of the nineteenth century:

> Darling, I read the play you wrote for me . . . you must make my part more important . . . Yes, yes, Morowski is a great actor . . . But, darling, I can say to you – *I* am more great . . . You must make me more always the centre . . . he makes me more great only, you see – but *always*, I must be the most important . . . I am the *raison d'être* of the play . . . (*she becomes restless*).[50]

Draper developed more monologues so the programmes became more variable, but she was still performing the same pieces in 1947 that she had premièred in the early 1920s.[51]

Ruth Draper performed throughout Europe and America, and was produced by Reinhardt in Germany and Lugné-Poe in France. In England, venues in which she appeared ranged from those in the West End to music halls and provincial theatres, where she was, early in her career, often accompanied on the bill by such acts as a performing seal.[52] At the beginning of her professional career she was being paid as much as £100 per week performing on the music hall circuits,[53] although, tired of the touring which her managers had arranged for her, she noted that she often got paid £40 just for one private recital. She managed continually to cross the bridge between one class of theatre clientele and another, seeing the music hall work as 'fun' where she could '"turn on" as it were, about three times as much power', but wanting to keep up her 'private recitals' and smaller venue work.[54] In the 1940s, Emile Littler, a member of the management cartel which controlled many of the London and touring venues during the inter-war period and beyond,[55] recognised that although the interval provided by the 1939–45 war meant that Draper would be working with a new audience, she could still guarantee attendance to such an extent that he was willing not only to cover any financial losses and expenses which might occur, but also to offer her 75 per cent of any money made on a tour she was proposing.[56] The point is that, from the late 1910s, Draper was consistently an economic viability within a commercial industry and her monologue performances sustained their currency over some forty years of cultural change, even though by the 1940s she was not adding any new items to her repertoire.

The monologues themselves asked for little in the way of staging but often required a visual transformation on stage as Draper moved from one character to another. Thus, in 'Three Generations in a Court of Domestic Relations' Draper used simple props such as a large shawl and altered physical posture to depict the three generations of women.[57] Many monologues were set in both domestic and public spaces, and often contained an acute social critique as well as a great deal of humour. Like Herford and Fisk, Draper often made fun of society women and their weakness for social fads and crazes. In 'Doctors and Diets', for example, Draper plays a woman taking out three of her friends for a pre-matinée lunch to a fashionable restaurant only to find that they are all on extreme diets: one can only eat boiled turnips, the other raw carrots, and the third the juice of eleven lemons. Draper's character reveals that her diet comprises *only* eating what she craves, and so she orders three chocolate éclairs. The hostess then proceeds to tell her guests all about a new doctor she has heard of who believes in 'mass cures': 'He never sees his patients. He is not interested in individuals, he prefers to treat a crowd. And he has organised these mass cures . . . and he cures thirty thousand people every Thursday. It only costs a dollar.'[58] As well as offering critiques of social types, Draper, whose ability to work with and manipulate different vocal registers is noted by critics, biographers and historians alike, also made sustained references to different national types, playing a Scottish peasant, an Irish woman and an aging central European. This was during a period when many national boundaries within Europe were fluid, and she moved between American and English characters at a historical point when the stereotyped distinctions between, and stereotyped characteristics of, the two nations were still in formation.

A female performer with the technique and agency to use the stage not only to story-tell, but to consciously reflect on cultural phenomena, Draper opened up the possibilities for actresses working with the monologue form. Not only did she sustain a remarkably long career, she refined the monologue as a form. One critic, in 1932, praised her work by referring to the specifics of her technique:

306

Not only have you appealed to their intellect and to their emotions, but you have opened up new vistas of technique, of gesture, of plastic rhythm and voice modulation . . . You are one of the only people, except Duse, who can produce drama by your immobility as well as by your movement.[59]

Cornelia Otis Skinner commented on the fact that Draper had 'one of the largest supporting companies' she had seen,[60] and it is certainly the case that what she was trying to create on stage was the *whole* world of the character portrayed – in this sense some of the scripts and even the late recordings have an almost filmic sense of energy and space where, in part because of the ways in which Draper is able to play with her voice and in part because of the layering of the text, you can feel the hustle and bustle of the bazaar, museum or restaurant, even though all you are hearing is a single voice (fig. 25).

Joyce Grenfell: taking the monologue into the recording studio

Unlike Draper, her distant English cousin Joyce Grenfell (1910–79) trained, if only for a short period, at RADA; like Draper, Grenfell found herself unable to work in a performance team. After working as a radio critic, she developed monologue performances for the professional stage, performing her sketches initially in Herbert Farjeon's *Little Revue* in London in 1939. The revue, a more intimate form in the context of the West End commercial theatre, survived the intervention of cinema in the popular performance market and often contained a strong element of social critique. Although Grenfell's stage career was relatively short, she is interesting because she established the monologue in more media than any of the solo women who had gone before her – working on stage, on radio and on screen. Grenfell performed to audiences who had grown up with both live and recorded media and adapted the monologue accordingly. She wanted to work with 'glimpses' as opposed to the 'full views' developed by Draper,[61] she wanted to create 'brief, shorthand sketches of characters, suggested rather than detailed'.[62] However, there are reverberations of Draper's social conscience as well as her style in many of Grenfell's texts. Thus, the 'Shirley' or the 'Women at Work' scripts are more than humorous takes on the different social classes; like the famous 'Free Activity Period' sketch they play out social difference in a performance context.[63] Grenfell's work did not carry the same sustained level of favour with the critics who, by the late 1950s, felt that her performances provided rather a 'tea-time view of life', her gangly upper-class persona failing to win them over.[64] She was, however, a household name in Britain and as far afield

Fig. 25. Ruth Draper as 'The American Tourist' in *In a Church in Italy*. (Mander and Mitchenson Theatre Collection.)

as Australia. Her solo shows in the 1950s and 1960s and her television work took the monologue[65] to a new audience, but lost the sense of live and fluid physical technique which Draper had developed. Grenfell gave her characters less time to develop on stage and, to some extent, relied more on the audience to recognise her characters and 'fill in the spaces'.

Joyce Grenfell, who came from an upper-class background,[66] appealed, like Draper, to both a popular and a more socially elite audience. Similarly, she had in common with Draper the ability to create a balance in her writing and performance between diegesis, the stating of a narrative, and mimesis, imitation or the playing out of the character. She became, perhaps more than any other solo performer, associated with the parts she played and with the characters she wrote, and this has somewhat distracted from any real analysis of the complexity of the material she was producing: critics and historians have tended to sideline her work because of her class and, ironically, because of her appeal to a commercial audience. She rarely features in analyses of professional theatre practice.

During the mid-twentieth century, actresses working with solo performance and the monologue form created layers of technique which made the form itself more complex and more performative. Nellie Wallace – a variety performer who often performed solo sketches on the variety circuits and who was still, during the Second World War, taking part in concerts with Grenfell – showed a lack of understanding of what Grenfell was attempting when she commented, 'What *does* she think she is doing out there on her own talking to herself?'.[67] Grenfell often actually cut across the fourth wall in performance and wasn't 'talking to herself' at all; yet Wallace, as a solo variety performer, did not recognise that she and Grenfell were doing the same thing but from different performance perspectives – she perhaps thought that Grenfell was *being* herself rather than *performing* imagined selves.

With Ruth Draper, as with others examined in this chapter, the monologue often blurs the relationships between the self, the script, the character, the audience, the location and space for performance, the distinction between mimesis and diegesis and *being* and *performing*. Such relationships are all part of a complex matrix of performative factors for the actress, whether from the nineteenth or the twenty-first century, working with the monologue, standing alone on stage, creating the world in which her characters come to life.

NOTES

1. Julia Varley, *Dona Musica's Butterflies* (Denmark: Odin Teatret, 1997), p. 10.
2. Varley has worked with Odinteatret, one of Europe's longest established and most acclaimed group theatres, for over thirty years, during which time she has made numerous solo performances.
3. Ina Beth Sessions, 'The Dramatic Monologue', *PMLA* 62.2 (June 1947), pp. 503–16, p. 503.

4. See Kay Ellen Capo, 'From Academic to Socio-political Uses of Performance', in David W. Thompson, ed., *Performance of Literature in Historical Perspectives* (Lanham, MD: University Press of America 1983), pp. 437–57.

5. See David W. Thompson, 'Early Actress Readers: Mowat, Kemble, and Cushman', in Thompson, ed., *Performance of Literature in Historical Perspectives*, pp. 629–50.

6. A. Dwight Culler, 'Monodrama and the Dramatic Monologue', *PMLA* 90.3 (May 1975), pp. 366–85, p. 384

7. John. S. Gentile, *Cast of One: One Person Shows from the Chautauqua Platform to the Broadway Stage* (Chicago: University of Illinois Press, 1989), p. 36.

8. See Charlotte Canning, 'Under the Brown Tent: Chautauqau in the Community Landscape', in Elinor Fuchs and Una Chaudhuri, eds., *Land/Scape/Theater* (Ann Arbor: University of Michigan Press, 2002), pp. 209–27.

9. Gentile, *Cast of One*, p. 95.

10. Ibid., p. 43.

11. Jacky Bratton, *New Readings in Theatre History* (Cambridge: Cambridge University Press, 2003), pp. 116–32.

12. Basil Francis, *Fanny Kelly of Drury Lane* (London: Rockcliff, 1950), p. 149.

13. Ibid., pp. 149–50.

14. Bratton, *New Readings*, p. 117.

15. Francis, *Fanny Kelly*, p. 150.

16. Susan A. Glenn, *Female Spectacle: The Theatrical Roots of Modern Feminism* (Cambridge, MA: Harvard University Press, 2000), p. 76.

17. Birth and death dates for Fisk have proved extraordinarily difficult to find. *The Times* records two performances of her work in England in 1909 and 1913. She married an English barrister, Captain Malcolm Campbell Johnson, in 1922, but *The Times* lists her, interestingly, as the 'American writer' (she published short stories and journalism as well as her monologues), rather than as a performer. I am very grateful to Gilli Bush-Bailey for introducing me to Fisk's work.

18. Warren Susman, *Cultural History: The Transformation of American Society in the Twentieth Century* (Washington, DC: Smithsonian Press, 2003), pp. 271–86.

19. Glenn, *Female Spectacle*, see ch. 3, 'The Strong Personality: Female Mimics and the Play of the Self', pp. 74–95.

20. Cornelia Otis Skinner, 'Monologue to Theatre: An Exponent of a Solo Art Discusses its Rise from the Ranks of the Amateurs', *New York Times*, 27 December 1931, p. 4.

21. Ibid.

22. May Isabel Fisk, *The Silent Sex* (New York: Harper and Brothers, 1923), p. 130.

23. Beatrice Herford, *Beatrice Herford's Monologues* (New York: Samuel French, 1937), pp. 54–7.

24. Beatrice Herford, *Monologues by Beatrice Herford* (New York: Charles Scribner's and Son, 1908), pp. 97–120, and Fisk's 'The London Char Lady', in May Isabel Fisk, *The Eternal Feminine: Monologues* (New York: Harper and Brothers, 1911), pp. 219–39.

25. May Isabel Fisk, *Monologues* (New York: Harper and Brothers, 1903), p. 22.

26. Fisk, *The Silent Sex*, pp. 145–6.

27. Ibid., pp. 154–5.

28. Stephanie Koziski, 'The Stand-up Comedian as Anthropologist: Intentional Culture Critic', *Journal of Popular Culture* 18.2 (1984), pp. 57–76, p. 61.
29. 'The Personality of the Popular Maker of Monologues – How She Compounds her Amusing Skits', in the *Boston Evening Transcript*, 21 March 1905, from the Allen and Brown Dramatic Collection, vol. 5, p. 118, quoted in Linda Sue Long, 'The Art of Beatrice Herford, Cissie Loftus and Dorothy Sands Within the Tradition of Solo Performance' (unpublished dissertation, University of Texas at Austin, 1982), p. 244.
30. Ibid., p. 246.
31. Ibid., p. 91.
32. Ibid., p. 60.
33. May Isabel Fisk, 'The Art of Giving Monologue', in May Isabel Fisk, *Monologues and Duologues* (New York: Samuel French, 1914), p. 9.
34. Ibid., p. 13.
35. Long, *The Art of Beatrice Herford*, p. 62.
36. Ibid.
37. John Gielgud, in *The Letters of Ruth Draper*, ed. Dorothy Warren (Carbondale: Southern Illinois University Press, 1999 [1979]), p. xiii.
38. Kenneth Tynan, from the London *Evening Standard*, 23 May 1952, quoted in Morton D. Zabel, ed., *The Art of Ruth Draper: Her Dramas and Character, with a Memoir by Morton Dauwen Zabel* (Oxford: Oxford University Press, 1960), pp. 114–15.
39. See *Ruth Draper and her Company of Characters* and *Ruth Draper and her Company of Characters: More Selected Monologues*, BMG Music, Special Products DRC 22685 and DRC 23085.
40. Virginia Woolf, *A Moment's Liberty: The Shorter Diary of Virginia Woolf*, ed. Anne Olivier Bell (New York: Harcourt Brace, 1990), p. 238.
41. See Glenn, *Female Spectacle*, pp. 74–95.
42. Zabel, *The Art of Ruth Draper*, pp. 100–1.
43. 'Interview with Ruth Draper', *New Yorker*, 6 March 1954, pp. 22–3.
44. Iris Origo, 'Ruth Draper and her Company of Characters', *Cornhill Magazine*, 1957–8, no. 1014, pp. 383–93, pp. 386–7.
45. Zabel, *The Art of Ruth Draper*, p. 101.
46. David Kaplan and Patricia Norcia, in Jo Bonney, ed., *Extreme Exposure: An Anthology of Solo Performance Texts from the Twentieth Century* (New York: Theatre Communications Group, 2000). For scripts see Zabel, *The Art of Ruth Draper*, pp. 167–74 and 350–69.
47. *The Letters of Ruth Draper*, ed. Warren, p. 29.
48. *The Times*, 30 January 1920, p. 10.
49. *The Times*, 11 November 1947, p. 9.
50. 'The Actress', in Zabel, *The Art of Ruth Draper*, pp. 343–9.
51. See the uncatalogued Ruth Draper file in the Theatre Museum, London, for details of programmes for performances from the early 1920s to the mid-1950s.
52. *The Letters of Ruth Draper*, ed. Warren, p. 27.
53. Ibid., p. 17. Lena Ashwell in 1914 suggested that the average annual wage for an actor was £70. Even allowing for the change in economic value of money as a result of the 1914–18 war, this places Draper amongst the high earners in the industry at an early stage in her career. See Michael Sanderson, *From Irving*

to *Olivier: A Social History of the Acting Profession* (London: Athlone Press, 1984), p. 85.

54. *The Letters of Ruth Draper*, ed. Warren, p. 23.

55. See Maggie B. Gale, *West End Women: Women on the London Stage 1918–1962* (London: Routledge, 1996).

56. Letter to Joan Ling, Ruth Draper's representative, dated 3 December 1946. From the estate of Emile Littler, Theatre Museum, London.

57. She often stored props – curtains and furniture – in London and New York ready for her next tour and so was not encumbered with stage sets whilst touring. See Margaret Rose, *Monologue Plays for Female Voices* (Turin: Tirrenia Stampatori, 1995), p. 57.

58. Zabel, *The Art of Ruth Draper*, pp. 255–65, p. 264.

59. Zabel, *The Art of Ruth Draper*, p. 79.

60. Ibid.

61. Rose, *Monologue Plays*, p. 60.

62. Joyce Grenfell, *Joyce Grenfell Requests the Pleasure* (London: Macdonald and Co., 1956), p. 253.

63. See Joyce Grenfell, *Turn Back the Clock* (London: Sceptre, 1983), *George Don't Do That* (London: Macmillan, 1977) and *Stately as a Galleon* (London: Macmillan, 1978) for scripts. There are also numerous recordings still available.

64. *The Times*, 9 October 1957, p. 3.

65. She also co-wrote songs and performed with Richard Addinsell, who had worked with Noel Coward and Clemence Dane.

66. See Jane Hampton, *Joyce Grenfell* (London: John Murray, 2002).

67. Grenfell, *Joyce Grenfell Requests*, p. 251.

FURTHER READING

Bonney, Jo, ed. *Extreme Exposure: An Anthology of Solo Performance Texts from the Twentieth Century*. New York: Theatre Communications Group, 2000.

Bratton, Jacky. *New Readings in Theatre History*. Cambridge: Cambridge University Press, 2003.

Draper, Ruth. *The Letters of Ruth Draper*, ed. Dorothy Warren. Carbondale: Southern Illinois University Press, 1999 [1979].

Ruth Draper and her Company of Characters and Ruth Draper and her Company of Characters: More Selected Monologues. BMG Music, Special Products DRC 22685 and DRC 23085.

Fisk, May Isabel. *The External Feminine: Monologues*. New York: Harper and Brothers, 1911.

Monologues. New York: Harper and Brothers, 1903.

The Silent Sex. New York: Harper and Brothers, 1923.

Francis, Basil. *Fanny Kelly of Drury Lane*. London: Rockcliff, 1950.

Gale, Maggie B. *West End Women: Women on the London Stage 1918–1962*. London: Routledge, 1996.

Gentile, John S. *Cast of One: One Person Shows from the Chautauqua Platform to the Broadway Stage*. Chicago: University of Illinois Press, 1989.

Glenn, Susan A. *Female Spectacle: The Theatrical Roots of Modern Feminism*. Cambridge, MA: Harvard University Press, 2000.

Grenfell, Joyce. *George Don't Do That*. London: Macmillan 1977.
Joyce Grenfell Requests the Pleasure. London: Macdonald and Co. 1956.
Stately as a Galleon. London: Macmillan, 1978.
Turn Back the Clock. London: Sceptre, 1983.
Herford, Beatrice. *Beatrice Herford's Monologues*. New York: Samuel French, 1937.
Monologues by Beatrice Herford. New York: Charles Scribner's & Son, 1908.
Rose, Margaret. *Monologue Plays for Female Voices*. Turin: Tirrenia Stampatori, 1995.
Sanderson, Michael. *From Irving to Olivier: A Social History of the Acting Profession*. London: Athlone Press, 1984.
Zabel, Morton D., ed. *The Art of Ruth Draper: Her Dramas and Character, with a Memoir by Morton Dauwen Zabel*. Oxford: Oxford University Press, 1960.

16

PENNY GAY

Changing Shakespeare: new possibilities for the modern actress

In the 1980s and 1990s there was plenty of evidence, in interviews with and articles by Shakespearean actresses, that the perspectives of second-wave feminism had influenced their thinking about the characters and stories of Shakespeare's plays.[1] The question arises, however, as to what difference, if any, this new awareness has made to what the twenty-first-century audience sees. Little in the record of Britain's Royal Shakespeare Company in recent years indicates any change in the relation between women performers and the Shakespeare industry. The few plays directed by women have been disliked or ignored by critics and other opinion-makers. As for the new generation of actresses, the older stars were still the dominant attraction. Judi Dench, for example, played the Countess in *All's Well That Ends Well* in 2004, to rave reviews that had a strong undertone of nostalgia and valediction: here was an actress who had blazed her way through an astonishing range of Shakespearean roles for nearly forty years (not to mention modern drama, film and television comedy), possibly playing her last major stage role. One critic's comments sum up Dench's unique contribution to Shakespearean acting in the second half of the twentieth century:

> What Judi Dench does as the Countess in *All's Well That Ends Well* goes way beyond acting. She combines humility with authority, she makes the world on the stage larger by the quality of her attention to others, she conceives her role in a large arc that takes her audience a mighty distance, and she plays it with an economy through which tiny movements and inflections pierce straight to the heart.[2]

This is the very opposite of 'stagey' acting; yet Dench was equally able, as Cleopatra in 1987, to imbue the performance with the character's extravagantly conscious theatricality and an astonishing, iconoclastic physicality.

So far, no young actress has indicated the potential that Dench first showed in her Viola in 1969. No young woman has been hailed on her debut as Rosalind as a brilliant star who revivified the role, as Vanessa Redgrave

314

did at the Royal Shakespeare Theatre in 1961. Other actresses who were young members of the RSC in the 1960s and 1970s – for example, Janet Suzman, Geraldine McEwan, Helen Mirren, Susan Fleetwood – were recognised immediately as mould-breaking performers of the standard Shakespearean female roles, re-energising them and allowing audiences to see the way feminist thinking of the period created meaningful new insights into Shakespeare's women, by encouraging a re-examination of the characters' situations and their potential for action.

A generation of committed feminist actresses carried this still powerful wave into the 1980s: those who saw the young Juliet Stevenson, Fiona Shaw, Josette Simon or Harriet Walter recognised that same intelligent, probing, committed rethinking of roles such as Rosalind, Celia, Isabella, Helena (*All's Well*). It has not been possible to say this of the RSC's productions in the 1990s and beyond, nor of the few Royal National Theatre or commercial British productions of Shakespeare. Actresses who break the mould of audiences' expectations – and make a success of it – remain, at the beginning of the twenty-first century, disappointingly rare.

Not just Juliet

A few names stand out in the 1990s and early twenty-first century as risk-takers within the Shakespearean canon. One such is Kathryn Hunter. After training at RADA she worked with the French-influenced English company Théâtre de Complicité, which had a strong commitment to physical theatre and story-telling. Hunter dominated the stage in a series of roles, often involving cross-gender doubling (for example, Paulina, Mamilius, and Old Shepherd in *The Winter's Tale*, 1992). This fearlessly exploratory approach to classical acting culminated in a King Lear, directed by Helena Kaut-Howson for the Haymarket Theatre, Leicester in 1997, and transferring to the Young Vic in London. (It is significant that this 'experiment' began its run in the provinces and that its London run was well away from the West End.) Hunter played the main role as a very old person of indeterminate gender, feisty, domineering, but post-sexual. Her deep husky voice and short stature contributed strongly to this representation: the famous speeches were delivered with a naturalism that arose from rethinking the character (in an early twentieth-century, vaguely middle-European setting) rather than employing the grandiose tones that male actors have usually felt obliged to adopt. The thematic focus was on the modern breakdown of bonds between parents and children – the fault of both – rather than revisiting the traditional tragic confrontation between man and the universe. After the scenes on the heath Lear was costumed in a long white nightgown, a sign simply of his/her enfeebled state (by contrast, Cordelia was in combat trousers, a woman looking deliberately boyish). 'The voice is that of a little, old and trembling creature, now briefly comical, now piercing in the pain of its hard-won wisdom. The sex of the actor is immaterial before such capacity to reach the core of an experience.'[3]

In 2003 Hunter played Richard III in an all-women production of the play at Shakespeare's Globe Theatre in London. Once again, Hunter was able to utilise her lack of height (and the remains of a limp caused by a major car accident some years earlier) to present a tiny, malformed, spider-like creature. This character, however, has both sexuality and charisma. Here Hunter's outstanding physical inventiveness, coupled with a wry, self-reflexive use of the language, allowed her to charm the audience both on and off stage. Physical, biological gender was subsumed into an extraordinarily knowing and detailed performance of charismatic masculine power.

The Globe management commendably went even further down this track with an all-women *Taming of the Shrew* in the same year, directed by Phyllida Lloyd (a male director was removed from the production during the rehearsal period). Their entirely reasonable assumption was that just as sixteenth-century conditions mandated all-male companies of actors whose performances of female roles audiences found perfectly acceptable, so twenty-first century conditions should allow acceptance of all-female companies. In the case of the *Shrew*, the gamble paid off (for audiences, certainly, and for the majority of critics). Tall, handsome, swaggeringly self-confident in his sexuality, Janet McTeer's Petruchio swept all but Kathryn Hunter's Katherine before him. The director and her principal actors were determined that the play should retain its modern feminist critique of the notion that women need 'taming'. Thus all the male characters were played with an edge of parody of typically male behaviours: heavy father, sentimental lover, cheeky servant, boisterous wooer. Petruchio whored, drank and even convincingly mimed urinating against one of the Globe's stage pillars – 'a beautifully observed parody of men behaving badly'.[4] Katherine's resistance to his wooing was an embodiment of the fury of the powerless woman in Elizabethan culture – until the point, late in the play, when she could turn his plan against him by over-performing the humility of the tamed wife. The couple were last seen in the bedroom/balcony above the stage, noisily engaged in another quarrel. The fact that this play, which focuses so strongly on gender relations, was performed by an all-female cast simply reinforced its power dynamics: it made clear that 'masculinity' or 'femininity' is always a performance informed by the dominant social ideology.

Isolated incidences of women performing major Shakespearean male roles, mostly from the tragedies, had continued to occur throughout the twentieth century, in a tradition – going back as far as the Restoration – of female Hamlets, Romeos, Oberons. Notable contributors to this tradition's persistence were Frances de la Tour's Hamlet (1979) and Fiona Shaw's Richard II (1995). Shaw, with her director Deborah Warner, opted for a barely adolescent Richard, his body under his kingly gown encased in wrappings that looked like swaddling clothes. Richard's ineffectual childishness, playing at being a king, was thus strikingly embodied. As Hamlet, de la Tour exploited her commanding presence and superb voice to recreate for some members of the audience the 'universal' angst-ridden Hamlet of many eighteenth- and nineteenth-century actresses. As Prospero, Vanessa Redgrave played an affectingly anxious – if somewhat bland – parental figure in the Globe's otherwise conventionally cast *Tempest* of 2000. Many reviewers did not care for the lack of 'vengefulness' in Redgrave's magus.[5] This judgement demonstrates how hard it is for any actor – much less a woman playing a male role – to break the mould of accepted interpretation of major classic roles.

Clearly these 'experiments', this grasping by ambitious actresses of the opportunity to explore roles outside those traditionally afforded them in Shakespeare, are not only personally and professionally challenging, but also enable new perspectives on the Shakespearean texts. In 1997 the director and drama teacher Helen Alexander wrote, 'The key to change is in the casting of existing texts . . . Isn't it time that the audience were challenged to accept the authenticity of a Queen Lear or a female Doctor Faustus? . . . By changing the gender you can make a brilliant story a different brilliant story.'[6] As acting theory moves further away from a simple naturalistic model, and, paradoxically, further towards recognising the sophistication of the Elizabethan all-male stage, more female performances of male roles should become normal, indeed unremarkable. Deborah Paige, 'determined to have a half female, half male company' in her 1992 production of *A Midsummer Night's Dream* for the Salisbury Playhouse, made Egeus a woman ('a mother instead of a father') and doubled her with 'Pat Quince', the female director of the mechanicals' play; Puck was also a woman.[7] This imaginative and effective practice offers an example that other directors and companies could follow, rather than complaining that Shakespeare's plays are overwhelmingly composed of male roles.

The most immediate field ready for female colonisation is probably that of Shakespearean clowns. Many smaller companies, wherever Shakespeare is played, have already cast women as, for example, Feste, Launce, Lear's Fool (a role that can be satisfyingly doubled with Cordelia) and any number of comic servants. The character's biological gender is not as important as his role as (frequently) musician, slapstick entertainer and commentator on the action. Not to be confused with rustic 'clowns' such as William in *As You*

Like It (a simple figure, the butt of the witty clown Touchstone), a list of such roles might include: Lance, Speed (*Two Gentlemen*), Grumio, Curtis, Biondello (*Shrew*), Moth (*Love's Labour's Lost*), Lancelot Gobbo (*Merchant*), the Gravediggers in *Hamlet*, Feste, Lavatch (*All's Well*), Lear's Fool, Macbeth's Porter, Cleopatra's serpent-bringer, Autolycus (*Winter's Tale*), Trinculo and Stephano (*The Tempest*).

A substantial experiment in cross-gender clowning was undertaken in a London production of *A Midsummer Night's Dream* (2001), directed by Matthew Francis. Set in the Second World War on the English home front, this West End production was unashamedly populist, and did not please all the critics, largely because of the perceived illogicality of the period setting (Surrey in 1940 did not have the same draconian laws as Shakespeare's 'Athens'). The historical basis for casting the Mechanicals as all (except Flute) female was that in the wartime period the Women's Volunteer Service did men's jobs in the community; notably, all-women amateur dramatic societies took to presenting Shakespeare as a way of upholding the cultural life of the nation. Selina Cadell impressed reviewers as 'Mrs Quince', a doughty WVS officer and 'superb, nervy busybody'.[8] But the trump card of the show was Dawn French's substantial 'Mrs Bottom'. French's popular television persona, as a fat comic with a genius for physical clowning, was well utilised in details of this production: 'changed by Oberon's spell, she's goofily appreciative of her newly acquired male parts; got up as Pyramus, she sinks, limbs flapping, under the weight of her armour'.[9] French 'has a great deal of presence, speaks Shakespeare very well and can warm up an auditorium just by walking onto the stage',[10] remarked the writer of *Shakespeare Survey*'s annual review of performances in England. This comment marks a shift in women's relation to comedy. Dawn French is one of a significant number of female comics who in the late twentieth century claimed the right to perform in anarchic sketch comedy (particularly on television) and live stand-up monologues in 'rough theatre' situations far removed from the genteel monologues performed on radio or in respectable theatres by the earlier generation of female monologists (see chapter 15). We have the achievements of post-1970s feminism to thank for this development – the acceptance of women's indecorous, even confrontational eloquence in clubs and pubs where a couple of generations ago they would not even have been admitted. There are exciting possibilities for taking these skills into Shakespeare's clowns, and also into reinterpretations of the comic heroines, who could be seen to have more in common with the clowns than traditional notions of these roles have envisaged.

Shakespeare seems to have tapped into this possibility of female clowning, at least early in his career: consider the comical adventures, including a hugely physical cat-fight, of Helena and Hermia in *A Midsummer Night's Dream*, and the first meeting of Katherine and Petruchio, with its coarse jokes and careerings around the stage. But physical comedy can also be used to express the dilemmas of more complex characters such as Viola, Olivia, Rosalind, Celia or Beatrice, once they are relieved of the obligation to always behave as ladies or even 'liberated women'.[11] Viola and Rosalind, in male attire for most of the play, can have enormous fun with the physical freedom this allows them. Rosalind's 'direction' of Orlando in *As You Like It*, act 4, scene 1, generally benefits from being played with 'boyish' restlessness and even awkwardness; the scene in *Twelfth Night* in which Olivia declares her love for 'Cesario' will often have a comically desperate Olivia leaping on the 'boy' and planting a hearty kiss on him. A major issue that the actress of Beatrice has to decide is how strongly to signal her difference from the other ladies of Leonato's household by gawkiness, mannishness or inventive physical clowning, particularly in the scene in which she is gulled into believing Benedick is in love with her (*Much Ado About Nothing*, act 3, scene 1).[12] And confiding in the audience in soliloquies – as Viola does, for example, in her 'ring' speech (*Twelfth Night*, act 2, scene 2) – offers the opportunity of creating the sort of empathy that a modern stand-up comic can achieve.

In almost all dramatic situations, class and/or profession is a more important marker of function than gender is. All members of serving professions – tailors, cooks, gardeners, schoolteachers, etc. (often comic figures in Shakespeare) – are potentially female in today's world. Even more interestingly, with the powerful professions, including law, politics, the judiciary and the military, now fully open to women, there is a vastly expanded range of possible roles for women in modern-dress productions of Shakespeare. A play such as *Julius Caesar*, so overwhelmingly masculine in traditional productions, yet so clearly relevant to modern politics in many parts of the world, has had many successful modern-dress productions featuring a female Cassius or Brutus, images that counter the powerlessness of the political wives Portia and Calpurnia. A striking rethinking of the iconic role of Chorus in *Henry V*, in Nicholas Hytner's production for the National Theatre (2003), had Penny Downie playing a female academic biographer of the king: at the end, the Chorus sounded 'unconvinced that the whole enterprise had been worth its cost, leaving the stage looking anxiously as though she had realized that she needed to do a good deal more thinking about the man to whose biography she had been dedicating her career'.[13]

Post-modernism's pleasure in irony and transgression has enabled actresses to find the comedy even in tragedy heroines. For example, Frances de la Tour played Cleopatra (to Alan Bates's Antony) for the RSC in 1999:

an immensely courageous performance that presented a middle-aged woman desperately trying to hang onto her lover, her girlishness a transparent pretence, every costume she was in danger of falling out of worn in the hope of looking younger. There was about this Cleopatra's self-awareness something extraordinary . . . She was funny, ironic, unpredictable, physically uninhibited and emotionally stormy – and she was also, as many of the reviewers solemnly pointed out, very unregal until her final scene.

Overall a performance 'undignified' and partly for that reason, deeply moving, argued Robert Smallwood.[14]

Harriet Walter played Lady Macbeth in 2000 in a production by Gregory Doran set in a contemporary war zone (Antony Sher was Macbeth):

Walter particularly excelled in finding the element of comedy of manners in Lady Macbeth's . . . social discomfitures. Her momentarily visible sense that Macbeth's dismissal of her among his other courtiers in 3.1 . . . was something of an affront, as well as a dreadful personal blow, was funny as well as poignant, as if she were brought up short by a memory of her mother's repeated warnings that she was marrying beneath her class.[15]

These more complex portrayals of tragedy heroines can be further enhanced when they have a female community to relate to. A late twentieth-century understanding of friendship between women, for example, has made the last few scenes of *Othello* newly memorable and even more moving for the warm bond between Desdemona and an increasingly young Emilia (a fine example is the 2004 *Othello* directed by Declan Donnellan for Cheek by Jowl), which not coincidentally makes more sense of the bawdy chat of each woman earlier in the play.

Just as we can explore new possibilities in portrayal of the comic heroines, we can also ask, are all the tragic heroines necessarily and only victims, or can they be seen as consciously making choices that contribute to their own demise? One-note performances of, for example, Ophelia as a pathetic innocent can be given complexity and thrilling contemporary relevance by assuming that she is complicit in both her sexual relation with Hamlet and the power games of her father and Polonius. For an example of this sort of rethinking from as early as 1984–5, see Frances Barber's essay in *Players of Shakespeare 2*[16] – and, just as significant, her account of the male director's resistance to her reading. This interpretation of the role has, in fact, been more commonly promulgated in the 1990s films of *Hamlet*, which are aimed at a general popular audience rather than the educated theatre-goers who have the expectation that Hamlet's is the only story worth telling.

What of the women on the edges of the political processes in the history plays? Is it possible for a modern actress to find power and personal autonomy in these roles? Revivals of the rarely performed *King John* demonstrate that eighteenth-century audiences were not wrong in seeing Constance as one of Shakespeare's major female roles, a wonderful vehicle for the talents of Sarah Siddons. Joan La Pucelle in *1 Henry VI* can be played with the feistiness of Shaw's St Joan; the active political intervention and the adulterous behaviour of Queen Margaret in *2 Henry VI* can anticipate the sexual enthusiasm of Cleopatra. And of course, Margaret is a survivor, making it through two more plays to *Richard III*, her eloquent speeches continually commenting on Richard's pursuit of power, even while the political processes marginalise her.

Finally, we should not forget that the Shakespearean canon contains approximately one hundred important and rich female roles. There is more to be explored here than just recounting the 'top twenty'. For example, both the young Helena and the old Countess in *All's Well That Ends Well* have some of the most eloquent speeches written in the period; the fact that Helena, like Cressida and the other women of Troy (*Troilus and Cressida*) or Imogen of *Cymbeline*, has to make her way in a world dominated by men behaving badly, is an exciting challenge to actress and director. Romantic comedies these are not: the playwright explores a cynical and more realistic view of love, one that modern women could well relate to.

Training the Shakespearean actress

As Sarah Werner, Richard Knowles and others have pointed out,[17] voice work, the keystone of classical actors' training, is perceived as a feminine field – largely because the most influential late twentieth-century theorists and teachers of voice were all women (and this is still the case with most drama schools and with many classical companies that retain a voice coach (see chapter 5)): 'Voice coaches have been figured as enablers (they help the actors to do their jobs) rather than as determiners (the province of the director), a configuration that both reflects and contributes to the gendering of the work.'[18] This may, indeed, reflect the response of female would-be directors to their closing-out from institutions such as the RSC, but there is a more entrenched ideological submission encapsulated in one of the commonest mantras to be found in the publications of these influential women: voice work enables the actor to 'serve the text', or 'honour the author' – Shakespeare – who at times seems to be given a god-like, and certainly patriarchal, status in relation to the project of voice training. As Werner points out, quoting Cicely Berry, 'Voice work's focus on a character's words as "a release of the inner life" prioritizes character reading above all other avenues of exploration, including consideration of Shakespeare's dramaturgy.'[19] Although these conditions clearly apply to male actors' voice training as much as to women's, the process of training for the most part will operate within the 'natural' gendered parameters. Rarely will a woman do her major vocal work on, say, Iago's confidences to the audience; or a man explore Lady Macbeth's 'Come you spirits that tend on mortal thoughts.' If they do, at the insistence of a voice coach who is trying to break down vocal habits and preconceptions, students will more often than not attempt to play what they consider to be the 'essential' gendered character – resulting, frequently, in awkward performances of external masculinity from the women and simpering campness from the men. Cross-cast professional productions are rarely free of this problem, although see my comments above on the overall success of the Globe's *Shrew*. The expectations of young actors at drama school here collude with conservative ideology: overwhelmingly, agents and casting directors will want to see a young actress's Juliet or Viola rather than her Lancelot Gobbo or Prospero. Few young women are going to 'waste their time' exploring such speeches, even though the training in eloquence and rhetorical variety that they might provide could prove extremely valuable in extending their vocal and emotional range.

The energy of the language in dramatic speech rarely depends absolutely on the actual gender of the speaker, but rather on a negotiation for power. Given the patriarchal structure of the society in and for which Shakespeare wrote, there is frequently an apparent straightforward correspondence between gender and power, or lack of it, in the dramaturgy of any scene or whole play. The critical project of deconstruction which emerged in the latter part of the twentieth century, however, enabled a more conscious 'playing against' the surface or 'natural' meaning of lines and speeches. Actresses can take part in this project by embracing the potential of their own presence, charisma and energy: their freedom to act and react in the moment. Training attempts to make this freedom possible; it will often mean, for women, a freedom to behave indecorously. The recent practice in progressive drama schools of single-sex casting for big classic plays, so that all genders and types get to 'be' all genders and types, is a healthy stretching of young actors' perceptions of the possibilities of their art. (It was not common even in the 1990s.) The aim is for the actors to 'own their process' in the story, rather than to just imitate the external signs of gender. But this experiment is conducted within the safety of the training institution, and rarely repeated on the professional stage.

Some drama schools at the beginning of the twenty-first century have expanded their undergraduate offerings to include courses in alternative theatre and new performance practices. Students who pursue this wider curriculum can, if they wish, top-up their classical acting skills with a one-year postgraduate course that will largely focus on becoming comfortable with the complex linguistic demands of Shakespearean drama. Regrettably, however, the theatrical market is flooded with 'product', largely female: more women than men apply for and complete drama school courses. What, then, can the talented, ambitious young actress do to make her mark in Shakespeare in the early twenty-first century? The answer would seem to lie outside the national theatrical institutions and commercial 'Theatreland' zones: self-generated co-operative shows, imaginatively thoughtful and rigorously directed with the highest attention to quality in speech, movement, and mise en scène (which is not to be confused with expensive scenery: after all, Shakespeare didn't have any). Cheap, off-beat venues, which have an attractive ambience; a lively and determined publicist; and – perhaps more often than not – a woman director.

Directing the Shakespearean actress

Elizabeth Schafer's ground-breaking book *Ms-Directing Shakespeare* (1998) demonstrated that 'women directors have been at the forefront of exploring new approaches to Shakespeare, and have directed some of the most exciting theatrical productions of our day'. Schafer writes of the achievements, and analyses the Shakespearean productions, of Joan Littlewood, Jane Howell, Yvonne Brewster, Di Trevis, Jules Wright, Helena Kaut-Howson, Deborah Paige, Jude Kelly and Gale Edwards. Yet even so, she points out, 'statistically [women directors of Shakespeare] are less likely to get the work than their male colleagues'[20] – or, if they do get it, it is in the provinces or on the fringe, rather than in London or at the RSC. This situation has not changed since Schafer's book was published, though several more women directors have entered the lists with high-profile London productions of the classics; most notably, Katie Mitchell and Phyllida Lloyd, who also work in opera and musicals. These two women had earlier been the focus of a failed experiment at the Royal Shakespeare Company in the mid-1990s:

> [Adrian] Noble wanted The Other Place to regain artistic credibility by appointing Phyllida Lloyd and Katie Mitchell to run the theatre, but this plan collapsed over the persistent problem of casting. Noble did not want the Lloyd/Mitchell company to be autonomous and isolated, and Mitchell took over alone in 1996. Her appointment and her work at The Other Place sig-nalled that the company had not stopped asking important questions. But in order to ask them, she felt obliged to create the very island Noble had feared and her leaving after three years encapsulated the RSC's artistic quandary . . . Mitchell was exhausted by the battles over casting and the performance space. She felt her brief to provoke and challenge was not supported institutionally.[21]

By 2005 there was, in fact, very little Shakespeare on either woman's illustrious CV. Most young female directors in Britain can get their chance at Shakespeare by working as guest directors in drama colleges, but this rarely develops into an appointment as an associate director at a prestigious classic company such as the RSC or the National Theatre.

Jude Kelly perhaps speaks for all modern female directors of Shakespeare when she comments that actresses 'recognise that as a woman director I am likely to be reading a piece of material and considering how the women in that material are dealing with the world and I will judge whether the playwright has understood how women may have felt about the world'. The corollary to this is a need to defuse the 'paranoia' of male actors, that they will 'somehow lose their masculine element if they have to fit in with some feminist scenario'.[22] It is unlikely that this underlying suspicion will soon disappear, particularly amongst the legions of older male actors who in any Shakespeare production still tend to have the numbers on their side.

Nevertheless, there are islands of enlightenment. Probably the single most influential woman in Shakespearean production at the beginning of the twenty-first century is the artistic director of the Oregon Shakespeare Festival, Libby Appel, who has directed a significant proportion of the Shakespearean canon in prestigious theatres all round the USA; she has pursued a particular mission to bring new perspectives to the 'masculine' histories and tragedies. The OSF, of which she became the first female artistic director in 1995, was founded in 1935; it is based in Ashland, Oregon (a town smaller than Stratford-on-Avon) and plays a full repertoire of Shakespeare, classic and modern plays in three state-of-the-art theatres for nine months of the year. Women of colour and of other ethnicities than Caucasian are regularly cast in major Shakespearean roles; imaginative and illuminating cross-casting is explored. The standard is world-class, the productions are adventurous and energetic. The core of the large company of actors return year after year, to the challenge and thrill of playing Shakespeare and other classics in front of a live and enthusiastic audience.

This model – which leads its audience into fresh fields rather than pandering to their expectations of traditional classical theatre – is followed in some smaller but highly successful regional companies in England, such as the West Yorkshire Playhouse at Leeds. Jude Kelly was the foundation artistic director of the WYP, from 1989 to 2002, building it into the country's largest regional theatre operation, and directing, amongst other fare, some strongly feminist Shakespeare – for example, a *Merchant of Venice* (1994) with Nicola McAuliffe as a fierce and bitter Portia who foreshadows Hedda Gabler. Gale Edwards's iconoclastic *Shrew* (Stratford, 1995), with another strong actress, Josie Lawrence, humiliating Petruchio in a heavily ironical final speech, probably reinforced the prejudices of the male establishment of the Royal Shakespeare Company against female directors, at least on the main stage. The fact that both McAuliffe and Lawrence have also appeared to acclaim as leading sopranos in musicals and as stars of television sit-coms suggests the charisma and technical range that both actresses are able to bring to such reinterpretations of the Shakespearean canon. It also reinforces the 'alternative' vision of their female directors as regards casting these roles. The RSC has yet to shake off the forty-year-old habit of being a 'men's club', and cede real power and space for women's re-visions of Shakespeare. Only then might a new generation of exciting Shakespearean actresses appear.

NOTES

1. See, for example, the essays by actresses in the series *Players of Shakespeare*, 6 vols. (Cambridge: Cambridge University Press, 1985–2004), variously edited by Philip Brockbank, Robert Smallwood and Russell Jackson; Carol Rutter, *Clamorous Voices: Shakespeare's Women Today* (London: The Women's Press, 1988).
2. Alistair Macaulay, *Financial Times*, 23 February 2004.
3. Jeremy Kingston, *The Times*, 4 July 1997.
4. Elizabeth Schafer, 'The Framing of the *Shrew*', *Around the Globe* 25 (Autumn 2003), pp. 14–16, p. 14.
5. E.g. Michael Dobson, 'Shakespeare Performances in England (2000)', *Shakespeare Survey* 54 (2001), p. 263.
6. Helen Alexander, cited in Dan Glaister, 'A Woman's Part – So Welcome Queen Lear', *Guardian*, 23 June 1997.
7. Elizabeth Schafer, *Ms-Directing Shakespeare* (London: The Women's Press, 1998), pp. 87–8.
8. Susannah Clapp, *Observer*, 25 March 2001.
9. Ibid.
10. Michael Dobson, 'Shakespeare Performances in England (2001)', *Shakespeare Survey* 55 (2002), p. 312.
11. For a survey of changes in the performance of these roles since the mid-twentieth century, see Penny Gay, *As She Likes It: Shakespeare's Unruly Women* (London: Routledge, 1994).
12. Josie Lawrence, as Beatrice in Helena Kaut-Howson's *Much Ado* for the Manchester Royal Exchange (1997), 'on hearing that Benedick loved her . . . fainted into the arms of a man sitting in the front row of the audience and then proceeded to steal his programme to use as "camouflage" in order to creep closer and hear what Hero and Ursula were saying' (Schafer, *Ms-Directing*, pp. 84–5). Yet at other points in the production she 'capture[d] the piercing sadness of a lonely woman whose spiky intelligence looks like dooming her to spinsterhood' (Charles Spencer, *Daily Telegraph*, 25 September 1997).
13. Michael Dobson, 'Shakespeare Performances in England, 2003', *Shakespeare Survey* 57 (2004), p. 284.

14. Robert Smallwood, 'Shakespeare Performances in England (1999)', *Shakespeare Survey* 53 (2000), p. 248.
15. Dobson, 'Shakespeare Performances in England (2000)', pp. 252–3.
16. Frances Barber, 'Ophelia in *Hamlet*', in Russell Jackson and Robert Smallwood, eds., *Players of Shakespeare* 2 (Cambridge: Cambridge University Press, 1988), pp. 137–50.
17. Richard Paul Knowles, 'Shakespeare, Voice, and Ideology: Interrogating the Natural Voice', in James C. Bulman, ed., *Shakespeare, Theory, and Performance* (London: Routledge, 1996), pp. 92–112; Sarah Werner, *Shakespeare and Feminist Performance: Ideology on Stage* (London: Routledge, 2001).
18. Werner, *Shakespeare and Feminist Performance*, p. 46.
19. Ibid., p. 40.
20. Schafer, *Ms-Directing*, pp. 2–3.
21. Colin Chambers, *Inside the Royal Shakespeare Company* (London: Routledge, 2004), pp. 103–4.
22. Schafer, *Ms-Directing*, p. 45.

FURTHER READING

Barber, Frances. 'Ophelia in *Hamlet*', in Russell Jackson and Robert Smallwood, eds., *Players of Shakespeare* vol. 2, pp. 137–50. Cambridge: Cambridge University Press, 1988.

Brockbank, Philip, Robert Smallwood and Russell Jackson, eds., *Players of Shakespeare*, 6 vols. Cambridge: Cambridge University Press, 1985–2004.

Gay, Penny. *As She Likes It: Shakespeare's Unruly Women*. London: Routledge, 1994.

Rutter, Carol. *Clamorous Voices: Shakespeare's Women Today*. London: The Women's Press, 1988.

Schafer, Elizabeth. 'The Framing of the *Shrew*', *Around the Globe* 25 (Autumn 2003), pp. 14–16.

Ms-Directing Shakespeare. London: The Women's Press, 1998.

Werner, Sarah. *Shakespeare and Feminist Performance: Ideology on Stage*. London: Routledge, 2001.

GENERAL READING

Aston, Elaine. *Feminist Theatre Practice*. London: Routledge, 1999.
  An Introduction to Feminism and the Theatre. London: Routledge, 1995.
Babington, Bruce, ed. *British Stars and Stardom*. Manchester: Manchester University Press, 2001.
Bassnett, Susan. *Magdalena: International Women's Experimental Theatre*. Oxford: Berg, 1989.
  'Struggling with the Past: Women's Theatre in Search of a History', *New Theatre Quarterly* 5.18 (1989), pp. 107–12.
Berlanstein, Lenard R. *Daughters of Eve: A Cultural History of French Theatre Women from the Old Regime to the Fin de Siècle*. Cambridge, MA: Harvard University Press, 2001.
Bolton, Betsy. *Women, Nationalism and the Romantic Stage*. Cambridge: Cambridge University Press, 2001.
Booth, Michael R., John Stokes and Susan Bassnett. *Three Tragic Actresses: Siddons, Rachel, Ristori*. Cambridge: Cambridge University Press, 1996.
Buonanno, Giovanna. *International Actresses on the Victorian Stage*. Modena: Edizioni Il Fiorino, 2002.
Burrows, Jon. *Legitimate Cinema: Theatre Stars in Silent British Films 1908–1918*. Exeter: Exeter University Press, 2003.
Cima, Gay Gibson. *Performing Women: Female Characters, Male Playwrights, and the Modern Stage*. Ithaca, NY: Cornell University Press, 1993.
Corbett, Mary Jean. 'Performing Identities: Actresses and Autobiographies', in Kerry Powell, ed., *The Cambridge Companion to Victorian and Edwardian Theatre*, pp. 109–28. Cambridge: Cambridge University Press, 2004.
Crouch, Kimberly. 'The Public Life of Actresses: Prostitutes or Ladies?', in Hannah Barker and Elaine Chalus, eds., *Gender in Eighteenth-Century England: Roles, Representations and Responsibilities*, pp. 58–78. London: Longman, 1997.
Davis, Tracy C. *Actresses as Working Women: Their Social Identity in Victorian Culture*. London: Routledge, 1991.
  The Economics of the British Stage. Cambridge: Cambridge University Press, 2000.
de Frece, Lady. *Recollection of Vesta Tilley*. London: Hutchinson and Co., 1934.
Dudden, Faye E. *Women in the American Theatre: Actresses and Audiences 1790–1870*. New Haven, CT: Yale University Press, 1994.

Eltis, Sos. 'The Fallen Woman on Stage: Maidens, Magdalens and the Emancipated Female', in Kerry Powell, ed., *The Cambridge Companion to Victorian and Edwardian Theatre*, pp. 222–36. Cambridge: Cambridge University Press, 2004.

'Private Lives and Public Spaces: Reputation, Celebrity and the Late Victorian Actress', in Mary Luckhurst and Jane Moody, eds., *Theatre and Celebrity in Britain 1660–2000*, pp. 169–90. Basingstoke: Palgrave Macmillan, 2005.

Erdman, Andrew L. *Blue Vaudeville: Sex, Morals and the Mass Marketing of Amusement 1895–1915*. Jefferson, NC: McFarland and Co. Inc., 2004.

Farfan, Penny. *Women, Modernism and Performance*. Cambridge: Cambridge University Press, 2004.

Ferris, Lesley. *Acting Women: Images of Women in Theatre*. London: Macmillan, 1990.

ed. *Crossing the Stage: Controversies on Cross-dressing*. London: Routledge, 1993.

Gale, Maggie B. 'Lena Ashwell and Autobiographical Negotiations of the Self', in Maggie B. Gale and Viv Gardner, eds., *Auto/biography and Identity: Women, Theatre and Performance*, pp. 99–125. Manchester: Manchester University Press, 2004.

West End Women: Women on the London Stage 1918–1962. London: Routledge, 1996.

Gardner, Viv. 'Gertie Millar and the "Rules for Actresses and Vicars' Wives"', in Jane Milling and Martin Banham, eds., *Extraordinary Actors*, pp. 83–96. Exeter: University of Exeter Press, 2004.

Gardner, Viv, and Susan Rutherford, eds. *The New Woman and her Sisters*. Basingstoke: Harvester Wheatsheaf, 1992.

Garelick, Rhonda K. *Rising Star: Dandyism, Gender and Performance in the Fin de Siècle*. Princeton, NJ: Princeton University Press, 1998.

Gay, Penny. *As She Likes It: Shakespeare's Unruly Women*. London: Routledge, 1994.

Gilder, Rosamond. *Enter the Actress*. London: George Harrap, 1931.

Gledhill, Christine. *Reframing British Cinema: 1918–1928*. London: BFI, 2003.

Glenn, Susan A. *Female Spectacle: The Theatrical Roots of Modern Feminism*. Cambridge, MA: Harvard University Press, 2000.

Green, Barbara. *Spectacular Confessions: Autobiography, Performative Activism and the Sites of Suffrage 1905–1938*. London: Macmillan, 1997.

Heys, Sandra. *Contemporary Stage Roles for Women*. Westport, CT: Greenwood Press, 1985.

Hill, Holly. *Playing Joan: Actresses on the Challenge of Shaw's Saint Joan*. New York: Theatre Communications Group Ltd., 1987.

Hollege, Julie. *Innocent Flowers*. London: Virago, 1981.

Howe, Elizabeth. *The First English Actresses*. Cambridge: Cambridge University Press, 1992.

John, Angela V. *Elizabeth Robins: Staging a Life, 1862–1952*. London: Routledge, 1995.

Kaplan, Joel H., and Sheila Stowell. *Theatre and Fashion: Oscar Wilde to the Suffragettes*. Cambridge: Cambridge University Press, 1994.

Kelly, Veronica. 'Beauty and the Market: Actress Postcards and their Senders in Early Twentieth Century Australia', *New Theatre Quarterly* 20.2 (2004), pp. 99–116.

Knepler, Henry. *The Gilded Stage*. London: Constable, 1968.

Marshall, Gail. *Actresses on the Victorian Stage: Feminine Performance and the Galatea Myth*. Cambridge: Cambridge University Press, 1998.

McDonald, Russ. *Look to the Lady: Sarah Siddons, Ellen Terry and Judi Dench on the Shakespearean Stage*. Athens: University of Georgia Press, 2005.

McManus, Clare. *Women on the Renaissance Stage: Anne of Denmark and Female Masquing in the Stuart Court (1550–1619)*. Manchester: Manchester University Press, 2005.

Nussbaum, Felicity. 'Actresses and the Economics of Celebrity, 1700–1800', in Mary Luckhurst and Jane Moody, eds., *Theatre and Celebrity in Britain 1660–2000*, pp. 148–68. Basingstoke: Palgrave Macmillan, 2005.

Orgel, Stephen. *Impersonations*. Cambridge: Cambridge University Press, 1996.

Peters, Margot. *Bernard Shaw and the Actresses*. New York: Doubleday and Company, 1980.

Powell, Kerry. *Women and Victorian Theatre*. Cambridge: Cambridge University Press, 1997.

Pullen, Kirsten. *Actresses and Whores: On Stage and in Society*. Cambridge: Cambridge University Press, 2005.

Richards, Sandra. *The Rise of the English Actress*. London: Macmillan, 1993.

Rutter, Carol. *Clamorous Voices: Shakespeare's Women Today*. London: The Women's Press, 1988.

Schofield, Mary Anne, and Decilia Macheski, eds. *Curtain Calls: British and American Women and the Theater 1660–1820*. Athens: University of Ohio Press, 1991.

Sentilles, Renée M. *Performing Menken: Adah Isaacs Menken and the Birth of American Celebrity*. Cambridge: Cambridge University Press, 2003.

Smith, Sidonie, and Julia Watson, eds. *De/Colonizing the Subject: The Politics of Gender in Women's Autobiography*. Minneapolis: University of Minnesota Press, 1992.

eds. *Interfaces: Women/Autobiography/Image/Performance*. Ann Arbor: University of Michigan Press, 2002.

Stokes, John. *The French Actress and her English Audience*. Cambridge: Cambridge University Press, 2005.

Stokes, John, Michael R. Booth and Susan Bassnett. *Bernhardt, Terry, Duse: The Actress in her Time*. Cambridge: Cambridge University Press, 1988.

Templeton, Joan. *Ibsen's Women*. Cambridge: Cambridge University Press, 1997.

Walter, Harriet. *Other People's Shoes*. London: Viking, 1999.

West, Shearer. *The Image of the Actor: Verbal and Visual Representation in the Age of Garrick and Kemble*. London: Pinter, 1991.

'Siddons, Celebrity and Regality: Portraiture and the Body of the Aging Actress', in Mary Luckhurst and Jane Moody, eds., *Theatre and Celebrity in Britain 1660–2000*, pp. 191–213. Basingstoke: Palgrave Macmillan, 2005.

Woddis, Carol. *Sheer Bloody Magic: Conversations with Actresses*. London: Virago, 1991.

INDEX

Cambridge Companions to...

AUTHORS

Edward Albee *edited by Stephen J. Bottoms*

Margaret Atwood *edited by Coral Ann Howells*

W. H. Auden *edited by Stan Smith*

Jane Austen *edited by Edward Copeland and Juliet McMaster*

Beckett *edited by John Pilling*

Aphra Behn *edited by Derek Hughes and Janet Todd*

Walter Benjamin *edited by David S. Ferris*

William Blake *edited by Morris Eaves*

Brecht *edited by Peter Thomson and Glendyr Sacks* (second edition)

The Brontës *edited by Heather Glen*

Frances Burney *edited by Peter Sabor*

Byron *edited by Drummond Bone*

Albert Camus *edited by Edward J. Hughes*

Willa Cather *edited by Marilee Lindemann*

Cervantes *edited by Anthony J. Cascardi*

Chaucer, *second edition edited by Piero Boitani and Jill Mann*

Chekhov *edited by Vera Gottlieb and Paul Allain*

Coleridge *edited by Lucy Newlyn*

Wilkie Collins *edited by Jenny Bourne Taylor*

Joseph Conrad *edited by J. H. Stape*

Dante *edited by Rachel Jacoff* (second edition)

Charles Dickens *edited by John O. Jordan*

Emily Dickinson *edited by Wendy Martin*

John Donne *edited by Achsah Guibbory*

Dostoevskii *edited by W. J. Leatherbarrow*

Theodore Dreiser *edited by Leonard Cassuto and Claire Virginia Eby*

John Dryden *edited by Steven N. Zwicker*

George Eliot *edited by George Levine*

T. S. Eliot *edited by A. David Moody*

Ralph Ellison *edited by Ross Posnock*

Ralph Waldo Emerson *edited by Joel Porte and Saundra Morris*

William Faulkner *edited by Philip M. Weinstein*

Henry Fielding *edited by Claude Rawson*

F. Scott Fitzgerald *edited by Ruth Prigozy*

Flaubert *edited by Timothy Unwin*

E. M. Forster *edited by David Bradshaw*

Brian Friel *edited by Anthony Roche*

Robert Frost *edited by Robert Faggen*

Elizabeth Gaskell *edited by Jill L. Matus*

Goethe *edited by Lesley Sharpe*

Thomas Hardy *edited by Dale Kramer*

Nathaniel Hawthorne *edited by Richard Millington*

Ernest Hemingway *edited by Scott Donaldson*

Homer *edited by Robert Fowler*

Ibsen *edited by James McFarlane*

Henry James *edited by Jonathan Freedman*

Samuel Johnson *edited by Greg Clingham*

Ben Jonson *edited by Richard Harp and Stanley Stewart*

James Joyce *edited by Derek Attridge* (second edition)

Kafka *edited by Julian Preece*

Keats *edited by Susan J. Wolfson*

Lacan *edited by Jean-Michel Rabaté*

D. H. Lawrence *edited by Anne Fernihough*

Primo Levi *edited by Robert Gordon*

David Mamet *edited by Christopher Bigsby*

Thomas Mann *edited by Ritchie Robertson*

Herman Melville *edited by Robert S. Levine*

Christopher Marlowe *edited by Patrick Cheney*

Arthur Miller *edited by Christopher Bigsby*

Milton *edited by Dennis Danielson* (second edition)

Molière *edited by David Bradby and Andrew Calder*

Nabokov *edited by Julian W. Connolly*

Eugene O'Neill *edited by Michael Manheim*

George Orwell *edited by John Rodden*

Ovid *edited by Philip Hardie*

Harold Pinter *edited by Peter Raby*

Sylvia Plath *edited by Jo Gill*

Edgar Allan Poe *edited by Kevin J. Hayes*

Ezra Pound *edited by Ira B. Nadel*

Proust *edited by Richard Bales*

Pushkin *edited by Andrew Kahn*

Philip Roth *edited by Timothy Parrish*

Salman Rushdie *edited by Abdulrazak Gurnah*

Shakespeare *edited by Margareta de Grazia and Stanley Wells*